D0268807

EU Environmental Law

Contemporary environmental regulation is facing significant challenges. These challenges are varied, and include the search for economic efficiency, popular mistrust of experts and frequent observation of poor practical results. At EU level, criticisms of regulatory activity are compounded by the significant questions that surround the legitimacy of certain EU institutions and processes. This book examines a range of substantive EU environmental law and policy, and considers far-reaching endeavours to improve environmental regulation. One striking feature of contemporary EU environmental law is its wholehearted preoccupation with the structure of decision-making. This development, and some of the serious tensions that arise in the legal conditions for decision-making, forms a major theme of this book.

Volume 6 in the Series Modern Studies in European Law

Modern Studies in European Law

EU Environmental Law:
Challenges, Change and Decision-Making

MARIA LEE

King's College London

·HART·
PUBLISHING

OXFORD AND PORTLAND, OREGON

2005

Hart Publishing
Oxford and Portland, Oregon

Published in North America (US and Canada) by
c/o International Specialized Book Services
5804 NE Hassalo Street
Portland, Oregon
97213-3644
USA

Hart Publishing is a specialist legal publisher based in Oxford, England.
To order further copies of this book or to request a list of other
publications please write to:

Hart Publishing, Salters Boatyard, Folly Bridge,
Abingdon Rd, Oxford, OX1 4LB
Telephone: +44 (0)1865 245533 Fax: +44 (0) 1865 794882
email: mail@hartpub.co.uk
WEBSITE: http//:www.hartpub.co.uk

British Library Cataloguing in Publication Data
Data Available
ISBN 1-84113–410–4 (paperback)

Typeset by Datamatics Technologies Ltd, India
Printed and bound in Great Britain by
Page Bros Ltd, Norfolk

Contents

Table of Cases

Numerical

Table of Legislation

EUROPEAN UNION

Decisions

Directives

Recommendations

Regulations

INTERNATIONAL

UNITED KINGDOM

UNITED STATES

Introduction

This book rests on the rather simple observation that contemporary environmental regulators are facing significant challenges. When environmental protection first became a mainstream political concern at the very beginning of the 1970s, solutions may have been far from obvious, but the responsibility of government to address the 'environmental crisis' by the direct regulation of industry was relatively uncontroversial. The broad consensus that regulation by bureaucracy is at worst a necessary evil was, however, rudely disturbed by the dominance of neo-liberal economic ideologies in the 1980s. The division between pro- and anti-regulation camps, arguably never as stark or rigid as it appeared, has however faded. The talk now is all of 'good governance' and 'better regulation', a series of debates around regulatory reform rather than de-regulation. These debates may imply criticism of traditional forms of 'government' activity, but the need for some intervention in complex environmental problems is, if anything, reinforced.

Environmental regulation has been subjected to sustained critique from a wide range of different and not always consistent perspectives. This has a considerable effect on the perceived legitimacy of environmental regulation, and the often fragile legitimacy of the EU and its institutions means that many more general criticisms resonate particularly strongly in this context. 'Legitimacy' is far from a straightforward concept, but for current purposes implies simply the broad social acceptability of processes, institutions, and results.[1] Most systems come to be judged against at least the criteria of effectiveness and democracy, and increasingly also efficiency or cost-effectiveness; EU environmental law is no exception. Three main categories of challenge faced in EU environmental law will be discussed in this book: the challenge from democracy, the challenge from the market, and the challenge from the 'implementation gap'. Each of these implicates both effectiveness and democratic legitimacy in its own way. When the democratic credentials of EU environmental regulation are challenged, democratic systems are presented not simply as the only legitimate way to make decisions, but, in their embrace of diverse perspectives, also as the most effective way of capturing the full complexity of environmental problems. From the perspective of the market, it may be argued not only that market regulation (for example 'green consumerism' or environmental taxation) is more effective and efficient than direct government regulation, but also that the market is a more legitimate locus for decision-making, involving a large number of unconstrained individual decisions rather than government command.

---

[1] For a flavour of the debate, see for example D Beetham and C Lord, *Legitimacy and the EU* (London, Longman, 1998); JHH Weiler, *The Constitution of Europe* (Cambridge, Cambridge University Press, 1999). C Lord and P Magnette, 'E Pluribus Unum? Creative Disagreement about Legitimacy in the EU' (2004) 42 *Journal of Common Market Studies* 183 review the different approaches to legitimacy in the EU.

More straightforwardly, poor implementation compounds these concerns: unimplemented law is ineffective; law that cannot command authority, quickly ceases to reflect public views.

Law is always challenged and always changing, and it is not suggested that the EU institutions, which in any event are far from possessing a single will, are in every case consciously responding to challenges to their authority. Many innovative or simply evolutionary steps in environmental policy can, however, be usefully assessed from the perspective of diverse legitimacy challenges, which have accordingly become an important element in the complex dynamics of European environmental integration. This book will examine a range of law and policy with that in mind. Although the need for regulatory innovation in the environmental field is barely controversial, important debates remain over its direction. As will be seen during the course of this book, EU environmental law appeals to a variety of different approaches to environmental regulation. A striking feature of much EU environmental law and policy is its preoccupation by the structure of decision-making. The various ways in which EU environmental law seeks indirectly to influence decisions at all levels (EU, national and sub-national, public and private) is a recurring theme in this book. There are real tensions, the most acute of which is between political and technical decision-making. Simple intuition is not likely to be capable of identifying and addressing environmental problems, which demand expertise. And yet environmental problems are also profoundly political, involving the distribution of benefits and burdens and implicating competing interests and significant public values. Technical information alone is an inadequate basis for decision-making.

Environmental law has always faced significant challenges, and chapter one will begin with some background. The vexed question of why governments regulate to protect the environment will be discussed here, as will the proper place for EU level action; both questions tend to receive the quickest response from economics. EU environmental policy was born of the single market, and hence began with an economic rationale; the tendency for economics to dominate contemporary environmental policy arises at several points in this book. Chapter one will introduce some of the limitations of an economic understanding of the environment, given the rather broad acknowledgement of the importance of politics and public values in environmental decision-making. Following a discussion of the historical development of EU environmental law, chapter one will also look to the future, in particular EU enlargement to twenty-five members. The new problems, new opportunities and new interests that arise with new and distinctive member states increase the complexity and unpredictability of all EU action.

Sustainable development, which will be the subject of chapter two, has exercised a profound influence over environmental policy worldwide. This chapter will examine the development of the concept from the Brundtland Report in the 1980s,[2] to the output of the Johannesburg World Summit on Sustainable

---

[2] World Commission on Environment and Development, *Our Common Future* (Oxford, Oxford University Press, 1987).

Development in 2003.[3] Sustainable development is suggestive of the potential for radical proposals for ecological and social change to be absorbed by 'business as usual'; the dominance of economics in regulation has the potential here to merge with the dominance of the market and the dominance of economic interests as fora of decision-making. From a somewhat different perspective, sustainable development is a sobering reminder that environmental protection competes for attention with other genuinely imperative public interests. Finally, some of the most acute tensions in environmental policy, including the respective roles of 'the people' and 'the expert', are captured by different approaches to sustainable development. It is a concept that is sometimes approached as a highly technical (scientific or economic) objective, requiring expert decision-making. Chapter two will take the alternative view that sustainable development is a normative objective, the complexity and values inherent in which demand political judgment. The ability of sustainable development to provide space for political debate is its most important contribution to environmental law.

The notorious 'implementation deficit' of EU environmental law, which has an undeniable if poorly defined impact on the development of EU environmental law, will be the focus of chapter three. This chapter will discuss empirical and theoretical scholarship on the exercise of enforcement powers by regulators on the ground, which is enormously important when the EU seeks to improve poor implementation by the Member States. It will then examine some of the distinctive difficulties that arise in respect of implementation and enforcement of EU environmental law, and some of the steps being taken in response. These include efforts to engage third party enforcers of environmental law, building on the development of direct effect, the negotiation of EU legislation that provides national regulators with additional tools of enforcement, and efforts to improve central enforcement against the Member States. An awareness of weak application of the law has also become an important driver of environmental policy much more generally. A range of 'new' approaches to environmental regulation, including voluntary agreements, market instruments and public participation, are called on in the interests of implementation. As a consequence, the challenge of implementation recurs many times in this book.

The politicisation of risk has been difficult to escape in recent years, as various crises from 'mad cows' to biotechnology have exposed elite and otherwise isolated forms of decision-making to public criticism. The EU has been heavily implicated in this politicisation. The governance of expertise, in particular the relationship between technical expertise and politics, has accordingly become a key question of EU legitimacy. The strength of the EU's institutional acceptance of the political nature of risk regulation will be examined in chapter four through discussion particularly of committees and agencies. One of the factors contributing to politicisation of risk is improved understanding of the uncertainty of science: uncertainty and fallibility make plain the elusiveness of neutral and inevitable technical

---

[3] Details can be found at: http://www.johannesburgsummit.org/.

judgments. EU policy on risk regulation explicitly acknowledges uncertainty and the limits of scientific information. The EU approach to the precautionary principle, which by allowing regulators to take uncertainty seriously could reinforce efforts to mediate between political values and technical rationality, is discussed in this chapter. The prioritisation in World Trade Organisation rules of scientific and technical 'facts' could have a problematic impact on EU efforts to allow politics into risk regulation, and this will form the final subject of chapter four.

Recent years have seen the emergence of a remarkable consensus around the importance of public participation in environmental decision-making, the subject of chapter five. In the absence of strong representative democracy, participation holds great appeal to the EU. The role of the 'people' is however far from straightforward. Any hope that participatory democracy will cut through the EU's democratic deficit is rather inflated, and there is a danger that the overreaching rhetoric will undermine the improvements that are achievable. More modest objectives are however increasingly placed centre-stage, in particular the potential for public participation to respond to a range of concerns about the quality and effectiveness of environmental decisions. Chapter five will examine the role of the public in EU level environmental decision-making, focusing on the three 'pillars' of the UN ECE Aarhus Convention,[4] that is access to environmental information, public participation in environmental decision-making and access to justice in environmental matters.

These three pillars are rather better established in EU legislative efforts to control decision-making processes within the Member States. Chapter six will examine the way in which 'hard' EU legislation gives teeth to the Member States' undertakings in the Aarhus Convention. The broader phenomenon of 'proceduralisation' of EU environmental law, the effort to stimulate environmentally beneficial reflection and learning within institutions, will also be discussed here. Much recent environmental legislation imposes constraints on national procedure: legislation on environmental assessment,[5] integrated pollution prevention and control,[6] and eco-management and audit[7] will be discussed in some detail. In providing for openness and participation, procedural law has the potential to enhance both the quality and the democratic credentials of that decision-making. Simultaneously, however, in a somewhat countervailing effort to improve the quality and accountability of expert decision-making, proceduralisation may emphasise 'expert' processes, such as formal risk assessment and cost benefit analysis. This could conflict with the apparent desire to expand the lay public's

---

[4] Convention on Access to Information, Public Participation in Decision-making and Access to Justice in Environmental Matters (1998), available at http://www.unece.org/env/pp/documents/cep43e.pdf.
[5] Dir 85/337 on the Assessment of the Effects of Certain Private and Public Projects on the Environment [1985] OJ L 175/40, as amended by Dir 97/11/EC [1997] OJ L 73/05; Dir 2001/42 on the Assessment of the Effects of Certain Plans and Programmes on the Environment [2001] OJ L 197/30.
[6] Dir 96/61 on Integrated Pollution Prevention and Control [1996] OJ L 257/26.
[7] Reg 761/2001 Allowing Voluntary Participation by Organisations in a Community Eco-Management and Audit Scheme (EMAS) [2001] OJ L 114/1.

participation in decision-making. It should also be noted that procedural constraints on the Member States are matched, at least superficially, by enhanced national discretion on substantive environmental standards. This de-centralisation of substantive decision-making is in part an issue of effectiveness/efficiency, based on arguments that centralised regulation is unable to respond to environmental needs. De-centralisation also responds to questions of democratic legitimacy, moving decisions 'closer to the people'. Changes to the complexion of environmental regulation in recent years suggest that if radical de-centralisation does not currently form a mainstream response to the EU's legitimacy problems, greater flexibility may. The EU intervention in national democratic processes that often goes along with this flexibility seems so far to have been accepted with little anxiety. It is perhaps viewed as an acceptable quid pro quo for substantive flexibility, but it is nevertheless a potentially momentous development.

Using the market to influence private decision-making is an alternative approach to criticisms of environmental regulation, and is discussed in chapter seven. A turn to the market to provide environmental protection does imply an element of public participation in decision-making, as all participate in markets; the sort of public participation envisaged is, however, very different from the more deliberative stance discussed particularly in chapter five. The market challenge to environmental regulation assumes more than any other critique that environmental regulation is based on the economic analysis of market failure, rather than on explicit collective decisions involving the non-economic value of environmental goods. Although market instruments are generally best conceptualised as instruments of implementation of environmental policy, rather than as instruments by which environmental policy is set, their potential to shift decision-making from collective government to the market should not be dismissed. Nevertheless, market instruments can be useful tools for environmental protection, and this chapter will discuss EU progress on minimum rates of taxation for energy products and electricity,[8] greenhouse gas emission allowance trading,[9] touching also on the 'new generation' of internal market disputes provoked by market instruments. Chapter seven will also consider the Environmental Liability Directive,[10] which started life as an instrument of cost internalisation, but ended up predominantly as a supplementary tool of implementation. The changing fortunes of this policy area suggest that preoccupation by the 'implementation gap' can deflect attention from other issues. This chapter will also discuss the role of 'green consumerism', looking particularly at the Eco-Labelling Regulation.[11]

---

[8] Dir 2003/96 Restructuring the Community Framework for the Taxation of Energy Products and Electricity [2003] OJ L 283/51.

[9] Dir 2003/87 Establishing a Scheme for Greenhouse Gas Emission Allowance Trading Within the Community and Amending Council Directive 96/61/EC [2003] OJ L 275/32.

[10] Dir 2004/35 on Environmental Liability with Regard to the Prevention and Remedying of Environmental Damage [2004] OJ L 143/56.

[11] Reg 1980/2000 on a Revised Community Eco-Label Award Scheme [2000] OJ L 237/1.

Although every chapter discusses different aspects of substantive environmental law, chapters eight and nine turn more explicitly to substantive law, discussing waste and genetically modified organisms (GMOs) respectively. Whilst these are important and interesting topics in their own right, they also demonstrate acutely many of the challenges faced in EU environmental law.

Notwithstanding its lack of obvious charisma, waste regulation is a fascinating area of study. It is extremely politically sensitive, and is often a highly visible manifestation of environmental damage and human profligacy. This immediately suggests that problems will be encountered if a highly technocratic approach is taken to regulation, and the role of public participation in waste management is an interesting contemporary feature of the law. Because of the vast numbers of tiny decisions that lead to waste production, waste regulation has also proven itself to be particularly amenable to, and in need of, 'alternative' regulatory approaches, particularly market and voluntary instruments. Chapter eight will discuss efforts to move beyond the 'end of pipe' regulation of waste management facilities, and some recent efforts to move waste up the waste hierarchy, including the Landfill Directive.[12] It will look at the alternative regulatory instruments of extended producer responsibility and voluntary agreements, particularly as provided in the End of Life Vehicles Directive.[13] Chapter eight will also discuss of some of the strangely lawyerly controversies that proliferate in waste regulation, in particular the difficult definition of waste itself. One final observation that might be made of waste law is the continued reliance on detailed substantive centralised standards, suggesting that proceduralisation and flexibility is not as far reaching as all that.

The regulation of genetically modified organisms (GMOs) in the EU has been highly controversial and strikingly political. Public and consumer opinion has been hugely, perhaps untypically, influential. The chaos into which this area of regulation descended in the late 1990s has left a legacy of extraordinarily complex and detailed legislation, and the ability of this regulatory framework to reconcile diverging views of the new technology is still in doubt. The regulation of GMOs illustrates a range of difficult issues around decision-making in EU environmental law. In particular, GMO regulation attempts to address conflict between lay and expert understandings of risk, controversial divisions of responsibility between EU and national authorities, and pressures from global trade liberalisation, all of which will be discussed in chapter nine. GMO regulation is also pervaded by a rhetoric of consumer choice, allowing a revisiting of 'green consumerism' in a very specific area. The regulation of GMOs brings out especially well the tension between highly technical and scientific proceduralisation, implied by the centrality of risk assessment, and the need for public participation in an area that provokes intense public concern and scrutiny. The proper role of public opinion in decision-making on controversial social issues is a topic that goes far beyond environmental questions, and has tested national governments

---

[12] Dir 1999/31 on the Landfill of Waste [1999] OJ L 182/1.
[13] Dir 2000/53 on End of Life Vehicles [2000] OJ L 269/34.

for many years; biotechnology is one of the areas pushing these decisions to the regional and international level.

The two chapters on waste and GMOs bring together some of the most important themes raised in this book. A very brief final chapter will make some further concluding observations.

Finally, I wish to thank a number of colleagues and friends for their comments on earlier drafts of parts of this book: Carolyn Abbot, Andrea Biondi, Michael Doherty, Sarah Hannett, Peter Oliver, and Joanne Scott all gave their time and expertise very generously, and their comments have undoubtedly improved the final text. Needless to say, the shortcomings are all my own. Different parts of this book have formed the basis of a number of conference and seminar papers, at the Universities of Exeter, Hamburg, Leuven, Manchester, and the Institute of Advanced Legal Studies, as well as King's College London. I am grateful to the organisers and participants for the opportunity to present some ideas and for useful feedback. Many thanks also to Natalie Cook and the Centre of European Law at King's College London for invaluable research assistance.

1

Environmental Regulation in the European Union

INTRODUCTION

T HE ORIGINAL EEC Treaty's silence on the subject of the environment is
hardly surprising. The new Communities faced the immediate and urgent
objectives of post-war economic recovery, and environmental protection
was in any event virtually invisible as a policy concern in the 1950s. Along with
governments around the world, the EC first ventured explicitly and systematically
into environmental policy in the early 1970s, on the basis of a generous interpretation of the original objectives of the Treaty by the European Council. The
European Council considered that the incorporation of non-material values was
crucial if the Community's economic objectives[1] were to be meaningful; and that
this implied efforts to combat pollution and nuisance, and to improve quality of
life and the environment. This led directly to the *First Environmental Action
Programme*,[2] setting out policy on the environment for the period 1973 to 1976.
The environment was now firmly on the European political agenda.

This chapter will consider some of the issues underlying the development of
EC environmental law from these early days, beginning by outlining the most
common justifications of regulating for environmental protection at all. The variety
and distinctiveness of the rationales for environmental regulation indicate that
even if there is broad agreement on the need to regulate to protect the environment, significant differences will remain over both the identification and the
resolution of environmental problems. The regulation of environmental protection at EC, rather than national, level will then be discussed. EC environmental
policy first emerged in support of the single market imperative, but gained independent and increasingly prominent status through successive treaty amendments.
More than three decades into EC environmental law, the precise scope of EC
competence in this area, however, remains subject to debate.

The EC Treaty's current environmental provisions have evolved since the
1986 Single European Act through an almost continual process of treaty
reform. The latest set of changes were perhaps intended to put a stop to that

---

[1] '[A] harmonious development of economic activities, a continuous and balanced expansion, an
increase in stability, and accelerated raising of the standard of living', Art 2 EEC.
[2] First Environmental Action Programme, adopted by Council Declaration on the Programme of
Action of the European Communities on the Environment [1973] OJ C 112/1.

process. The Laeken European Council in 2001 convened a 'Convention on the Future of Europe',[3] which submitted a draft *Treaty Establishing a Constitution for Europe* to the European Council in July 2003.[4] A new Constitution based on this text was agreed by the Member States at intergovernmental conference in June 2004, following rather prolonged political debate and disagreement. This Treaty now faces a drawn out and uncertain process of ratification in the Member States. Central to the constitutional changes, and a significant challenge for the development of EC environmental law, is the historic accession of ten new Member States to the EU in May 2004.[5] The possible challenges that ten new members, eight central and eastern European countries, plus two Mediterranean countries, will pose for EC environmental regulation, will be the final subject of this chapter.

WHY REGULATE?

Various reasons, selfish, altruistic, political or personal may motivate environmental regulation.[6] Regardless of whether or how these motives operate, public interest rationales are needed to justify environmental regulation in the public sphere; a number of such rationales, economic, political and ethical, compete for attention. Economic justifications for environmental regulation generally prevail in EC law, perhaps because of the dominant economic objectives of the polity. Rather than attempt to analyse and critique the different justifications for environmental regulation, this section will provide a brief introduction to the economic perspectives that will recur in this and later chapters, followed by a brief consideration of some criticisms and alternatives.

Garrett Hardin's classic article, 'The Tragedy of the Commons'[7] provides a vivid fable for the economic understanding of environmental problems. To take

---

[3] [2001] OJ C 80/85. The text of the Laeken Declaration is available at http://european-convention. eu.int/pdf/LKNEN.pdf.

[4] [2003] OJ C 169/1. The Treaty establishing a Constitution for Europe can be found at [2004] OJ C 310/1, also available at http://europa.eu.int/constitution/index_en.htm

[5] The ten new entrants are the Czech Republic, Cyprus, Estonia, Hungary, Latvia, Lithuania, Malta, Poland, Slovakia and Slovenia. For discussions of the relationship between constitutional reform and enlargement, see JHH Weiler, 'A Constitution for Europe? Some Hard Choices' (2002) 40 *Journal of Common Market Studies* 563; N Walker, 'Constitutionalising Enlargement, Enlarging Constitutionalism' (2003) 9 *European Law Journal* 365; A Wiener, 'Finality vs Enlargement: Constitutive Practices and Opposing Rationales in the Reconstruction of Europe' in JHH Weiler and M Wind (eds), *European Constitutionalism Beyond the State* (Cambridge, Cambridge University Press, 2003); B De Witte, 'The Impact of Enlargement on the Constitution of the European Union' in M Cremona (ed), *The Enlargement of the European Union* (Oxford, Oxford University Press, 2003).

[6] See for example C Hilson, *Regulating Pollution: A UK and EC Perspective* (Oxford, Hart Publishing, 2000), especially ch 1; R Baldwin and M Cave, *Understanding Regulation: Theory, Strategy, and Practice* (Oxford, Oxford University Press, 1999).

[7] G Hardin, 'The Tragedy of the Commons' (1968) 162 *Science* 1243. The article has been criticised as failing to capture the actual potential for management of traditional commons, but that does not detract from its explanatory force. See DH Cole, *Pollution and Property: Comparing Ownership Institutions for Environmental Protection* (Cambridge, Cambridge University Press, 2002) for a discussion of the complexity of the relationship between property regimes and environmental protection.

Hardin's example, each herder using a common pasture has an economic incentive to add one more animal to the pasture. The herder will benefit individually from the extra cattle, but the burden on the pasture will be shared by all users. Individually rational economic decisions therefore lead to potentially disastrous results, as every herder adds one more beast until the pasture collapses through overgrazing. Hardin applies this thinking to pollution: each individual benefits from adding a unit of pollution to a common sink such as air or a river, but the burden is shared. Collective action, rather than individual changes to behaviour, is likely to be necessary to resolve the tragedy of the commons. The link between individual behaviour and environmental harm is often not obvious.[8] Even if the link is obvious, free riding is likely to be a significant problem and the incentive to change is in any event low: each individual can make only a small contribution to the solution, but possibly at high individual cost. Collective action by regulation can then be justified:

> The tragedy of the commons as a food basket is averted by private property ... But the air and waters surrounding us cannot readily be fenced, and so the tragedy of the commons as a cesspool must be prevented by different means, by coercive laws or taxing devices.[9]

Hardin's tragedy of the commons builds on the concept of 'externalities', which is another crucial economic metaphor. Externalities are costs of producing a product which are not reflected in the final cost of the product. Farmers whose crops die because of the smoke from a factory, government or consumers who pay to remove the factory's emissions from drinking water, and communities living around the factory which suffer the health effects of its emissions, all bear some of the factory's external costs. The operator has to purchase machinery, raw materials and labour, but in an unregulated market does not have to purchase the use of the water or air, reducing the cost of production. Not only is this intuitively unfair, but from an economic perspective, artificially low prices lead to an inefficient level of production (too much production). Regulation is justified as an attempt to internalise externalities, bringing them within operating costs.

Environmental economics provides some powerful arguments for regulatory action to protect the environment, and, importantly, is able to put those arguments within dominant political discourse around economic prosperity.[10] Without the insight of environmental economists, it would have been difficult to get past the undeniable 'failure of the economic system to take account of the valuable services which natural environments provide'.[11] Many concerned with environmental

---

[8] For example climate change, depletion of the ozone layer, destruction of the rain forests.

[9] Hardin, above n 7, p 1254. Note that there are many efforts now to simulate markets in the use of the commons as 'cesspool', that is in pollution. See further ch 7 below.

[10] DW Pearce, EB Barbier and A Markandya, *Blueprint for a Green Economy* (London, Earthscan, 1989) popularised environmental economics, which whilst far from a new discipline, had then nothing like the policy influence that it does now.

[11] D Pearce and EB Barbier, *Blueprint for a Sustainable Economy* (London, Earthscan, 2000), p 1.

protection are, however, deeply uneasy about economic approaches to environmental regulation, for a number of reasons.

One fundamental reason for mistrust of environmental economics is that economic assessments attach no moral significance to environmental destruction. Environmental harm is simply the neutral activity of any rational economic actor. Nor does an economic approach view the environment as a distinctive or autonomous concern: it is simply one element of overall human welfare, and human welfare is assumed to be the primary concern of environmental policy. This charge of anthropocentrism against environmental economics clearly sticks, and the place of elements of the natural world that are without human benefit (the scientifically uninteresting, commercially valueless, aesthetically ordinary) is vulnerable in even broadly defined anthropocentric environmental ethics. Although it is important to be reminded of the possibility that the environment has a value unconnected with human welfare, anthropocentrism is probably always going to be difficult to escape in law. Ethical approaches that place a fundamental and intrinsic value on nature,[12] independent from, unconnected with, and prior to human concerns, would have to *prohibit* the continued exploitation of nature.[13] Such a radical change is not about to find any imminent favour in EC (or any Member State) official policy, which prefers just to manage the exploitation of the environment more effectively. Policy-makers are hardly likely to start empathising with the bears.[14] 'Enlightened anthropocentrism',[15] which brings non-material values into play by emphasising the complexity and value of human relationships with nature, might however be sought in real life environmental policy. The difficulty, of course, is in checking its implementation; no doubt economists could measure it.

A more concrete criticism of the economic approach to regulation arises out of the concern that it leads to an overemphasis of the goal of economic efficiency, at the expense of environmental protection and other social goals, and at the expense of open discussion of the values involved in social decision-making. The prevalence of cost benefit analysis (CBA) in regulatory activity strengthens this concern.[16] CBA involves a comparison of the costs and benefits of a proposal, and

---

[12] Intrinsic value does not depend on human value. This is sometimes contrasted with 'inherent value', which refers to non-use values such as the value that people place on the beauty of a natual resource, or on simply knowing that a resource exists, R Attfield, *Environmental Ethics: An Overview for the Twenty-First Century* (Cambridge, Polity Press, 2003), p 12.

[13] This is not the place for a detailed discussion of environmental ethics: see generally Attfield, *ibid*; A Dobson, *Green Political Thought* (London, Routledge, 2000), especially chs 1 and 2; J Alder and D Wilkinson, *Environmental Law and Ethics* (Basingstoke, Macmillan Press, 1999).

[14] Dobson, *ibid*, p 50, citing Robert Aitken: 'Deep ecology ... requires openness to the black bear, so that honey dribbles down your fur coat as you catch the bus to work'. Arne Naess is the founder of the 'deep ecology' movement, which urges the identification with all life, see A Naess, *Ecology, Community and Lifestyle* (Cambridge, Cambridge University Press, 1989); A Naess, 'The Shallow and the Deep, Long-range Ecology Movement: A Summary' (1973) 16 *Inquiry* 95.

[15] Dobson makes a slightly different distinction between 'strong' anthropocentrism (meaning 'human instrumentality') and 'weak' anthropocentrism (meaning 'human centredness'), Dobson, *ibid*, p 51. See also Attfield, above n 12, ch 1.

[16] Art 174(3) EC in the Environment Title requires the Community to 'take account of ... the potential benefits and costs of action or lack of action'.

in theory only measures that are demonstrated to be efficient, that is creating more benefit than cost, are pursued. Although the EU approach to CBA is somewhat less rigid than this description might suggest,[17] its presence can nevertheless place efficiency at the centre of policy.

Although an economic rationale for regulating does not require CBA or the monetary valuation of the environment, environmental economists argue that this puts environmental goods on an equal footing with other goods.[18] The attribution of a monetary value to environmental goods raises concerns even beyond questions of 'intrinsic' value. One category of criticisms of CBA of regulatory initiatives, and indeed an economic approach to environmental regulation more generally, points to the highly disputed and variable outcomes of environmental valuation.[19] The direct and indirect financial costs of externalities such as failed crops, ill health or dirty water, can in theory be calculated. However, the physical effects of an activity and its regulation are complex and unpredictable, as well as hard to price. The necessary information is difficult and expensive to acquire; the regulated industry is best placed to provide the information, but generally has incentives to overestimate the costs and underestimate the benefits of regulation. In any event, the value to human beings of environmental goods goes far beyond physical effects, and as economists pursue a comprehensive assessment, the 'inherent' and 'non-use' values of environmental goods are assessed. These include, for example, the value of aesthetic or spiritual appreciation of landscape, and the value individuals attribute to environmental resources with which they have had in the past and anticipate in the future no personal connection at all. Enormous controversy revolves around the monetary calculation of these values,[20] which is also often an expensive and unpredictable exercise. 'Revealed preference' methods involve calculating what people actually pay for environmental resources, for example by reference to relative property values, or to the cost of travelling to an environmental resource for recreation. 'Hypothetical preference' methods are based on surveys of individuals' willingness to pay for the receipt of environmental benefits, or willingness to accept payment for their removal. The accuracy of inherent and non-use valuation is even more profoundly uncertain than valuation

---

[17] See the discussion in ch 4 below.

[18] Pearce and Barbier, above n 11.

[19] By way of example, see the vastly different assessments of the benefits to be gained by improving visibility at the Grand Canyon, M Sagoff, 'Cows Are Better Than Condos, Or How Economists Help Solve Environmental Problems' (2003) 12 *Environmental Values* 449, p 458; or by regulating arsenic in drinking water, C Sunstein, *Risk and Reason: Safety, Law and the Environment* (Cambridge, Cambridge University Press, 2002), ch 7. J Froud, R Boden, A Ogus and P Stubbs, *Controlling the Regulators* (Basingstoke, MacMillan, 1998), ch 5, discuss the problematic assessment of the costs of Dir 1999/31 on the Landfill of Waste [1999] OJ L 182/01.

[20] It is not appropriate to consider the extensive literature on environmental valuation here. See Pearce and Barbier, above n 11, especially ch 3; M Jacobs *The Green Economy* (London, Pluto Press, 1991), especially ch 17; DA Farber, *Eco-pragmatism: Making Sensible Environmental Decisions in an Uncertain World* (Chicago, University of Chicago Press, 1999), especially ch 2.

of physical impacts. Although techniques are increasingly refined, uncertainty remains endemic.

An economic approach to environmental protection also raises distributional concerns. In the absence of compensating mechanisms, it is likely to prioritise the environmental problems of the rich over the environmental needs of the poor. The value placed on environmental goods, relative to the value created by environmentally damaging activity, is likely to depend on the wealth of those participating in real or hypothetical markets, as well as their social circumstances.[21] Similarly, *who* bears the benefits and burdens of regulation may be a crucial factor in social decisions. Regulation is inherently distributive of burden and benefit, a subject at the heart of any ordinary approach to politics. It is possible, and perhaps desirable, to adjust economic calculations to account for these distributional concerns,[22] but this incorporation of value judgment undermines the apparent objectivity of the process.

The most fundamental criticism of environmental valuation questions whether the full complexity of the value of environmental resources, even only their value to human beings, is even *capable* of expression in monetary terms. The *reductio ad absurdum* of the economic basis for environmental regulation can be seen in the 'plastic trees' debate.[23] Plastic trees and piped birdsong may be cheaper, longer lasting, and easier to maintain than the real thing. Given time and education, we may even learn to love them, and the relative welfare provided by plastic as opposed to real trees would reflect that. If plastic trees turn out to provide greater welfare, they could or should replace real trees. Intuitive distaste for such a proposition suggests that something important is missing from the analysis, some value that cannot be captured by economic analysis, or cannot ever be replicated by plastic trees. More prosaically, although perhaps more urgently, this debate from the mid-1970s looks very different from the beginning of the 21st century. We now have a far better understanding of the role of trees, in, for example, climate regulation and the mitigation of air and noise pollution, as well as an improved understanding of how little we know about the complexity of ecosystems. The *instrumental* benefits of real trees are perhaps clearer than they were, and increase as trees become less common. These factors could and should go into a sensitive CBA. One cannot help but observe how unlikely that would have been in the 1970s. Our limited understanding of the world means that even the most narrowly anthropocentric utilitarian should use CBA with great caution; the chance that the efficient number of trees could be miscalculated seems unacceptably high.

---

[21] See G Smith, *Deliberative Democracy and the Environment* (London, Routledge, 2003), p 36; CR Sunstein, 'Endogenous Preferences, Environmental Law' (1993) 22 *Journal of Legal Studies* 217.

[22] W Beckerman, 'Sustainable Development: Is it a Useful Concept?' (1994) 3 *Environmental Values* 191.

[23] MH Kreiger, 'What's Wrong With Plastic Trees?' (1973) 179 *Science* 446 (his reply to that question is 'very little', p 453); L Tribe, 'Ways Not to Think About Plastic Trees: New Foundations for Environmental Law' (1974) 83 *Yale Law Journal* 1315; M Sagoff, 'On Preserving the Natural Environment' (1974–75) 84 *Yale Law Journal* 205; L Tribe, 'From Environmental Foundations to Constitutional Structures: Learning From Nature's Future' (1974–75) 84 *Yale Law Journal* 545.

And of course we have the paradox that the dedicated scientific endeavour on which improved knowledge would be based is in many cases outside the market system upheld by economic justifications of environmental regulation.[24]

One might respond to the uncertainty problems by relying on the precautionary principle, which provides space for regulation to take account of uncertainty and ignorance. The precautionary principle will be discussed in chapter four below. To pre-empt that discussion a little, the precautionary principle provides no easy solution to the difficulties of existing approaches to CBA, although on some approaches it reinforces arguments that CBA is not an appropriate mechanism of decision-making. More generally, however, one might buttress anthropocentric arguments for environmental protection by environmental principles such as the precautionary principle, the polluter pays principle and the preventive principle. We do not have to agree with his adoption of a 'post-modern' analysis of law to enjoy Nicholas de Sadeleer's argument that environmental principles provide rationality in an increasingly complex legal world.[25] Although the content and application of the environmental principles are disputed, they are very widely accepted as 'good things', and this consensus means that they can be called on by those seeking a 'general truth' to justify environmental regulation. General principles do not and cannot, however, resolve detailed questions as to who regulates or how. Just as they can at best provide only guidance in particular difficult cases,[26] they cannot make simple the choice between particular approaches to, or understandings of, environmental problems. For example, the polluter pays principle is called on both as an economic tool and as a tool of 'environmental justice'; the precautionary principle can be approached as a guide to the use of scientific knowledge, and/or as a mechanism to move beyond conventional scientific knowledge.[27] The environmental principles themselves cannot resolve any debate over the justifications for environmental regulation, although they do generally assume an anthropocentric understanding of environmental problem, which is presumably an inevitable part of their embrace by the legal establishment.

One final criticism of economic approaches to environmental regulation lies in the value judgments that are necessarily made at every stage of a CBA,[28] from deciding whose costs and values count, that is the scope of the 'community of concern',[29] to interpreting the results. One example of the introduction of non-economic value

[24] DA Kysar, 'Some Realism About Environmental Skepticism: The Implications of Bjørn Lomborg's *The Skeptical Environmentalist* for Environmental Law and Policy' (2003) 30 *Ecological Law Quarterly* 223.

[25] N de Sadeleer, *Environmental Principles: From Political Slogans to Legal Rules* (Oxford, Oxford University Press, 2002).

[26] See MG Doherty, 'Hard Cases and Environmental Principles: An Aid to Interpretation?' vol 3 *Yearbook of European Environmental Law* 57.

[27] The polluter pays principle will be discussed in ch 7 below; the precautionary principle in ch 4 below. Sustainable development is the subject of ch 2 below.

[28] See the articles cited above n 23; D Kennedy, 'Cost-Benefit Analysis of Entitlement Problems: A Critique' (1980–81) 33 *Stanford Law Review* 387, pp 401 and onwards.

[29] Smith, above n 21, pp 39–45; C Hilson, 'Greening Citizenship: Boundaries of Membership and the Environment' (2001) 13 *Journal of Environmental Law* 335, discusses the different values arrived at in the measurement of non-use value of a stretch of river, depending on whether all of the water company's customers were included in the valuation, or just those within the affected catchment area.

judgments into the process is the question of 'intrinsic value'. If they pursue CBA, policy makers have presumably disregarded the belief that aspects of the environment have an intrinsic value incapable of expression in monetary terms. However, if that belief is held by any of the individuals taking part in a 'hypothetical preference' survey, things become more complicated. The individuals involved may refuse to give any figure, or put an enormous figure on an environmental resource. To avoid skewing the values used in the policy process by these 'protest bids', protest bids will generally be discounted in the CBA. However, this involves an incorporation of non-economic criteria and professional judgment that undermines the apparent objectivity and inevitability of the exercise. Similarly, a survey of 'willingness to pay' (that is what individuals would pay to keep an environmental resource) provides consistently lower figures than a survey of 'willingness to accept' (that is the sum that would be accepted as compensation for the destruction of a resource); deciding which question to ask in these circumstances is quite blatantly not a neutral task. This is not to criticise the individuals involved in environmental valuations, who may properly be following best professional practice, but to note that the values of the profession may be called on almost without being noticed. Even taking human wants as the ultimate frame of reference is an important judgment, as is the decision that efficiency is a good in itself.[30]

Given that CBA is far from a neutral exercise, we might question the wisdom of leaving decisions on environmental protection entirely to its practitioners. It should be possible to respond to concerns about the normative nature of CBA (or other economic assessments of environmental protection) by ensuring that it is used simply to provide information among a range of information for an explicitly *political* judgment, and that it is not a judgment in itself.[31] There are nevertheless two opposite dangers. The first is that leaving non-material values such as environmental values out of the CBA, to be addressed separately in a political decision, may mean that they are unable to compete with the more immediate economic objectives of the policy process. Conversely, their inclusion creates an illusion of comprehensiveness, concealing uncertainty and rendering implicit necessary value judgments. A deliberate and concerted effort is necessary to ensure that the decision remains open at the political stage.

Which brings us to Mark Sagoff, a prominent figure in the plastic trees debate, who has made important criticisms of economic understandings of environmental problems.[32] Sagoff provides an account of the *political* nature of environmental decision-making. As well as bringing public values to the attention of

---

[30] L Tribe, 'Ways Not to Think', above n 23; M Sagoff, *The Economy of the Earth: Philosophy, Law and the Environment* (Cambridge, Cambridge University Press, 1988); R Dworkin, 'Is Wealth a Value?' (1980) 9 *Journal of Legal Studies* 191.
[31] Sunstein, above n 19, advocates the 'cost benefit state' as a means to improve the rationality of risk regulation. Rather than abandoning CBA because of concern that values will be ignored, he argues that care should be taken precisely *not* to ignore those values, but to require them to be articulated.
[32] Sagoff, above n 30.

decision makers, the political process shapes and determines those values, which emerge from debate and discussion.[33] Political value judgments, rather than economic calculations, are required to justify decisions. The distinction between values on the one hand, and interests or preferences on the other, is central to Sagoff's thesis. Preferences or interests are measured by economists, and are assumed to be pre-formed, static factors; by contrast, values emerge from society as a result of argument and debate, and are, Sagoff argues, far more likely to invoke the public good than the private interest. Private preferences and public values may diverge in the same individual. For example, as a consumer of cheap tourist flights that fail to internalise all of their environmental costs, an individual might hold an environmentally destructive preference; whilst as a political citizen, the same individual might value environmental protection, for example, by voting for politicians promising high taxes on aviation fuel. Of course, another word for 'divided preferences' might simply be hypocrisy.[34] However, it is not necessary to argue that divided preferences make a good basis for public policy, to agree that 'not all political decisions are economic', or that environmental regulation should be the product of rational discussion and debate, rather than economic analysis.[35]

This dispute over the nature of environmental problems is a perennial debate, the question of whether environmental problems can be assessed as economic questions, or only as questions of value. It is reflected especially in the recurrent tension between economically focused decision-making (and other highly technical tools of decision-making) and explicitly political decision-making, which will be returned to throughout this book. The aim here has been simply to illustrate how contentious this very basic question (Why regulate?) is. Criticisms of environmental regulation are not simply pragmatic critiques of effectiveness, but reflect profound divisions as to the sort of world in which we believe we live, and the sort of world in which we want to live. And far beyond the environmental sphere, these debates are about the ways in which society should take difficult decisions on which reasonable people disagree.

WHY EC REGULATION?

The next question is why the EC, rather than the Member States, should take action to protect the environment. The principle of subsidiarity is a useful starting

---

[33] See the discussion of 'deliberation' in ch 5 below.

[34] Examples Sagoff provides, apparently from his own experience, include the bribe of a judge to fix a speeding ticket (consumer preference) and voting against the corrupt judge at the next election (citizen value), and the display of an 'ecology now' sticker on a car that leaks oil, Sagoff above n 30, pp 52–3. DA Farber, 'Environmentalism, Economics and the Public Interest' (1989) 41 *Stanford Law Review* 1021 is scathing.

[35] Whilst Sagoff rejects CBA and the pursuit of efficiency as a social goal, he elsewhere applauds certain contributions of environmental economics, particularly in achieving cost effective implementation of a politically determined environmental aim, Sagoff, above n 23. In that he is not so far from Farber, above n 20, who in some respects is highly critical of Sagoff, Farber, above n 34.

point. It was first introduced into the new environment title of the Treaty in the Single European Act, before being 'promoted' to a general principle by the Maastricht Treaty.

> In areas which do not fall within its exclusive competence, the Community shall take action, in accordance with the principle of subsidiarity, only if and insofar as the objectives of the proposed action cannot be sufficiently achieved by the Member States and can therefore, by reason of the scale or effects of the proposed action, be better achieved by the Community.
>
> Any action by the Community shall not go beyond what is necessary to achieve the objectives of this Treaty.[36]

The relevance of subsidiarity, which does not apply when the Community has exclusive competence, in the environmental field is not disputed; although determining areas of exclusive competence can be problematic, shared environmental competence is generally accepted.

At the time of its introduction into the main part of the Treaty, subsidiarity was politically extremely significant, and broad concerns about national sovereignty meant that it was presented in some Member States as a real limit on Community competence. Most would now discuss subsidiarity in terms of identifying the optimal level of regulation, rather than as *per se* de-centralising. Identifying the optimal level of regulation could require consideration of process, such as rights of participation or the willingness of the different levels to take action,[37] a perspective that might include the possibility that centralised decision-making bodies are likely to be more democratically remote, and less responsive than the local. Subsidiarity in the Treaty, however, is concerned with the privileges of the Member States, rather with citizen rights or lower levels of government.[38] The debate in EC environmental law, in any event, tends to focus on the *effectiveness* of action.

There are at least three commonly cited justifications for EC level action on the environment: physical, economic and 'psychic' 'spillovers' (or externalities).[39] The first, embracing primarily transboundary pollution, should be the least problematic area. Not only is centralised regulation necessary to address physical externalities, but in the absence of central action the local regulator has every reason to encourage the export of pollution, for example by requiring its own polluters to install tall chimneys to disperse air pollution. Physical spillovers, however, justify relatively little environmental legislation, as the effects of much regulated pollution

---

[36] Art 5 EC.

[37] There is no guarantee that the national level *will* take action, once it has asserted the right to take action.

[38] G de Búrca, 'Reappraising Subsidiarity's Significance after Amsterdam' *Harvard Jean Monnet Working Paper 7/99* discusses 'executive subsidiarity' as opposed to 'democratic subsidiarity'. Note that the Treaty Establishing a Constitution for Europe does refer action that 'cannot be sufficiently achieved by the Member States, either at central level or at regional and local level', Art I–11(3).

[39] G Cross, 'Subsidiarity and the Environment' [1996] *Yearbook of European Law* 197; J Scott, *EC Environmental Law* (London, Longman, 1998), pp 10–22; J Jans, *European Environmental Law* (Groningen, Europa Law Institute, 2000) pp 12–14.

remain local. It is nevertheless a very important basis for EC level regulation of environmental protection. Particularly at a time when the Community institutions need to seek greater engagement with the citizen, environmental policy emphasises the physical interdependence of the Member States, and should demonstrate the capacity for improved responses at the central level.[40]

Economic spillover as a rationale for central action relies on the argument that differing levels of environmental protection in different states distort competition between economic operators, because an operator in a state with very stringent environmental standards faces higher costs than an operator in a Member State with lower standards.[41] Whilst this justification for centralised regulation is subject to considerable criticism, its perceived importance to the internal market means that it is very solidly placed in EC environmental law.[42] However, distortion of competition arguments provide only relatively weak guidance in particular cases. Almost anything can be said to interfere with the internal market in some way, begging the question as to how developed an internal market we want; reference to subsidiarity does not in itself answer that pre-existing political question.[43] An important follow on from the notion of competitive disparities, is the 'race to the bottom' argument.[44] This makes two assumptions: first, that industry migrates to areas with laxer environmental standards in order to gain a competitive advantage[45]; secondly that states compete for economic investment in part on the basis of environmental regulation, leading to a ratcheting down of environmental standards. The 'race to the bottom' phenomenon is controversial both empirically and theoretically. *Empirically* it is difficult to establish that firms do move to take advantage of less severe environmental regulation, given the many factors that influence location decisions, and the sunk costs once that decision has been taken.[46] At a general level, however, we do observe that polluting activities are established in parts of the world with weak social regulation or weak enforcement,

[40] See D McGillivray and J Holder, 'Locating EC Environmental Law' (2001) 20 *Yearbook of European Law* 139.

[41] See Case 92/79 *Commission v Italy* [1980] ECR 1115, discussed below. Protocol No 7 to the Treaty of Amsterdam on the Approach of the Parties to Subsidiarity and Proportionality, requires the Community legislator to consider whether: 'actions by Member States alone or lack of Community action would conflict with the requirements of the Treaty (such as the need to correct distortion of competition or avoid disguised restrictions on trade or strengthen economic and social cohesion) or would otherwise significantly damage Member States' interests', para 5.

[42] Many of the criticisms of centralised environmental regulation come from the perspective of well developed federal states (particularly the US) where the political impetus of market integration is absent. See R van den Bergh, 'Economic Criteria for Applying the Subsidiarity Principle in European Environmental Law' in RL Revesz, R Sands and RB Stewart (eds), *Environmental Law, the Economy and Sustainable Development* (Cambridge, Cambridge University Press, 2000).

[43] de Búrca, above n 38.

[44] See RB Stewart, 'Introduction' in Revesz, Sands and Stewart, above n 42.

[45] 'Migration' includes new operations locating partly on the basis of environmental regulation. See also the 'stuck in the mud' alternative, suggesting not that states reduce environmental standards, but that they are reluctant unilaterally to improve them, discussed in APJ Mol, *Globalization and Environmental Reform: Ecological Modernization of the Global Economy* (Cambridge, Massachussets, The MIT Press, 2001), p 86.

[46] van den Bergh, above n 42, pp 85–6.

and moreover, industry migration only has to be a credible threat to set regulatory competition into motion. *Theoretically*, it is argued that regulatory competition is a good thing. If it is accepted that preferences for levels of environmental quality vary between regions, and that costs and benefits of regulation vary, regulatory competition should lead to an efficient level of regulation, that is a level for which a society's members are prepared to pay.[47] This alternative route to economic integration, through competition rather than harmonisation, has effectively been rejected by the EC institutions, and again, whatever the controversy, the race to the bottom theory is widely accepted as a rationale for EC environmental regulation.

Physical spillovers are relatively straightforward, and competitive spillovers, whilst more controversial in other jurisdictions, are highly consistent with internal market objectives. It is also clear, however, that EC environmental law regulates environmental goods in ways that are not readily analysed in economic or physical terms. Nature conservation measures, for example, are not obviously about economic or physical spillover. The protection of migratory species provides physical justification for regulation, as does the possibility that a minimum scale of habitat, crossing borders, is necessary to allow species to flourish in the long term[48]; associated land use restrictions may also have a marginal impact on competitiveness. The Community's conservation directives, however, rely on the idea of 'common heritage'[49] and 'the Community's natural heritage',[50] to explain centralised action. In practical terms, even a general acknowledgement that there is such a thing as a common heritage does little more than restate the question of *which* natural resources attract common interests and responsibilities. One attempt to bring less tangible concerns into a clearer framework, alongside physical and economic spillovers, is by reference to 'psychic spillover', which occurs when environmental damage would have 'psychic' effects on the citizens of other Member States.[51] Again, that largely restates the question, since it does not tell us which 'psychic' effects qualify for action. It is common to resort once again to an economic cost benefit analysis, to determine which of these externalities merits action, effectively measuring the 'non-use'

---

[47] R Revesz, 'Federalism and Environmental Regulation: an Overview' in Revesz, Sands and Stewart, above n 42; van den Bergh, *ibid*. Contrast J Ferejohn, 'The Political Economy of Pollution Control in a Federal System' in Revesz, Sands and Stewart, above n 42.

[48] Scott, above n 39, p 17, fn 45.

[49] Dir 79/409 on the Conservation of Wild Birds [1979] OJ L 103/1; Case C–44/95 *R v Secretary of State for the Environment, ex parte RSPB (Lappel Bank)* [1996] ECR I–3805. See also Case 247/85 *Commission v Belgium* [1987] ECR 3029, para 9.

[50] Dir 92/43 on the Conservation of Natural Habitats and Wild Fauna and Flora [1992] OJ L 206/7. See McGillivray and Holder, above n 40.

[51] W Wils, 'Subsidiarity: Taking People's Concerns Seriously?' (1994) 6 *Journal of Environmental Law* 85. The alternative framing of this as a 'preservation spillover', RB Stewart, 'Environmental Law in the United States and European Community: Spillovers, Cooperation, Rivalry, Institutions' [1992] *University of Chicago Legal Forum* 41, captures the fact that this is primarily, although not exclusively, concerned with the conservation of special sites or sights, rather than pollution or more mundane environmental degradation.

value of a resource to individuals from other Member States.[52] Economics proves rather difficult to escape.

Because it is so closely aligned with proportionality, subsidiarity addresses how the Community should act, as well as whether it should take action at all. The Amsterdam *Protocol on Subsidiarity and Proportionality* provides that:

> other things being equal directives should be preferred to regulations and frame-work directives to detailed measures ... Community measures should leave as much scope for national decision as possible ...[53]

This preference for a 'light touch' is apparent in certain changes of approach in environmental regulation since Maastricht. There seems to be a greater use of framework directives, and more willingness to explore voluntary agreements and other alternatives to traditional 'command and control' legislation. Subsidiarity at least reinforces contemporary shifts in thinking on regulation. This can be seen in the *Fifth Environmental Action Programme*,[54] which followed the Maastricht debate on subsidiarity quite quickly. The *Fifth Environmental Action Programme* states that it 'combines the principle of subsidiarity with the wider concept of *shared responsibility*'[55] between public authorities at all levels (not just EC / national), the private sector, environmental interest groups and individuals; it also links sub-sidiarity with the cost-effectiveness of regulatory instruments.[56] These two links point towards broadening the range of regulatory tools that will be used, includ-ing regulation of information provision, economic instruments and voluntary agreements as well as command and control regulation. Whilst 'shared responsi-bility' is quite a leap from the ostensibly simple choice between centralised and national action found in the Treaty approach to subsidiarity, it is perhaps a more realistic approach to the nature of action on the environment. It also fits very well with the *Fifth Environmental Action Programme*'s preoccupation with 'alternative' regulatory instruments, the pursuit of which will be considered throughout this book. Shared responsibility does not, of course, provide any inherent limits on Community action.

The Treaty status of subsidiarity suggests that it should have some legal 'teeth'. However, whilst discussion of the justiciability of subsidiarity has been overtaken by the willingness of the European Court of Justice (ECJ) to hear arguments on the issue,[57] the ECJ has so far taken a cautious approach and subsidiarity remains

---

[52] Wils, *ibid*; Ferejohn, above n 47. The reductionism of this approach is rejected by Scott, above n 39.
[53] *Protocol on Subsidiarity and Proportionality*, above n 41, paras 6–7.
[54] Fifth Environmental Action Programme, *Towards Sustainability: A European Community Programme of Policy and Action in Relation to the Environment and Sustainable Development* [1993] OJ C 138/5.
[55] *Ibid*, p 78.
[56] *Ibid*, p 16.
[57] The *Protocol on the Application of the Principles of Subsidiarity and Proportionality* provides that 'Compliance with the principle of subsidiarity shall be reviewed in accordance with the rules laid down by the Treaty', para 13.

a relatively peripheral issue in judicial review. So for example, in tangentially environmental litigation,[58] the Netherlands challenged the validity of the Biotechnology Directive,[59] which requires the Member States to protect biotechnological inventions through their patent laws. The Netherlands argued, *inter alia*, that the Directive was invalid for breach of the principle of subsidiarity, or alternatively because it failed to make an explicit statement of reasons on subsidiarity. The Court rejected both arguments in short measure. On the substantive argument, the Court stated simply that the objective of ensuring smooth operation of the internal market in this area could not be achieved by action taken by the Member States alone. And although the recitals to the Directive contain no explicit reference to subsidiarity, the Court held that statements to the effect that developments in the different Member States impede the proper functioning of the internal market provide sufficient reasons for Community action.[60] Detailed evidence in support of that conclusion is not demanded by the Court.

The Court's 'hands off' approach is understandable given the complex political and social judgments necessary to determine the most effective level of regulation. The abruptness of the Court's dismissal of the subsidiarity complaints might however be a cause for concern. To leave subsidiarity entirely in the control of the Community legislators ultimately allows the allocation of powers to be determined by majorities in the legislative bodies, rather than by the more rigorous procedure of Treaty revision.[61] A willingness to review subsidiarity more stringently, albeit at the margins, may enhance explicit consideration of the limits of Community action when legislation is proposed and negotiated; better that this decision is explicit and contestable, at least politically. A Protocol attached to the new EU Constitution requires the Commission to provide a 'detailed' statement on subsidiarity in its legislative proposals.[62] However, in a worrying hint that an economic approach to subsidiarity questions is to be formalised, the Protocol requires this statement to be 'substantiated by qualitative and, wherever possible, quantitative indicators'. As well as explicitly confirming the jurisdiction of the ECJ on subsidiarity, the Protocol provides an interesting alternative to judicial oversight, allowing a more active role for national parliaments in monitoring the operation of subsidiarity. Certain documents produced during the legislative process would be provided to each national parliament, which is given the opportunity to produce a 'reasoned opinion' if it is of the view that the proposal breaches the principle of subsidiarity. The legislative institutions would have to 'take account' of the reasoned opinions. If sufficient parliaments support the reasoned opinion, the Commission is required to 'review' its proposal, and although it need not

---

[58] Case C–377/98 *Netherlands v European Parliament* [2001] ECR I–7079. This is in line with other decisions, see Case C–84/94 *UK v Council (Working Time Directive)* [1996] ECR I–5755; Case C–233/94 *Germany v Parliament and Council* [1997] ECR I–2405.

[59] Dir 98/44 on the Legal Protection of Biotechnological Inventions [1998] OJ L 213/13.

[60] *Netherlands*, above n 58, paras 32–3.

[61] There may be parallels with the interplay between legislation and litigation in the development of EC competence on the environment, discussed below.

[62] Protocol on the Application of the Principles of Subsidiarity and Proportionality, Art 5.

withdraw or amend it, it must give reasons for its decision. Whilst the Protocol gives the national parliaments no authority over the course of legislation, this introduction of external monitoring could prove to have some effect on at least the explanation of environmental policy.[63] Given the continued controversy over subsidiarity in the environmental field, and the frequently lightweight justifications for action provided in legislation, this is potentially very significant.

The allocation of powers in the European Community is a complex legal and political question, going to the heart of the legitimacy of Community action. The principle of subsidiarity to a large degree simply restates the question,[64] providing one way of conceptualising the path through the debate, but without in itself providing any clear answers. As with the prior question of why a society should regulate to protect the environment at all, economics tends to dominate in this area. Contributing to the debate on the legitimacy of EC environmental regulation other than in economic terms can be something of a challenge. The alternative to relying on economics is, again as with the prior 'why regulate?' question, to establish the common interest by strength of argument, including economic arguments. This involves far more obviously normative, political decisions, both about the physical world in which we want to live, and the appropriate role of the EU in achieving that world.

LEGAL AND POLITICAL EVOLUTION

Environmental protection has a clear and significant place in the objectives of the European Community, which provide for 'a high level of protection and improvement of the quality of the environment'.[65] Although environmental protection is just one objective among many, this provides an important point of reference for law-making, albeit without answering the subsidiarity question. The development of environmental policy from inauspicious beginnings is a well-rehearsed story,[66] but a brief summary will be attempted here. Environmental policy provides a clear demonstration of the interaction between legal and constitutional change and the political process, which Joseph Weiler argues has been crucial in the 'transformation of Europe'.[67] Legal intervention has been both

---

[63] J Jans and J Scott, 'The Convention on the Future of Europe: An Environmental Perspective' (2003) 15 *Journal of Environmental Law* 323.

[64] See de Búrca, above n 38; Cross, above n 39.

[65] Art 2 EC. The full text provides:

The Community shall have as its task, by establishing a common market and an economic and monetary union and by implementing common policies or activities referred to in Articles 3 and 4, to promote throughout the Community a harmonious, balanced and sustainable development of economic activities, a high level of employment and of social protection, equality between men and women, sustainable and non-inflationary growth, a high degree of competitiveness and convergence of economic performance, a high level of protection and improvement of the quality of the environment, the raising of the standard of living and quality of life, and economic and social cohesion and solidarity among Member States.

[66] See especially Scott, above n 39, pp 4–10.

[67] J Weiler, 'The Transformation of Europe' (1991) 100 *Yale Law Journal* 2403.

shaped by and legitimised by political alliances; legal change has in turn pushed the politics.

It was observed at the beginning of this chapter that by the early 1970s, environmental policy was firmly on the EC political agenda. Political agreement, even unanimous political agreement, does not, however, provide legislative competence in any field. Legislative competence can be found only in the powers set out within the Treaty. Until 1986, when the Single European Act introduced an environmental Title to the Treaty, there was no explicit Treaty base for environmental action. With the vital support of the ECJ, the Commission and Council used Articles 94 (ex 100) and 308 (ex 235) to develop a body of environmental legislation. Article 94 provides for the 'approximation' of Member State laws that 'directly affect the establishment or functioning of the common market', and was the main vehicle for environmental regulation; Article 308 provides for action 'necessary to attain, in the course of the operation of the common market, one of the objectives of the Community', where the Treaty itself has not provided necessary powers.

The ECJ confirmed the viability of Article 94 as the legal base for environmental legislation, accepting that national differences in environmental regulation could distort competition.[68] This approach meant that environmental legislation developed in this period as a policy dependent on, and supportive of, the internal market paradigm.[69] In *ADBHU*,[70] the ECJ confirmed that the less commonly used Article 308 sufficed as a legal basis for environmental legislation, holding that environmental protection is 'one of the Community's essential objectives',[71] sufficient to justify certain restrictions on the free movement of goods. This important decision allowed for the possibility of an autonomous environmental policy, independent of the market. The continued vitality of internal market justification is nevertheless clear from the orientation of the subsidiarity debate discussed above.

This expansion of Community environmental competence during the 'mutation' of EC law[72] was initially relatively unproblematic. Interestingly, and counter-intuitively, a significant expansion of EC environmental regulation took place during the 1980s, when at least some Member States were heavily influenced by neo-liberal economic ideologies fiercely opposed to regulation. This contradiction may in part be explicable by a real failure to anticipate the significance of these first steps into environmental regulation[73]: environmental policy was perceived to be domestically popular, and there were few short-term costs since the early directives generally postponed implementation and compliance for some

---

[68] Case 92/79 *Commission v Italy*, above n 41.

[69] See McGillivray and Holder, above n 40; D Chalmers, 'Environmental Protection and the Single Market: An Unsustainable Development. Does the EC Treaty Need a Title on the Environment?' (1995) 1 *Legal Issues of European Integration* 65.

[70] Case 240/83 *Procureur de la République v Association de Défense des Bruleurs d'huiles Usagées* [1983] ECR 531.

[71] *Ibid*, para 13.

[72] Weiler, above n 67. The expansion was by no means limited to the environmental sphere.

[73] P Sands, 'European Community Environmental Law: The Evolution of a Regional Regime of International Environmental Protection' (1991) 100 *Yale Law Journal* 2511; Weiler, *ibid*.

years.[74] It is perhaps just as important that environmental regulation was designed to be supportive of the development of the single market[75]; it is now very familiar ground that de-regulatory, competitiveness focused strategies in fact imply not only de-regulation, but equally *re*-regulation, leading in time to a strategy of regulatory reform. Perhaps the key factor in the relative absence of controversy is the requirement under both Articles 94 and 308 for unanimity in Council (in consultation with the European Parliament): Member States retained their sovereignty. The fact of unanimity does not mean that expansion of competence is necessarily benign; action at EC level tended to enhance the autonomy of the executive within the Member State. Nevertheless, these factors together made for an 'easy start' to environmental regulation, providing the foundations of a far stronger and more politically delicate environmental competence.

The Single European Act instituted the first changes. It effectively codified the *status quo* on decision-making in the environmental arena, by providing an explicit legal base for environmental legislation in Articles 174–6 (ex Articles 130(r)–(t)), requiring unanimity in Council, in consultation with the European Parliament. These new provisions also established a coherent legal basis for environmental action, and began to set out a framework and principles for pro-active decision-making. For many, whilst this new environmental title added nothing to legislative competence, it provided a welcome a response to concerns that environmental policy dependent on market integration objectives was unnecessarily conservative, *ad hoc* and reductionist.[76]

Changes introduced in the Single European Act to enable completion of the single market were at least as significant as the introduction of an environment Title. Under Article 95 (ex Article 100A), measures 'which have as their object the establishment and functioning of the Internal Market' could be enacted on the basis of qualified majority voting, in co-operation with the European Parliament. The stronger role for the European Parliament under Article 95 compared with Article 175, led to inevitable disagreement over choice of legal basis. In *Titanium Dioxide*,[77] the adequacy of Article 95 for measures to protect the environment was confirmed by the ECJ. The decision has been much criticised,[78] and with the convergence of internal market and environmental decision-making procedures,

---

[74] P Sands, *ibid*; A Jordan, 'European Community Water Standards: Locked in or Watered Down?' (1999) 37 *Journal of Common Market Studies* 13, argues that the British government did not appreciate the costs of the legislation it was negotiating.

[75] PM Hildebrand, 'The European Community's Environmental Policy, 1957 to "1992": From Incidental Measures to an International Regime' [1993] *Journal of Environmental Politics* 13.

[76] See Chalmers, above n 69, arguing that these problems are more apparent than real.

[77] Case C–300/89 *Commission v Council (Titanium Dioxide)* [1991] ECR 2867.

[78] See for example Scott, above n 39; S Crosby, 'The Single Market and the Rule of Law' (1991) 16 *European Law Review* 451. In holding that the legislation at issue was 'concerned, indissociably, with both the protection of the environment and the elimination of disparities in conditions of competition', para 13, the Court explains why in theory either legal basis would be suitable; after observing that the conflicting procedures in the two articles mean that a choice has to be made, the Court holds that the measure should have been based on Art 95, but without explaining why Art 175 was insufficient. The Court appears simply to prefer Art 95 because of the enhanced role for the European Parliament.

the controversy over choice of legal base for environmental directives has lost at least some of its political significance.[79] However, the importance of *Titanium Dioxide* should not be underestimated; Treaty revision at Maastricht in 1992 again followed practice, introducing qualified majority voting to the environment Title. The Court's decision in *Titanium Dioxide* was supportive of this fundamental change in the politics of environmental legislation. Perhaps even more significantly, it also perpetuated and reinforced the understanding of environmental legislation as a tool of market integration. This rationalisation remains difficult to move beyond, even with well-developed environmental competence.

THE FUTURE

The most recent enlargement of the European Union poses unique challenges for environmental regulation.[80] The May 2004 enlargement is different from former enlargements in part because of simple scale: it involves a large increase in state actors (from 15 to 25), in geographical area (increase of 34 per cent) and in population (increase of 105 million). In addition, the positive political and symbolic implications of 're-unifying' Europe after the divisions of the Cold War bring with them unfamiliar administrative traditions and relatively poorly performing economies. For current purposes, we need to speculate on the possible effect of enlargement on the environments of the new Member States, and on the future development of the environmental policy of the EU.[81]

One of the most serious challenges for everybody is the existence of major disparities in economic performance between the new ten and the old fifteen.[82]

The orthodox position is now to look for a single 'primary aim' of legislation, rather than to allow the possibility of a dual aim: see Cases C–164/97 and C–165/97 *Parliament v Commission* [1999] ECR I–1139. Note also, however, *Opinion 2/00* [2001] ECR I–9713: 'By way of exception, if it is established that the measure simultaneously pursues several objectives which are inseparably linked without one being secondary and indirect in relation to the other, the measure may be founded on the corresponding legal bases', para 23; in that case, the main (environmental) purpose was however identifiable.

[79] Note the continued potential for disagreement over choice of legal basis (not limited to Arts 175/95): Cases C–164/97 and C–165/97 *Parliament v Commission, ibid*; *Opinion 2/00 of the Court, ibid*. Note also that Articles 175 and 95 make different provisions for the maintenance or introduction of higher environmental standards in national law. It is possible that Case C–376/98 *Germany v Council (Tobacco Advertising)* [2000] ECR I–8419, in which on the basis of a narrow reading of Art 95 the Court annulled a directive for exceeding competence, suggests a willingness to look more closely at internal market arguments for social regulation.

[80] European Commission, *Accession Strategies for Environment: Meeting the Challenge of Enlargement with Candidate Countries in Central and Eastern Europe* COM (1998) 294 sees this as the most challenging enlargement yet from an environmental perspective; see also European Commission, *2003 Environmental Policy Review: Consolidating the Environmental Pillar of Sustainable Development* COM (2003) 745 final.

[81] See the excellent collection of papers in the spring 2004 special issue of *Environmental Politics*, also published as J Carmin and SD VanDeveer (eds), *EU Enlargement and the Environment: Institutional Change and Environmental Policy in Central and Eastern Europe* (New York, Frank Cass Publishers, 2004).

[82] Although note that the long process of accession has put some of the new members in a much stronger position than might otherwise have been expected, see M Schreurs, 'Environmental Protection in an Expanding European Community: Lessons from Past Accessions' in Carmin and VanDeveer, *ibid*.

In 2002 the acceding states' GDP per capita averaged only 47 per cent of the EU fifteen average.[83] In a specifically environmental context, poor economic performance raises concerns as to the ability and willingness of government, industry and the general population to comply with environmental requirements. Practical implementation of environmental law, and meaningful involvement in the evolution of new policy, both require significant financial and human resources. However, whilst the depth and breadth of the disparity is far greater in the current enlargement, the EU has had poorer new members before; and even with well established members, the EU has long lived with radical regional differences of economic performance.[84] Nevertheless, limited resources are likely to exacerbate every one of the challenges discussed here.

The implementation of the '*acquis communautaire*', the 'common rules, standards and policies that make up the body of EU law' before accession[85] was one of the so-called 'Copenhagen criteria'[86] applied to all recent applicants for EU membership. The complexity and scale of the *acquis* puts enormous pressure on limited expertise and resources, which might suggest that even though they face distinctive environmental issues (many are suffering from major industrial pollution from the Soviet era[87]; many also enjoy large areas of rich and undisturbed biodiversity), the new Member States will have little opportunity to develop purely national environmental priorities.[88] The new Member States will follow western European priorities and approaches even if they are not the most appropriate response to the particular situation they face. Nor is this an issue limited to the existing *acquis*, that is environmental law developed before full membership. The capacity of the new Member States to influence ongoing environmental priorities, and the response of the new EU to the environmental challenges that were until recently outside its borders, remain to be seen. It is also feared that the prioritisation of *formal* implementation of the *acquis*, that is the adjustment of domestic law, has at least to some extent been at the expense of building capacity for implementation of environ-

---

[83] Eurostat, *Statistics in Focus*, Economy and Finance, 64/2003, 'Purchasing Power Parities and Related Economic Indicators for EU, Acceding and Candidate Countries and EFTA'.

[84] Ipeiros in Greece enjoys 42% of the EU average GDP *per capita*; parts of inner London, 243%. See the figures cited in Schreurs, above n 82.

[85] See M Maresceau, 'Pre-Accession' in Cremona, above n 5 on the demands made of the latest entrants relative to former enlargements; P Nicolaides, 'Preparing for Accession to the European Union: How to Establish Capacity for Effective and Credible Application of EU Rules', also in Cremona, above n 5.

[86] Copenhagen Council, 1993. The new members must have the ability to take on the obligations of membership. The first, political Copenhagen criterion is for a stable democracy, respecting human rights, the rule of law, and the protection of minorities; new members must also have a functioning market economy, and the capacity to cope with competitive pressure and market forces within the Union.

[87] Commission (1998), above n 80 discusses the gap in the level of environmental liabilities and environmental protection between certain new members and the fifteen. See also European Environment Agency, *Environment in the European Union at the Turn of the Century*, available at http://reports. eea.eu.int/92–9157–202–0/en. The total investment costs of meeting the environmental acquis were estimated by the Commission as ECU 100–120 billion for the ten candidates from central and eastern Europe, ie including Bulgaria and Romania, see Commission (1998), *ibid*.

[88] See R Greenspan Bell, 'Further Up the Learning Curve: NGOs from Transition to Brussels' in Carmin and VanDeveer, above n 81.

mental standards on the ground.[89] True implementation is an ongoing endeavour, requiring practical day to day implementation of environmental law,[90] and placing considerable demands on administrations and judiciaries at all levels. In this respect, the distinctive recent administrative and political traditions in the new Member States may compound the capacity challenges created by relatively weak economies.[91] Many of the new Member States are young democracies in which meaningful environmental policy is still short-lived. Marc Maresceau expresses 'astonishment' at:

> the ease with which the EC has been willing to close the negotiating chapter on environment ... It is very doubtful whether the majority of the enumerated candidates are really capable in terms of human resources, know-how, and infrastructure of complying with EC environmental law.[92]

The implementation of the *acquis* will undoubtedly have a major impact on the environment of the new Member States, and notwithstanding the reservations expressed above, one might expect that impact to be largely positive. EU membership at the very least forces environmental issues on to a potentially crowded agenda. The non-environmental impacts of membership, such as the construction of road networks linking west and east Europe, are however equally important for the expanded EU environment. Some old habits in the new Member States are environmentally positive[93]: certain new members are well ahead on matters such as recycling rates, and have relatively low levels of private car use, as well as less intensive land use practices. Whether these practices will survive trade liberalisation and anticipated increases in prosperity remains to be seen. Although the scale effects of the increased consumption that is likely to follow increased wealth add to environmental pressures, one might also speculate that the expected increase in wealth is necessary to mitigate the financial cost of implementing the environmental *acquis*, not to mention pressing ahead with future environmental policy.

The impact of enlargement on the future of EC environmental policy is likely to be just as complex as the impact of EC environmental policy on the environments of the new Member States. It is often assumed that enlargement will have a primarily negative effect, as economic pressures in the new Member States push

---

[89] See the concern expressed in, for example, P Jehlicka and A Tickle, 'Environmental Implications of Eastern Enlargement: the End of EU Progressive Environmental Policy?' in Carmin and VanDeveer, above n 81.

[90] See ch 3 below for a detailed discussion of implementation of EC environmental law. The older Member States find compliance far from straightforward.

[91] The EU is of course used to difference. Greece, Portugal and Spain all joined the EU after the establishment of democracy following decades of right wing dictatorships.

[92] See Maresceau, above n 85, p 23, fn 38. For the purposes of accession, the *acquis* has been divided by subject area into chapters, which were negotiated separately.

[93] See Z Gille, 'Europeanising Hungarian Waste Policies: Progress or Regression?' in Carmin and VanDeveer, above n 81; P Pavlínek and J Pickles, 'Environmental Pasts / Environmental Futures in Post-Socialist Europe' in Carmin and VanDeveer, *ibid*.

the environment down the domestic agenda, making the new Member States less than enthusiastic participants in the improvement of environmental standards at EU level. EC environmental policy is expected to become more conservative, as the influence of the traditional policy leaders in both Council and Parliament is diluted, and the new Member States ally themselves with the environmental 'laggards' of the existing fifteen.[94] Less pessimistic commentators, however, point out that some of the new Member States may well take a more progressive approach than this assumes.[95] The potential for new and fruitful collaborations and innovations is significant, as is the enhancement of the EU's regional and global leadership role. On previous enlargements to take in poorer member states with less well developed administrative traditions of environmental protection, there appears to have been no overall weakening of environmental standards, and indeed some policy innovation.[96] However, as with implementation, the role of the new Member States at EU level depends largely on the institutional capacities of the state and national interest groups; lack of expertise or resources may inhibit the ability to take a full role in policy development.[97] The real future of EC environmental policy is unpredictable, and of course depends on many economic, environmental and political variables, operating in different ways in all 25 Member States.

A related question is what has been dubbed the 'fourth Copenhagen condition',[98] that is 'the Union's capacity to absorb new members, while maintaining the momentum of European integration'.[99] As the diversity of interests represented in the EU's decision-making bodies increases, policies that would benefit all are harder to find, and reaching decisions becomes correspondingly more difficult. Consensus decision-making becomes problematic, and coalition building for majority voting, more complex and unpredictable. Mere increase in the size of institutions (such as the Commission and courts) may eventually make them too unwieldy for effective discussion. Even the addition of new languages increases costs and puts additional barriers in the way of effective communication. The Nice Treaty took some limited steps to address these questions, but whilst constitutional change was never a pre-requisite of enlargement,[100] the two issues have

---

[94] See the outline of the 'leaders and laggards' theory in A Sbragia, 'Environmental Policy: The "Push-Pull" of Policy-Making' in H Wallace and W Wallace (eds), *Policy-Making in the European Union* (Oxford, Oxford University Press, 2002).

[95] See Jehlicke and Tickle, above n 89. Their research suggests that some of the new Member States are more likely to have an affinity with the 'leaders' such as Denmark and the Netherlands.

[96] Schreurs, above n 84, discusses the cases of Greece, Portugal and Spain.

[97] The ability of 'grass roots' environmental movements to participate in EU level decision-making does not look promising, LK Hallstrom, 'Eurocratising Enlargement? EU Elites and NGO Participation in East Central European Environmental Policy' in Carmin and DeVeers, n 81 above. See also Greenspan Bell, above n 88; B Hicks, 'Setting Agendas and Shaping Activism: EU Influence on Central European Environmental Movements' in Carmin and VanDeveer, above n 81. Note, however, that similar limitations arise with respect to the role of 'civil society' in the older member states, see further ch 5 below.

[98] Cremona, above n 5, p 3.

[99] See more generally de Witte, above n 5.

[100] The Nice Declaration stated that enlargement was not dependent on further reform.

become entwined. The real impact of the institutional reforms agreed in 2004 will only become clear over many years.

It would be wrong to characterise all new entrants from central and eastern Europe as lacking either environmental consciousness or effective structures for environmental protection. Most countries of central and eastern Europe had environmental laws in place before 1989, although enforcement was generally weak. Environmental issues and environmental interest groups even seem to have played a significant role in the overthrow of the communist regimes in some, although not all, central and eastern European countries[101]; questioning achievements on a particular issue, to which the government was ostensibly committed, was a relatively 'safe' way to criticise the regime. And although the promise of this environmental movement was not entirely fulfilled after the end of communist rule, the early 1990s did see the development of environmental legislation and institutions. It is also important not to see the new entrants as a monolithic block. There are as many variations within and between the new Member States as within and between the fifteen. And nothing has so far been said about the Mediterranean entrants. Whilst they do face capacity challenges of their own,[102] as well serious environmental problems such as those brought about by intensive coastal tourism in Cyprus,[103] without the recent history of state socialism, and with relatively strong economies,[104] those challenges are less distinctive.

The overall appeal of enlargement to the older Member States, at least among the political elites, included the expectation of political and security gains, as well as longer-term economic gains. Alongside the expectation of instrumental advantage, it has been suggested that a sense of historic duty and solidarity with the countries of central and eastern Europe has been a factor in enlargement.[105] The overall risks include in particular the possible exacerbation of legitimacy problems by resentment at the costs (to new and old members) of expansion. The continued capacity for effective and efficient internal action, as well as the risk of instability from the shifting of external borders are also important challenges. For current purposes, the recent enlargement of the EU raises questions as to both future environmental policy and legislation at EU level, and environmental quality in the new Member States. In neither case is the nature of impact on the European environment likely to be simple. A complex

---

[101] See Hicks, above n 97; Greenspan Bell, above n 88.

[102] See EcoTech Research and Consulting et al, *Administrative Capacity for Implementation and enforcement of EU Environmental Policy in the 13 Candidate Countries*, available at: http://europa.eu.int/ comm/environment/enlarg/pdf/administrative_capacity.pdf for details.

[103] See European Environment Agency, above n 87.

[104] Cyprus GDP per capita is 76% of the EU fifteen average; Malta's is 69%, see Eurostat, above n 83. These are the highest proportions of the new Members. Note that Greeece and Portugal GDP per capita rests at 71% of the EU fifteen average according to the same report.

[105] See H Sjursen, 'Why Expand? The Question of Legitimacy and Justification in the EU's Enlargement Policy' (2002) 40 *Journal of Common Market Studies* 491, for an interesting account of the motivations behind enlargement.

combination of costs and benefits is likely to accrue both to EC policy, and to the new Member States.[106]

CONCLUSIONS

This book aims to examine certain contemporary challenges faced within EC environmental law, and possible responses in recent legislation and policy developments. The purpose of this introductory chapter has been to illustrate that the subject has always faced questions as to its scope and its very purpose; those early questions are unlikely to be resolved any time soon. Of the range of distinctive justifications for environmental regulation, economic approaches have an obvious intuitive appeal in a body dedicated to market integration. This appeal was institutionalised during the development of environmental policy, and is reinforced by the priority of market integration in the ongoing debate about subsidiarity. Indeed, the apparently unassailable place of economic liberalisation, economic integration and economic growth at the heart of the whole European project suggests that the radical change urged by some environmentalists will not be found in EC law. Environmental awareness might change the management of certain activities, but always within the normal rules of the market game.

This book discusses change in EC environmental law; the focus is not however on the most transparent changes currently on the agenda, which are undoubtedly enlargement and constitutionalisation. Constitutional change could affect profoundly the future development of EC environmental regulation. Changes to decision-making procedures are immensely important. In the environmental context, it should also be recalled that whilst the central status of environmental policy in the Treaty framework had seemed impregnable, the early versions of the draft *Treaty Establishing a Constitution for Europe* were distinctly discouraging, suggesting a potential downgrading of environmental policy relative to other policy areas.[107] That the final agreed Constitution contains environmental provisions in line with the status quo, as indeed had the final draft Constitution submitted by the Convention in 2003, is as much a matter for relief as celebration.[108] Enlargement not only raises complex questions around effectiveness, as discussed above. Increased diversity within the EU also re-ignites old debates about the appropriateness of uniformity on environmental matters, a debate that goes to the heart of the legitimacy of centralised action. The possibility of groups of Member States entering into 'enhanced cooperation agreements' under the Treaty gained political visibility as negotiations over the draft *Constitution* fell acrimoniously

---

[106] See SD VanDeveer and J Carmin, 'Assessing Conventional Wisdom: Environmental Challenges and Opportunities Beyond Eastern Accession' in Carmin and VanDeveer, above n 81.

[107] For detail, see Jans and Scott, above n 63.

[108] See particularly the environment title, Arts III–233–234, and the objectives of the Union.

apart in December 2003.[109] Less confrontational responses, more likely in the environmental sphere, are also available. First, if the costs of a measure are 'deemed disproportionate for the public authorities of a Member State', temporary derogations can be introduced into new legislation; this is a very common form of flexibility.[110] Most significantly, there has in any event been a considerable shift in EC environmental regulation to allow more Member State flexibility in the implementation of environmental legislation. This more subtle approach to difference was noted above in the discussion of subsidiarity, and will be returned to below.[111] Whether it will suffice to hold the environmental policy of the 25 together remains to be seen. Amidst all of this dissent and uncertainty, it is perhaps paradoxical that the vigour of EC environmental law remains apparently undaunted: 'the union constitutes a very "productive" and maturing system of public policy-making'.[112] It is, at least for now, an accepted forum for environmental legislation, and the mainstream debate is currently limited to nuanced appeals to flexibility and 'better' regulation. Much more radical de-centralisation of environmental responsibilities would of course be one response to criticisms of EC environmental law. The pressure is likely to continue, particularly given recently increased representation of euro-sceptic politics in the European Parliament, and the popular anxiety represented by that development. How EC environmental regulation responds to contemporary challenges will to a large extent dictate its continued effectiveness and importance.

---

[109] Provision for enhanced cooperation is contained in Art 4 EC, introduced in the Amsterdam Treaty, and amended by the Nice Treaty.
[110] Art 175(5) EC. See the discussion of flexibility in Scott, above n 39, pp 37–43.
[111] Especially ch 6.
[112] J Richardson, 'Policy-Making in the EU: Interests, Ideas and Garbage Cans of Primeval Soup' in J Richardson (ed), *European Union: Power and Policy-Making* (London, Routledge, 1996), p x.

2

Sustainable Development

INTRODUCTION

LIKE JUSTICE, LIBERTY and truth, 'sustainable development' is an objective from which few would openly dissent; like justice, liberty and truth, however, sustainable development can be rather slippery in its operation. In spite of, or perhaps because of, its elusiveness, sustainable development has been extraordinarily widely accepted and embraced in environmental policy across the world. The World Commission on Environment and Development published the seminal work on sustainable development in 1987, exercising an enormous influence on international, European and domestic law and policy for nearly two decades. The 'Brundtland Report'[1] set out an approach to sustainable development that quickly became the dominant framework within which environmental protection must be pursued. The Brundtland Report has been built on at an international level, most prominently at the UN Convention on Environment and Development (the famous Rio Earth Conference) in 1992,[2] and more recently at the 2002 *World Summit on Sustainable Development* in Johannesburg.[3] These international developments have had a profound influence on EU environmental policy. The Single European Act, introducing environmental policy explicitly into the Treaty, was completed at around the same time as 'sustainable development' entered the mainstream political lexicon; not surprisingly, an explicit Treaty commitment to sustainable development followed only later. Sustainable development is now one of the core tasks of the European Community under Article 2 EC,[4] and will remain so under the new Treaty Establishing a Constitution for Europe.[5]

---

[1] Named for its chair, Gro Harlem Brundtland: World Commission on Environment and Development, *Our Common Future* (Oxford, Oxford University Press, 1987). Note also the 1972 Stockholm *Conference on the Human Environment*, which first linked human development and the environment.

[2] The main outputs of the conference were the *Rio Declaration on Environment and Development* and *Agenda 21*, a plan of action. Both are available at: http://www.un.org/esa/sustdev/documents/docs.htm.

[3] Details of the summit can be found at: http://www.johannesburgsummit.org/. Two main documents were agreed: the *Johannesburg Declaration on Sustainable Development* and the *Johannesburg Plan of Implementation*, available by following links at: http://www.un.org/esa/sustdev/index.html. Details of the agreements reached at Johannesburg can be found in L Kimball, FX Perez and J Werksman, 'The Results of the World Summit on Sustainable Development: Targets, Institutions and Trade Implications' (2002) 13 *Yearbook of International Environmental Law* 3.

[4] Following a somewhat controversial appearance under the guise of 'sustainable growth' in the Maastricht Treaty. Art 2 TEU also contains a commitment to sustainable development.

[5] Art I–3(3) and (4), plus preamble to Part II.

The most widely quoted 'definition' of sustainable development comes from the Brundtland Report, according to which sustainable development is development that 'meets the needs of the present without compromising the ability of future generations to meet their own needs',[6] a definition adopted by the EU on numerous occasions.[7] Of the many alternative definitions available, the emerging competitor is perhaps the reference to 'the interdependent and mutually reinforcing pillars of sustainable development — economic development, social development and environmental protection', found in the *Johannesburg Declaration on Sustainable Development* (the Johannesburg Declaration).[8] This 'three pillar' approach may lack the elegance of the earlier definition, but it does very directly reflect dominant contemporary understandings of sustainable development. It appeals to a number of different perspectives on the 'good life', attempting to reconcile otherwise competing objectives. That the pursuit of 'economic development, social development and environmental protection' should attract widespread consensus is unsurprising; the debate and dissent begins when one attempts to identify the precise meaning of sustainable development in particular cases. At this point, the consensus can reveal itself to be something of an illusion.

Sustainable development can perhaps best be viewed as an objective, something to be aimed for and worked at, rather than an environmental principle. Like the environmental principles, however, sustainable development can provide a framework for the process of legal reasoning, and a flexible guide to decision-making. By laying down common language and mutual objectives, sustainable development provides a starting point for debate.[9] From an environmental perspective, competing conceptions of sustainable development tend to divide between 'business as usual' managerial approaches to environmental protection, and much more radical challenges to existing ways of carrying on. This is a division that is commonly observed in environmental policy more generally, for example in Andrew Dobson's distinction between 'ecologism' and 'environmentalism': environmentalism 'argues for a managerial approach to problems, secure in the belief that they can be solved without fundamental changes in present values or patterns of production and consumption'; ecologism on the other hand 'holds that a sustainable and fulfilling existence presupposes radical changes in our relationship with the non-human natural world, and in our mode of social and political life'.[10] Radical and reformist approaches not only provide different

---

[6] Brundtland Report, above n 1, pp 8 and 43.

[7] See for example European Commission, *A Sustainable Europe for a Better World: A European Union Strategy for Sustainable Development* COM (2001) 264 final (the *Sustainable Development Strategy*), p 2. Note that subsequent European Council conclusions have added to the original *Sustainable Development Strategy*.

[8] Above n 3, para 5.

[9] See especially M Jacobs, 'Sustainable Development as a Contested Concept' in A Dobson (ed), *Fairness and Futurity: Essays on Environmental Sustainability and Social Justice* (Oxford, Oxford University Press, 1999).

[10] A Dobson, *Green Political Thought* (London, Routledge, 2000), p 2. D McGillivray and J Holder, 'Locating EC Environmental Law' (2001) 20 *Yearbook of European Law* 139, apply this to EC environmental law.

responses to environmental and social problems, but even provide very different understandings of what might constitute a problem. The complexity and profound ambiguity of sustainable development means that in the absence of continued debate, rather than providing progressive impulses in environmental regulation, sustainable development could instead simply provide a moral cloak for 'business as usual'. Together with the need to work towards such an ambitious and comprehensive social objective, this presents extraordinary challenges for EC environmental law.

This chapter will begin with an examination of the main elements of sustainable development, specifically the place of future generations, the role of social development in sustainable development, the relationship between economic growth and the environment, and the Johannesburg approach to sustainable development. There is much controversy surrounding the implementation and application of sustainable development, with competing frameworks provided by economics, science and more political perspectives, and the second half of this chapter will discuss these different approaches.

ELEMENTS OF SUSTAINABLE DEVELOPMENT

As a definition, the Brundtland soundbite on sustainable development, development that 'meets the needs of the present without compromising the ability of future generations to meet their own needs',[11] is not particularly helpful. In fact, it is a single phrase selected from a report that runs to almost 400 pages, and cannot fully encompass even all of the concerns of the Brundtland Report, let alone the huge academic and political literature on sustainable development. It highlights, however, the absolute centrality to sustainable development of justice to future generations. By concentrating on 'needs', it also, if less explicitly than elsewhere in the Report, brings out the concern of the Brundtland Commission to reconcile the opposing perspectives of developing nations (pursuing development) and industrialised nations (pursuing environmental protection). Environmental protection and development have often been perceived to be inconsistent objectives, making progress on either subject extremely difficult. The Brundtland Report confirmed the legitimacy and necessity of continued economic development, even in the face of environmental problems, and the imperative of environmental protection in the face of poverty.

A single, all-embracing definition of sustainable development is probably not possible or desirable. The crucial aspect of sustainable development, which allows it the potential to be more than fashionable jargon for 'environmental protection', or indeed for 'development', is its embrace of different areas of concern that may otherwise be thought of as distinct and even conflicting. The three pillar approach to sustainable development, bringing economic development, social development

[11] Above n 6.

and environmental protection together, is highly significant. The balance between the different facets of sustainable development is constantly shifting and contested, but if any one aspect of sustainable development overpowers the others, sustainable development loses much of its appeal. Although one might question whether it is always realistic, the denial or avoidance of fundamental conflict between basic social aims has set the tone of environmental debate in recent years. For the EU, sustainable development has become a crucial part of the contemporary rhetoric that economic prosperity and environmental protection are mutually supportive objectives.

Although one might object that the elements of sustainable development should properly be considered holistically, this section will consider social and economic development separately, and from the perspective of their relationship with environmental protection. First, however, I will examine the Brundtland question of future generations, before turning to the place of social development and then economic development. This section will conclude by looking at the Johannesburg approach to the pillars of sustainable development.

Future Generations

The appeal to the needs of future generations is the most distinctive element of sustainable development. The Brundtland Report was groundbreaking in putting the very long-term on the political agenda. By contrast, the very long-term was decidedly neglected in the conclusions emerging more recently out of the Johannesburg World Summit on Sustainable Development.[12] Although the Johannesburg Declaration does contain some vague references to 'the generations that will surely inherit this earth'[13] and a 'long-term perspective',[14] the future is mainly perceived through by the much shorter-term perspective offered by the 'children of the world'.[15] Indeed, even the Brundtland Report itself pays relatively little attention to future generations, certainly compared with justice within the current generation. It is perhaps strange in these circumstances that the reference to future generations has had such staying power in academic and policy analysis of sustainable development. It is constantly reinforced by use of the Brundtland 'definition',[16] and by attempts to apply economic measurement tools to sustainable development, which will be discussed below.

Much of the theoretical debate on future generations revolves around the feasibility of formulating duties and rights in respect of people who do not yet, and

---

[12] Even more so than the Rio Declaration, above n 2, which is also short on this point: 'the right to development must be fulfilled so as to equitably meet developmental and environmental needs of present and future generations', Principle 3.

[13] *Johannesburg Declaration*, above n 3, para 37.

[14] *Ibid*, para 26.

[15] *Ibid*, paras 3 and 46.

[16] That is, development that 'meets the needs of the present without compromising the ability of future generations to meet their own needs', above n 6.

indeed may never,[17] exist.[18] For current purposes, whatever the theoretical basis, intuitive notions of justice that assume responsibilities in respect of future generations are widely accepted. This impulse of responsibility in respect of future generations is most difficult in its detail. The detail of implementation will be returned to below, but for current purposes, the inclusion of the future as an interest in policy debate is most significant for its ability to bring environmental protection centre stage. Not all agree: some argue that future generations are best served by the creation and maintenance of secure institutions for the protection of human rights, rather than by environmental protection[19]; many others assume that economic growth and technological development provide best for future generations. The debate is unavoidably over the right balance between the different pillars of sustainable development. Notwithstanding the desirability of other bequests to the future, depleting environmental resources is the clearest way in which we prejudice future generations: 'the results of present profligacy are rapidly closing the options for future generations'.[20]

We set ourselves a difficult task when we try to provide for future generations. I, for example, find it hard to believe myself worse off for the industrial revolution, although it undoubtedly degraded much of Europe's natural environment, and few environmentalists would argue that it constituted a 'sustainable' form of development. My view may of course be irrelevant, perhaps because my options have been so twisted by the industrial revolution that I have grown to love the (metaphorical) plastic trees.[21] Or perhaps the relevant future generation is further down the line; or perhaps Europeans are not the right people to ask, given that we reap disproportionate benefits from industrialisation. Alternatively, the question may not be sufficiently sophisticated, and alternative development paths through the industrial revolution, with a better balance between the three pillars of sustainable development, could have reduced burdens relative to benefits. Whatever the provisos, this illustrates what tricky ground one is on when attempting to consider the future, and the inability of the mere concept of sustainable development to provide clear answers. Any assertion that sustainable development demands or prohibits a particular course of action should be treated with caution.

This is not to deny that sustainable development is capable of providing arguments in favour of some options and away from others, particularly at the extreme: to reiterate, although some will insist that the exploitation of people

---

[17] 'Parfit's paradox', to simplify, assumes that any effort to improve the prospects of future generations will mean that different individuals will exist. For discussion see A Carter, 'Can We Harm Future People?' (2001) 10 *Environmental Values* 429; E Partridge, 'The Future — For Better or Worse' (2002) 11 *Environmental Values* 75; J Alder and D Wilkinson, *Environmental Law and Ethics* (Basingstoke, Macmillan Press, 1999), p 133.

[18] For discussion see A Dobson, *Justice and the Environment: Conceptions of Environmental Sustainability and Theories of Distributive Justice* (Oxford, Oxford University Press, 1998), especially pp 102–28; B Barry, 'Sustainability and Intergenerational Justice' in Dobson, above n 9.

[19] W Beckerman and J Pasek, *Justice, Posterity, and the Environment* (Oxford, Oxford University Press, 2001).

[20] Brundtland Report, above n 1, p 8.

[21] See ch 1 above.

and nature was an unavoidable element of industrial growth, it may be that a different path through the industrial revolution would have maintained a better balance between the three elements of sustainable development. And whilst specific development paths, or specific bequests, for the future cannot be dictated by sustainable development, if the concept is seen as an injunction to leave the greatest possible range of options for future generations,[22] more guidance can be provided. However, this involves a spin on the meaning of sustainable development that would be disputed by some; the tighter the definition of sustainable development, the better able it is to provide guidance. The cost of tightening the definition of sustainable development is that some of the space that sustainable development provides for debate is lost, as well of course as the risk that the angels lose the debate over definition. The cost, then, is rather high.

Social Development and Sustainable Development

The 'social development' pillar of sustainable development, as it has become in the Johannesburg Declaration, is concerned with questions of equality and justice within the current generation. Much of the appeal of sustainable development at an international level rests on its efforts to side step the perception that environmental protection is a hobby of the rich, and to respond to the legitimate complaint that whilst the rich industrialised world continues to reap the benefits of enormously damaging historical and contemporary patterns of industrial development, we try to prevent poor countries from developing along similar paths, in the name of environmental protection.[23] This approach to social development is concerned with the question of economic development on a global scale, which it might be objected should more properly be discussed under the 'economic development' pillar of sustainable development. However, the economic pillar in EU policy is more often concerned with economic *growth* for wealthy economies, rather than the complex question of development: 'economic *growth*, social cohesion and environmental protection must go hand in hand'.[24] To keep the question of intra-generational justice and growth of wealthy economies separate, the former will be discussed here.

The links between 'poverty, inequality and environmental degradation'[25] are a major theme of the Brundtland Report.[26] The connections between environmental

---

[22] A Dobson, *Citizenship and the Environment* (Oxford, Oxford University Press, 2003), ch 4.

[23] For discussion of longstanding and persistent tensions between developing and developed countries in international environmental law, see L Rajamani, 'From Stockholm to Johannesburg: The Anatomy of Dissonance in the International Environmental Dialogue' (2003) 12 *Review of European Community and International Environmental Law* 23.

[24] *Sustainable Development Strategy,* above n 7, p 2, emphasis added. Note however that the *Sustainable Development Strategy* is concerned with the *internal* pursuit of sustainable development; the external perspective receives separate consideration, and is more concerned with development in the sense discussed here, see European Commission, *Towards a Global Partnership for Sustainable Development* COM (2002) 82 final.

[25] Brundtland Report, above n 1, p xii.

[26] Brundtland Report, *ibid.* This pervades the Report, but see in particular pp 2–3; 28–30; ch 5 on food security, and ch 9 on the 'urban challenge'.

protection and poverty eradication are drawn from the observation that the poor generally bear the brunt of environmental degradation, being more likely to live in environmentally degraded areas[27]; more likely to rely directly on environmental resources (forests, soil, climate) for food, shelter and warmth; and less able to protect themselves from the effects of environmental degradation such as climate change. And just as the poor suffer from environmental degradation, the desperately poor may degrade the environment in search of survival. To a great extent these links are indisputable, and the Brundtland Report contributed to a broad understanding that eradicating poverty is a crucial element of environmental protection, and environmental protection a crucial element of development policy. One might feed into this a general acceptance that a certain level of prosperity is necessary before environmental protection becomes either desirable by a society or technically feasible.[28] However, the link between poverty and environmental protection is not entirely convincing. It is at best counter-intuitive to argue that in normal circumstances a subsistence farmer has a more damaging environmental impact than a rich western consumer. The relationship between development and environment is not a *necessary* relationship, and improving one will only improve the other if a special effort is made to ensure that it does so.[29] Perhaps we should be satisfied for now that compatibility between development and environmental protection should be the *aim* of sustainable development.

A key element of the futurity formula in the Brundtland Report, which resonates strongly in the promise of economic development, is the reference to current and future 'needs'. The Brundtland Report is concerned with 'in particular the essential needs of the world's poor, to which overriding priority should be given'.[30] There is however no very scrupulous examination of the notion of needs in the Brundtland Report. Alongside the emphasis on 'essential' needs, the Brundtland Report also discusses culturally and socially determined needs, including the opportunity for people to 'satisfy their aspirations for a better life'.[31] As 'needs' become indistinguishable from 'wants', absolute economic *growth* becomes crucial. Whether such absolute and enormous levels of growth as would be necessary, in

---

[27] This applies also in industrialised regions such as the EU. A link might be made in this respect with the environmental justice movement in the US.

[28] This is in part a broad political argument, but is sometimes discussed by reference to the 'environmental Kuznets curve', which posits that environmental degradation can be seen first to increase, but then to decline, with an increase in per capita income. The conclusion is sometimes drawn that economic growth will necessarily take care of environmental degradation. For detail, see D Pearce and EB Barbier, *Blueprint for a Sustainable Economy* (London, Earthscan, 2000), pp 24 ff. For a concise outline of some of the flaws of assumptions based on the Kuznets curve, see DA Kysar, 'Some Realism About Environmental Skepticism: The Implications of Bjørn Lomborg's *The Skeptical Environmentalist* for Environmental Law and Policy' (2003) 30 *Ecological Law Quarterly* 223.

[29] Dobson, above n 18, argues that the relationship between sustainability and justice is essentially an empirical issue; see by contrast O Langhelle, 'Sustainable Development and Social Justice: Expanding the Rawlsian Framework of Global Justice' (2000) 9 *Environmental Values* 295, arguing that sustainability and justice are inherently linked.

[30] Brundtland Report, above n 1, p 43.

[31] *Ibid*, ch 2 and p 44. Note also that culturally and socially determined needs might include improved environmental protection; it is not inconceivable that we want a better environment than we need.

the absence of massive redistribution, to achieve global equality can be reached without severely downgrading the importance of environmental protection is at least questionable. The central position of the 'limits to growth' thesis, most influential in the 1970s, is that the resources of the earth are finite.[32] Reluctance to take the identification of 'needs' seriously amounts to a denial of the possibility that there are absolute limits on the capacity of the earth to support human activity. Whilst the Brundtland Report accepts certain limits (for example some resources are non-renewable), it asserts that limits are equally determined by technological and social organisation; and 'technological and social organisation can be both managed and improved to make way for a new era of economic growth'.[33] Believers in 'limits to growth' by contrast deny the ability of human ingenuity always to design our way out of environmental apocalypse: technological fixes to environmental problems will at best postpone, rather than prevent, environmental collapse. There is a clear divergence of approach between the 'limits' and the 'sustainable development' theses, and one that is unlikely to have gone unnoticed by the architects of sustainable development. Sustainable development provides a softer, less confrontational *alternative* to the limits rhetoric of the 1970s, which had been at the heart of the impasse between development/environment, developing countries/industrialised countries. The serious disruption to social practice, to human values and even to morality that are implied by an acceptance of limits is deliberately absent.

Ending inequality and impoverishment was a core ideal of the Brundtland Report, and remains a core element of sustainable development. Arguing for the end of poverty is an extremely sharp and immediate challenge to existing institutions, practices and distributions of power. Even though the Brundtland Report blunts its own sharp edge by emphasising growth (catching up) over redistribution, the Brundtland goal of ending poverty was initially much less readily absorbed by industry and the rich than the environmental limb of sustainable development. It is fair to say that the emphasis of developed nations has largely been on the environmental protection/economic growth linkage of sustainable development, rather than on social development.[34] Indeed, in EC 'hard law' on global sustainable development, which aimed to integrate sustainable development into external development funding, sustainable development was defined as:

> the improvement of the standard of living and welfare of the relevant populations within the limits of the capacity of the ecosystems by maintaining natural assets and their biological diversity for the benefit of present and future generations.[35]

[32] DH Meadows *et al*, *Limits to Growth: A Report for the Club of Rome's Project on the Predicament of Mankind* (New York, Basic Books, 1972).

[33] Brundtland Report, above n 1, p 8.

[34] Although some were disappointed by the emphasis in the Rio Declaration on development over the environment, see M Pallemaerts, 'International Environmental Law from Stockholm to Rio: Back to the Future' in P Sands (ed), *Greening the Treaty* (London, Earthscan, 1993).

[35] Reg 2493/2000 on Measures to Promote the Full Integration of the Environmental Dimension in the Development Process of Developing Countries [2000] OJ L 288/1, Art 2.

This definition suggests that the social development aspect of sustainable development is contingent on the environmental aspect. Whilst consistency is of course important, this hints at an inappropriate hierarchy between the different pillars of sustainable development.[36]

Successful co-option of sustainable development by the environmental movement is likely to underplay commitments to the poor. The social elements of sustainable development have, however, resurfaced with a vengeance. The Johannesburg documents place considerable emphasis on questions of global poverty and social development. There is inevitably some rhetorical bluster, but there are also some clear and ambitious commitments to development, the most headline grabbing of which has been the promise to halve poverty by 2015.[37] This, however, is a restatement of an earlier commitment.[38] That is not in itself a problem, given that the Johannesburg Summit was designed to be an implementation conference, but it might be appropriate to limit the fanfare. Similarly, both the commitment to increase development aid from industrial countries[39] and the consideration of debt relief[40] are in themselves admirable and redistributive, but are also unmet commitments from previous agreements.[41] The 'world solidarity fund' that is to 'eradicate poverty' is subject to voluntary contributions, and 'the role of the private sector and individual citizens relative to Governments in funding the endeavours' is to be encouraged.[42] Only rather ambiguous vestiges of redistribution come out of Johannesburg. Even the relatively modest indirect redistribution implied by the concept of 'common but differentiated responsibilities',[43] which provides that

[36] Note that more recent Commission policy has addressed the abolition of poverty and the role of trade more directly, Commission, above n 24; European Commission, *The World Summit on Sustainable Development One Year On: Implementing Our Commitments* COM (2003) 829 final.

[37] The governments commit to action to '[h]alve, by the year 2015, the proportion of the world's people whose income is less than \$1 a day', *Johannesburg Plan of Implementation*, above n 3, ch II, para 6. The same chapter, entitled 'Poverty Eradication', contains, inter alia, commitments to action to halve 'the proportion of people who suffer from hunger and, by the same date, to halve the proportion of people without access to safe drinking water'; and to '[improve] access to reliable and affordable energy services'.

[38] The commitment is contained in the UN *Millenium Development Goals* 2000. Detail is available at http://www.undp.org/mdg/.

[39] To increase overseas development assistance to 0.7% of GNP, *Johannesburg Plan of Implementation*, above n 3, para 79(a).

[40] Distinct ambivalence can in any event be detected in the wording: 'debt relief measures should, where appropriate, be pursued vigorously and expeditiously, [...] while recognizing that debtors and creditors must share responsibility for preventing and resolving unsustainable debt situations', *Johannesburg Plan of Implementation, ibid*, para 83.

[41] The commitment on overseas development aid is left over from Rio, see Rajamani, above n 23. The discussion of debt 'supports' the Monterrey Consensus on Financing for Development, available at http://www.un.org/esa/ffd/0302finalMonterreyConsensus.pdf. For discussion of the 'reaffirmation' of previous commitments at Johannesburg, see Kimball, Perrez and Werksman, above n 3.

[42] *Johannesburg Plan of Implementation*, above n 3, para 7(b).

[43] 'States shall cooperate in a spirit of global partnership to conserve, protect and restore the health and integrity of the Earth's ecosystem. In view of the different contributions to global environmental degradation, States have common but differentiated responsibilities. The developed countries acknowledge the responsibility that they bear in the international pursuit of sustainable development in view of the pressures their societies place on the global environment and of the technologies and financial resources they command', *Rio Declaration*, above n 2, Principle 7. The Rio approach is confirmed in the *Johannesburg Plan of Implementation*, above n 3, for example paras 2 and 75.

the costs of sustainable development (or on some interpretations, the costs only of the environmental pillar of sustainable development) should be borne in accordance with ability and with contribution to the harm, proved controversial, with developing countries arguing for a far broader understanding of the concept than developed countries.[44] The mechanisms proposed at Johannesburg for ending poverty are largely consistent with the interests and perspectives of dominant groups from industry and developed countries.[45] In particular, the route to development is free markets, efficiency and growth; social development is often contingent on private sector assistance, and often hedged around by the requirement of consistency with free trade rules.[46]

So far, this section has concentrated on economic development for the global poor, given that the 'economic development' pillar has been largely co-opted by the pursuit of economic growth in wealthy economies. This is however too narrow. Social development also embraces a wide range of social justice and equality issues *within* nations and regions. Alongside the recent increase in the attention paid to global poverty (albeit in an unchallenging framework), more space has been devoted to efforts to tie local questions of social justice into sustainable development. So, at the EU level, whilst sustainable development began life as a predominantly environmental policy,[47] chiefly concerned with minimising the trade off between economic growth and environmental protection, the three-pillared approach is far more apparent in the *Sustainable Development Strategy*.[48] The 'main threats' to sustainable development identified in the *Sustainable Development Strategy* include poverty and social exclusion alongside more clearly environmental issues.[49] At Lisbon, the European Council set itself the goal of becoming 'the most competitive and dynamic knowledge-based economy in the world, capable of sustainable economic growth with more and better jobs and greater social cohesion'.[50] 'Social cohesion' has become a central concern of sustainable development as the EU sustainable development strategy has been absorbed within the much broader 'Lisbon strategy'.[51]

[44] See Rajamani, above n 23; Kimball, Perrez and Werksman, above n 3.

[45] See N Middleton and P O'Keefe, *Rio Plus Ten: Politics, Poverty and the Environment* (London, Pluto Press, 2003) for heavy criticism along these lines.

[46] See particularly *Johannesburg Plan of Implementation*, above n 3, ch X on implementation. Note also, simply by way of example, the reference in ch II to 'innovative financing and partnership methods' for water (para 7(f)), and 'public-private partnerships' in respect of energy projects (para 8(g)). Technology transfer also features in ch II, which may, although need not, involve an element of redistribution.

[47] Fifth Environmental Action Programme, *Towards Sustainability: A European Community Programme of Policy and Action in Relation to the Environment and Sustainable Development* [1993] OJ C 138/5.

[48] Above n 7. Note however that Commission, above n 36 pays more attention to environmental than social questions in its discussion of the *internal* implementation of the Johannesburg commitments.

[49] *Sustainable Development Strategy*, above n 7, boxed text, para 1.

[50] Lisbon Council Conclusions, March 2000, see further: http://europa.eu.int/comm/lisbon_strategy/key/index_en.html The Gothenburg European Council in 2001 brought the sustainable development strategy within the Lisbon process.

[51] See especially European Commission, *Choosing to Grow: Knowledge, Innovation and Jobs in a Cohesive Society. Report to the Spring European Council, 21 March 2003 on the Lisbon Strategy of Economic, Social and Environmental Renewal* COM (2003) 5 final/2.

There is a danger that the recently discovered primacy of social development within the sustainable development agenda will squeeze out environmental protection. This is particularly the case if regional social development becomes almost indistinguishable from the pursuit of economic growth, as one might argue is happening at the global level. There is cause for concern in the EU. For example, a strong plank of social development policy is increasing employment.[52] This is entirely unobjectionable and indeed laudable. It could however very easily become indistinguishable from economic growth.[53] In the absence of a very strong environmental protection perspective, there is a danger that the pursuit of economic growth will be subject to fewer and fewer environmental constraints. Without wishing to downplay the importance of social development, its prominence in contemporary sustainable development policy serves as a reminder that environmental policy should not be subsumed entirely within sustainable development policy.[54] Importantly, the EU does maintain independent environmental policy review within the sustainable development rubric.[55]

Economic Growth and the Environment

One of the real achievements of sustainable development is the decoupling of economic development from environmental degradation, certainly at a rhetorical level, but to some extent also at a practical level. Considerable endeavours have been devoted to establishing the possibility of environmentally benign economic growth, and economically beneficial environmental protection. Environmental *degradation*, rather than environmental *protection*, is posed as the challenge to economic growth, and the ability of environmental problems to erode the resource base on which economic prosperity rests becomes an important focus of attention.[56]

Scientific and technological development, without which 'adjustment to sustainable development will have to happen much more through changes in our consumption patterns',[57] is crucial to a strategy of delinking growth and environmental degradation. In this respect, the EU approach to sustainable development can usefully be considered alongside theories of ecological modernisation,[58]

---

[52] Commission, *ibid.*

[53] Note the focus on employment and productivity in European Commission, *Delivering Lisbon: Reforms for the Enlarged Union* COM (2004) 29 final.

[54] See A Ross-Robertson, 'Is the Environment Getting Squeezed Out of Sustainable Development?' [2003] *Public Law* 249, arguing that the environment pillar of sustainable development is in danger of being neglected in the UK government approach to sustainable development.

[55] European Commission, *2003 Environmental Policy Review: Consolidating the Environmental Pillar of Sustainable Development* COM (2003) 745 final.

[56] The *Johannesburg Plan of Implementation*, above n 3, devotes a chapter to 'the natural resource base of economic and social development', ch IV.

[57] *Sustainable Development Strategy*, above n 7, p 7.

[58] See M Hajer, *The Politics of Environmental Discourse: Ecological Modernization and the Policy Process* (Oxford, Oxford University Press, 1995); D Chalmers, 'Environmental Law' (1996) 15 *Yearbook of European Law* 449.

which take the good environmental performance of wealthy nations as evidence of the possibility of win-win solutions to environmental problems. The exhaustion of policies that provide economic and environmental benefits should of course be a priority; again, however, we see the effort of sustainable development debate to avoid or delay as much as possible any discussion of conflict between objectives.

The emphasis of Article 2 EC is arguably on the economic side of the delicate balance of sustainable development. It is concerned with 'a sustainable development of economic activities', and clearly links sustainable development with growth, albeit alongside 'a high level of protection and improvement of the quality of the environment' and 'social cohesion'. Even the *Sustainable Development Strategy* refers to economic *growth* rather than development as one of its three objectives[59]; the very title of the Commission's 2003 Report to the European Council is even more suggestive: *Choosing to Grow*.[60] Whilst growth *need* not be measured purely in quantitative terms, it tends to evade the qualitative focus of sustainable development. The concession of 'sustainable' growth, as in Article 2, does suggest staying power, and so the maintenance of the environmental (and social) base that will sustain economic growth. The concern remains that reliance on growth will allow environmental protection to be captured by economic dialogue, particularly at times of economic slow down. The *Treaty Establishing a Constitution for Europe* does nothing to lessen this concern, providing that sustainable development should be 'based on balanced economic growth', again as well as 'a high level of protection and improvement of the quality of the environment'.[61] The goal of economic growth drives the project of economic integration that is at the heart of the EU; its 'sustainability' is assumed in EU sustainable development policy, as indeed it is throughout the Brundtland Report.

EC judicial commentary on sustainable development is so far sparse. Because the content of sustainable development is so uncertain and so political, it is appropriate that its judicial employment should generally be restrained. There has, however, been at least one enthusiastic adoption of the environment/economy linkage. *First Corporate Shipping*[62] concerned a challenge by a property owner against the UK government's notification of a site to the Commission for designation under the Habitats Directive.[63] In his discussion of the relevance of economic

---

[59] Above n 24.

[60] Commission, above n 51.

[61] Art I–3(3): 'The Union shall work for sustainable development of Europe based on balanced economic growth and price stability, a highly competitive social market economy, aiming at full employment and social progress, and a high level of protection and improvement of the quality of the environment. It shall promote scientific and technological advance.'

[62] Case C–371/98 *R v Secretary of State for Environment, Transport and the Regions, ex parte First Corporate Shipping* [2000] ECR–I 9235. For discussion, see D McGillivray, 'Valuing Nature: Economic Values, Conservation Values and Sustainable Development' (2002) 14 *Journal of Environmental Law* 85.

[63] Dir 92/43 on the Conservation of Natural Habitats and of Wild Fauna and Flora [1992] OJ L 206/7.

considerations in the designation of sites under the Directive, Advocate General Léger makes the following comment:

> sustainable development does not mean that the interests of the environment must necessarily and systematically prevail over the interests defended in the context of the other policies pursued by the Community ... On the contrary, it emphasises the necessary balance between various interests which sometimes clash, but which must be reconciled.[64]

Whilst the idea that there are difficult decisions to be made is unobjectionable, this approach demonstrates that just as sustainable development can legitimise environmental constraints on economic development, so can it enhance the status of economic concerns in environmental decisions. On the particular facts of the case, it allows economic concerns to creep into a decision that it is strongly arguable should properly be taken on ecological grounds alone.[65] Whilst the ECJ did not refer to this part of the Advocate General's Opinion, the potential for distraction from environmental protection is clear.

The notion of sustainable development could raise rather serious questions about the social and economic order of contemporary Europe. A radical approach to sustainable development would need to put the very real tension between economic development, social development and environmental protection at the forefront of the debate, and resist the current inclination to reason it away as much as possible. Whilst long-term, and in the aggregate, economic and environmental benefits may indeed be consistent, short term conflicts are real. Importantly for the broader sustainable development debate, it should also be recalled that it is not just environmental policy that risks dilution by the inexorable pursuit of economic growth; concern has also been expressed that the social objectives of the welfare state may be subordinated to economic policy through a process of integration.[66]

More positively, it would be churlish to deny the importance or the positive contribution of win/win approaches to sustainable development, and whilst EU policy seeks to maximise them rhetorically as well as on the ground, the need for difficult decisions between competing interests is also generally acknowledged.[67] It should be recalled that the reconciliation of economic growth and environmental protection is the *aim* of sustainable development. Sustainable development remains a useful pragmatic response to the prophesies of doom that can characterise parts of the environmental movement. By providing an alternative to either hand wringing or revolution, it has so far proved consistently effective at keeping environmental issues in the mainstream of political debate.

---

[64] *First Corporate Shipping*, above n 62, Advocate General's Opinon, para 54.

[65] McGillivray, above n 62. Once the conservation of land has been legally established by designation according to ecological criteria, a balance can be drawn with economic interests when development permission is sought.

[66] See D Chalmers and M Lodge, 'The Open Method of Co-ordination and the European Welfare State' *CARR Discussion Paper 11*, June 2003.

[67] See for example *Sustainable Development Strategy*, above n 7, p 4.

Johannesburg: Markets and Sustainable Development

Sustainable development has always been about reconciling competing policy objectives, and has always embraced at least the three elements of social development, economic development and environmental protection. The relationship between the 'three pillars' is, however, always contentious. Before Johannesburg, the developed world had focused primarily on the environment/economy connection. Attention in Johannesburg, however, seemed to shift away from environmental protection. Although environmental questions clearly are addressed,[68] the language is largely vague or permissive,[69] and the approaches to implementation unchallenging, with 'technical fixes' (including the as yet undiscovered) and private funding (including the as yet undonated) figuring prominently.[70] The most striking aspect of Johannesburg is the way in which the social development pillar of sustainable development has finally been settled into the dominant economic paradigms. The Johannesburg *Plan of Implementation* promises much for liberalised markets and private initiatives. This is not new: the outputs of the Earth Summit at Rio also demonstrated a commitment to trade as part of the path to sustainable development, and indeed one of the significant innovations of the Brundtland Report was to emphasis the importance of working with the private sector. Johannesburg is simply a renewed demonstration of this enthusiasm at the heart of sustainable development.

There is undoubtedly something in the promise of trade and private resources. Trying to address the world's problems only with public finances, and without addressing the development and environmental possibilities of trade, would miss a very important part of the picture. Freer export markets should bring fresh financial resources to developing countries, and imports expand the range of goods available, as well as the efficiency of their production. This can tackle problems of underdevelopment, and increased prosperity is then thought to create the space for environmental protection. Technological fixes can bring low cost environmental improvement, and international trade and the stimulation of private investment might be expected to increase the technology available. The direction of private funds to public ends is in any event extremely attractive around the world

---

[68] *Johannesburg Plan of Implementation*, above n 3, ch III addresses 'unsustainable patterns of consumption and production', focusing on the 'delinking' of economic growth and environmental degradation, a discussion familiar from the Brundtland Report onwards. Ch IV is concerned with 'the natural resource base of economic and social development'.

[69] So for example, *Johannesburg Plan of Implementation*, ibid, commits to a 'significant reduction in the current rate of loss of biological diversity' by 2010, para 42; on fisheries, to 'Maintain or restore stocks to levels that can produce the maximum sustainable yield with the aim of achieving these goals for depleted stocks on an urgent basis and where possible not later than 2015', para 31(a); to pursue 'the aim of giving a greater share of the energy mix to renewable energies', para 20(c); there is much 'encouragement', 'enhancement' and 'promotion'; 'programmes, policies and approaches' will be drawn up, and 'initiatives' will be 'supported'. On climate change, 'States that have ratified the Kyoto protocol [on climate change] strongly urge States that have not already done so to ratify the Kyoto protocol in a timely manner', para 36.

[70] See above n 46, and note also the dominance of these mechanisms in ch IV.

at time of pressure on public finances, and is a recurring theme in EC environmental policy, as will be seen in later chapters.

A certain amount of suspicion is, however, inevitable. The 'development' potential of free trade has in the past been decidedly neglected,[71] and although the trade and development agenda is beginning to receive some attention,[72] there is at the moment little to suggest any fundamental alteration to existing distributions of power and resources. The prospects for poverty alleviation and enhanced equality are there, but uncertain; the danger is that rather than alleviating poverty, market forces will even exacerbate economic inequalities within and between states. In the absence of concerted effort, it seems likely that the most significant benefits of globalisation will continue to flow to the rich.[73]

Environmentalists have equally strong, if somewhat different, reasons to be suspicious of the free trade paradigm. As discussed above, unconstrained economic growth poses serious difficulties for anybody who still wishes to argue that policy should respond to physical 'limits to growth'. The simple scale effects of increased trade and increased production and consumption will not necessarily be compensated by improved environmental management. Further, global norms of trade liberalisation in certain circumstances constrain national and regional (EU) freedom to set standards of environmental protection.[74] Developing countries often see the environmental protection measures of industrialised countries as simple barriers to the entry of their products to wealthy markets. For many developing countries, free trade is indeed not free enough. Any emerging responsibility explicitly to consider development when striking the balance between free trade and the environment could provide further impetus towards reduced environmental standards. As for private initiatives, again there are real benefits to be sought; however, the very possibility of conflict between private profit and public good is ignored if reliance on the private sector becomes unbalanced.

Whilst the global justice strand of sustainable development seems to have re-emerged from the shadows of environmental debate, the mechanisms proposed are deeply controversial, and pose a risk of downgrading the 'third pillar' of environmental protection. Free trade has no necessary or automatic relationship with the end of poverty, and there must be even greater concern as to the possibility of increasing trade without increasing environmental damage. Similarly, the (legitimately) private motives of the private sector must be borne in mind when they are appealed to for public purposes. The elite acceptance that free trade, environmental protection and social justice can be consistent, alongside the current

---

[71] SE Gaines, 'International Trade, Environmental Protection and Development as a Sustainable Development Triangle' (2002) 11 *Review of European Community and International Environmental Law* 259.

[72] *Johannesburg Plan of Implementation,* above n 3, discusses trade, paras 84–93. See Kimball, Perrez and Werksman, above n 3 for discussion of how Johannesburg relates to existing initiatives in this respect.

[73] Note the awareness of this issue in Commission, above n 24. Translating this into action will be the test. See also Commission, above n 36.

[74] Discussed further in chs 4 and 9 below.

reality that certain patterns of trade exacerbate both inequality and environmental degradation, can only enhance popular disquiet about globalisation. 'Sustainable development' initially concentrated on the tension between the objectives of environmental protection and of economic development or economic growth. Its role seems increasingly to be in the denial or amelioration of conflict between global justice and trade liberalisation. The effort now belongs in the detail, in ensuring that social and environmental policies are indeed enhanced alongside and within trade liberalisation.[75]

IMPLEMENTING SUSTAINABLE DEVELOPMENT

Sustainable development is multi-dimensional and dynamic. Whilst the major policy concerns embraced by sustainable development are generally divided into three, as discussed, each embraces a range of issues, capable of evolving to meet new concerns; the *Johannesburg Declaration*, for example, ranges from hunger through xenophobia to disease in a single article.[76] Capturing, and especially measuring, this complexity in practice is difficult. However, although sustainable development means more than the proposition that something must be sustained, and some economic approaches to sustainable development might be criticised for concentrating on durability to the exclusion of all else, a consideration of implementation might begin from the understanding that sustainable development at least implies that something must be sustained, probably long into the future. Even at its simplest, that is the proposition that human life on earth should be capable of continuation, sustainable development provokes some difficult questions, for example around assumed population levels[77] and assumed technological development. And few would limit themselves to the modest ambition of survival. It is not necessarily the case, however, that we must try to second guess the needs of the future in any determinate way. Andrew Dobson's argument that sustainable development implies an obligation to leave for the future the widest range of physical and mental opportunities is a useful and environmentally focussed starting point.[78] This approach still, however, leaves the appropriate balance between the three pillars of sustainable development open for normative debate.

The debate on tools for measuring sustainable development has long been dominated by economists. The *Blueprint* approach to sustainable development[79] encapsulates what has become known as 'weak' sustainability, although it should be noted that just as 'sustainable development' has no fixed and stable meaning,

---

[75] See M Pallemaerts, 'International Law and Sustainable Development: Any Progress in Johannesburg?' (2003) 12 *Review of European Community and International Environmental Law* 1.
[76] Johannesburg Declaration, above n 7, Art 19.
[77] This chapter will not discuss population growth, which was however a crucial part of the Brundtland Report, above n 1.
[78] Dobson, above n 22. Dobson recognises that this leaves open very tricky questions, especially p 164.
[79] DW Pearce, EB Barbier and A Markandya, *Blueprint for a Green Economy* (London, Earthscan, 1989).

nor do notions of 'weak' or 'strong' sustainability.[80] Generally speaking, however, the dispute between strong and weak sustainability lies in disagreement over whether 'natural capital has a unique or essential role in sustaining human welfare'.[81] Weak sustainability requires the bequest of at least equal amounts of 'total capital stock' to future generations. Total capital stock is comprised of natural capital, physical capital and human capital; so one can include technology, works of art and factories as well as forest, fossil fuels and an intact ozone layer. Natural, human and physical capital are essentially substitutable. 'Weak' sustainable development is not readily distinguishable from ordinary welfare economics, seeking the maximisation of human welfare.[82] The distinctiveness is perhaps the *necessity* of considering questions of distribution (inter- and intra-generational equity),[83] alongside the attribution of value to environmental resources. 'Strong' sustainability on the other hand denies the fungibility of human and natural capital. It instead requires that natural capital be maintained, although disagreement over the meaning of 'natural capital' means that the significance of that proviso can vary.

Weak and strong sustainability may be less starkly divided than they appear. Both are predicated on 'capital', and subject to the criticisms of economic approaches familiar from the discussion in chapter 1 above. And neither argues for either infinite or zero substitutability[84]: weak sustainability would not provide that everything (the ozone layer for example) is capable of substitution; nor does strong sustainability absolutely deny the possibility of depleting natural capital in all circumstances.[85] However, the possibility of technical fixes means that nothing is really out of bounds for weak sustainable development; quite what is out of bounds for strong sustainability is difficult to pin down. The controversy revolves around the degree of permissible substitution; perhaps one could say, the concept of limits. Welfare economics provides that whether a substitution of natural by man-made capital is acceptable depends on whether such a substitution will maximise welfare; this quickly becomes circular,[86] as it returns to the question of what sort of capital contributes most to welfare. Moreover, the fact that an economist could choose to answer this question by

---

[80] Or indeed 'very weak' and 'absurdly strong' sustainability, see A Holland, 'Substitutability: Or Why Strong Sustainability is Weak and Absurdly Strong Sustainability is not Absurd' in J Foster, *Valuing Nature? Economics, Ethics and The Environment* (London, Routledge, 1997).

[81] Pearce and Barbier, above n 28, p 23.

[82] W Beckerman, 'Sustainable Development: Is it a Useful Concept?' (1994) 3 *Environmental Values* 191.

[83] Distributional issues can be an element of welfare economics, Beckerman, *ibid.*

[84] Holland, above n 80.

[85] H Daly, 'On Wilfred Beckerman's Critique of Sustainable Development' (1995) 4 *Environmental Values* 49.

[86] Beckerman above n 82. An aside in European Commission, *Bringing our Needs Together- Integrating Environmental Issues with Economic Policy* COM (2000) 576 final, Annex I, illustrates this: the Commission states that different types of capital are substitutable, but not wholly substitutable; the emphasis is on allowing future generations 'the same level of well being' as the current generation; we do that by striking 'the right balance between the accumulation and depletion of economic, social and environmental assets'. Taking us nicely back to the initial question as to what maximises well being.

measuring the welfare provided by the different forms of capital does not detract from the fact that this is ultimately a value judgment.

It can also be argued that both weak and strong sustainability, indeed any economic approach to sustainable development, tends to devalue the future[87]; which after all is (or at least used to be) at the heart of sustainable development. The 'discounting' of future costs and benefits is entirely legitimate in economic terms: the promise of one Euro in the future is worth less than one Euro now. But whilst discounting reflects an important truth in respect of money, and perhaps also in respect of latent injury to a current individual (avoiding the loss of my arm, or life, now, is worth more to me than avoiding such loss in thirty years), its simple transfer to harm to future generations is much more difficult to justify.[88] Aside from the moral question of valuing other human life, it affects the distinctiveness of sustainable development as a policy instrument, because discounting can mean that the long term has very little practical impact on current decisions. The hard question posed by sustainable development is quite what we are prepared to sacrifice to the future, and that is not easily answered by economics.

There are many approaches to sustainable development that attempt to resist the call of economics, whilst maintaining a technical focus. 'Carrying capacity', for example, is a notion that has been developed to identify the ability of the environment to continue to act as a source of raw materials, and as a sink for the outputs of economic processes. So, for example, waste emissions should be within the capacity of the environment to absorb waste, without diminishing its future waste-absorption capacity; renewable resources should be mined or harvested within the capacity of the environment to regenerate; and non-renewable resources no faster than the rate at which substitutes are developed. If clear limits are not set, however, a physical approach to sustainable development can become very open-ended.[89]

So far, the approaches considered have tended to emphasise the environmental pillar of sustainable development. Along with many national governments, the EU has developed 'indicators' to measure practical progress towards sustainable development.[90] Indicators should avoid the over-prioritisation of any single aspect of sustainable development, although that depends entirely on the indicators selected. There are benefits of using measurable indicators in a journey towards sustainable development, including enhanced accountability of decision-makers

---

[87] M Jacobs, *The Green Economy: Environment, Sustainable Development and the Politics of the Future* (London, Pluto Press, 1991).

[88] RL Revesz, 'Environmental Regulation, Cost-Benefit Analysis, and the Discounting of Human Lives' (1999) 99 *Columbia Law Review* 941.

[89] See for example Case C–36/98 *Spain v Council* [2001] ECR I–779. AG Léger equates sustainable development with 'rational use', para 77, which in respect of renewable resources 'must aim to encourage moderate use, thereby allowing their regular renewal', para 79; in respect of non-renewable resources 'the measures imposed must prevent their rapid exhaustion', para 80; there is no discussion of any relationship between use and replacement.

[90] European Commission, *Structural Indicators* COM (2003) 585. The indicators are attached to the Lisbon Strategy rather than the *Sustainable Development Strategy* specifically, but monitoring of sustainable development has been largely incorporated into the Lisbon process, see above n 50.

and more transparent objectives. In a specifically EU context, common indicators also allow comparison and spread of good practice between Member States.[91] There is nevertheless a risk that indicators could turn into a poorly focused effort to measure all manner of 'good things'. The proposed indicators for the EU for 2004 run from 'GDP per capita', through poverty and research and development expenditure, to greenhouse gas emissions.[92] Care should be taken that indicators do not actually impoverish sustainable development debate; as with economic analysis, the concentration on technical measurement can squeeze out debate about values. Sustainable development is much more complex than even a high number of discrete indicators might suggest.

Whether sustainable development should be conceptualised as a technical or a moral/ethical criterion is a central and unresolved dispute that parallels the difficulties around conceptualising environmental problems discussed in chapter one. Ignorance about the short and long-term effects of human actions precludes clear answers to questions about sustainability. Even in the absence of this inevitable uncertainty gap, the illusion of clarity and objectivity provided by technical analysis is deeply problematic. Unless the uncertainties and value judgments behind a decision are explicit, cost benefit analysis and technical conclusions on whether something is 'sustainable' obfuscate rather than enlighten. After any technical debate, there is a judgment to be made about the world in which we want to live, the world we want to leave behind, and the price we are prepared to pay for the privilege. Technical uncertainty is compounded by the uncertainty inherent, and not undesirable, in these political judgments around public values. Sustainable development provides a useful point of reference in decision-making, emphasising the breadth of social objectives and the moral claim from the future; done properly, the technical input is only one part of the equation.

The indeterminacy of sustainable development in any particular situation makes process very attractive. An open, participative process of decision-making would allow the values involved in difficult decisions to be explicitly discussed, capturing also the multi-dimensionality of sustainable development more readily than economics. This participative perspective on sustainable development has found an easy reception in parts of EC environmental law and policy, and will be discussed in more detail in later chapters.[93] Open-ended as to result, a participatory approach leaves room to explore the distributive and value quandaries of sustainable development, as well as, if done with a 'democratising' intent, in itself constituting action on the 'social development' aspect of sustainable development.

The conscious effort to 'integrate' different policy concerns also resorts (primarily) to procedural obligations in an effort to capture the complexity of sustainable development. At its simplest, a policy of integration attempts to act on the recognition that more can be achieved by incorporating environmental concerns

---

[91] See the discussion in AB Atkinson, E Marlier and B Nolan, 'Indicators and Targets for Social Inclusion in the European Union' (2004) 42 *Journal of Common Market Studies* 47.
[92] Commission, above n 90.
[93] See especially chs 4, 5 and 6.

within other policy areas, than by leaving them as a ring-fenced special interest. Article 6 EC provides:

> Environmental protection requirements must be integrated into the definition and implementation of the Community policies and activities ... in particular with a view to promoting sustainable development.[94]

The integration principle is clearly of considerable consequence to sustainable development, and its position at the head of the Treaty is symbolically significant. Although its removal to Part III of the Constitution reduces the visibility of the integration principle, however, its inclusion continues to enhance the legal weight of sustainable development. The integration principle at least legitimises the incorporation of environmental considerations into other areas of policy,[95] and arguably even obliges decision-makers to take account of environmental considerations, for example in the interpretation of internal market law.[96] The predominant legal manifestation of the integration principle is procedural.[97] However, whilst courts are not likely to set substantive environmental standards by default, it is arguable that egregious environmental degradation *may* be indicative of failure to integrate.[98] The Commission's periodic 'stocktaking' of integration also takes a more substantive approach, looking at actual laws and policies, although less at substantive results on the ground.[99] Moreover, the *Sustainable Development Strategy* seems to introduce a

---

[94] The integration principle appears in its current form Art III–119 the Treaty Establishing a Constitution for Europe, and in the Charter of Fundamental Rights, incorporated into the Treaty, Art II–97.

[95] For example, see Case C–300/89 *Commission v Council (Titanium Dioxide)* [1991] ECR 2867, discussed in ch 1 above. Holding that the single market provisions of the Treaty could form the basis for legislation that protects the environment, the Court relied on the requirement in the environmental title that 'environmental protection requirements shall be a component of the Community's other policies' (para 21), as well as the requirement in the single market provisions for measures taken under that provision 'to take as a base a high level of protection in matters of environmental protection' (para 24).

[96] 'Article 6 is not merely programmatic; it imposes legal obligations', Case C–379/98 *PreussenElektra AG v Schleswag AG* [2001] ECR I–2099, Opinion of AG Jacobs, para 231.

[97] On efforts to put in place institutional procedures for integration, see R Macrory, 'The Amsterdam Treaty: An Environmental Perspective' in D O'Keefe and P Twomey (eds), *Legal Issues of the Amsterdam Treaty* (Oxford, Hart Publishing, 1995); A Lenschow, 'New Regulatory Approaches to "Greening EU Policies"' (2002) 8 *European Law Journal* 19.

[98] For example by way of analogy with the approach taken by the ECJ to the objectives in Art 4 of Dir 75/442 on Waste [1975] OJ L 194/39, which requires that that Member States 'take the necessary measures to ensure that waste is recovered or disposed of without endangering human health and without using processes or methods which could harm the environment'. In Case C–365/97 *Commission v Italy (San Rocco)* [1999] ECR I–7773, the Court held that whilst Art 4 'does not specify the actual content of the measures that must be taken ... it is nonetheless true that it is binding on the Member States as to the objective to be achieved whilst leaving to the Member States a margin of discretion in assessing the need for such measures', para 62. The Court found that although there could be no automatic assumption that because a situation is not in conformity with Art 4 there is a breach, 'if that situation persists and leads in particular to a significant deterioration in the environment over a protracted period without any action being taken by the competent authorities, it may be an indication that the Member States have exceeded the discretion conferred on them by that provision' (para 68). The legal context is very different from that provided by Art 6, but nevertheless suggestive of a role for certain principles *in extremis*.

[99] European Commission, *Integrating Environmental Considerations into other Policy Areas — A Stocktaking of the Cardiff Process* COM (2004) 394 final. The 'Cardiff process' refers to the request of

hierarchy that is absent from the Treaty: 'All policies must have sustainable develop-ment as their *core concern*'[100]; the multi-dimensionality of sustainable development, however, suggests that this hierarchy is not likely to be unduly testing.

The focus on *environmental* policy in Article 6 only begins to capture the den-sity of sustainable development. The dangers of such a narrow approach might be appreciated from the approach of the Advocate General in *First Corporate Shipping*, who seems to understand to the integration principle and sustainable development to be virtually one and the same thing,[101] concerned particularly with the relationship between economic development and environmental protec-tion. However, 'integration' is now part of the *Sustainable Development Strategy*, and as such is broader than in Article 6, requiring a consideration of economic, environmental and social impacts of any decision. The introduction of 'sustain-able impact assessment'[102] as a contribution to 'a more coherent implementation of the European Strategy for Sustainable Development'[103] is an important ele-ment of moving towards sustainable development in practical terms. Impact assessment applies to 'all major initiatives'[104]; if assessing environmental impacts, and integrating environmental policy is proving difficult, however, meaningful sustainable impact assessment is likely to be enormously challenging.

The *Sustainable Development Strategy* and related documents are pervaded by the idea that integration means that the different elements of sustainable devel-opment 'go hand in hand', and should be considered holistically. However, inte-gration seems to be less ambitiously used as a responsibility to bring environmental concerns *into* other sectors, for example by assessing the environmental impact of a sector or policy or attempting to achieve 'policy coherence'.[105] Whilst this may be a conceptually limited approach to integration,[106] and should in fact be part of any policy process, it may nevertheless promote practical environmental progress. The principle has played an important role in efforts, of varying success, to 'green' a number of major policy areas.[107] The Community institutions put enormous,

the European Council in 1998 for different Council formations to prepare strategies and programmes aimed at environmental integration.

[100] *Sustainable Development Strategy*, above n 7, emphasis added.
[101] *First Corporate Shipping*, above n 62: 'The concept [sustainable development] originates in a com-munication of the Commission to the Council of 24 March 1972 on an environmental programme of the European Communities, in which it stated that the proposals made on 22 July 1971 on the policy of the Community in this respect should henceforth be implemented in accordance with the principle of integration' (footnotes omitted), para 55.
[102] European Commission, *Impact Assessment* COM (2002) 276 final, p 2.
[103] *Ibid*, p 2.
[104] *Ibid*, p 2, defined as 'those which are presented in the Annual Policy Strategy or later in the Work Programme of the Commission'.
[105] See Commission, above n 36.
[106] WM Lafferty and E Hovden, 'Environmental Policy Integration: Towards An Analytical Framework' (2003) 12 *Environmental Politics* 1.
[107] The main policy areas implicated by Art 6 are agriculture, development, energy, enterprise, fish-eries, internal market, research, structural funds, trade and external relations, transport, economic and financial affairs, a fairly comprehensive list: see http://europa.eu.int/comm/environment/integration/integration.htm. See also the discussion of progress in Commission, above n 99.

perhaps undue, faith in the power of environmental integration.[108] Its importance, and its limitations, are enhanced by the latest enlargement of the EU, given antic-ipated economic growth and related increase in consumption and production in the new Member States. Whether integration will create sufficient environmental improvements in policies related to consumption and production to compensate remains to be seen. Although there might be concern that the enormous task of implementing the *acquis* will mean that the new Member States neglect the more sophisticated problems of sustainable development, the Commission remains confident: 'the enlargement of the EU constitutes one important, self-standing contribution to sustainable development'.[109]

CONCLUSIONS

Sustainability is 'now one of the most contested words in the political vocabu-lary'[110]; perhaps paradoxically, it is also a virtually uncontroversial reference point in all manner of policy debates. The promise that genuinely positive social objec-tives can be reconciled is simply irresistible.

Sustainable development both responds to and poses significant challenges to EC environmental regulation, giving comfort to various phenomena that charac-terise contemporary EC environmental law and policy. The remarkable tension between democracy and technocracy in contemporary EC environmental law and policy is clearly reflected in different conceptualisations of sustainable develop-ment. An approach to sustainable development that concentrates on the impor-tance of public participation in decision-making is highly consistent with the EU's self-description as an organisation close to the peoples of Europe,[111] and the efforts being made to follow through on a commitment to public participation in environmental legislation suggest an evaluative understanding of sustainable development. Simultaneously, however, the EU looks to a range of technical, expert responses to the conundrum of sustainable development, for example through the selection of structural indicators, and economics. The contemporary emphasis on supposedly more efficient market instruments of regulation[112] is a key aspect of sustainable development's efforts to reconcile economic growth and environmental protection, which underscores the role of economics in environmental policy.

Sustainable development is clearly profoundly ambiguous and uncertain, which some fear undermines its practical appeal to policy makers and lawyers. However:

---

[108] Integration appears throughout Decision 1600/2002 Laying Down the Sixth Community Environment Action Programme [2002] OJ L 242/1; see also Commission, above n 55; Commission, above n 36.

[109] Commission, above n 36, paras 3 and 3.4.

[110] Dobson, above n 10, p 62.

[111] See especially chs 5 and 6 below.

[112] See ch 7 below.

> [l]ike other political concepts ... sustainable development has two levels of meaning. One of these is well defined; the other is the site of political contest.[113]

In the essay from which this quotation is taken, Michael Jacobs argues that contestation around a core of accepted meaning is politically advantageous.[114] The general acceptability of sustainable development provides a veneer of policy legitimacy beneath which the most radical manifestations of sustainable development can be discussed in the political mainstream. The potential to stimulate debate is perhaps the most valuable contribution of sustainable development to environmental policy, but only for as long as the site of contestation remains truly open. If one perspective on sustainable development is able to dominate debate and fix meanings, it becomes far less realistic to assert that sustainable development is a locus for discussion. The moral authority provided by sustainable development cuts both ways, and can be appropriated by powerful interests; some would argue that that is precisely what happened in Johannesburg.

In this respect, the pattern of contestation identified by Jacobs should be noted. He suggests that the radical and mainstream approaches to sustainable development differ along four main faultlines: the degree of environmental protection required; the importance of 'equity'[115]; the role of public participation; and the scope of the subject matter. Jacobs suggests that a radical, challenging approach to sustainable development will tend to argue for higher levels of environmental protection, a central role for equity and public participation, and for a broad scope to the subject matter covered by sustainable development; whilst a 'business as usual' approach would take the opposite perspective. The boundaries seem to have moved in recent years, as formerly radical perspectives are rapidly incorporated into something approaching a 'business as usual' approach to sustainable development. So whilst the level of environmental protection remains controversial along the parameters suggested by Jacobs, equity has transformed itself into 'social development' and been co-opted by the mainstream; public participation no longer holds the fear for the mainstream that it perhaps once did; and the dominant view puts a mass of detailed policy into the rubric of sustainable development. Perhaps this is an indication that the radicals have won; it is however far too soon to be sure that the radicals have not already lost.

This chapter should end positively. Sustainable development is a fundamentally optimistic premise, perhaps overly optimistic; we can have our cake, eat it and

---

[113] Jacobs, above n 9, p 23.

[114] Although even the core can be disputed, see R Attfield, *Environmental Ethics: An Overview for the Twenty-First Century* (Cambridge, Polity Press, 2003), for disagreement with Jacobs' analysis of the core, p 129.

[115] This covers the issues discussed under the Johannesburg heading of 'social development'; the different terminology may suggest that Johannesburg has a less challenging understanding of this element of sustainable development than Jacobs.

even give some away. Optimism at this level is perhaps unusual in environmental debate, almost jarring. And indeed, compared with the striking confidence of the Brundtland Report, perhaps one detects a level of disillusionment by the time we reach Johannesburg. Nevertheless, for all its faults, Johannesburg reaffirms many fine principles, and introduces some concrete commitments. To return to the comparison made at the very beginning of this chapter: justice, liberty and truth are also slippery and capable of misuse; we do not reject them for that reason.

3

The Implementation Gap

INTRODUCTION: THE CHALLENGE

T
HE NOTORIOUS AND persistent 'implementation deficit' in EC environmental law has become a major influence on the development of policy, with the full application, enforcement and implementation of environmental legislation gaining the status of a 'strategic priority' in the *Sixth Environmental Action Programme*.[1] Preoccupation with implementation is closely related to the legitimacy issues that plague EC environmental regulation: *effective* action could go a long way to providing *de facto* legitimacy; and conversely, the credibility of a legal instrument, or of an institution, that is not capable of producing compliance is likely to be undermined. The remedying of the implementation deficit is however a difficult and sensitive project, and the challenges are only likely to increase with enlargement, given the human, financial and institutional resources that implementation demands from the new Member States.[2] Implementation of EC law is primarily the responsibility of the Member States, and reasons for breach are complex and diverse.[3] For example, Member States often encounter political or practical difficulties if responsibility for environmental regulation cuts across sensitive national distributions of power and responsibility.[4] It is verging on legendary that Italy's administrative and political culture, with complex relationships between different levels of government and relatively unstable central governments, complicates implementation. Political dilemmas are also being seen in the UK's difficulties implementing the Landfill Directive: the construction of new waste incinerators is crucial if the Directive's obligations to

[1] *Sixth Environmental Action Programme Environment 2010: Our Future, Our Choice* COM (2001) 31 final, p 13; Decision 1600/2002 Laying Down the Sixth Community Environment Action Programme [2002] OJ L 242/1, Art 3.

[2] See P Nicolaides, 'Preparing for Accession to the European Union: How to Establish Capacity for Effective and Credible Application of EU Rules' in M Cremona (ed), *The Enlargement of the European Union* (Oxford, Oxford University Press, 2003).

[3] See for example, C Demmke, 'Trends in European Environmental Regulation: Issues of Implementation and Enforcement' vol 3 *Yearbook of European Environmental Law* 329; C Demmke, 'Towards Effective Environmental Regulation: Innovative Approaches in Implementing and Enforcing European Environmental Law and Policy' *Harvard Jean Monnet Working Paper 05/01*; C Knill and A Lenschow, 'Coping with Europe: The Impact of British and German Administrations on the Implementation of EU Environmental Policy' *EUI Working Paper 1997/57*.

[4] For an interesting discussion in respect of a number of Member States, see A Weale *et al*, *Environmental Governance in Europe: An Ever Closer Ecological Union?* (Oxford, Oxford University Press, 2000), ch 8.

divert waste from landfill are to be met, but the siting of incinerators, which hardly make popular neighbours, has turned out to be politically sensitive and very slow.[5] Whilst there is a consistent line of EC jurisprudence to the effect that no state can rely on internal administrative, political or practical difficulties to justify a failure to implement, it is clear that simple punishment or exhortation leaves many genuine difficulties unaddressed.

To add to the complexity, the 'full implementation' objective may be misplaced in any event. Activities that pollute are in an important sense socially and economically desirable, and over-deterrence of those activities should be avoided at the enforcement, as well as standard setting, stage of regulation. Moreover, there comes a point at which further implementation becomes disproportionately onerous, the 'last 10 percent problem'[6]; again, this is a concern that should be addressed when regulatory standards are set, but which may recur in enforcement. The prioritisation of enforcement resources between different areas of environmental regulation, not to mention other political demands, means that not all compromises on implementation are pernicious. Moreover, because implementation is inevitably a moving target in the environmental sphere (environmental conditions change, knowledge and regulation evolve), it is unrealistic to anticipate a moment at which compliance is 'complete'.[7]

Notwithstanding these provisos, it is clear that adequate levels of implementation provide a particular challenge in the environmental arena[8]; equally, that implementation concerns are driving policy development. This chapter will begin by examining national responsibilities for implementation of EC environmental law, and the different approaches that might be taken by regulators on the ground. The regulation literature discussed here suggests that it would be a mistake to assume that swift and harsh enforcement action is necessarily the best way to improve application of the law; cooperation with the regulated, backed up by a wide range of enforcement tools, seems to be effective in many cases. This observation should be borne in mind in efforts to enhance the implementation of EC

---

[5] Dir 99/31/EC on the Landfill of Waste [1999] OJ L 182/01. See S Tromans, 'Alternatives to Landfill — Can the Planning System Deliver?' [2001] *Journal of Planning and Environmental Law* 257; M Lee, 'Implementation of the Landfill Directive and the End of Life Vehicles Directive in England' in A Biondi, M Chechetti, S Grassi, M Lee (eds), *Scientific Evidence in European Environmental Rule-Making: The Case of the Landfill and End of Life Vehicles Directives* (The Hague, Kluwer, 2003).

[6] S Breyer, *Breaking the Vicious Circle: Toward Effective Risk Regulation* (Cambridge, Mass, Harvard University Press, 1993), p11 and generally.

[7] In Case C–278/01 *Commission v Spain*, 25 November 2003, not yet reported, a case about Spain's failure to comply with an Art 226 judgment on bathing water standards, the ECJ seems to assume that compliance can at a particular point be deemed to be complete, once and for all and forever. This is perhaps a necessary fiction, but it should be recalled that compliance with water quality standards is an ongoing process, likely to fluctuate according to weather conditions and agricultural and industrial activity.

[8] Although the level of enforcement activity cannot be an entirely accurate indicator of levels of compliance, some indication of the scale of the challenge can be seen in the fact that in 2002, one third of all infringement cases investigated by the Commission were in the environmental sector, notwithstanding the sector's small size relative to other policy areas such as agriculture, social policy or trade: European Commission, *Fourth Annual Survey on the Implementation and Enforcement of Community Environmental Law, 2002* SEC (2003) 804, p 6.

environmental law. This chapter will then discuss the enforcement of EC environmental law against the Member States, and some of the well-known limitations of traditional mechanisms, before turning to some of the different tactics being pursued in efforts to address the implementation deficit.

NATIONAL RESPONSIBILITIES

The nature of the Community enterprise thus far means that there is no centralised environmental inspection and investigation. The primary responsibility for ensuring that public and private enterprise complies with environmental legislation is with the Member States, which enjoy a broad discretion as to mechanisms of enforcement. This discretion is bounded by the requirements of the legislation at issue, and by the general requirements that enforcement be non-discriminatory, that is no less favourable than in respect of equivalent national law, and 'effective'.[9]

There is a long-standing debate about the relative merits of different approaches to enforcement of environmental law. Although the labels characterise extremes on a spectrum of approaches to enforcement, a distinction is commonly drawn between 'compliance' approaches, where the environmental regulator seeks to work with a polluter and improve performance, and 'deterrence' approaches, where the full force of the law, often through criminal prosecutions, is brought to bear on polluters.[10] Empirical and theoretical work suggests that a compliance approach is widespread, and can be successful, particularly if it is backed up with the credible threat of sanctions.[11] In fact, whether a regulator is deemed to be exercising a compliance or a deterrence approach in any particular case depends to a large extent on the structure of the law. If criminal offences are only available for the most culpable breaches, the chances are that resort will be had to criminal courts whenever there is a good chance of conviction. In many jurisdictions, including the UK, criminal status attaches in theory to routine and relatively minor breaches of regulation: environmental offences are strict liability and require no evidence of environmental harm. Frequent decisions not to prosecute are not surprising in those circumstances.

---

[9] See C Harding, 'Member State Enforcement of European Community Measures: The Chimera of "Effective" Enforcement' (1997) 4 *Maastricht Journal of European and Comparative Law* 5.

[10] AJ Reiss Jr, 'Selecting Strategies of Social Control Over Organisational Life' in K Hawkins and JM Thomas (eds), *Enforcing Regulation* (The Hague, Kluwer-Nijhoff Publishing, 1984); K Hawkins, *Environment and Enforcement: Regulation and the Social Definition of Pollution* (Oxford, Clarendon, 1984); BM Hutter, *The Reasonable Arm of the Law? The Law Enforcement Procedures of Environmental Health Officers* (Oxford, Clarendon, 1988); P Grabosky and J Braithwaite, *Of Manners Gentle: Enforcement Strategies of Australian Business Regulatory Agencies* (Melbourne, Oxford University Press, 1986). We might refer to an 'adversarial' as opposed to a 'co-operative' approach, see C Hilson, *Regulating Pollution: A UK and EC Perspective* (Oxford, Hart Publishing, 2000), p 149.

[11] See the sources cited above n 10. For a more critical view, see C Wells, *Corporations and Criminal Responsibility* (Oxford, Clarendon Press, 1993). Wells is not discussing environmental crime in particular, but regulatory offences in general; many of her examples relate to breaches of health and safety law and resulted in a number of deaths.

A non-adversarial approach to enforcement has a number of potential advantages. Briefly, these include, first, the maintenance of relationships between regulator and regulated over the long term. Compliance with environmental law requires environmental quality or performance standards to be met on an ongoing basis, rather than a one-off 'event' of compliance.[12] Legal and practical goalposts move, for example because of enhanced monitoring capacities, changed understandings of harm, or changing environmental conditions. An immediately confrontational attitude may reduce a polluter's inclination to co-operate in the longer term.[13] Secondly, the regulated party may have the best information on regulation. A co-operative attitude can mean that the regulator gains necessary information for ongoing, perhaps more formal, relationships with the regulated. Thirdly, a compliance approach is said to minimise the diversion of resources to the sanctioning process. The regulator may be able to devote resources more profitably to other regulatory activity, and the regulated to improvement of environmental performance.

Regulation scholarship suggests that enforcement is most effective if the full continuum of approaches is available. For example, one of the classic models used to explain corporate non-compliance with regulation focuses on three (overlapping) types of firm: the *amoral calculator* is motivated by profit and will comply only if it costs more not to; the *political citizen* is inclined to comply, and believes in the rule of law, but will not comply with a rule to which it has principled objections; and the *organizationally incompetent* would comply, but fails for various organisational reasons.[14] Persuasion, advice, and even a degree of intimidation,[15] could be effective with the latter two; a resort to formal sanctions is more likely to be necessary in the first case. Smaller or less sophisticated firms are also apparently more likely to be persuaded or intimidated into compliance, since they are more dependent on the expertise of the regulator.[16] This variation in the motives of the regulated suggests that a single approach to enforcement will not be the most successful. The work of Ian Ayres and John Braithwaite on 'responsive regulation' reinforces this conclusion, in its effort to mediate between the (perhaps overstated[17]) conflict between advocates of 'deterrent' and 'compliance' approaches to regulation. They emphasise flexibility and diversity in enforcement, arguing that over-reliance on persuasion will be exploited by some within the regulated community, and that over-reliance on punishment will undermine the inherent good will of others.

---

[12] See above n 7.

[13] Hawkins, above n 10.

[14] RA Kagan and JT Scholz, 'The "Criminlogy of the Corporation" and Regulatory Enforcement Strategies' in Hawkins and Thomas, above n 10. See also A Mehta and K Hawkins, 'Integrated Pollution Control and its Impact: Perspectives From Industry' (1998) 10 *Journal of Environmental Law* 61; I Ayres and J Braithwaite, *Responsive Regulation: Transcending the Deregulation Debate* (Oxford, Oxford University Press, 1992), discussed further below.

[15] See Hawkins, above n 10, on the importance of 'bluff'. Note that this is inherently more likely to be successful with an unsophisticated regulatee.

[16] Mehta and Hawkins, above n 14.

[17] Or at least it seems so now; this work was published in 1992, and perhaps has simply helped in overcoming that dichotomy.

The most significant aspect of Ayres and Braithwaite's work for current purposes is the 'enforcement pyramid', which they argue avoids too consistent a reliance on *either* a punitive (deterrent) or a co-operative (compliance) strategy. Regulators, argue Ayres and Braithwaite, are best able to achieve compliance when they are 'benign big guns', with serious enforcement sanctions at their disposal, but a desire to persuade and co-operate. The enforcement pyramid provides for an escalation of regulatory responses (to a particular polluter, industry or problem) with increasing intrusiveness as the problem goes on, from persuasion, through civil and criminal penalties, to revocation of a licence.

The flexible approach to enforcement that this work implies does suffer from dilemmas of accountability and transparency. Flexibility involves the exercise of a broad discretion by regulators, which can be difficult to control. Theories of regulatory 'capture', for example, posit that the relationship that develops between regulators and the regulated is likely to be to the detriment of stringent or consistent enforcement. A variety of explanations have been put forward for the phenomenon of capture,[18] which perhaps at its crudest rests on a 'revolving door' theory. This assumes that enforcers have either recently left the industry they are regulating, and so are sympathetic to its problems, or have an eye to more lucrative future employment in the industry, and so are eager to please those they regulate. This could be particularly problematic in highly specialist areas, in which there are few experts available. The result of capture, whatever its cause, is that regulators act, not in the public interest, but in accordance with the interests of the regulated. Drawing a line between a sensible and effective 'compliance' approach to regulation and 'capture' will never be easy, increasing difficulties of accountability; even the revolving door enhances the understanding necessary for useful co-operation as well as for capture. The discretion and co-operation that are vital elements of 'responsive regulation' nevertheless leave open the possibility of capture, corruption, or simple incompetence within the regulatory body.

Responsive regulation attempts to respond to problems of accountability by 'tripartism', that is the involvement of environmental interest groups in enforcement.[19] Public interest groups would have all the information available to the regulator, be present at negotiations, and be able to sue or prosecute. The use of tools of openness and participation to enhance environmental regulation is attractive to the EU for all sorts of reasons, discussed in chapters five and six. The role of tripartism in enforcement is not, however, entirely straightforward.[20] First, there

---

[18] T Makkai and J Braithwaite, 'In and Out of the Revolving Door: Making Sense of Regulatory Capture' (1995) 1 *Journal of Public Policy* 61, argue that what is called capture takes a number of forms and arises differently in distinct situations; GK Wilson, 'Social Regulation and Explanations of Regulatory Failure' (1984) *Political Studies* 203, reviews capture theories and emphasises the important influence of electoral politics on regulators.

[19] Ayres and Braithwaite, above n 14, ch 3.

[20] See for example M Gunningham and P Grabosky, *Smart Regulation: Designing Environmental Policy* (Oxford, Oxford University Press, 1998), which generally views increased third party involvement positively, pp 104–6; MS Grieve, 'The Private Enforcement of Environmental Law' (1990) 65 *Tulane Law Review* 339.

is a risk of capture of the interest groups, in respect of which Ayres and Braithwaite recommend 'contestable guardianship'; public interest groups would have to compete for access to the 'smoke filled rooms' where the business of enforcement takes place. There is also a danger that interest groups will shift regulatory priorities in directions that do not necessarily reflect the general environmental (let alone general public) interest. In particular, and in parallel with their ability to break into unduly cosy relationships between regulated and regulator, environmental interest groups could compromise an effective and efficient compliance relationship, taking an unhelpfully inflexible approach to enforcement. Ayres and Braithwaite devote considerable space to ensuring that third parties will be 'rational PIGs [public interest groups]', not 'zealous PIGs'; zealous PIGs are inappropriately adversarial, requiring enforcement action when co-operation would more effective. Ayres and Braithwaite argue that it is their very lack of power (in respect of tangible benefits) that makes the activities of PIGs combative and litigious, and that the pursuit of symbolic victories would be reduced if real environmental benefits were within their grasp. Problems of accountability would return with real power.

It is not intended to suggest that responsive regulation is the only, or necessarily the best, approach to environmental regulation. Nor is the advocacy of diverse and flexible sanctions, together with the use of third parties to ensure probity, unique to responsive regulation. Both of these elements of regulation have much to offer in the EC context. Independent and discretionary enforcement is on most accounts a necessary part of effective regulation, but the danger of sloth, inefficiency, capture or even straightforward corruption increases with the autonomy of the regulator. The 'access principles', access to information, public participation in decision-making (including overall enforcement strategies as well as individual enforcement decisions) and access to justice, can perform a modest instrumental role in encouraging regulators to keep the public interest at the forefront of regulation.[21]

The range of tools at the disposal of national regulators, and the level of discretion they enjoy, will vary. There seems to be a historical / cultural aspect to the regulatory 'style' that prevails in different jurisdictions or different agencies.[22] It is important to keep the subtlety of regulatory enforcement in mind when responding to the 'implementation deficit'.

---

[21] See chs 5 and 6 below.

[22] The most well researched, although perhaps peripherally relevant here, is the distinctively legalistic and coercive approach taken in the US. See D Vogel, *National Styles of Regulation: Environmental Policy in Great Britain and the United States* (New York, Cornell University Press, 1986). See also, although not in the context specifically of enforcement, the discussion of national policy approaches in Weale *et al*, above n 4. A more formalistic approach seems to be taken in Germany, see Knill and Lenschow, above n 3; B Lange, 'National Environmental Regulation? A Case-Study of Waste Management in England and Germany' (1999) 11 *Journal of Environmental Law* 59, reviews the literature comparing German and English approaches. Lange concentrates on the local level, and finds no significant difference between the German and English authority examined, with a flexible and cooperative approach dominating.

FORMAL TREATY ENFORCEMENT

The Commission's role as 'guardian of the treaty', and its powers under Article 226 EC to bring a Member State before the European Court of Justice (ECJ), are sufficiently well known to need little rehearsal here. The limitations of the centralised enforcement of environmental law under Article 226 are considerable.[23]

Community law obligations are formally owed by central government. The obligations on Member States under environmental legislation tend however to be diffuse. EC environmental legislation may require operators to work under a licence, or subject to other administrative arrangements; product standards may have to be applied; substantive environmental quality standards, for example as to the amount of particular pollutants in water or air, may be imposed; national or local strategies on a particular environmental issue may have to be published. Central government control over certain of these questions is likely to be indirect. Most obviously, the actual breach of Community environmental law, for example failure to comply with a licence or failure to meet quality standards, may have been committed in the final instance by a private sector polluter; if their action has been authorised or ignored by the state, that is likely to mean a decentralised regulator. In formal terms, there is no enforcement gap, as the 'state' is deemed responsible for all breaches, and the Commission can take action against the central government in respect of the breaches elsewhere in the system.[24] The inability of the Commission to take action against private polluters or decentralised administrators, however, means that the Commission is reduced to indirect enforcement, and even after enforcement action continues to rely on the capacity of the central government to ensure compliance. It also makes monitoring still more complex than it would anyway be, given the possible variations in implementation within any single Member State.[25] The integration of EC law into national legal systems is its great strength, particularly by comparison with its international law heritage. The roundabout way of tackling practical breaches by private polluters or devolved organs of the state is also, however, an obvious frustration, and is likely to emphasise diplomacy and politics in enforcement.

The notion of implementation covers a range of issues around making environmental law effective, including not just the *formal* implementation of directives into national law, but also the far more difficult task of *practical* implementation,

---

[23] See R Macrory, 'The Enforcement of Community Environmental Laws: Some Critical Issues' (1992) 29 *Common Market Law Review* 347; L Kramer, *EC Environmental Law* (London, Sweet & Maxwell, 2003), ch 12; Weale *et al*, above n 4, ch 8; W Grant, D Matthews and P Newell, *The Effectiveness of European Union Environmental Policy* (Basingstoke, MacMillan Press, 2000). See also European Commission, *Implementing Community Environmental Law* COM (96) 500.

[24] Including even legislative interpretation by the national courts, Case C–129/00 *Commission v Italy*, 9 December 2003, not yet reported.

[25] It seems also that devolved responsibilities in the Member States and a resulting absence of consolidated information often complicates reporting of implementation, see Lenschow and Knill (1997), above n 3.

that is ensuring that standards of environmental quality are in place on the ground.[26] The Commission's ability to monitor the formal implementation of directives is supported by obligations on the Member States to report to the Commission.[27] Failure to report is a straightforward breach of EC law, the establishment of which requires little in the way of administrative effort; patently inadequate transposition may also be spotted at this stage. Checking that purported implementation is actually consistent with the obligations in the Directive is more complex, and may require a sophisticated understanding of national law,[28] particularly if the Member State is relying on existing legislation, or the new material cuts across a number of established areas. By far the most demanding breach, however, which is particularly problematic in the environmental sector, is inadequate practical application of the law. For example, notwithstanding the introduction of appropriate national legislation, the regulatory authority may fail to ensure that a particular operation is in fact complying with a properly awarded licence, or fail to meet substantive environmental standards as to water or air quality. Identifying and confirming a suspected practical breach is complex, and may well require the exercise of considerable expert judgment. The Commission has no powers, and in any event inadequate resources, to investigate practical compliance. Obligations in directives to report on practical implementation, as with formal implementation, can support the Commission in respect of a simple failure to report or a clearly inadequate report. Under-reporting, or 'creative' reporting is more difficult to identify; and environmental conditions are always changing.

The Commission relies heavily on complaints from third parties (environmental interest groups, industry, individuals) to alert it to possible practical breaches of environmental legislation. Whilst this is a useful (and cheap) source of information, it forces the Commission into a reactive position, and could compromise the development of an independent and strategic approach to enforcement.[29] Moreover, the difficulties faced by the Commission are faced also by third parties. Substantiation of, for example, breach of water quality standards can be very demanding; moreover, compared to questions such as economic loss by traders prevented from moving goods across borders, there is little immediate gain for individuals from going to this trouble. Environmental interest groups are most likely to provide substantial information on practical compliance. Reliance on interest groups is only an erratic response to the basic problem. In particular, it assumes a strong and well-resourced interest group, something that varies between jurisdictions and environmental sectors.

[26] See for example Case C–337/89 *Commission v UK* [1992] ECR I–6103.

[27] Dir 91/692 Standardizing and Rationalizing Reports on the Implementation of Certain Directives Relating to the Environment [1992] OJ L 377/48, standardises reporting obligations. Note that the Commission places considerable emphasis on the importance of improving obligations to report, see European Commission, *Better Monitoring of the Application of Community Law* COM (2002) 725 final; Commission, above n 8.

[28] J Jans, *European Environmental Law* (Groningen, Europa Law Institute, 2000) provides a number of interesting examples, pp 152–4.

[29] The Commission is seeking to prioritise its enforcement efforts more effectively, see Commission, above n 27, and discussion below.

The Commission is, moreover, distinctly ambivalent about third party complainants. It recognises that 'complaints are a vital means of detecting infringements of Community law',[30] but on the other hand emphasises 'the bilateral nature of the infringement procedure' (and so the absence of a role for the third party complainant) as well as its own discretion in infringement matters.[31] Commission enforcement processes have in fact been notoriously isolated from the public and lacking in transparency.[32] Prompted by the European Ombudsman, the Commission has voluntarily undertaken to provide certain basic information to complainants on the steps taken by the Commission, including prior notice of a decision to close a case,[33] but formal rights remain elusive.[34] The Commission also publishes enforcement decisions on the internet, albeit it not documents themselves, such as correspondence.[35] The Article 226 procedure is also however in principle covered by legislative rights of access to documents, limited by the ability to refuse access 'where disclosure would undermine the protection of ... court proceedings and legal advice' or 'the purpose of inspections, investigations and audits', subject to 'an overriding public interest in disclosure'.[36] The 'protection of investigations' is the exception to access most often invoked by the Commission, reflecting its use in respect of requests for access to documents relating to infringement proceedings.[37] Clearly a balance between the interest in disclosure and the interest in protecting proceedings is necessary; whilst consideration of the overriding public interest provides for such a balancing of interests, it is how this is put into practice that is the key. The judiciary has generally supported the Commission in maintaining the confidentiality of infringement proceedings: Member States are 'entitled to expect the Commission to guarantee confidentiality during investigations'.[38]

---

[30] Commission, above n 25, p 12.

[31] European Commission, *Communication on Relations with the Complainant in Respect of Infringements of Community Law* COM (2002) 141 final, p 2.

[32] R Rawlings, 'Engaged Elites, Citizen Action and Institutional Attitudes in Commission Enforcement' (2000) 6 *European Law Journal* 28; R Williams, 'Enforcing European Environmental Law: Can the Commission be Held to Account?' (2000) 1 *Yearbook of European Environmental Law* 271.

[33] Commission, above n 30. The Commission sets itself time limits for dealing with complaints. Note the European Ombudsman's comment in the 2002 annual report that properly applied, these principles should prevent the sorts of maladministration that arose for consideration in that Report, see European Ombudsman, *Annual Report 2002*, available at: http://www.euro-ombudsman.eu.int/report/en/default.htm, pp 105–6.

[34] Note that European Commission, *Proposal for a Council Decision on the Conclusion, on behalf of the European Community, of the Convention on Access to Information, Public Participation in Decision-making and Access to Justice in Environmental Matters* COM (2003) 625 final explicitly excludes Arts 226–8, see ch 5 below.

[35] Commission, above n 30, p 8; the information is available at http://europa.eu.int/comm/secretariat_general/sgb/droit_com/index_en.htm#infringements.

[36] Reg 1049/2001 Regarding Public Access to European Parliament, Council and Commission Documents [2001] OJ L 145/43, Art 4. This Regulation is discussed in detail in ch 5 below.

[37] And also in competition matters. European Commission, *Report on the Implementation of the Principles in EC Regulation No 1049/2001 Regarding Public Access to European Parliament, Council and Commission Documents* COM (2004) 45 final, p 22. Note that L Kramer, 'Access to Letters of Formal Notice and Reasoned Opinions in Environmental Law Matters' [2003] *European Environmental Law Review* 197, argues that these matters do not fall within the exception at all.

[38] Case T–191/99 *Petrie v Commission* [2001] ECR II-3677, para 68, citing Case T–105/95 *WWF v Commission* [1997] ECR II–313. Note that these decisions preceded Reg 1049/2001, above n 36.

The Commission enjoys a very generous discretion on enforcement action. One of the major concerns about the free hand given to the Commission is the absence of a clear separation between the Commission's political role, in steering proposals through the legislative process, and its enforcement role.[39] A lengthy period of negotiation between Commission and the Member State precedes litigation under Article 226.[40] This implies considerable effort to settle without litigation, the importance of which is strengthened by the conceptualisation of the objective of the proceedings as 'an amicable resolution of the dispute' by the Court of First Instance (CFI).[41] This approach has undoubted advantages, maintaining the relationship between Commission and Member State, and preserving the resources of both parties. It does however allow political considerations to enter the assessment of compliance at any stage. Whilst the Commission's consistent integrationist stance and policy might suggest that it is not likely to be 'captured' by Member State interests,[42] it does face a conflict of interests. Political sensitivity may even be particularly acute in the environmental sector.[43] An alleged infringement that involves a particular project or development, such as a road or a waste facility,[44] has a more immediate political salience than a more abstract (to most people) claim that, for example, legislation on free movement has been inadequately transposed. Although this could cut both ways, enhancing compliance by bringing political pressure to bear on Member States, the relatively closed nature of the process certainly provides opportunities for the misuse of discretion. Moreover, the difficulty of substantiating claims that the Commission makes inadequate use of its enforcement powers is not helped by the general assumption of confidentiality that persists in this area. Even if there is no actual abuse, widespread disillusionment with the Commission's enforcement process could be damaging, particularly when considered alongside the reliance on third party information in environmental law.

Reducing the Commission's discretion on enforcement, requiring more immediate formal enforcement action, would be difficult. Article 226 is about long term compliance, not just about penalties, and ongoing compliance may be improved by cooperative bi-lateral negotiations; indeed improved cooperation is a major element of Commission efforts to improve implementation.[45] Because an Article 226 ruling by the Court is largely symbolic, overuse of Article 226 could reduce its impact[46]; the Commission's high success rate before the Court might also be

---

[39] This point has been made very strongly in respect of environmental law, see R Williams, 'The European Commission and the Enforcement of Environmental Law: An Invidious Position' (1994) 14 *Yearbook of European Law* 351. Williams, above n 32, suggests that this is precisely why the Member States are reluctant to move away from Commission enforcement.

[40] For discussion of the Art 226 process, see Kramer, above n 23, ch 12; Hilson, above n 10, ch 8.

[41] *Petrie*, above n 38, para 68.

[42] See P Craig, 'Once Upon a Time in the West: Direct Effect and the Federalisation of EEC Law' (1992) 12 *Oxford Journal of Legal Studies* 453.

[43] Macrory, above n 23.

[44] See Williams, above n 39, for a detailed account of some infringement activity in respect of controversial UK road building projects.

[45] Commission, above n 27. See discussion below.

[46] Hilson, above n 10.

expected to enhance the threat of litigation. The farrago surrounding regulation of GMOs in EC law, a story that will be pursued in more detail in chapter nine below, might also be considered. The relevant regulation ceased to function in quite a dramatic manner in the late 1990s, with a moratorium on new authorisations of GMOs, and a mushrooming of Member State 'safeguard' action, banning the import of authorised GMOs. The Commission undoubtedly could have pursued Member States for infringement much more aggressively than it has.[47] The perhaps unprincipled point should be made that those urging rigid enforcement in the environmental cause are perhaps also quite happy to see a blind eye turned in this case: we should be careful what we wish for. More importantly, the failure to apply the relevant regulation was due to a major popular political controversy about the commercialisation of GMOs, and resolution was sought through negotiation of a new and more appropriate legislative framework. Legal conflict between the Commission and a large number of Member States would be unlikely to have helped in that process.

However, if I would prefer to see the lack of action on GMOs as a sensible use of discretion to allow a long-lasting political solution to a problem, rather than a short term legalistic one, others might see the breakdown of the GMO regulation, together with the Commission's inaction, as a flagrant breach of the rule of law. The 'victims' of the breakdown, the international agricultural biotechnology industry, have well-defined economic interests, and the resources to pursue national or EC legal remedies. The fact that they did not choose to pursue legal action on a large scale suggests that they made a similar calculation to that made by the Commission. This reserve option of 'privatised enforcement' is, however, as discussed in this chapter and elsewhere,[48] frequently unavailable in environmental law. This makes the accountability of the Commission in Article 226 process particularly important.[49] The argument that the need for political support on new regulation should be a legitimate factor in weighing the exercise of discretion on enforcement is not an easy one. The potential for abuse, and the inequalities it is likely to provoke between the Member States, makes such an exercise of discretion eminently suitable for judicial review.

The availability of judicial review in extreme cases, together with further openness of the process, would ease many of the concerns about Commission discretion under Article 226. It is also a much more feasible response to a genuine problem than one of the main alternative suggestions, which would involve the separation

---

[47] Action was first taken against France, see Case C–296/01 *Commission v France*, 20 November 2003, not yet reported; action is promised against other member states. Note also that the Community institutions were also failing to apply the law, leading to a danger of double standards if the Commission took action against the Member States.

[48] See especially ch 5 below on access to justice.

[49] Little in the way of additional safeguards against Commission inaction can be found in mutual supervision by the Member States. Art 227 EC allows one Member State to take action against another for breach of EC law, but the diplomatic and political sensitivity of any such action makes it virtually unusable. Moreover, Member States, according to the most basic principles of EC law, cannot retaliate, or engage in 'self help' if they suspect that another Member State is not meeting its obligations, see for example Case C–5/94 *R v Ministry of Agriculture ex parte Hedley Lomas* [1996] ECR I–2553.

of enforcement powers from the Commission's political, legislative, role.[50] This would be bound to prompt concern that it constituted the beginnings of a European enforcement agency, as well as eliminating entirely any positive synergy from the political context of negotiations.

One longstanding limitation on the effectiveness of Article 226, the absence of concrete sanctions against a Member State in breach of EC law, was remedied in the Maastricht Treaty. Article 228 allows the Commission to seek financial penalties against Member States that fail to comply with an Article 226 judgment.[51] This is a powerful resource, and is clearly a major advance on the purely declaratory nature of a decision before Maastricht; in negotiations with a Member State following an Article 226 judgment, the Commission has a far stronger hand than it would otherwise. However, in the case of real Member State defiance, where it understands its vital national interest to be at stake, there is no way to force a Member State to pay, any more than they could be forced to comply with an Article 226 decision.[52] This is not a counsel of despair; simply a reminder that ultimately, implementation relies on mutual cooperation, and on the power of the law *per se*. It is to national capabilities, as well as to national cynicism, that attention should be directed. Another major challenge under Article 228 is to set payment at a level that has a deterrent effect, without harming other important interests, including, given the diversion of resources, environmental protection.[53] The Commission performs a calculation based on the seriousness of the infringement, the duration of the infringement, and a combination of GDP and weighting of votes in Council, deemed to indicate the Member State's ability to pay. It prefers a daily penalty to a lump sum fine, as encouraging swifter compliance.[54] The Court is not bound to follow the Commission's suggestions, which 'merely constitute a useful point of reference'[55] for the Court's own assessment of duration, seriousness and ability to pay.[56]

In conclusion, formal enforcement of Community law under Articles 226–8 faces considerable problems, which are to a large extent inherent in the nature of Community law. Although Community law has moved far beyond classic international law, some tension between central law and national implementation responsibilities is perhaps inevitable.[57] That tension is, however, compounded by

---

[50] Williams, above nn 32 and 39.

[51] Article 228(2) EC. See Case C–387/97 *Commission v Greece* [2000] ECR I–5047; *Commission v Spain*, above n 7. Note that the *Treaty Establishing a Constitution for Europe* provides for financial penalties to be applied in respect of failure to notify measures transposing European legislation, Art III–362(3).

[52] See TC Hartley, *Constitutional Problems of the European Union* (Oxford, Hart Publishing, 1999). The Commission could withhold money due to the Member State, as was threatened in the case against Greece, *ibid*, but the Member State could equally withhold money due to the Community.

[53] See Hilson, above n 10.

[54] The Court applied a daily penalty in *Greece*, above n 51, but rejected the imposition of a daily penalty in *Spain*, above n 7, where compliance can only be assessed annually, and imposed an annual fine.

[55] *Spain, ibid*, para 41.

[56] *Spain, ibid*, para 52; *Greece*, above n 51, para 92.

[57] JHH Weiler, 'The Community System: The Dual Character of Supranationalism' (1981) 1 *Yearbook of European Law* 268; A Jordan, 'The Implementation of EU Environmental Policy: A Policy Problem without a Political Solution?' (1999) 17 *Environment and Planning C* 69.

specific difficulties faced in the environmental sphere. Moreover, because private mechanisms of enforcement tend to be relatively weak, as discussed below, an additional premium must be placed on public mechanisms of enforcement.

INNOVATIONS IN IMPLEMENTATION

Although the practical impact of EC environmental legislation was for a long time a neglected subject, implementation questions have become a real driver of policy, given additional urgency by enlargement. The Commission has stated that litigation under Article 226 'is not the only, nor often the most efficient way to resolve the current problem',[58] and is pursuing a number of different approaches to improving implementation; whilst one might worry about ultimate coherence of the regulatory system, the single-mindedness is admirably practical.

Privatising Enforcement: Direct Effect and Beyond

In the absence of a powerful public enforcer of EC law, the ECJ developed techniques to involve private parties in implementation very early in the life of the Community. Whilst hardly a recent innovation, direct effect provides an alternative mechanism to encourage Member States to meet their EC law responsibilities. It allows private parties to use even unimplemented EC law in the national courts, thus appropriating 'the vigilance of individuals concerned to protect their rights' to the supervision process.[59]

Early *environmental* case law, however, developed predominantly through centralised enforcement mechanisms, rather than the national courts, for a number of reasons. Private parties willing to invest in litigation over diffuse interests, such as environmental protection, are few and far between. Individual losses are likely to be small, even if total losses are high, and so the benefits of litigation will often not match the investment. This contrasts starkly with the enforcement of free trade rules by traders across national borders, where there is a direct financial benefit in ensuring that the law is applied.[60] We might turn to environmental interest groups, or even unusually dedicated individuals, to fill this gap in interests. The practical limitations in respect of diffuse interests are, however, institutionally reinforced by traditional liberal legal ideas about the assertion of rights. Direct effect was traditionally as concerned with the protection of individual rights as with the effectiveness of Community law.[61] A narrow approach to direct effect,

---

[58] Commission, above n 8, p 6.

[59] Case 26/62 *Van Gend en Loos* [1963] ECR 1, p 13.

[60] See S Weatherill, 'Addressing Problems of Imbalanced Implementation in EC law: Remedies in an Institutional Perspective' in C Kilpatrick, T Novitz and P Skidmore (eds), *The Future of Remedies in Europe* (Oxford, Hart Publishing, 2000).

[61] F Snyder, 'The Effectiveness of European Community Law: Institutions, Processes, Tools and Techniques' (1993) 56 *Modern Law Review* 19.

which defines the concept by reference to the capacity of a provision of EC law to confer rights on individuals, dominated until recently. The language of rights is problematic, not only because of its 'indiscriminate' use,[62] but also because the environment is a classic public good, whilst legal 'rights' are generally highly individualised. In the early 1990s, the identification of environmental provisions designed to protect human health began to open up the 'rights' issue to environmental lawyers,[63] and some use has also been made of coincidences between environmental quality and economic interests.[64] Nevertheless, environmental directives are not happily analysed in terms of individual rights. Rights talk might empower individuals in core EC economic law, but it can have perverse effects in environmental law.[65]

The ECJ has placed less emphasis on 'rights' in recent years, greatly expanding the legal scope for national environmental litigation to call on unimplemented EC law. The ECJ has developed a line of case law, dubbed 'public law effect',[66] which has concentrated on the effectiveness of directives. The pivotal case is *Kraaijeveld*,[67] a case involving the application of the Environmental Impact Assessment Directive.[68] By marked contrast with its Advocate General and the referring court, the ECJ avoided consideration of whether the relevant provisions of the Directive were capable of direct effect. Instead, it held that where a Community measure imposes a clear obligation on a Member State, national courts must be able to use that provision to review the legality of the Member State's exercise of discretion. The line of cases following *Kraaijeveld* does not raise the question of rights for individuals, but concentrates on effectiveness. *Linster*, for example, confirmed that:

> the effectiveness of [a directive] would be diminished if individuals were prevented from relying on it in legal proceedings and if national courts were prevented from

---

[62] S Prechal and L Hancher, 'Individual Environmental Rights: Conceptual Pollution in EU Environmental Law?' (2001) 2 *Yearbook of European Environmental Law* 89, p 92; see also C Hilson and T Downes, 'Making Sense of Rights: Community Rights in EC Law' (1999) 24 *European Law Review* 121.

[63] See for example similar cases concerning the obligation to transpose directives by binding law: Case C–361/88 *Commission v Germany* [1991] ECR I–2567; Case C–59/89 *Commission v Germany* [1991] ECR I–2607; Case C–58/89 *Commission v Germany* [1991] ECR I–4983; Case C–298/95 *Commission v Germany* [1996] ECR I–6747.

[64] *Bowden v South West Water Services Ltd* [1999] Env LR 438.

[65] S Prechal, 'Does Direct Effect Still Matter?' (2000) 37 *Common Market Law Review* 1047, considers the potential of direct effect to *limit* the application of EC law by member states, rather than extend it. See also C Hilson, 'Community Rights in Environmental Law: Rhetoric or Reality?' in J Holder (ed) *The Impact of EC Environmental Law in the United Kingdom* (Chichester, John Wiley, 1997).

[66] J Scott, *EC Environmental Law* (London, Longman, 1998) p 157; Hilson and Downes, above n 62.

[67] Case C–72/95 *Aanemersebedrijf PK Kraaijeveld BV v Gedeputeerde Staten van Zuid-Holland* [1996] ECR I–5403.

[68] Dir 85/337 on the Assessment of the Effects of Certain Private and Public Projects on the Environment [1985] OJ L 175/40, as amended by Dir 97/11/EC [1997] L 073/05. The plaintiff in the national proceedings challenged Dutch legislation authorising certain construction work, in particular on dykes and canals. The work would leave the plaintiff without access to an inland waterway, and so affect its commercial interests.

taking it into consideration ... in determining whether the national legislature ... had kept within the limits of its discretion.[69]

The development of powers, or in some circumstances obligations[70] on courts to raise Community law of their own motion emphasises this move from a focus on the individual, to a focus on the impact of Community law. Obligations on national administrations to apply Community law where it has not been correctly transposed into national law takes this further[71]; the effectiveness rationale increasingly dominates the 'rights' side of the direct effect equation.

This line of cases raises not only the question of 'rights', but also the 'horizontal' effect of directives; direct effect is traditionally subject to a fundamental proviso that directives (unlike treaty provisions or regulations) cannot have direct effect against private parties.[72] A review of the legality of state action, however, may well affect private rights; the illegality of granting development consent without an environmental impact assessment, for example, clearly affects the third party developer. The duty on national courts to interpret national law consistently with EC law ('indirect effect'), even in litigation between private parties, can also bypass the state/private dichotomy.[73] The Court has on the whole avoided addressing the effect of the *Kraaijeveld* case law on individuals. More recently, the point was directly raised in another reference on the EIA Directive:

> the principle of legal certainty prevents directives from creating obligations for individuals ... Consequently, an individual may not rely on a directive against a Member State where it is a matter of a State obligation *directly* linked to the performance of another obligation falling, pursuant to that directive, on a third party ... On the other hand, *mere adverse repercussions* on the rights of third parties, even if the repercussions are certain, do not justify preventing an individual from invoking the provisions of a directive against the Member State concerned (emphasis added).[74]

---

[69] Case C–287/98 *Luxembourg v Linster* [2000] ECR I–6917, para 32; again, the approach of the Advocate General, which dealt more explicitly with direct effect, was not followed. See also Case C–435/97 *World Wildlife Fund v Autonome Provinz Bozen* [1999] ECR I–5613.

[70] *Kraaijeveld*, above n 67.

[71] Case C–198/01 *Consorzio Industrie Fiammiferi* [2003] 5 CMLR 16 deals with the application of the duty to disapply national legislation that contravenes Community law to all organs of the State, including administrative authorities; note the Court's concern that private parties are not penalised. See also Case 103/88 *Constanzo* [1989] ECR I–1839, and discussion in S Prechal, 'Community Law in National Courts: The Lessons from *van Schijndel*' (1998) 35 *Common Market Law Review* 631.

[72] Case 152/84 *Marshall v Southampton and South West Hampshire Area Health Authority* [1986] ECR I–723.

[73] Case 14/83 *Von Colson v Land Nordrhein-Westfalen* [1984] ECR 1891; Case 79/83 *Harz v Deutsche Tradax GmbH* [1984] ECR 1921; Case C–106/89 *Marleasing v La Comercial Internacional de Alimentación SA* [1990] ECR I–4135. See further G Betlem, 'The Doctrine of Consistent Uncertainty: Managing Legal Uncertainty' (2002) 22 *Oxford Journal of Legal Studies* 397.

[74] Case C–201/02 *The Queen on the application of Wells v Secretary of State for Transport, Local Government and the Regions* [2004] 1 CMLR 31, paras 56–7, citations omitted. Note also that in this case the Court did not rely on the *Kraaijeveld* line of case law.

This rather subtle distinction between direct obligations and 'adverse repercussions' does not contribute greatly to the difficult task of identifying impermissible situations of 'horizontal direct effect' and situations where the provisions of a Directive can be applied. For current purposes, it is however clear that individuals are increasingly empowered to monitor national application of EC environmental law.

Unimplemented directives are now used in litigation between individuals in a range of situations, dependent to a large degree simply on the justiciability of the directives, a development predicted by Pescatore some time ago.[75] Alongside any other benefits, this introduces an important independent policing of national implementation of EC environmental law. Another legal mechanism that enhances the potential for individual vigilance over the implementation of EC environmental law, is the action for state liability for damage caused by breach of EC law, arising out of the *Francovich* line of case law.[76] *Francovich* is an indirect remedy, involving suit against the state rather than the polluter.[77] The possibility in Community law for the action to be brought against the decentralised regulator, could enhance the incentives for compliance on those front line institutions.[78]

Much of the case law and academic literature on state liability has focused on the question of whether the breach by the state is 'sufficiently serious', and the question of causal link between the breach and the damage.[79] These questions are of course likely to be significant in an environmental context. Equally importantly, *Francovich*, like classical approaches to direct effect, is based on parallel objectives of effectiveness together with the judicial protection of individual rights, and requires that the rule of law in question be intended to confer rights on individuals. Whilst the relationship between the two principles of effectiveness and rights protection has been fundamentally rebalanced in recent case law on direct effect, it has not yet been much discussed in respect of state liability. It has been convincingly argued that state liability is more about penalties than about compensating individuals,[80] and it may well be then that the Court is more concerned by effectiveness than the protection of individual rights. Nevertheless, the rights issue seems set to persist in *Francovich* cases, if only because somebody needs to be compensated for some damage.[81] The notion of 'damage' has not been

---

[75] P Pescatore, 'The Doctrine of "Direct Effect": An Infant Disease of Community Law' (1983) 2 *European Law Review* 155.

[76] Case C–6/90 and C–9/90 *Francovich and Bonifaci v Italian State* [1991] ECR I–5357.

[77] The responsibility of the state extends to 'manifest infringements' of Community law committed even by the courts, Case C–224/01 *Kobler v Austria* [2003] 3 CMLR 28. This is an extremely controversial innovation. For discussion, see PJ Wattel, '*Kobler, CILFIT* and *Welthgrove*: We Can't Go on Meeting Like This' (2004) 41 *Common Market Law Review* 177.

[78] Case C–424/97 *Haim v Kassenzahnärztliche Vereinigung Nordrhein* [2000] ECR I–5123.

[79] T Tridimas, 'Liability for Breach of Community Law: Growing up and Mellowing Down?' (2001) 38 *Common Market Law Review* 301, discusses the development of the case law.

[80] C Harlow, '*Francovich* and the Problem of the Disobedient State' (1996) 2 *European Law Journal* 199.

[81] Note that the *Kraaijeveld* line of case law, by avoiding the language of rights, manages to allow the national use of unimplemented legislation without opening up the possibility of state liability; the possibility of compensation is however raised in *Wells*, above n 74.

clarified by the ECJ, but the approach of the English Court of Appeal in *Bowden*[82] illustrates the likelihood that environmental quality will remain contingent on other interests. A mussel fisher brought an action against the state in respect of breach of environmental directives, and resultant poor water quality, which threatened his livelihood. The Court was able to identify certain rights for those who might benefit from equal conditions of competition and the common market in shellfish. But although these rights existed for those economically active in the sector, there were no 'environmental rights'. Beyond economic rights, the clearest question for liability is harm to human health. Proof of causation is, however, likely to be extremely problematic. Disease, a more likely harm than traumatic injury in environmental cases, is often impossible to link to the breach, particularly if there is a high background incidence of the disease in the general population; the claimant may have succumbed to the disease for reasons entirely independent of the breach.[83] Beyond actual illness, the public may be prevented from bathing in or drinking particular water. Such diffuse harm is very difficult to address through normal mechanisms of civil liability, although provision could be made for action by environmental interest groups.[84]

It is not necessary here to go into further detail on judicial development of the individual use of EC environmental law, which is clearly at an important, and very complex, stage of its development. Traditional direct effect seems to be losing its pre-eminence in the use of unimplemented directives in national legal systems, and there are increasing opportunities for third parties to 'enforce' unimplemented EC environmental law within their national legal systems.

The historical effectiveness of third party enforcement of EC law is a lesson well learned by the other EU institutions, and is reflected in numerous initiatives to empower individuals and interest groups against polluters or national regulators. National rules on standing have the potential to dictate the role of EC environmental legislation in the national courts. The usual Community law provisos of non-discrimination and effectiveness apply, restricting national freedom of action to a limited degree. This question is also however increasingly being pre-empted by 'access to justice' provisions in directives. For example, whilst early proposals to enhance tort claims against polluters by individuals and public interest groups have not survived,[85] the Environmental Liability Directive explicitly makes room for individuals and interest groups to seek judicial review of a regulator's decisions on liability.[86] This sidesteps any question as to standing for interest groups, or indeed as to direct effect, and is

---

[82] Above n 64.

[83] J Stapleton, *Disease and the Compensation Debate* (Oxford, Oxford University Press, 1986) discusses the longstanding difficulties of civil actions for disease rather than traumatic injury. Austria's argument that the private party's act is an intervening event that breaches the chain of causation was rejected in Case C–140/97 *Rechberger v Austria* [1999] ECR I–3499.

[84] European Commission, *White Paper on Environmental Liability* COM (2000) 66 final, raised the possibility of such an action.

[85] Commission, *ibid*.

[86] Dir 2004/35 on Environmental Liability with Regard to the Prevention and Remedying of Environmental Damage [2004] OJ L 143/56, Art 13.

a potentially powerful monitoring tool. Provision for judicial review, with explicit standing for environmental interest groups, has also been introduced to environmental impact assessment and integrated pollution prevention and control, and is being developed in respect of environmental litigation more generally.[87]

Even the Court's increasingly expansive approach to the effectiveness of EC law provides in principle no claim against a private polluter for breach of EC environmental law, certainly in respect of directives.[88] Environmental liability, an obligation to pay to remedy breaches of environmental law, is a useful tool at many levels, providing considerable incentives for compliance, as well as funds for the restoration of environmental harm. Early discussion of environmental liability at EC level could have provided some space for individual or environmental interest group suits against polluters, an attractive shift of enforcement costs from the public to the private sector. The Environmental Liability Directive as ultimately agreed, however, provides a purely administrative tool, through which regulators can require those who breach environmental law to pay to restore the effect of their breaches.[89]

A strong role for third parties is often at least part of the prescription for various forms of regulatory failure, including capture, inefficiency, incompetence. As discussed above in respect of the Article 226 process, this monitoring function is only weakly and very recently emerging at EU level. It is on the other hand very long established in respect of national implementation, and the traditional limitations of private action in the environmental sphere are currently subject to considerable renewed attention. Many of the participatory innovations discussed elsewhere in this book could be viewed from the perspective of implementation, including especially access to information and access to justice, as well as self-regulatory approaches such as eco-management and audit systems and environmental agreements.[90]

National Tools of Enforcement

As well as looking to the supervision of national regulators by private parties, EC law is beginning to address the enforcement tools available to national regulators.

---

[87] See ch 6 below. Dir 2003/35 Providing for Public Participation in Respect of the Drawing Up of Certain Plans and Programmes Relating to the Environment and Amending with Regard to Public Participation and Access to Justice Council Directives 85/337/EEC and 96/61/EC [2003] OJ L 156/17; European Commission, *Proposal for a Directive on Access to Justice in Environmental Matters* COM (2003) 624 final.
[88] Case C–253/00 *Antonio Munoz v Frumar Ltd* [2002] ECR I–7289 provides that rights provided in a regulation must be capable of enforcement by means of civil proceedings. This is part builds on the distinction between regulations and directives in respect of horizontal and vertical direct effect, see especially Advocate General Geelhoed's Opinion. Case C–453/99 *Courage Ltd v Crehan* [2001] ECR I–6297 held that there should be no national bar on damages to a claimant injured by an agreement that is illegal under EC competition rules.
[89] Dir 04/35, above n 86. Commission, above n 84, considered the provision of a right for public interest groups to sue in respect of environmental damage. This disappeared by the time of European Commission, *Proposal for a Directive on Environmental Liability with regard to the Prevention and Restoration of Environmental Damage* COM (2002) 17 final. For discussion of the change, see M Lee, 'The Changing Aims of Environmental Liability' [2002] *Environmental Law and Management* 189.
[90] See especially chs 6 and 8 below.

The enlargement of the EU perhaps emphasises the importance of this approach, given the young administrative law systems in many of the new Member States. It should however be noted that regulators in older Member States such as the UK lack certain key enforcement tools, such as the routine ability to impose penalty payments on polluters in administrative law[91]; similar gaps and surprises no doubt occur around the EU. Small steps have been taken in respect of common EC administrative and criminal law tools of enforcement, which will be discussed here.

Administrative Tools

There is a range of possible administrative responses by a regulator to a breach of environmental law. Most systems allow for the withdrawal by a regulator of a licence to operate, 'corporate capital punishment'.[92] Less dramatically, many systems allow regulators to demand penalty payments from polluters, or to serve administrative notices requiring compliance or the temporary cessation of operations. Administrative mechanisms generally do not require the full rigours of criminal prosecution and proof, and so absorb fewer administrative resources than criminal prosecution. Anthony Ogus and Carolyn Abbot explain the deterrence effect of administrative penalty payments in law and economics terms: essentially, rational firms comply with the law when the costs of violation are greater than the costs of compliance; the availability of administrative penalty payments increases the likelihood that violation will incur a cost, since they are more likely to be used than either resource intensive criminal prosecution or the extreme response of licence revocation.[93] Even accepting that firms do not always behave as rational economic calculators,[94] but are motivated by a complex range of factors, good, bad and indifferent, the administrative sanction can give regulators extra flexibility to respond to different situations, and allow them to 'escalate' sanctions where necessary.[95] They do not currently form part of the 'common' EC environmental law toolbox, save in a couple of instances. First, the obligation on Member States to impose a fixed financial penalty on those who breach certain elements of the EU greenhouse gas emissions allowance trading scheme is a very unusual specification of sanctions in a particular piece of legislation, with apparently no flexibility for the regulator.[96] If this new legislation is indicative of a new tactic in enforcement, it suggests a real change to the relationship between

---

[91] A Ogus and C Abbot, 'Sanctions for Pollution: Do We Have the Right Regime?' (2002) 14 *Journal of Environmental Law* 283.

[92] Ayres and Braithwaite, above n 14, p 53.

[93] Ogus and Abbot, above n 91; see also Hilson, above n 10, p 154.

[94] See R Baldwin, 'The New Punitive Regulation' (2004) 67 *Modern Law Review* 351, on the often poor response to regulatory risk of even sophisticated regulated entities.

[95] Ayres and Braithwaite, above n 14.

[96] Dir 2003/87 Establishing a Scheme for Greenhouse Gas Emission Allowance Trading Within the Community and Amending Council Directive 96/61/EC [2003] OJ L 275/32, Art 16. See ch 7 below.

Community and Member State on implementation. It is however possible that the reasons for the innovation lie in the nature of the scheme at issue, as will be discussed in chapter seven below. Secondly, administrative sanctions appear in the very specific guise of an obligation to pay for the restoration or prevention of environmental damage, to which I will now turn.

The Environmental Liability Directive requires the Member States to put in place an administrative scheme under which regulators are able to require polluters to finance the restoration of environmental damage.[97] Whilst the EC's environmental liability scheme was initially developed on the basis of a range of rationales, the objective of improving enforcement moved centre-stage during its development. The deterrence aim is 'to induce operators to adopt measures and develop practices to minimise the risks of environmental damage so that their exposure to financial liabilities is reduced'.[98] Enforcement objectives can also be detected in the close relationship between environmental liability and existing, substantive environmental legislation: both environmental damage and those subject to strict environmental liability are defined by reference to existing legislation.[99] In addition, although the scheme is prima facie strict liability, Member States are able to provide a defence for polluters that cause damage in spite of having complied with a licence; again, that relationship between compliance and liability points towards an implementation concern, rather than a concern that environmental externalities be internalised, or that environmental damage be restored.[100] The Directive's hard-edged language also suggests an enforcement concern: competent authorities 'shall' require the operator to take the preventive or remedial measures determined under the Directive.[101] The language in the Directive will be open to interpretation, and certainly there is inherent discretion in identifying damage or imminent threats of damage, as well as in identifying the most appropriate measures to be taken in response.[102] Nevertheless, there seems to be an intention to cut down the regulator's discretion, reducing attendant problems of accountability and transparency. Limiting the scope of regulators to take a 'compliance' rather than a 'deterrence' approach to enforcement will not necessarily, however, improve implementation. Further, the absence of regulatory discretion would give the entitlement of individuals and interest groups to 'request action' of the competent authority and subsequently seek judicial review real teeth, going quite deeply into the relationship between regulator and

---

[97] Dir 04/35, above n 86.

[98] *Ibid*, Recital 2.

[99] *Ibid*, Art 2 provides for three categories of environmental damage: damage to protected species and habitats, defined by reference to EC nature conservation legislation; water damage, defined by reference to EC water legislation; land damage, defined by reference to risk to human health, given the absence of EC level legislation. Annex III lists the relevant occupational activities subject to strict liability. Fault based liability applies to 'occupational activities' not listed, in respect of damage to protected species and habitats only, Art 3(1)(b).

[100] *Ibid*, Art 8(4). This applies only in the absence of fault.

[101] *Ibid*, Arts 5(4) and 6(3).

[102] Note the emphasis on discretion, *ibid*, Recital 24.

regulated.[103] The limitation of discretion does not seem to have received the attention it deserves, and it will be interesting to see how it develops.

In any event, environmental liability is a potentially powerful tool of implementation of EC environmental law. It provides an additional deterrent for polluters, an additional tool for regulators, and an additional point of entry for third parties. Currently, it is the only free-standing attempt to address poor implementation by providing national regulators with administrative sanctions.

Criminal Law

Developments in criminal environmental law at EC level also seek to ensure that national regulators are fully equipped for their task. The Commission is of the view that availability of criminal sanctions is vital to the enforcement of EC environmental law.[104] It is certainly arguable that criminal environmental law both reflects society's condemnation of environmental wrongs, and exercises a deterrent effect.[105] The deterrence effect of different sanctions is however notoriously difficult to assess, even in respect of 'ordinary' crime, let alone predominantly corporate environmental crime. It is perhaps simplistic to claim that criminal sanctions, because they are symbolically powerful are always the most effective sanctions. For example, revocation of a licence, by taking away a polluter's livelihood, is an extremely serious penalty that need not be attached to criminal conviction. Similarly, Ogus and Abbot demonstrate that administrative penalties may be as influential an element of an overall enforcement strategy as criminal law, in part because they are a more credible and immediate threat.[106] Although the Commission is perhaps guilty of overstating its case on the contribution of criminal penalties to environmental law, or even of naivety,[107] a criminal conviction does carry with it an important social stigma that may not be available from other sanctions, as well as providing an additional enforcement tool to regulators.

Both Commission and Council have been pursuing measures in environmental criminal law. The Council has adopted a *Framework Decision on the Protection of the Environment through Criminal Law*[108] under the third pillar of the EU treaty.[109] The third pillar is a forum for inter-governmental decision-making on police and judicial cooperation on criminal matters, requiring consensus in

---

[103] *Ibid*, Arts 12 and 13.
[104] European Commission, *Proposal for a Directive on the Protection of the Environment through Criminal Law* COM (2001) 139 final, amended COM (2002) 544 final, p 2; Council Framework Decision 2003/80/JHA on the Protection of the Environment through Criminal Law [2003] OJ L 29/55 suggests that criminal sanctions constitute a 'tough response' to breach of environmental law, Recital 2.
[105] C Abbot, 'Friend or Foe? Strict Liability in English Environmental Licensing Regimes' [2004] *Environmental Law and Management* 67.
[106] Ogus and Abbot, above n 91.
[107] M Faure, 'European Environmental Criminal Law: Do We really Need It?' [2004] *European Environmental Law Review* 18.
[108] Decision 03/80, above n 104.
[109] Title VI TEU.

Council, and largely excluding the Commission and the European Parliament. Before adoption of the Framework Decision, the Commission had adopted a Proposal for a Community (first pillar) Directive on the same subject.[110] The Commission is of the view that although the EC Treaty does not provide competence in relation to criminal matters per se, the Community can oblige Member States to provide for criminal sanctions if necessary for the achievement of Community objectives. It has commenced proceedings before the ECJ challenging the Council's use of a Framework Decision,[111] and it remains to be seen whether the Framework Decision or the proposed Directive will apply. Although there are strong arguments in favour of the Commission's position,[112] demanding a particular method of implementation of EC law is a development that should not be taken lightly, given the long-standing flexibility on implementation. Moving beyond the 'non-discriminatory' and 'effective' standard[113] implies a shift in the relationship between Community and Member State on implementation. Regardless of any differences in content or effect of the two environmental crime initiatives, the action before the ECJ is a constitutionally important challenge.

Both initiatives provide for minimum standards of criminal environmental law; Member States can go further. A list of offences is set out in both instruments. In the Commission's proposal, these are explicitly related to a breach of Community law or rules adopted by Member States to comply with Community law[114]; the Framework Decision covers also breach of purely national provisions.[115] The Framework Decision, however, addresses only breaches of regulation that cause or are likely to cause harm,[116] whilst the Commission's proposal applies in many cases without proof of damage. The latter approach puts the emphasis of the criminal law on risky behaviour rather than on the fortuitous avoidance of damage. This has the advantage of limiting difficulties of proof, and avoiding interpretative debate if the criminal law is used to support regulation that attempts to improve an already heavily polluted environment.

Both initiatives on environmental crime cover breaches of law committed with intention or serious negligence, leaving strict liability to the discretion of the Member States. The different standards of criminal liability are subject to considerable theoretical and practical debate,[117] but for current purposes, a requirement for intention or serious negligence will always create problems of proof, exacerbated

---

[110] Commission, above n 104.

[111] Case C–176/03 *Commission v Council* [2003] OJ C 135/21.

[112] See F Comte, 'Criminal Environmental Law and Community Competence' [2003] *European Environmental Law Review* 147.

[113] Above n 9.

[114] Commission, above n 104, Annex.

[115] Commission, *ibid,* Art 1(a), definition of 'unlawful'. The framework Decision does not need to keep within the terms of the EC Treaty.

[116] For example, 'the unlawful disposal, treatment, storage, transport, export or import of waste, including hazardous waste, which causes or is likely to cause death or serious injury to any person or substantial damage to the quality of air, soil, water, animals or plants', Decision 03/80, above n 104, Art 2(c).

[117] See Abbot, above n 105 for a very useful review in an environmental context.

in respect of a corporate entity. A major drawback of pursuing criminal penalties through the courts, as far as regulators are concerned, is that enormous resources are required for successful prosecution, and the more elements the prosecution is required to prove, the greater the resources absorbed. However, assuming that adequate alternative penalties are available for less severe cases, reserving criminal sanctions for very serious cases avoids inappropriately stigmatising largely 'blameless' defendants and the risk of diluting the moral opprobrium implied by criminal sanctioning. In countries such as the UK, with generously defined criminal offences, the 'moral' and 'symbolic' elements of criminal law are reflected in discretion to prosecute, which seems to be reserved by regulators for serious cases,[118] and in discretion on sentence.[119] The major argument in favour of strict liability criminal environmental law is to make a successful prosecution feasible in the worst cases, in which proof of mental states would otherwise be very difficult. It should also be recalled that the more onerous the prosecution, the less likely a regulator is to resort to criminal sanctions, and economically rational polluters in these circumstances are likely to discount the risk of prosecution.[120]

In a number of Member States, corporate bodies cannot be prosecuted for a criminal offence.[121] Both Commission and Council would in principle apply criminal environmental law against legal persons, although the Commission's proposal would allow non-criminal penalties' to avoid the need to make fundamental changes to national legal systems.[122] The Commission is clearly trying to anticipate resistance from the Member States on this issue, but its approach does demonstrate a certain inconsistency in its faith in criminal sanctions. Prosecution of a corporate body can be useful if the offence reflects a 'systemic' failure, or a training or monitoring failure, for which no individual can be held responsible; or if it is necessary to deter all company officers rather than just those with direct pollution control responsibilities; or it may simply reflect the fact that just as a company can run a factory and take profits, it can break the law.[123] The prosecution only of the individual within the company who makes the final error or decision can seem to be unfair scapegoating. The ability to prosecute individuals as well as the company is nevertheless crucial, often concentrating the mind more effectively than corporate liability, although it will not be appropriate in every case.

Sanctions have to be 'effective, proportionate and dissuasive', and the possibility of imprisonment is explicitly raised in both initiatives.[124] However, companies

---

[118] Abbot, *ibid.*

[119] P de Prez, 'Excuses, Excuses: The Ritual Trivialisation of Environmental Prosecutions' (2000) 12 *Journal of Environmental Law* 65, suggests that a defendant inevitably puts these factors before the court.

[120] Ogus and Abbot, above n 91.

[121] See the studies at http://europa.eu.int/comm/environment/crime/#studies for a discussion of corporate criminal liability in the Member States.

[122] Commission, above n 104, p 5. More elaborate provisions for the liability of legal persons are made in the Framework Decision, above n 104, Art 6.

[123] Hilson, above n 10, p 139.

[124] Commission, above n 104, Art 4(a); Framework Decision, above n 104, Art 5(1).

and public sector organisations have 'no soul to damn, no body to kick'.[125] Imprisonment of the company is not an option, although removal of a permit similarly 'disables' the polluter from committing the same crime in future. Possible corporate penalties under the two initiatives discussed here include fines, judicial supervision, 'disqualification from the practice of commercial activities', exclusion from entitlement to public benefits or aid.[126] A fine is the usual penalty against companies. The fine in many legal systems simply passes into general public funds, and so is not available for environmental restoration; in environmental terms, the resources involved in prosecution, defence and penalties may often be better spent on a less coercive approach. Moreover, setting the fine is very difficult. If it is low, a fine is not an effective sanction, but simply becomes part of the firm's operating costs. A high fine, on the other hand, could have negative social impacts, an even more acute problem with a public sector defendant. An English Court of Appeal decision indicates some of the problems. The case concerned the grounding, due to serious errors on the part of the pilot employed by the defendant, of the tanker *Sea Empress* as it entered the port of Milford Haven.[127] Many thousands of gallons of oil were spilled in an area of considerable conservation value. The Court of Appeal was of the view that although a penalty must recognise the seriousness of the offence and provide a level of deterrence, it should not 'cripple' the defendant's business or 'blight' the local economy, and considerably reduced the initial sentence.[128] However, this concern that the penalty will rebound on the innocent (employees, shareholders, taxpayers, customers) should perhaps be no greater than with respect to individual offenders, where penalties similarly affect the innocent, particularly the offender's family, to relatively little general concern. And in any event, none of these 'innocent' groups should gain an advantage (employment, dividends, cheaper goods and services) from illegal acts. It remains the case however that the negative social side-effects of a genuinely deterrent financial penalty could be excessive.

Rather than concentrating on the fine, the focus might be placed on the moral opprobrium that attaches to a criminal conviction, and judicious use of publicity by regulators could have an effect beyond any punishment imposed by the court.[129] As well as the fixed penalty discussed above, the EU's emissions trading

---

[125] The striking phrase became widely used following JC Coffee Jr, ' "No Soul to damn, no Body To Kick": An Unscandalised Enquiry into the Problem of Corporate Punishment' (1981) 79 *Michigan Law Review* 386. It is also rare for the officers or employees of a large corporation to be imprisoned.

[126] Commission, above n 104, Art 4; Framework Decision, above n 104, Art 7. The latter includes 'the obligation to adopt specific measures in order to avoid the consequences of conduct such as that on which the criminal liability was founded'.

[127] *R v Milford Haven Port Authority* [2000] Env LR 632.

[128] *Ibid*, p 648. The Court of Appeal reduced the fine from the £4 million imposed at first instance, to £750,000.

[129] See P de Prez 'Beyond Judicial Sanctions: The Negative Impact of Conviction for Environmental Offences' (2000) 12 *Environmental Law Review* 91. Mehta and Hawkins, above n 14, suggests that larger organisations are more concerned about negative publicity, smaller firms (in their study, firms with under 500 employees) about the financial costs of prosecution. Note the possibility in some Australian jurisdictions for court ordered publicity, at the cost of the defendant, discussed in C Abbot, 'The Regulatory Enforcement of Pollution Control Laws: The Australian Experience', forthcoming.

legislation requires the identity of those who infringe certain elements of the scheme to be published.[130] Celia Wells discusses a number of other possible sanctions against companies, including corporate probation and community service.[131] Probation, or 'judicial supervision' in the terms of the Commission and Council interventions, could involve a court-controlled revisiting of the company's decision-making structure. This has obvious appeal in an environmental context, although one has to ask oneself whether that is not exactly what regulators should do in a 'compliance' approach. As for 'community service', it is not difficult to envisage useful environmental projects; most obviously perhaps, a requirement to fund environmental restoration, available in many jurisdictions, sometimes attached to a criminal conviction, or sometimes independently of conviction, as in the Environmental Liability Directive.[132] Certainly, imaginative responses to corporate crime are required, and we may not need to look too far for them; the Council and Commission initiatives are however open-ended on the subject.

It has been suggested that the Commission's proposals would imply the availability of criminal penalties to the exclusion of all alternatives.[133] This would be a major step back for environmental law, flying in the face of decades of research on the flexibility of effective law enforcement. An assumption that the criminal law should always be enforced to the hilt would be burdensome for everybody involved, and ultimately perhaps corrosive of the stigmatising power of the criminal law. Considerable discretion is inherent in prosecution decisions, particularly if the offences are very generously defined. Sole reliance on criminal law is probably not a necessary interpretation of the Commission's proposal, and is certainly nowhere stated. If a flexible approach is intended, however, it is surprising that no accountability mechanisms are discussed in either the Framework Decision or the Commission's proposal. The Commission, rather strangely, suggests that criminal prosecution inherently goes some way to avoiding regulatory capture, providing 'an additional guarantee of impartiality', because it is removed from the decisions on licensing and policy.[134] That is certainly not the case in England and Wales, where the Environment Agency makes both licensing and prosecution decisions.

Conclusions

From a pragmatic environmental perspective, the efforts discussed here to ensure that all regulators have the full range of tools at their disposal are a useful practical response to poor implementation. Poor implementation, however, is a product of a far more complex set of factors than the simple unavailability of enforcement tools, and certainly these tools in themselves provide no panacea. There are other efforts to influence national regulators.

[130] Dir 03/87, above n 96, Art 16.
[131] Wells, above n 11, pp 36–8.
[132] Dir 04/35, above n 86.
[133] Faure, above n 107.
[134] Commission, above n 104, p 2.

The creation of the EU 'Network for the Implementation and Enforcement of Environmental Law' (IMPEL) attempts to go beyond simply providing tools for regulators. Arising out of the perceived weakness of practical application of environmental law, IMPEL provides mechanisms to encourage institutional learning. It is an informal network of national environmental inspectorates that examines and reports on various enforcement concerns, and aims to encourage learning and exchange of best practice between Member States and between sectors. Rather than looking to central government, IMPEL more realistically looks to the 'disaggregated state' for enforcement opportunities.[135] Amongst its day to day work, the IMPEL network has developed common minimum criteria for national environmental inspections of certain operators, formalised in a Council and Parliament Recommendation.[136] Monitoring and inspecting are the primary elements of most enforcement models, and vital for ensuring practical effectiveness. The Recommendation defines minimum criteria relating to the organisation, implementation, follow-up and publication of the results of environmental inspections. Particularly when coupled with requirements in legislation to inspect,[137] soft law on minimum standards of inspections could make considerable demands of the Member States.

Central Enforcement

Alongside efforts to empower Member State regulators and to supplement regulators by empowering third parties, efforts are being made to enhance the ability of the Commission to enforce EC environmental law. An obvious, perhaps simplistic, response to poor enforcement of EC environmental law would be to create a centralised regulatory agency with strong powers of investigation and enforcement against private and public polluters. This would end the reliance on national regulators, and avoid the politicisation of Commission enforcement decisions. Although rare, supranational enforcement is not unheard of in the Community context; the Commission was granted strong enforcement powers in competition law early in the life of the Community.[138] The idea of strong environmental enforcement agencies at EU level has not so far found much favour with either the Commission or the Member States. Even more modest proposals, such as the

---

[135] The phrase comes from A-M Slaughter, *A New World Order* (Princeton, Princeton University Press, 2004), which includes discussion of 'information networks' such as IMPEL.
[136] Recommendation 2001/331 of the European Parliament and of the Council [2001] OJ L 118/41.
[137] Case C–392/99 *Commission v Portugal*, 10 April 2003, not yet reported, concerns a requirement in Dir 75/439 on the Disposal of Waste Oils [1975] OJ L 194/23 that permit holders 'shall be inspected periodically by the Member States, particularly as regards their compliance with the conditions of their permits.' According to the Court, the national legislation has to require that the undertakings 'are in fact inspected periodically', para 168.
[138] The Commission was given enforcement powers from the beginning, see Reg 17/62 First Regulation Implementing Articles 85 and 86 of the Treaty [1962] OJ L 13/204; Reg 1/2003 on the Implementation of the Rules on Competition Laid Down in Articles 81 and 82 of the Treaty [2003] OJ L 1/1 grants enforcement powers also to the national authorities.

establishment of a Community 'audit' inspectorate, monitoring the policies and performance of national regulators, have proved beyond the pale, although IMPEL is a consensual and cooperative step in that direction. Centralised investigation and enforcement would be extraordinarily sensitive politically, and indeed something of a revolution in the current Community distribution of powers. It would remove one of the Commission's foremost responsibilities and powers,[139] and by a wholesale transfer of national prerogatives, would also be a highly political statement about the changing nature of EC environmental law. Just as importantly, it is far from obvious that a centralised body would not suffer from all the faults of its parent national regulators, with a few extras just for itself. The exercise of discretion, with all of the attendant dangers and benefits, would simply be shifted to a different, and arguably more distant and obscure, level. Resources for environmental regulation are always vulnerable, and the controversy may well increase if the responsibility is no longer perceived to be national. Moreover, the ability to rely on national administrations, customs and relationships is a strength as well as a weakness of EC environmental regulation, a resource that should only be diminished if there are clear advantages in doing so.

In the absence of more radical change, the Commission is instead attempting to rationalise its existing approach to enforcement. It emphasises the importance of prevention of breaches, and prioritisation of enforcement activities.[140]

Prevention is in part about cooperation, and the Commission extends assistance to Member States before implementation becomes a problem, for example by meetings with the Member States, by technical assistance, by 'reminders' of transposition dates.[141] All of this, reminiscent of a 'compliance approach' to regulation, is eminently sensible, if perhaps limited in its ambition. Improving legislation, aiming for clearer laws, which pay attention to the complexity of de-centralised implementation is another important attempt to prevent problems. The Commission claims that it 'strives to anticipate implementation problems when it is designing Community environmental legislation'.[142] However, implementation problems are not always readily predictable at the drafting stage. The divergent administrative traditions in the EU mean that different Member States are likely to face very different challenges in the implementation of law[143]; even EC legislation that looks like a 'good fit' with national regulatory style is not necessarily successfully

---

[139] Although the final decision to 'prosecute' a polluter or a Member State could be left with the Commission; there are many different ways of introducing agencies.

[140] Commission, above n 27.

[141] See Commission, *ibid*; Commission, above n 8.

[142] Commission, above n 8, p 6. This question of the quality of legislation has been considered by the EU institutions fairly regularly in their history, most recently, in European Commission, *Better Law Making* COM (2002) 278 final; see also IMPEL, *Effective Enforcement Needs a Good Legal Base: Final Report of the IMPEL Better Legislation Project*, available at http://europa.eu.int/comm/environment/impel/better_legislation.htm.

[143] C Knill and A Lenschow, 'Change as "Appropriate Adaptation": Administrative Adjustment to European Environmental Policy in Britain and Germany' *European Integration Online Papers* (1998) 2; Knill and Lenschow, above n 3.

implemented, adding to unpredictability.[144] In addition, the negotiation of legislation between the members of Council and the European Parliament makes clarity difficult. As well as disparities between language versions, and sheer sloppiness, legislation may even be deliberately ambiguous, perhaps for cynical reasons, or more often because of the need to get a measure agreed and through the legislative process in a reasonable time.

It is however possible to identify certain changes in environmental legislation that aim to prevent implementation problems. Given that they are able to reflect local conditions, flexible environmental standards should be easier for Member States to comply with. Whether they will be easier to enforce is an entirely different question; Han Somsen, for example, argues that because detecting the breach of flexible standards (such as 'best available techniques', or 'good ecological quality') is more difficult than detecting the breach of more precise quantitative standards, there will be an overall negative effect on implementation.[145] This argument is characteristic of a basic division in views on the role of legislation in implementation pressures. Some argue that clear and detailed obligations, clear responsibilities and minimal discretion enhance implementation; others that this is precisely the problem, and more flexible approaches are needed to improve overall environmental quality and compliance. Perhaps partly in an effort to mediate between these approaches, flexible standards in EC environmental legislation generally go hand in hand with procedural mechanisms, such as mandatory consultation or information provision, designed to encourage 'institutional learning' and external policing. The deep roots of a turn to third parties in EC environmental law have been mentioned, and this is a subject to which we will return in later chapters, especially chapters five and six. However, 'procedural' directives are not necessarily any less ambiguous or more easily applied than more traditional legislation, and the difficulties of implementation remain entrenched.[146] Somsen reminds us of the great, and as yet unproven, faith being placed in procedure.

Information plays many crucial and complex roles in EC environmental law, with patterns of both policy formation and implementation depending heavily on the type of information available and the way it is used. Information is a key element of efforts to extend the cast of environmental 'regulators'. So for example, improving the information available to industry is thought to enable more effective self-regulation; improving information to third parties is thought to allow the monitoring of regulated and regulator.[147] IMPEL on the other hand is primarily about improving information and knowledge within regulators, looking to develop good practice. It is only one of many efforts being made to link improved

---

[144] Knill and Lenschow, *ibid;* C Knill and A Lenschow (eds) *Implementing EU Environmental Policy: New Directions and Old Problems* (Manchester, Manchester University Press, 2000).
[145] H Somsen, 'Current Issues of Implementation, Compliance and Enforcement of EC Environmental Law' in L Kramer (ed), *Recht und Um-Welt: Essays in Honour of Prof Dr Gerd Winter* (Groningen, Europa Law Publishing, 2003).
[146] See generally Knill and Lenschow, above n 144.
[147] See chs 5 and 6 below.

information with improving performance in environmental law. The Commission's annual report on implementation also attempts to use information to enhance implementation. The development of an 'implementation scoreboard' that compares national performance, and the 'name, shame and fame' events designed to embarrass Member States into compliance, attempt to move beyond the limitations of a purely legalistic approach to enforcement.[148] The creation of the European Environment Agency also rests on the importance of good information. Its primary objective is to 'provide the Community and the Member States with ... objective, reliable and comparable information at the European level'.[149] Rather than creating new data, the European Environment Agency is supposed to allow more effective use of existing data by aggregation and standardisation. This control of information is by no means a neutral task.[150] The provision of comparative information on, for example, bathing water quality, could have a 'peer pressure' effect between Member States, could stimulate Commission intervention, or could lead to pressure from private parties.

Prioritisation of infringement actions is another objective pursued by the Commission. An *ad hoc* approach to responses to infringements of environmental law is not the most fruitful way of using scarce resources. The Commission intends to focus on serious matters such as repeated infringements and cross-border infringements, as well as prioritising formal over practical implementation, placing a far greater emphasis on the role of national institutions (including courts) in ensuring practical implementation.[151] This prioritisation of certain infringements is not a sea-change, but reflects existing priorities,[152] albeit that they have not so far always been pursued in practice.[153] Although practical implementation is indeed a national responsibility, and establishing practical failures is indeed highly resource intensive for the Commission, in a sector involving public goods, any more generalised dependence on private enforcers is still a matter of concern. The legal enhancement of the policing potential of third parties in the environmental sector is a necessary counterpoint to any reprioritisation by the Commission.

---

[148] Commission, above n 8, p 7; note also Commission, above n 27. Assessing comparative national implementation is however extremely difficult. The Commission depends for most of its data on reports provided by the Member States. Additional information from third parties reflects the obviousness and political profile of the particular environmental problem, and the level of environmental interest group activity, as well as relative compliance.

[149] Reg 1210/90 on the Establishment of the European Environment Agency and the European Environment Information and Observation Network [1990] OJ L 120/1, as amended.

[150] See B Wynne and C Waterton, 'Public Information on the Environment: the Role of the European Environment Agency' in P Lowe and S Ward (eds), *British Environmental Policy and Europe* (London, Routledge, 1998).

[151] Commission, above n 27, pp 15–17. The prioritisation is: (a) Infringements that undermine the foundations of the rule of law; (b) Infringements that undermine the smooth functioning of the Community legal system; (c) Infringements consisting in the failure to transpose or the incorrect transposal of directives, pp 11–12.

[152] Commission, above n 23; C Harlow, *Accountability in the European Union* (Oxford, Hart Publishing, 2002), p 72.

[153] E Hatton, 'The Implementation of EU Environmental Law' (2003) 15 *Journal of Environmental Law* 271. This raises considerable accountability issues.

CONCLUSIONS

Institutional efforts to address the implementation gap's challenge to the credibility of EC environmental law are wide-ranging and highly visible. The attention being paid to implementation is admirable, and the range of initiatives, impressive. That the target remains elusive is perhaps not surprising. Given that national systems of enforcement determine levels of compliance, the key must be to ensure that national regulators are able to be effective, particularly if the Commission is to de-prioritise practical over formal implementation of directives in its activities under Article 226. In this respect, lessons need to be learned from the socio-legal scholarship on practical environmental regulation. This chapter has concentrated on English language literature from primarily common law jurisdictions, and one can safely predict that there will be variations in research from civilian systems. However, although the empirical and theoretical work leaves a lot of questions unexplored, it is now reasonably familiar, and it is surprising that more attention is not paid to it in EU initiatives. Ensuring that national regulators are fully equipped with a range of legal tools of enforcement is however a useful starting point for the Community legislator. Responsive regulation, for example, requires the possibility of very tough sanctions, and a wide range of sanctions: 'regulators will be more able to speak softly when they carry big sticks (and crucially, a hierarchy of lesser sanctions)'.[154] The EC measures attempted in this area so far are minimalist, which is in part an indication of how fraught the involvement of Community law in the practicalities of national enforcement can be. There are hints in these measures of a subtly changing relationship between the centre and the Member States on the subject of implementation. This shift fits in well with the move to regulate procedure over substance to be discussed in chapter six below, and, like that development, deserves considerable attention.

The scholarship on enforcement also suggests that regulatory discretion is crucial; the temptation to constrain discretion should be resisted. One of the major challenges in designing schemes of regulatory enforcement is to remain alive to the very productive possibilities of negotiation and cooperation between regulator and regulated, whilst ensuring accountability and rigour. A common response in the literature to the thorny problem of accountability in the exercise of discretion, is to turn to third parties, a response that has been seized with alacrity by Community institutions. This approach fits in well with both the historic success of third party enforcement activities in EC law, and the emerging paradigm of 'access' to environmental decision-making. It is a subject to which we will return.

---

[154] Ayres and Braithwaite, above n 14, p 19.

4

Perils, Politics, Precaution: Risk Regulation in the EU

INTRODUCTION

THE EU HAS experienced the political heat of risk in debates over nuclear energy, salmonella in eggs, 'mad cow disease', through to contemporary concern about biotechnology. The pre-occupation of long-lived and healthy societies by risk may seem paradoxical, but these periodic crises have gripped public attention and shown the fallibility of administrative decision-making. The EU is thoroughly implicated in these risk crises, which have highlighted not only the potential for conflict between different national approaches to risk, and attendant dangers for the internal market,[1] but also the vulnerability of EU claims to legitimate decision-making. The potential of EU level regulation both to ease free movement and to contribute to the EU's popular legitimacy by responding to popular concern makes risk regulation an increasingly central element of market integration.[2] As soon as environmental law ceased to be limited to a simple reaction to obvious physical harm, risk became one of its keystones. As such, legal responses to risk provide an important perspective from which to examine the development of environmental law.

A classical approach to risk implies understanding and calculability; technical risk assessment focuses on identifying the nature of a hazard and the likelihood of its occurrence. As well as this technical calculation, however, the regulation of risk profoundly affects diverse public values and competing private interests. The contemporary EU response to this political aspect of risk will be the first subject of this chapter. The relationship between expertise and the public, between technocracy and politics, is one of the key dilemmas of risk regulation, and one of the key challenges in environmental regulation. Whilst expertise, particularly scientific expertise, is an inescapable part of environmental risk regulation, recent very

---

[1] Note in particular the BSE saga, see Case C–241/01 *National Farmers Union v Secretariat General du Gouvernement* [2002] ECR I–907; Case C–1/00 *Commission v France* [2001] ECR I–9989; Case C–180/96 *UK v Commission* [1996] ECR I–3903.

[2] EC regulation is said to have become more risk averse in recent years, see D Vogel, 'The Politics of Risk Regulation in Europe and the United States' vol 3 *Yearbook of European Environmental Law* 1. The relative precaution exercised in different areas is however difficult to assess, JB Weiner, 'Whose Precaution After All? A Comment on the Comparison and Evolution of Risk Regulatory Systems' (2003) 13 *Duke Journal of Comparative and International Law* 207.

bruising public encounters with the limitations of science have put an end to the assumption that 'scientific facts' provide adequate authority for regulation. The working out of this tension in the legal development of EU committee and agency structures will be explored in the next section of this chapter. And whilst the politicisation of risk rests on many and complex factors, it is greatly enhanced by increased awareness of the uncertainties in scientific knowledge. The need to act when the facts are not certain poses enormous challenges for risk regulators. The use of the precautionary principle as a legal principle by which to address questions of scientific uncertainty will be examined below. Finally, whilst the EC is arguably beginning the task of facing up to the politics of risk, the scientific focus of World Trade Organisation (WTO) rules appears to be more persistent. The EU and its Member States are bound by WTO rules on risk regulation, and that will be the final topic of this chapter.

RISK AND THE EU

Although scholarly research on risk is not always clear or consistent, the political, contextual and value-based nature of risk management has for some time been a fairly common theme. The acceptability of risk depends not simply on how likely any particular bad outcome is, but also of the type of world in which we want to live; even this is not simply a question of physical environment, but also of distribution of benefits and burdens and the proper role of the state or the EU in managing the physical environment. Differing perspectives on risk among different groups of people is now a well-known phenomenon, and defies any understanding of risk as purely technical fact. So the cultural and social background to a risk affect which risks are selected for concern, and which dismissed as unimportant.[3] The perception of a risk's significance could, for example, be influenced by its social and political implications, such as concern that nuclear technology leads to more authoritarian state security, or that agricultural biotechnology increases reliance on large corporate entities for food production. The more personal context in which risk arises is also thought to affect risk perception, so that, for example, an unfamiliar risk is more worrying than a familiar risk, a freely chosen risk less worrying than one imposed from outside.[4] Finally, sociological theories of 'risk society'[5] describe a society in which risk creates new lines of political conflict, escaping the old class divides. Whether or not one sympathises with its

---

[3] See M Douglas and A Wildavsky, *Risk and Culture* (Berkley, University of California Press, 1983); Special Issue on Risk (1999) 8(2) *Environmental Values*.

[4] See C Starr, 'Social Benefit Versus Technological Risk' (1969) *Science* 1232; B Fischoff *et al*, *Acceptable Risk* (Cambridge, Cambridge University Press, 1981); P Slovic, *The Perception of Risk* (London, Earthscan, 2000). Note that concepts such as voluntariness are not mechanically applicable, which might undermine any efforts to draw conclusions from such distinctions: CR Sunstein, *Risk and Reason: Safety, Law and the Environment* (Cambridge, Cambridge University Press, 2002), pp 67–70.

[5] U Beck, *Risk Society: Towards a New Modernity* (London, Sage Publications, 1992).

central claims, the thesis of risk society usefully exposes the political nature of risk decisions. The pervasiveness of 'manufactured risk', that is risk created by human advances in science and technology is another central element of risk society, and highlights a further paradox in contemporary risk debates more generally: science and technology are blamed for harm, looked to for solutions to harm, and then blamed again for not finding them.

The different perspectives on risk are not readily captured by a technical process, but can be better reflected in a political process. Increased acceptance that the regulation of risk is a political question has led to a reassessment of the position of scientific and technical expertise in government. This issue has received considerable recent attention in the Commission's 'European governance' project.[6] Ensuring ultimate political decision-making responsibility, whilst at the same time ensuring adequately influential scientific and technical advice, is a complex task. The solution in the EU is to attempt to institutionalise a clear division between the decision-making responsibility of political institutions, and the purely advisory role of expert advisors. This is by no means a new solution,[7] but has certainly been reinforced recently. In its White Paper on the *Precautionary Principle*,[8] the Commission sets out a 'structured approach' to risk analysis that comprises three distinct stages of risk assessment, risk management and risk communication. For current purposes, the crucial distinction is drawn between risk assessment, a technical process for expert institutions, and risk management, a political process for political institutions. This distinction that has been followed through in legislation[9] and case law.[10]

Whilst the recognition of the political significance of risk management is welcome, the distinction between the technical and the political is not as clear-cut as the EU's risk dichotomy might suggest. The technical and evaluative parts of risk regulation are intrinsically linked. First of all, even if risk assessors refrain from overt policy recommendations, some level of signalling seems inevitable, and the late involvement of the policy makers means that they may be presented with very limited options. There is also a danger that entrenching the divisions between political decision-makers and experts will leave the uncertainties and value judgments of the prior technical stage of risk assessment unexamined. And

---

[6] Discussed also in ch 5 below. See European Commission, *White Paper on European Governance* COM (2001) 428 final; European Commission, *Communication on the Collection and Use of Expertise By the Commission: Principles and Guidelines* COM (2002) 713 final; European Commission, *The Operating Framework for the European Regulatory Agencies* COM (2002) 718 final. See also L Levidow and C Marris, 'Science and Governance in Europe: Lessons from the Case of Agricultural Biotechnology' [2001] *Science and Public Policy* 345.

[7] See for example Case C–405/92 *Mondiet v Armement Islais SARL* [1993] ECR I–6133, para 80.

[8] European Commission, *Communication on the Precautionary Principle* COM (2000) 1 final.

[9] Reg 178/2002 Laying Down the General Principles and Requirements of Food Law, Establishing the European Food Safety Authority and Laying Down Procedures in Matters of Food Safety [2002] OJ L 31/1.

[10] Albeit without consistency of language. See for example Case T–70/99 *Alpharma Inc v Council* [2002] ECR II–3495, paras 162–9; Case T–13/99 *Pfizer Animal Health SA v Council* [2002] ECR II–3305, paras 149–56.

risk assessment cannot be a wholly objective exercise. Not only is it shaped by the policy background against which it is carried out, but also by the values and beliefs of the practitioners, and the judgments of the profession.[11] This is not to criticise scientific endeavour, or even to doubt that there are truths 'out there' to be discovered; it is simply to highlight the elusiveness of objective, neutral facts. In particular, assumptions will need to be made at every stage of the process, the accuracy or appropriateness of which is likely to be debated.[12] To give just one example, estimates of the effect of a low, but perhaps lengthy, human exposure to a particular pollutant may be made on the basis of high exposure of laboratory animals; predictions will rely on modelling, extrapolations, averaging, compositing, and numerous other techniques, all of which require the exercise of professional judgment. The entirely legitimate, and necessary, exercise of professional judgment not only creates additional space for error, but also undermines the apparent inevitability and objectivity of decisions based on science. The 'hole' in the ozone layer illustrates the paradox: the depletion of the ozone layer is a problem that can only be perceived through science; its identification was, however, delayed because computer models were designed to ignore measurements that diverged too much from the expected norm.[13] This pursuit of simplification, which is also commonly seen in the neglect of interactions between different substances or between and within ecosystems, is crucial in day-to-day scientific activity, which in turn is crucial to environmental protection. It undermines, however, arguments that science reveals neutral and inevitable 'facts' about risk.

These observations suggest that the EC's approach to the political nature of risk regulation, whilst important, is inadequate, because it fails to recognise the value judgments implicit in the first, risk assessment, stage of the process. One of the most important concerns with respect to the split between risk assessment and risk management is that it will be used to justify sheltering scientific bodies from public scrutiny, allowing the values and uncertainties of the risk assessment to go unexamined. A rhetoric of openness, especially with regard to uncertainty and disagreement, has however become a conventional element of the 'governance' of expertise in the EU.[14] It is important that this is carried through, so that judgments, uncertainties and even biases in scientific assessments are exposed.

From the opposite perspective, others resist *any* overt politicisation of risk, and would entirely remove final authority from political bodies. Stephen Breyer, for

---

[11] See for example, S Jasanoff, *The Fifth Branch: Science Advisors as Policymakers* (Cambridge, Mass, Harvard University Press, 1990); KS Schrader-Frechette, *Risk and Rationality* (Berkley, University of California Press, 1991).

[12] See the discussion in S Breyer and V Heyvaert, 'Institutions for Regulating Risk' in RL Revesz, R Sands and RB Stewart (eds), *Environmental Law, the Economy and Sustainable Development* (Cambridge, Cambridge University Press, 2000).

[13] This example is discussed by S Eden, 'Public Participation in Environmental Policy: Considering Scientific, Counter-Scientific and Non-Scientific Contributions' (1996) 5 *Public Understanding of Science* 183, p 187.

[14] See especially Commission (2001), above n 6; Commission COM (2002) 713, above n 6, also discussion below.

example, argues in the US context that risk regulation should be de-politicised, and kept out of the hands of the irrational public (including their representatives in Congress), whose influence prevents the rational prioritisation of risks.[15] Giandomenico Majone is the most prominent commentator to take this highly technical view of EC risk regulation. Majone sees the increasing politicisation of the Commission, and indeed of economic and social regulation more generally, as an important credibility problem for the EC, and is an advocate of powerful, independent expert agencies for risk regulation.[16] These technical approaches to risk are certainly respectable. The main concern is consistency of risk regulation, particularly the prioritisation of risk, including the trade-offs that must be made between risk, which imply in turn a rational use of resources. Cass Sunstein is another academic who is highly sceptical about the role of 'public opinion' in risk regulation, explaining convincingly how 'people often think poorly' about risk.[17] Sunstein advocates cost benefit analysis (CBA) of different risk regulation measures, not primarily on economic grounds, but as a means to aid prioritisation and overcome this 'poor thinking'.

A technical approach to risk, however, needs to take into account the possibility that very good contextual, social or cultural reasons justify treating statistically similar risks differently. The isolation of the autonomous expert ignores the centrality of values to risk decisions, and struggles fully to acknowledge the inherent fallibility of even the best scientific and technical arrangements. The relative role of the experts and the public (or their representatives) depends in part on whether one believes that a dissenting public has simply got its facts wrong, or that disagreement reflects the richness of intuitive social or cultural judgments. To take the polarised debate on genetically modified organisms (GMOs) as an example, parts of the British press have condemned GM food as 'Frankenfood'. This emotive and obscure language must be the nightmare of bureaucrats charged with listening to the public. However, if one views the Frankenstein story as a parable of punishment for interference with nature, it becomes necessary to consider the possibility that deeper public values are being aired. It would certainly be difficult and controversial, itself vulnerable to abuse, but an effort in serious cases to pull out some of the reasons behind opinion provides a basis for deciding whether public disagreement with the experts rests on misunderstanding, or on a richer framework of decision-making.[18]

Certainly, scientific and technical information is too important to be ignored or lightly overridden; space for alternative values, however, should be ensured.

---

[15] S Breyer, *Breaking the Vicious Circle: Toward Effective Risk Regulation* (Cambridge, Mass, Harvard University Press, 1993); Breyer and Heyvaert, above n 12.

[16] G Majone, *Regulating Europe* (London, Routledge, 1996); G Majone, 'What Price Safety? The Precautionary Principle and its Policy Implications' (2002) *Journal of Common Market Studies* 89; G Majone, 'The Credibility Crisis of Community Regulation' (2000) 38 *Journal of Common Market Studies* 273.

[17] Sunstein, above n 4, p viii.

[18] On regulators as 'interpreters' in this context, see J Black, 'Regulation as Facilitation: Negotiating the Genetic Revolution' (1998) 61 *Modern Law Review* 621.

Sunstein's approach to CBA is interesting here. Notwithstanding his doubts, Sunstein ultimately prioritises political decision-making, advocating CBA as a democratic tool to provide information to decision-makers and the public. Its conclusions can be overridden by other concerns, such as distribution, or even widespread fear.[19] This is not a million miles from the stated EC approach to the role of technical evidence in risk regulation, although Sunstein places greater emphasis on *quantitative* CBA. So for example, the *Sixth Environmental Action Programme* emphasises the importance of 'sound science' and economic assessments, but also that these tools should 'support' an 'open dialogue with all interested groups'.[20] This is however much more easily said than done. The concern remains that notwithstanding a recognition that decisions are political, the 'magic of numbers' overwhelms the politics, which effectively rubber stamps economic or other technical exercises. CBA and similar technical approaches to risk regulation may also fail fully to capture the complexity of uncertainty. Sunstein's proposal that a 'range' of figures be produced to avoid the illusion of precision, and that uncertainty be expressly acknowledged in the CBA, would go some way to making uncertainty clearer. The exercise of professional judgment (rather than the simple application of neutral expertise) however, may remain hidden in that range of numbers, which looks even more comprehensive than it would otherwise, and revisiting that exercise of judgment may be difficult.

The limitations of an exclusively technical rationality can be seen in the debate on GMOs, as it emerged in the early 1990s. Opposition to GMOS was dismissed as 'irrational', because it was not based on established science,[21] an approach that clearly fails to take into account other concerns, ranging through the gaps and uncertainties in scientific understandings of the technology, ethical questions around interfering with nature, to socio-economic concerns about corporate control over the food sector. A willingness to hear only scientific reasons pre-empts discussion of these values.[22] The contemporary political conflicts over fishing stocks, however, illustrate the other edge of the populist knife. Some fishing communities call on their local, situated knowledge, claiming basically that there must be plenty of fish in the sea because their catches are good; this common sense proposition is not unattractive. Scientists use a statistical approach, identifying massive reductions in fish stocks, which justifies regulatory restrictions on fishing. How to distinguish between scientific knowledge that needs to be constrained by contextual knowledge, and scientific knowledge that needs to be protected from contextual knowledge (ignorance?) is by no means obvious; a call on objectivity,

---

[19] Although note that Sunstein, above n 4, p 112, emphasises the *costs* of even unjustified fear, taking us back to CBA.

[20] European Commission, *Environment 2010: Our Future, Our Choice* COM (2001) 31 final, p 61.

[21] See for example the speech of David Byrne, European Commissioner for Health and Consumer Protection, 'Risk Versus Benefit', Brussels, 22 November 2001, available at http://europa.eu.int/comm/food/food/biotechnology/resources/speeches_en.htm. He refers to 'risk paranoia' in respect of GMOs, and takes the classic approach of those who reject the legitimacy of public perceptions of risk, comparing GMOs with road and tobacco deaths.

[22] Levidow and Marris, above n 6.

rationality and even weight of numbers does not help.[23] A political judgment between different positions is necessary; this political judgment should be based on some understanding of the reasons behind the disagreement.

If one accepts the importance of non-technical aspects of risk, the monopoly of technical experts on 'good judgment' becomes problematic, and sheltering environmental regulators from democratic influences becomes unacceptable. Although flawed, the EC approach of drawing lines between risk assessment and risk management at least explicitly recognises the ultimately political nature of risk decisions. This should in turn allow the grounds for decisions to be expanded beyond scientific or technical information. It also directs responsibility and accountability more clearly to the political institutions, which are much better suited than technical bodies for placing in the public domain the value judgments behind decisions.

SCIENCE AND POLITICS IN THE EU

The relationship between environmental regulation and science is complex. Whilst science and technical assessments remain at the heart of environmental regulation, the political nature of that regulation is explicitly accepted. The relationship between the experts and the politicians, and between expert opinion and public opinion, is a significant dilemma that will be returned to in various contexts throughout this book. Of the many methods for incorporating scientific evidence that have been developed by the Community administration, this section will look at committees and agencies, and particularly the legal relationships developed between politics and expertise in those fora.

Committees, Politics and Expertise

Community administration involves a bewildering variety of committees, at every stage from the preparation of policy to the implementation of legislation. Committees proliferated outside formal Treaty provisions primarily as an attempt to provide the institutions with technical and scientific information.[24] This section

---

[23] Appeal is constantly made to 'mainstream' or 'majority' scientific opinion on climate change, for example, where environmentalists seem to find a certain comfort in numbers; in other cases, environmentalists are more likely to appeal to minority science. S Yearley, 'Green Ambivalence About Science: Legal-Rational Authority and the Scientific Legitimation of a Social Movement'(1992) 41 *British Journal of Sociology* 511, discusses the environmental movement's very complex relationship with science.

[24] Apart from the committees discussed here, the most significant of the other Community committees are probably the 'standardisation committees', in which private standard setting bodies come together to set standards for products on the basis of broad objectives set out in so-called 'new approach' legislation. Many of the issues raised in this section apply to standardisation committees. In particular, the decisions taken are political as well as technical, and the composition and openness to external critique of standardisation committees, which tend to be dominated by industry, is much

will concentrate on the 'comitology' committees, through which Member State representatives supervise Commission implementation of legislation,[25] and the scientific committees set up in various fields to provide scientific advice to the institutions.[26]

Scientific committees are in place in various fields to provide technical advice to the Community institutions. Some legislation on the regulation of risk provides for mandatory consultation of an expert committee.[27] Although a Community institution is not bound to accept the conclusions of such a committee,[28] if it reaches a different conclusion the institution 'must provide specific reasons', and the reasons must be 'of a scientific level at least commensurate with that of the opinion in question'.[29] In the case of legislation that does not put in place an obligation to consult the relevant committee, but merely a power, the Court of First Instance (CFI) has held that only in 'exceptional circumstances' can measures relying on an assessment of complex facts of a technical or scientific nature be adopted without consulting the relevant EU level scientific committee, and in any event only when there are 'adequate guarantees of scientific objectivity' from another source.[30] The CFI, in the judgments from which these quotations are taken, confirms the boundary between the responsibilities of technical and political institutions. Even accepting the political nature of decisions, however, the Court requires those decisions to rest on a robust scientific basis; the possibility of a conclusion based on non-scientific criteria does not seem to be contemplated. This is potentially troubling, although legislative efforts to expand the decision-making base will be discussed below.

Scientific committees are not supposed to be political, and whilst they consist of Member State experts, they are not supposed to 'represent' the Member States; indeed the Member States are not equally represented.[31] The lines between political and technical decision-making are, however, as easily confused in committees as

disputed. The environmental impact of these committees is acknowledged: European Commission, *Communication on the Integration of Environmental Aspects into European Standardisation* COM (2004) 130 final. Note also the committees that assist the Council in responding to Commission proposals, including the Committee of Permanent Representatives. Interest group committees, composed of representatives from different sectors implicated by Community action may be consulted by the Community institutions, although their influence seems to be weak.

[25] Implementation is delegated under Art 202 EC; comitology procedures are set out in Decision 1999/468 Laying Down the Procedures for the Exercise of Implementing Powers Conferred on the Commission [1999] OJ L 184/23.

[26] See Commission Decision 2004/210 Setting up Scientific Committees in the Field of Consumer Safety, Public Health and the Environment [2004] OJ L 66/45.

[27] Case C–212/91 *Angelopharm* [1994] ECR I–171.

[28] *Alpharma*, above n 10; *Pfizer*, above n 10; see also *Mondiet* above n 7; Case 331/88 *R v MAFF ex parte Fedesa* [1990] ECR I–4023.

[29] *Pfizer, ibid*, para 199.

[30] *Alpharma*, above n 10, para 213.

[31] See Commission Decision 2004/210, above n 26, Art 3 on membership: the Scientific Committee on Consumer Products and the Scientific Committee on Health and Environmental Risks have 19 members 'appointed on the basis of their expertise and consistent with this a geographical distribution that reflects the diversity of scientific problems and approaches in the Community'; the Scientific Committee on Emerging and Newly Identified Health Risks has 13 members, appointed on the same basis.

anywhere else. The danger that committees will provide for self-interested bargaining, rather than the subjection of expert evidence to good argument, came to the fore in the post mortem on the BSE scandal. The scientific committees dealing with BSE had been dominated by British experts, and heavily influenced by the British political agenda. Although it is initially surprising that the country with the most to lose should dominate scientific proceedings, it is also quite predictable that the country with the most experience of BSE should also possess the most expertise, and indeed show the most interest in EC committees[32]; this illustrates again the elusiveness of disinterested expertise, and the dangers of an obscure system.

The EC judiciary is prepared to police the adequacy of the science used in regulation, even to the extent of examining the expertise of a Community committee on which the institutions do choose to rely.[33] This seems to include a level of monitoring of the 'governance' obligations applied to scientific expertise: for example, the CFI has rejected the possibility that consultation of a political committee (even one assisted by experts) could fulfil an obligation to consult a scientific committee, because a political committee cannot be said to supply 'scientific advice based on the principles of excellence, transparency and independence'.[34] These are core principles that have been given considerable importance in post-BSE policy on expertise,[35] in the governance of both scientific committees and agencies, which form the subject of the next section. Whilst the reality of transparency will doubtless be much discussed, the principle is much better embedded in respect of scientific committees than in comitology, to which we now turn.

'Comitology' is a term strictly applicable only to the committees, composed of Member State representatives, that supervise powers of implementation delegated to the Commission in legislation. Implementation, which might include considering applications for authorisation under EC legislation, setting standards, amending legislation to provide for scientific and technical progress, is by no means a neutral technical task; on the contrary it can have a radical effect on the content or operation of legislation.[36] Comitology recognises the political sensitivity

---

[32] GR Chambers, 'The BSE Crisis and the European Parliament' in C Joerges and E Vos (eds), *EU Committees: Social Regulation, Law and Politics* (Oxford, Hart Publishing, 1999); K St Clair Bradley, 'Institutional Aspects of Comitology: Scenes From the Cutting Room Floor' in Joerges and Vos, *ibid*; C Harlow, *Accountability in the European Union* (Oxford, Oxford University Press, 2002), p 69.

[33] Case C–269/90 *Technische Universitat Munchen v Hauptzollamt Munchen-Mitte* [1991] ECR I–5469: 'the group of experts cannot properly carry out its task unless it is composed of persons possessing the necessary technical knowledge ... or the members of that group are advised by experts having that knowledge', para 22.

[34] *Alpharma*, above n 10, para 236; *Pfizer*, above n 10, para 285.

[35] Decision 04/210, above n 26, and the 'core principles' of 'quality', 'openness' and 'effectiveness' in Commission (2002) COM 713, above n 6.

[36] M Onida, 'The Determination of EC Environmental Technical Rules, With Specific Regard to the Implementation Procedures of the Commission' in A Biondi, M Chechetti, S Grassi and M Lee (eds), *Scientific Evidence in European Environmental Rule-Making: The Case of the Landfill and End of Life Vehicles Directives* (The Hague, Kluwer, 2003), discusses the enormous significance of certain implementation decisions under waste directives. See also the examples and criticisms in House of Lords Select Committee on the European Union, 2002-3 47th Report, *Waste Management Policy* HL 194.

of implementation decisions, and indeed the often fuzzy line between executive and legislative acts, by providing the Member States with some control over implementation. Comitology subjects the Commission's implementation powers to one of a number of different procedures involving committees of Member State representatives. These procedures range from consultation with an 'advisory committee', to the submission of a proposal to a 'regulatory committee', which, if it rejects the proposal by qualified majority voting, is able to return problematic decisions to Council.[37]

Comitology committees are political bodies, and as such they are often involved, with the Commission, in the risk management decisions reserved for political bodies in the EU's 'structured approach' to risk analysis. In this respect their role differs from the scientific committees discussed above, which provide technical advice. However, lines of political accountability in the EU are blurred; delegating a decision to an institution deemed to be political does not imply any necessary connection with public concerns. Comitology committees consist mainly of national technical experts, and there is a danger that committees sharing a common professional background, largely sheltered from the public gaze and from high level political attention, may reconceptualise political decisions as purely technical questions, ignoring their important political implications.[38] This is perhaps less likely in very controversial and high profile issues, such as the authorisation of genetically modified organisms (GMOs); in the vast majority of cases, however, committees are much less exposed to political concerns.

Implementation through comitology to a considerable degree escapes the scrutiny of the European Parliament, and also largely excludes the public, including the media, and those affected by the decision.[39] In most cases, comitology committees agree with the Commission. Even when a regulatory committee disagrees with the Commission (returning the issue to Council) decisions have been known to evade systematic Council control. These are the occasions on which the mismatch between the politically contentious decision, and the relatively de-politicised decision-making process, is clearest. So for example, one of the important implementing powers delegated to the Commission under the EC legislation on GMOs is the consideration of applications for the authorisation of a GMO. As the procedure stood until recently,[40] an application for authorisation of a GMO

---

[37] Decision 1999/468, above n 25.

[38] C Landfried, 'The European Regulation of Biotechnology by Polycratic Governance' in Joerges and Vos, above n 32; Onida, above n 36. See also the discussion in CR Sunstein, 'Deliberative Trouble? Why Groups Go to Extremes' (2000) 110 *Yale Law Journal* 71, on the tendency of discussion between the like-minded to move them to more extreme end of their initial position.

[39] See generally the contributions to Joerges and Vos, above n 32; G de Búrca, 'The Institutional Development of the EU: A Constitutional Analysis' in P Craig and G de Búrca (eds), *The Evolution of EU Law* (Oxford, Oxford University Press, 1999); M Rhinard, 'The Democratic Legitimacy of the European Union Committee System' (2003) 15 *Governance* 185; Harlow, above n 32, ch 3; E Vos, 'The Rise of Committees' (1997) 3 *European Law Journal* 212. See also House of Lords Select Committee on the European Union, above n 36, criticising the poor availability of minutes and agenda.

[40] Dir 90/220 on the Deliberate Release into the Environment of Genetically Modified Organisms [1990] OJ L 117/15. The current regime is discussed in detail in ch 9 below.

would be made to the competent authority of one Member State; if that initial competent authority gave a positive response, and no objection was maintained by any other Member State or the Commission, authorisation could proceed; if however, there was disagreement between the Member States, the Commission was required to submit a draft decision on the application to a 'regulatory' committee, and thence to Council. Under the comitology decision then in force, the Commission's draft could only be rejected by unanimity in Council.[41] The very fact that the comitology procedure had been brought into play, however, meant that unanimity in Council was unlikely; at least one Member State had thought authorisation appropriate, and at least one had objected.[42] In a particularly notorious case, the Commission was able to adopt its decision in the teeth of vociferous objections from a number of Member States, a European Parliament resolution urging the segregation of GMOs, and the positive approval of only one Member State in Council.[43] The ability under comitology simply to discount these political objections contributed to the morass into which the regulation of GMOs subsequently descended.

Comitology now provides somewhat more balance between the Member States and the Commission. Under the regulatory procedure, if the committee does not agree with the Commission proposal, the Council can accept or reject the Commission proposal by qualified majority voting; there is no longer any requirement for unanimity to reject the Commission's proposal. However, if, as is perfectly possible in a contentious area, the Council is unable to muster a qualified majority in either direction, 'the proposed implementing act shall be adopted by the Commission',[44] an imperative that suggests a lack of discretion. This avoids regulatory impasse, but because of the high political stakes, those cases where qualified majorities cannot be reached are precisely the cases in which it is problematic to neglect national concerns. A Commission declaration attached to the Comitology Decision provides that in 'particularly sensitive sectors' the Commission will 'avoid going against any predominant position which might emerge within the Council'.[45] The interpretation of the 'predominant' position is problematic, when by definition it has proven impossible to reach a qualified majority in Council. The Commission recently proceeded with authorisation of a GMO for food use, notwithstanding the inability of a deeply divided Council to reach a decision, and considerable public disquiet about the whole issue.[46]

---

[41] Council Decision 1987/373 [1987] OJ L 197/33.
[42] See TK Hervey, 'Regulation of Genetically Modified Products in a Multi-Level System of Governance: Science or Citizens?' (2001) 10 *Review of European Community and International Environmental Law* 321. The only situation, other than a national change of view, in which unanimity would be possible, is if the initial objection came from the Commission, not a Member State.
[43] Commission Decision 97/98 OJ [1997] L 31/69. See Hervey, *ibid*; Bradley, above n 32.
[44] Decision 1999/468, above n 25, Art 5(6).
[45] Declaration No 3 on Council Decision 1999/468 Laying Down the Procedures for the Exercise of Implementing Powers Conferred on the Commission [1999] OJ C 203/1.
[46] See European Commission, *Proposal for a Council Decision Authorising the Placing on the Market of Sweet Corn from genetically Modified Maize Line Bt 11 as a Novel Food or Food Ingredient under*

Moreover, the role of the European Parliament is still limited under the current comitology process; it simply monitors that the decision is within the terms of the legislative act, with no political influence over the substance of the decision. The Commission has proposed amendments to comitology that would put the European Parliament on a more equal footing with Council in respect of the implementation of legislation that was itself passed by co-decision between European Parliament and Council.[47] However, in a desire to avoid the possibility of 'impasse', neither Parliament nor Council would be able to block Commission implementation under these proposals, enhancing the role of the Commission.[48] The political feasibility of Commission action in the face of Council or Parliament objections would depend on the context; again, the mere fact of objections suggests a certain sensitivity.

Whilst comitology is subject to considerable criticism, which is not likely to be put to rest by the Commission's proposals for revision, some argue that it in fact *provides* legitimacy to Community decision-making. Comitology is said to create mechanisms for 'deliberative supranationalism'.[49] 'Deliberation' will be discussed further in chapter five below; for current purposes, 'deliberative supranationalism' involves making the case that comitology rests on 'good arguments', formulated in terms of the public interest, and can be contrasted with a process of negotiation around positions of (here, national) self-interest. The potential for comitology to legitimise decision-making by valuing good arguments is an extremely important observation, particularly as a response to tension between centralised decision-making and the Member States.[50] However, as well as empirical disputes about whether committees actually do deliberate (rather than bargain from self-interested positions),[51] risk management on the basis of closed deliberation by an unelected elite (national experts) does not in itself respond to the most pressing concerns

Regulation 258/97 COM (2004) 10 final; European Commission Press Release, *Commission Authorises Import of Canned GM-sweet Corn under New Strict Labelling Conditions — Consumers can Choose* IP/04/663. See the discussion in ch 9 below.

[47] European Commission, *Proposal for a Council Decision amending Decision 1999/468/EC Laying down the Procedures for the Exercise of Implementing Powers Conferred on the Commission* COM (2002) 719 final; European Commission, *Amended Proposal for a Council Decision amending Decision 1999/468/EC Laying down the Procedures for the Exercise of Implementing Powers Conferred on the Commission* COM (2004) 324 final.

[48] The measure only reaches Council and Parliament if the committee is not in favour. If there are objections from either institution, the Commission, 'taking account of the positions of the European Parliament and the Council' can put forward a proposal for legislation, adopt the original draft, adopt a modified draft or withdraw its draft; new Art 5a(5). The Commission would be required to provide reasons for its actions.

[49] C Joerges and J Neyer, 'From Intergovernmental Bargaining to Deliberative Process: The Constitutionalisation of Comitology' (1997) 3 *European Law Journal* 273; E Vos, 'EU Committees: The Evolution of Unforeseen Institutional Actors in European Product Regulation' in Joerges and Vos, above n 32; C Joerges, ' "Good Governance" Through Comitology?' in Joerges and Vos, *ibid*.

[50] Note that Vos, *ibid*, sees comitology as a form of subsidiarity.

[51] M Egeberg, GF Schaefer and J Trondal, 'The Many Faces of EU Committee Governance' (2003) *West European Politics* 19, argues that comitology committees are characterised by a strongly intergovernmental (rather than supranational) focus.

about comitology as a political institution.[52] And whilst it will inevitably create some difficulties for the ability of elites to deliberate in the general EU interest, the enhancement of transparency and sometimes participation is broadly accepted as a minimum concession to the reality of the decisions taken by comitology. Indeed, scholarly discussion of the 'problem' of committees generally, political or expert, focus on procedure, particularly greater transparency and consultation, and varying degrees of citizen and European Parliament participation.

The dilemmas posed by committee decision-making, which broadly reflect the politics of risk regulation more generally, are not likely to go away. Not only is there increasing need for expert advice, but the contemporary enthusiasm for regulatory 'networks'[53] and for new forms of decision-making suggests the longevity of old debates on political responsibility for decisions based on a mixture of expertise and value judgment. So for example the *White Paper on Governance* discusses 'co-regulation', a combination of 'binding legislative and regulatory action with actions taken by the actors most concerned', building on the 'practical expertise' of private parties, as part of the strategy for 'better and faster regulation'. Co-regulation is, however, 'only suited to cases where fundamental rights or major political choices are not called into question'[54]; the difficulty of distinguishing the non-political from the political perhaps need not be restated.

Agencies and Expertise

Agencies could play a number of different roles in risk regulation. Independent expert agencies could provide a complete alternative to the risk regulation process provided by technical and political committees, allowing expert decision-making to take place independently of political influence or control. Majone is perhaps the most prominent advocate of strong agencies in the EU, arguing that the associated improvement in both outputs (because of expertise) and credibility (because the regulators would be sheltered from short term electoral influences) would improve legitimacy as well as and via improved performance.[55] Regulatory agencies at EU level are increasing in number and have diverse powers,[56] and the *White Paper on Governance* is positive about the potential

---

[52] JHH Weiler, 'Epilogue: "Comitology" as Revolution — Infranationalism, Constitutionalism and Democracy' in Joerges and Vos, above n 32; de Búrca, above n 39.

[53] See the preparatory document for Commission (2001), above n 6: Report of Working Group, *Networking People for a Good Governance in Europe*, May 2001.

[54] Commission (2001), *ibid*, pp 20–1. See also the discussion of 'environmental agreements' in ch 8 below.

[55] Majone (2000), above n 16.

[56] See the discussion of the different models in Commission COM (2002) 718, above n 6. On agencies in the EU, see for example D Geradin and N Petit, 'The Development of Agencies at EU and National Levels: Conceptual Analysis and Proposals for Reform' *Jean Monnet Working Paper No 1/04*; E Vos, 'Reforming the European Commission: What Role to Play for EU Agencies?' (2000) 37 *Common Market Law Review* 1113; E Chiti, 'The Emergence of a Community Administration: The Case of European Agencies' (2000) 37 *Common Market Law Review* 309.

of agencies.[57] The role of agencies in EU risk regulation, however, tends to be rather limited, certainly relative to Majone's proposals, and also relative to the models of many national administrations. Alongside principled doubts about the possibility of divorcing technical decisions from the political aspects of risk, the development of powerful agencies is impeded by the already sensitive distribution of powers in the EU. Legally supported by a narrow reading of the *Meroni* doctrine,[58] there is both a reluctance of existing institutions to cede power, and an awareness of the fragility of the EU's social legitimacy. The tension is clear from the *White Paper* confirmation that agencies 'cannot be granted decision-making power in areas in which they would have to arbitrate between conflicting public interests, exercise political discretion or carry out complex economic assessments'.[59] Perhaps more worrying than the very limited role for agencies that this implies, the reluctance openly to delegate political power could disguise the inevitably political nature of agency responsibilities, with associated accountability problems.

Two agencies will be discussed here: the European Food Safety Agency (EFSA) and the European Environment Agency (EEA). Both are primarily providers of independent scientific expertise, and as such are not entirely distinct from the scientific committee system discussed above.[60] To begin with the EFSA, the 2002 Food Regulation,[61] which sets up the EFSA, entrenches the division of 'risk analysis' into separate stages of 'risk assessment', 'risk management' and 'risk communication'.[62] Risk assessment is the primary tool, as well as the primary responsibility, of the EFSA; risk management is for the political institutions.

Recent history would suggest that influence, and perceived influence, from industry is damaging to the quality and credibility of risk regulation. Independence is a key governance requirement on the EFSA.[63] Although the EFSA is institutionally independent, however, independence is not necessarily easy to follow through in practice. In particular, there is some tension between independence and the emphasis on contacts with stakeholders, including industry.[64] Whether it is realistic (or even desirable) for science to be conducted in complete independence of the food industry is debatable. Aside from anything else, the

---

[57] Commission (2001), above n 6.
[58] In Case 9/56 *Meroni v High Authority* [1957/8] ECR 133 the ECJ set out conditions for the delegation of power to new bodies; the possibility of delegating wide discretionary powers was rejected.
[59] Commission (2001), above n 6, p 24. The same tension is apparent in Commission COM (2002) 718, above n 6.
[60] Both the European Food Safety Agency and the European Environment Agency rely on advice from committees, and in the case of the EFSA, scientific committees are co-opted into the agency structure. Both also cede to political committees, comitology, in respect of the implementation of risk regulation measures.
[61] Reg 178/2002, above n 9. On the EFSA, see D Chalmers, ' "Food for Thought": Reconciling European Risks and Traditional Ways of Life' (2003) 66 *Modern Law Review* 532; G Majone (2002), above n 16.
[62] Reg 178/2002, *ibid*, Arts 3(9)–(13) and 6.
[63] *Ibid*, Art 37.
[64] 'The Authority shall develop effective contacts with consumer representatives, producer representatives, processors and any other interested parties', *ibid*, Art 42.

EFSA will not have the resources to carry out all necessary research itself, and is likely to need information from industry. In these circumstances, openness to other perspectives, in this instance especially consumer groups, is a necessary balance; although provided for in the Regulation,[65] care needs to be taken that the consumer voice is not overwhelmed by better resourced industry interests.

The relationship with national risk regulators will also be crucial. The EFSA is required to promote 'the European networking of organisations' operating in its area:

> to facilitate a scientific cooperation framework by the coordination of activities, the exchange of information, the development and implementation of joint projects, the exchange of expertise and best practices.[66]

'Networking' of risk assessors through agency structures, like networking through the involvement of national experts in committee, attempts to bring national risk regulators into the EU fold. This sort of network is nothing new in Community administration,[67] but provides a crucial foil to the centralisation of authority otherwise inherent in the creation of the EFSA.[68] Networks have become an important part of Community decision-making, in the expectation that they will provide for improved common action, whilst avoiding over-centralisation of power.[69] In themselves, however, networks do not resolve problems of effectiveness or popular legitimacy, particularly if the network is simply composed of like-minded elites. Participants in the EFSA network (as in committees) are technical experts. As with committees, it is not far-fetched to be concerned that their common technical perspective will lead them to resolve political decisions as if they were purely technical; unselfish deliberation does not in itself respond to that concern. If, as seems likely, less formal networks are developed including other 'stakeholders', there may be some alternative input, but still from within a technical framework.[70]

Networking implies the openness of scientific views to critique from other technical experts. This openness is reinforced by the centrality of transparency in the legal framework of the EFSA. The EFSA is required to 'ensure that it carries out its activities with a high level of transparency', with obligations to make public many of its documents, and to hold certain meetings in public.[71] As part of its risk communication responsibilities:

---

[65] *Ibid.*
[66] *Ibid,* Art 36.
[67] TA Borzel, 'Organizing Babylon — On the Different Conceptions of Policy Networks' (1998) 76 *Public Administration* 253; Working Group, above n 53.
[68] Majone (2000), above n 16, is of the view that centralisation would compound the 'credibility crisis'; see also R Dehousse, 'Regulation by Networks in the European Community: The Role of European Agencies' (1997) 4 *Journal of European Public Policy* 246.
[69] See the discussion in A-M Slaughter, *A New World Order* (Princeton, Princeton University Press, 2004), which looks at the global rather than specifically EU context; see also Dehousse, *ibid.*
[70] Note that much discussion on networks assumes private participation, and often also less formal structures, see Slaughter, above n 69; Borzel, above n 67; Working Group, above n 53.
[71] Reg 178/2002, above n 9, Art 38.

where there are reasonable grounds to suspect that food or feed may present a risk for human or animal health, then, depending on the nature, seriousness and extent of that risk, public authorities shall take appropriate steps to inform the general public of the nature of the risk to health.[72]

Whilst the value of transparency is clear in this provision, an attempt to avoid past mistakes, its contingency on political judgment is equally so. Similarly, the EFSA is to provide not only 'objective' and 'reliable' information, but also information that is 'easily accessible'.[73] This could just mean physically accessible information, but the EFSA is also required to 'develop and disseminate information material for the public'.[74] Whilst it is important that the lay public can understand the information it is given, this again emphasises the judgment involved at all stages of risk regulation. The centrality of 'transparency' to governance and democratisation debates, and its complexity, is discussed further in chapters five and six below.

The requirements on the EFSA in the case of 'diverging scientific opinion' also rely in part on transparency to respond to previous poor practice. The EFSA is required to 'exercise vigilance' in respect of potential sources of divergence with other bodies' scientific opinions. There is an obligation to identify the relevant body, to ensure the sharing of scientific information and the identification of potentially contentious scientific issues. There is then an obligation to cooperate in order either to resolve the divergence, or to prepare and publish a joint document 'clarifying the contentious scientific issues and identifying the relevant uncertainties in the data'.[75] The EFSA has no arbitral responsibilities; dealing with the uncertainties generated by disagreement is a political task.

The EFSA has been created as a technical body, providing information to the Community's political institutions for the political decision on risk management. The legislation provides that the grounds for risk management by these political institutions need not be purely technical: 'scientific risk assessment alone cannot, in some cases, provide all the information on which a risk management decision should be based'[76]; 'other factors legitimate to the matter under consideration'[77] may be an element of risk management. 'Other factors' include 'societal, economic, traditional, ethical and environmental factors and the feasibility of controls'[78]; politics and values are clearly not systematically ignored as irrelevant. Notwithstanding

---

[72] *Ibid*, Art 10.

[73] *Ibid*, Art 40(2).

[74] *Ibid*.

[75] *Ibid*, Art 30. Community or Member State bodies are obliged to cooperate. Note that if the diverging opinion comes from a Community body, the joint document is 'presented to the Commission'; if it is a national body, it is simply prepared and made public. There is a comparable provision in Decision 2004/210, above n 26, under which the committees are to 'assist the Commission in identifying ...', Art 13. If judgments between central and national risk asessors continue to diverge, the ability of Member States to take independent action varies in complex and not always readily explicable ways, see Chalmers, above n 61.

[76] Reg 178/2002, *ibid*, Recital 19.

[77] *Ibid*, Art 6.

[78] *Ibid*, Recital 19.

the breadth of legitimate grounds for decisions, however, the scientific and technical information provided by the EFSA, or similar bodies, is likely to prove difficult to resist.

The risk assessment/risk management dichotomy may, paradoxically, enhance the authority of risk assessment. Adding non-scientific concerns at the margins of decision-making only makes it marginally easier to feed them into decisions. The isolation of the risk assessment from the political cut and thrust reinforces the appearance of scientific neutrality, in turn enhancing the appeal of the advice to politicians faced with controversy. This is underlined by the CFI's approach to scientific expertise, discussed above: disagreement with scientific advice needs to be matched by alternative scientific evidence. The CFI's acceptance only of scientific evidence presumably would not directly be applied to a legislative context that explicitly refers to 'other factors'; this judicial risk philosophy nevertheless provides an incentive to risk managers that would tend to limit the authority of 'other factors'. In addition, powers have to be exercised mainly or exclusively for the purposes for which they were granted,[79] and so 'other factors' need to find a basis in those purposes. The Food Regulation is dominated by safety objectives (human, animal and plant health, and the environment), which reinforces the primacy of scientific risk assessment. There is, however, some room in the legislation for softer values, particularly consumer interests and animal welfare,[80] but also 'diversity in the supply of food including traditional products'.[81] Moreover, even in the pursuit of public health objectives, 'the restoration of consumer confidence can ... be an important objective'[82]; albeit that exercising a public health power with the sole aim of creating 'a favourable political impression in the press and with public opinion' would be unlawful.[83]

It would be churlish to dismiss the efforts of the EC legislators to embrace the political nature of risk regulation. The Food Regulation crucially allows for a transparent explanation of the reasons for a decision on a broad basis, which should be welcomed. Moreover, it may indeed be appropriate that only occasionally will politics overrule science, and it should be recalled that 'other factors' are as likely to be argued by industry as by environmental groups. The barriers to any routine consideration of whether non-scientific criteria justify regulatory action or inaction are, however, significant and unacknowledged. Similarly, there is no acknowledgement that policy considerations are highly likely already to be operating at the risk assessment stage. There is, rightly, much opportunity for the contestation of the EFSA's scientific claims; that however is in a distinctly technical framework. The relationship between experts and politics remains to be worked out.

---

[79] See for example Case C–84/94 *UK v Council* [1996] ECR I–5755, para 69; *Fedesa*, above n 28.
[80] Reg 178/2002, above n 9, Art 5, 'General Objectives', in section I of the Regulation, headed 'General Principles of Food Law'.
[81] Reg 178/2002, *ibid*, Art 1, 'Aims and Scope'.
[82] *Pfizer*, above n 10, para 462.
[83] *Ibid.*

No authoritative Community body comparable to the EFSA exists for risk assessment in respect of environmental protection. Whilst environmental crises do periodically arise, they have not yet provoked the same level of popular concern, or the level of interference with internal trade, as food issues. Although the EFSA has certain core environmental responsibilities, particularly in respect of GMO authorisations,[84] it has only subsidiary concern for environmental issues.[85] The European Environment Agency (EEA) has nothing like the profile of the EFSA, but many of the observations made above about the constitution of the EFSA apply to a greater or lesser degree to the EEA. Like the EFSA, the EEA is primarily a provider of information. The creation of a network (the European Environment Information and Observation Network), with the EEA at the centre, is a prime aim of the Regulation setting up the EEA.[86] The EEA/EEION is to provide 'objective, reliable and comparable information at European level',[87] targeting the fragmented, disparate and *ad hoc* nature of information on the environment. The bulk of the information used by the EEA comes from the Member State authorities, although in principle it can use information from any source.[88] The 'governance' aspects of agencies, such as transparency and independence, are perhaps less heavily emphasised in respect of the EEA. Because the EEA does not provide the same direct input into legislative or implementation decisions as the EFSA, there seems to be an assumption that the information it generates requires less vigilance. Information duties need not, however, be banal or neutral.[89] Even without formally feeding into decision-making, the provision of information can drive policy, and policy makers will be required to justify their actions in the light of scientific knowledge provided. Indeed the power of information is an increasingly important part of EC environmental policy, both in its ability to influence regulators, and also in its potential influence over individuals (consumers, producers, citizens) and the empowerment of private vigilance over public goods.[90]

Conclusions

This section has discussed themes that will arise again and again in this book. The centrality of science and technical skills to risk regulation is undeniable; the

---

[84] Ch 9 below.
[85] The EFSA is to 'contribute to a high level of protection of human life and health, and in this respect take account of animal health and welfare, plant health and the environment', Art 22(3).
[86] Reg 1210/90 on the Establishment of the European Environment Agency and the European Environment Information and Observation Network [1990] OJ L 120/1, as amended.
[87] *Ibid*, Art 1(2).
[88] R Dilling, 'Improving Implementation by Networking: The Role of The European Environment Agency' in C Knill and A Lenschow (eds), *Implementing EU Environmental Policy* (Manchester, Manchester University Press, 2000), discusses the need to enhance possibilities for information generation and dissemination outside of the dominant relationship with the Member States.
[89] B Wynne and C Waterton, 'Public Information on the Environment: the Role of the European Environment Agency' in P Lowe and S Ward (eds), *British Environmental Policy and Europe* (London, Routledge, 1998).
[90] See also chs 5 and 6 below on the power of information.

importance of politics is becoming so. Attempts to enable a productive relationship between political and scientific judgments at EU level seem to be genuine, but do raise their own questions, and face unacknowledged legal and political barriers. To that science/politics relationship must be added the role of the 'public', the non-elite political input into decision-making, which will receive closer attention in chapters five and six below.

THE PRECAUTIONARY PRINCIPLE

The politicisation of risk is in part a reflection of the uncertainty of scientific knowledge: greater awareness of the extent of scientific uncertainty, and a less deferential public attitude to science, weakens a call on 'the facts' as the only rational basis for decisions.[91] The precautionary principle acknowledges the place of scientific uncertainties at the centre of decision-making.

The notion of scientific uncertainty is by no means straightforward. Numerous categorisations have been made of the different types of uncertainty that lie alongside 'risk'; whilst the categorisations are not important for current purposes, the concepts behind them are vital to understanding the limits of risk assessment.[92] In technical terms, 'risk' usually implies that the odds of adverse effect are known, with some level of certainty. There are also situations in which the parameters of the risk are understood, but the likelihood is currently unknown.[93] Perhaps the most significant form of scientific uncertainty in environmental risk regulation is the 'we don't know what we don't know' problem: nobody initially thought to investigate the impact of CFCs on stratospheric ozone, and who knows what we are currently failing to investigate. 'Indeterminacy' is a different form of uncertainty, which arises where the validity of scientific knowledge depends on certain circumstances, but real life effects depend on open-ended and unpredictable natural environments and human behaviour.

Article 174 EC provides that EC environmental policy shall be 'based on' the precautionary principle, and the principle has now also been recognised by the CFI as an autonomous principle, stemming from and applying to all Treaty responsibilities for public health, safety and the environment.[94] Attempting to

---

[91] See E Fisher, 'Precaution, Precaution Everywhere: Developing a 'Common Understanding' of the Precautionary Principle in the European Community' (2002) 9 *Maastricht Journal of International and Comparative Law* 7.

[92] The following relies particularly on the characterisation of uncertainty in B Wynne, 'Uncertainty and Environmental Learning: Reconceiving Science and Policy in the Preventive Paradigm' [1992] *Global Environmental Change* 111.

[93] An important distinction might be drawn between cases where historical data provide a basis for a 'frequentist' measure of probability, and those in which experts apply assumptions to arrive at a level of belief about odds, see for example the discussion of frequentist/Bayesian approaches in MD Adler, 'Risk, Death and Harm: The Normative Foundations of Risk Regulation' (2003) 87 *Minnesota Law Review* 1293.

[94] *Alpharma* and *Pfizer*, above n 10; more explicitly in Cases T–74/00, T–76/00 and T141/00 *Artegodan and Others v Commission* [2002] ECR II–4945, para 184; Case T–392/02 *Solvay Pharmaceuticals BV v*

define the precautionary principle in such a way that it could be simply and comprehensively applied to give clear answers in any particular case is a thankless and probably pointless task; principles simply do not provide answers in that way.[95] It is however possible to draw out certain elements of the EC law approach to the precautionary principle from the Treaty, an important Commission *Communication on the Precautionary Principle*,[96] the use of the principle by the EC judiciary,[97] and the Food Regulation, which provides the most explicit legislative consideration of the principle.[98]

'Weak' approaches to the precautionary principle rely on 'sound science' and cost benefit assessment. The *Rio Declaration* is most commonly cited:

> Where there are threats of serious or irreversible damage, lack of full scientific certainty shall not be used as a reason for postponing cost-effective measures to prevent environmental degradation.[99]

The Rio requirement for 'serious or irreversible damage' does not appear in EC discussions of the precautionary principle, and indeed the Commission refers rather vaguely to the need to identify 'potentially negative effects'.[100] There are however frequent references to cost benefit analysis and proportionality in EC risk regulation,[101] which inevitably involves addressing the magnitude of harm. Indeed, reference to costs and benefits (in Rio, 'cost effectiveness') is a defining factor of a weak approach to the precautionary principle. Cost benefit analysis (CBA) does not simply put up a hurdle for precautionary action; because CBA assumes the predictability of effects and their impacts, it also denies much of the

---

Council, 21 October 2003, not yet reported, para 121. The Commission decisions challenged in *Artegodan* were annulled by the CFI; the Commission's unsuccessful appeal to the ECJ did not provoke any discussion of the precautionary principle, Case C–39/03 P *Artegodan and Others v Commission* [2003] ECR I–7785.

[95] See for example N de Sadeleer, *Environmental Principles: From Political Slogans to Legal Rules* (Oxford, Oxford University Press, 2002); E Fisher, 'Is the Precautionary Principle Justiciable?' (2001) 13 *Journal of Environmental Law* 315; P van Zwanenberg and A Sterling, 'Risk and Precaution in the US and Europe: A Response to Vogel' vol 3 *Yearbook of European Environmental Law* 43.

[96] Commission, above n 8.

[97] See especially *Alpharma* and *Pfizer*, above n 10; *Artegodan*, above n 94; *Solvay*, above n 94; Case C–6/99 *Greenpeace v Ministère de l'Agriculture et de la Pêche* [2000] ECR I–1651; Case C–236/01 *Monsanto Agricoltura Italia SpA v Presidenza del Consiglio dei Ministri*, 9 September 2003, not yet reported.

[98] Reg 178/2002, above n 9: 'In specific circumstances where, following an assessment of available information, the possibility of harmful effects on health is identified but scientific uncertainty persists, provisional risk management measures necessary to ensure the high level of health protection chosen in the Community may be adopted, pending further scientific information for a more comprehensive risk assessment', Art 7(1). Art 7(2) provides for conditions as to proportionality, trade restriction, technical and economic feasibility, and review.

[99] *Rio Declaration on Environment and Development* (1992) available at http://www.un.org/esa/sustdev/documents/docs.htm, Principle 15.

[100] Commission, above n 8, p 13.

[101] See for example Commission, above n 8; CFI decisions in *Alpharma* and *Pfizer*, above n 10; Reg 178/2002, above n 9, requires regard to be had to 'economic feasibility', Art 7. Art 174(3) EC requires the Community to 'take account of ... the potential benefits and costs of action or lack of action.

potential radicalism of the precautionary principle. The European approach to CBA is, however, not as formal as might be assumed. The CFI has aligned CBA with the principle of proportionality in risk management, effectively providing a new criterion by which to assess the 'proportionality' of a measure.[102] A measure would be disproportionate if:

> in the framework of a cost/benefit analysis ... disadvantages are disproportionate by comparison with the advantages which would ensue if no action were taken.[103]

A move to replace the potentially more evaluative balancing exercise of proportionality with economic CBA would be alarming; the 'magic of numbers' can drown out softer values. However, the intention seems to be the other way around, and CBA seems in this context simply to involve a weighing up of the pros and cons of the various options, without necessarily attributing numerical values to them.[104] Similarly, the Commission's *Communication on the Precautionary Principle* provides that although an economic CBA should be carried out 'when this is appropriate and feasible',[105] the obligation to consider costs and benefits is much broader, and includes questions such as the efficacy of possible options and the acceptability of measures to the public, although these issues could of course also be subjected to economic valuation.[106] The Commission's commitment to carry out 'impact assessment' of major policy proposals also includes an element of CBA, alongside 'qualitative' assessment.[107] Moreover, impact assessment is supposed to provide information for political decisions, rather than to replace political decisions. This flexible approach to CBA may ease some of the concerns about economic understandings of environmental protection discussed in chapter one above. However, the recurrent emphasis on CBA and its potential to undermine political debate should be noted.

The weak approach to the precautionary principle is resisted by some for being inadequately protective of the environment, and by others simply because it is a common sense proposition of good practice, given that decision-makers never operate in conditions of full scientific certainty. However, some brief examples indicate the continued importance of precautionary thinking, even in this relatively prosaic sense. Concern has intensified in recent years about the development by bacteria of resistance to particular antibiotics, which would make the

---

[102] *Alpharma*, above n 10, para 323; *Pfizer*, above n 10, para 410. The three familiar criteria are: a measure would be disproportionate, first, if it is 'a manifestly inappropriate means of achieving the objective pursued'; secondly, if 'other, less onerous, measures could have been taken'; thirdly if 'the disadvantages caused by the contested regulation are manifestly disproportionate to the objective pursued'.

[103] *Alpharma*, *ibid*, para 326; *Pfizer*, *ibid*, para 413.

[104] *Alpharma*, *ibid*, paras 359–68; *Pfizer*, *ibid*, paras 464–75; although note that the CFI did consider the relevance of CBAs carried out on the relevant issue for other purposes.

[105] Commission, above n 8, p 19.

[106] There is a worrying a hint to that effect: '[a] society may be willing to pay a higher cost to protect an interest, such as the environment or health, to which it attaches priority', *ibid*.

[107] European Commission, *Communication on Impact Assessment* COM (2002) 276 final.

treatment of disease by that antibiotic ineffective. In response to concern that antibiotic resistance developed in animals, through exposure to antibiotics in feed, could be transferred to humans, the EC withdrew the authorisation of certain antibiotics for use in animal feed. At the hearing of its challenge to this measure, Pfizer was asked what proof in its view would have justified intervention. Its rather stark response was 'the first dead man'.[108] Even after qualifying this with 'the first infection, or ... the first proof of colonisation, or the first proof of transfer in a human',[109] it is clear that Pfizer's standard of scientific evidence would only be satisfied if harm was done. The Court's response that this is 'based on an incorrect interpretation of the precautionary principle'[110] is probably indisputable; one might even query whether Pfizer's approach is consistent with the much less radical 'preventive principle'.[111] It is similarly salutary to recall the refusal of the UK government to respond to concerns that the pollution exported from British power stations precipitated as damaging 'acid rain' on the other side of the North Sea, in advance of scientific proof.[112] And finally, the UK government reassured the public that BSE in cattle posed no risk to human health for many months, notwithstanding considerable uncertainty. These may well simply be examples of bad decision-making, which need no special principle to be condemned. They do however illustrate that normal processes of decision-making are all too capable of disregarding uncertainty. Wide acceptance of the precautionary principle helps to counter disingenuous demands that unambiguous proof be provided for regulatory action.

By comparison with the 'weak' approach, a strong version of the precautionary principle would provide that where there are threats to the environment or health, the proponent of an activity must prove its safety, without reference to costs and benefits. There are unavoidable difficulties with this approach: proof of 'no risk' is rarely if ever available, and a consistent refusal to innovate in the absence of such proof would lead to technological stagnation.[113] This approach to the precautionary principle is rarely found in official circles. The Commission rejects what it considers to be an unrealistic search for 'zero risk',[114] as does the CFI.[115] The Community institutions seem to be concerned to reject any suggestion that positive proof of absolute safety (never available) might be required. In approving the parties' agreement that 'a "zero risk" does not exist, since it is not

---

[108] Note the extraordinary removal of this statement from the final report, WTH Douma, 'Fleshing Out the Precautionary Principle by the Court of First Instance' (2003) 15 *Journal of Environmental Law* 372, p 399.

[109] *Pfizer*, above n 10, para 379.

[110] *Ibid*, para 381.

[111] Also contained in Art 174(2) EC.

[112] Note Ludwig Krämer's reference to this dispute as the origin of the incorporation (at the UK's insistence) of the reference to 'available scientific and technical data' in Art 174, L Krämer, 'On Integration of Scientific and Technical Evidence into EU Environmental Rule-making', in Biondi *et al*, above n 36.

[113] Majone (2002), above n 16; CR Sunstein, 'Beyond the Precautionary Principle' (2003) 151 *University of Pennsylvania Law Review* 1003. As Sunstein puts it, the problem with a strong approach to the precautionary principle is not that it 'leads in the wrong directions, but that it leads in no direction at all', because regulation also involves risks, which should also be avoided, p 1054.

[114] Commission, above n 8, p 8.

[115] *Alpharma*, above n 10, para 158; *Pfizer*, above n 10, para 145; *Solvay*, above n 94, para130.

possible to prove scientifically that there is no current or future risk associated with the [activity]',[116] the CFI condemns any attempt to base risk regulation on a 'purely hypothetical approach to the risk',[117] contrasted with a risk that is 'adequately backed up by the scientific data available at the time'.[118] The phrase 'zero risk' is somewhat ambiguous. Whilst it is clear that regulation cannot be based on an inability to prove absolute safety, it is less clear that attempts to reduce the probability of an identified hazard to zero would be illegitimate. So for example, the WTO Appellate Body rejects a response to 'theoretical risk',[119] but has also asserted that a determination to 'halt' a particular risk is legitimate.[120] This statement was made in the context of a ban on the import of asbestos; few substances have such uncontroversial adverse effects. In an earlier Report, however, the Appellate Body notes that:

> it is important to distinguish ... between the evaluation of risk in a 'risk' assessment and the determination of the appropriate level of protection ... the 'risk' evaluated in a risk assessment must be an ascertainable risk; theoretical uncertainty 'is not the kind of risk which ... is to be assessed'. This does not mean, however, that a Member cannot determine its own appropriate level of protection to be 'zero risk'.[121]

A later Appellate Body report seems to introduce an element of proportionality to the setting of national levels of protection, comparing the measures taken with the risk faced. This suggests that it will not in every case be permissible to seek to reduce an identified risk to zero.[122] It seems nevertheless in principle to be legitimate under WTO rules at least in some cases to seek to eliminate a risk. The EC judiciary has also confirmed the legitimacy of a 'zero tolerance' approach to risk, which might be contrasted with a search for 'zero risk'.[123] The phrase 'zero risk' has the potential unnecessarily to restrict the setting of high protective standards, and as such is perhaps simply best avoided.

In any event, a regulatory response to 'hypothetical' risk, by which I mean an inability to prove safety, is clearly deemed to be illegitimate by the Commission, the CFI and the WTO Appellate Body. And it is true that as a matter of fact, society

---

[116] *Alpharma, ibid*, para 158; *Pfizer, ibid*, para 145.

[117] *Alpharma, ibid*, para 156; *Pfizer, ibid*, para 143; *Solvay*, above n 94, para 129.

[118] *Alpharma, ibid*, para 157; *Pfizer, ibid*, para 144.

[119] *Beef Hormones, EC Measures Concerning Meat and Meat Products (Hormones)* WT/DS26/AB/R, WT/DS48/AB/R, 16 January 1998, para 186.

[120] *European Communities — Measures Affecting Asbestos and Asbestos Containing Products* WT/DS135/AB/R, 12 March 2001, para 174.

[121] *Australia — Measures Affecting Importation of Salmon* WT/DS18/AB/R, 20 October 1998, para 125. Footnotes omitted. The Appellate Body cited its own Report in *Hormones*, above n 119.

[122] *Japan — Measures Affecting the Importation of Apples* WT/DS245/AB/R, 26 November 2003, which confirms that the 'clearly disproportionate' nature of measures taken against a 'negligible' risk constitutes evidence that there was no rational relationship between the scientific evidence and the measures taken, paras 163–8, confirming the Panel approach. The appropriate approach depends on the particular case, especially para 164.

[123] C–121/00 *Hahn* [2002] ECR I–9193 in respect of national measures; *Solvay*, above n 94, in respect of Community measures.

does not demand proof of no risk; if we had, the world would be a very different, and arguably poorer, place. In itself, however, 'so far so good' does not respond to concern about ignorance of the 'we don't know what we don't know' variety. It seems odd to preclude so absolutely (presumably even when 'other factors' than the risk assessment may form a basis for the decision[124]) the possibility of democratic discussion about the 'acceptability' of a 'theoretical risk', particularly if combined with ethical or contextual factors, or doubtful social benefits to set against the unknowns.

A measure cannot be based on a 'purely hypothetical' approach to the risk, founded on a 'mere conjecture which has not been scientifically verified'.[125] It can however, according to the CFI, be based on a risk which:

> although the reality and extent thereof have not been 'fully' demonstrated by conclusive scientific evidence, appears nevertheless to be adequately backed up by the scientific data available at the time.[126]

The boundaries between these two positions remain unspecified, as does quite what they would mean to technical risk assessors. It would be artificial, not to mention somewhat at odds with the nature of the precautionary principle, to attempt to define a level of scientific evidence at which the precautionary principle can be invoked. We know from *Alpharma* and *Pfizer* that the evidence does not have to be certain; we also know that little ever is. The notion of *adequate* scientific evidence goes to the heart of the operation of the precautionary principle, and to a large degree determines what the precautionary principle adds to more traditional approaches to sound decision-making.[127] It is, however, clear that a scientific risk assessment is a necessary first step to any regulatory activity. The precautionary principle depends, perhaps paradoxically, on as complete a scientific risk assessment as possible, and as discussed above, the EC judiciary is willing to examine in some detail the scientific evidence relied upon.

The Commission sees the precautionary principle as a tool to be applied in the risk management stage of risk regulation, when political actors are determining the appropriate *levels* of risk. In this context of setting appropriate standards, one of the most striking aspects of the precautionary principle in EC law is its prioritisation of social protection over economic interests. The CFI has confirmed the place of this prioritisation at the centre of the precautionary principle:

> the precautionary principle can be defined as a general principle of Community law requiring the competent authorities to take appropriate measures to prevent specific

---

[124] As under Reg 178/2002, above n 9; ignorance, not surprisingly, does not feature in the indicative list of 'other factors', above text at n 78.

[125] *Alpharma*, above n 10, para 156; *Pfizer*, above n 10, para 143.

[126] *Alpharma, ibid*, para 157; *Pfizer, ibid*, para 144.

[127] See also *Artegodan*, above n 94, which requires 'solid and convincing evidence which ... may reasonably raise doubts as to the safety and/or efficacy of the medicinal product', para 192.

potential risks to public health, safety and the environment, by giving precedence to the requirements related to the protection of those interests over economic interests.[128]

The precautionary principle looks 'stronger' by the minute. It would, however, be unwise to assume that protection of human health or the environment is always an absolute objective. Not only does EC policy on the precautionary principle generally assume a reference to costs and benefits, but the existence of risk/risk tradeoffs challenges any simplistic assertion that health or environmental protection can always be easily prioritised. In *Artegodan*, the case from which this quotation is taken, the dispute revolved around medicinal products, which very clearly raises health/health trade-offs in situations of uncertainty; there were even suggestions in *Pfizer* and *Alpharma* that the routine use of antibiotics has certain environmental benefits in terms of the waste produced by livestock.[129] Less directly, although arguments that wealth and health are closely connected at a societal level remain controversial, the importance of economic wellbeing to other social goods cannot automatically be rejected if one wishes to avoid exposing the most vulnerable to new risks.[130] Although prioritisation of social goods provides very important shelter for protective action, the crucial question that no principle can answer in the abstract is precisely the costs we are prepared to accept for a particular level of protection. The elusiveness of easy tradeoffs in areas of uncertainty is likely to be emphasised by the efforts of industry to rely on the precautionary principle in its own protection. It is perfectly plausible, for example, that in a case with similar facts to *Artegodan* it could be argued that withdrawal of a medicine increases overall risk; similarly that the biotech industry will argue that failing to authorise GMOs increases overall risks. The use of the precautionary principle, and indeed the exploitation of uncertainty, by industry groups should not be surprising; legal entrenchment of protection, however well designed, is always likely eventually to be called on by those with the best legal resources.[131]

The dominant approach to the precautionary principle in the EC institutions is as a tool of risk management that begins with, and ultimately returns to, scientific knowledge. Other approaches to the precautionary principle would shake up risk regulation much more significantly. Nicholas de Sadeleer, for example, argues that the precautionary principle politicises, and even democratises, otherwise wholly technical debates.[132] This is consistent with a line of thinking that sees the precautionary principle as a new and radical approach to environmental decision-making,

---

[128] *Artegodan, ibid*, para 184. See also *Alpharma*, above n 10, para 356; *Pfizer*, above n 10, para 456; *UK v Commission*, above n 1; Commission, above n 8: 'requirements linked to the protection of public health should undoubtedly be given greater weight that *(sic)* economic considerations'. Note that the Commission distinguishes the precautionary principle from the caution exercised by scientists and risk assessors, and so there need be no constraint on scientific judgment.

[129] This argument is rejected by the CFI.

[130] See Sunstein, above n 4; Weiner, above n 2.

[131] M Galanter, 'Why the "Haves" Come Out Ahead: Speculations on the Limits of Legal Change' (1974) *Law and Society* 95, argues that there are limits to what can be achieved by changes to substantive legal rules. See also ch 5 below.

[132] de Sadeleer, above n 95.

which de-prioritises the scientific method, bringing into play factors external to scientific and technical expertise, including more qualitative, personal, experience.[133] On this understanding, the precautionary principle points towards increasingly open, deliberative decision-making. Without subscribing to any particularly radical understanding of 'lay science' or the like, the Community approach to the precautionary principle does confirm its political nature, and enables dissenters to challenge scientific orthodoxies, or at least to bring into the open the values involved in scientific assessment. The European Court of Justice (ECJ) has even made an oblique suggestion that when the science is too disputed to provide the sole authority for a decision, it might be legitimate to look to public opinion.[134]

The precautionary principle is used in two main contexts: justification of decision-making at an internal level; and justification of regulation externally, in the context of free trade regimes. The precautionary principle is particularly contentious when it is used to justify protective measures that affect trade. Both internal EU trade rules and external international trade rules allow, broadly, regulatory interruptions to trade in order to protect certain legitimate interests, including the environment or human health. Scientific uncertainty is, however, likely to plague the relationship between the measures taken and the interest protected, hence the potential importance of the precautionary principle. As well as wishing to assert the Community's regulatory autonomy, the Commission is keen to discipline misuse of the precautionary principle; one of the aims of the *Communication on the Precautionary Principle* is to 'avoid unwarranted recourse to the precautionary principle, as a disguised form of protectionism'.[135] Although the background of uncertainty is likely complicate the assessments, long-standing principles associated with the control of trade restrictions are allied to the precautionary principle in the EC: precautionary action must be proportionate, non-discriminatory and consistent.[136] The international perspective on this issue could have a major impact on EC level regulation, and the next section will return to this subject.

In the former context of justifying decisions internally, the use of the precautionary principle as a shield in defence of controversial risk averse decisions is now well-established in the EU. Although in these cases the courts are prepared to engage in detailed review of the evidence and expertise used in reaching the decision, the precautionary principle essentially expands the substantive discretion of

---

[133] Fisher, above n 95.

[134] *Fedesa*, above n 28. When there are divergent scientific opinions, an operator is not entitled to expect measures to be based purely on scientific information, para 10. The concerns expressed by the European Parliament, the Economic and Social Committee and by several consumer organisations were apparently relevant to the decision, para 9. See J Scott and E Vos, 'The Juridification of Uncertainty: Observations on the Ambivalence of the Precautionary Principle within the EU and the WTO' in C Joerges and R Dehousse (eds), *Good Governance in Europe's Integrated Market* (Oxford, Oxford University Press, 2002).

[135] Commission, above n 8, p 2.

[136] Commission, *ibid*, para 6.3. 'Consistency' is most familiar from WTO law. Inconsistency of levels of protection in a 'warning signal' of illegitimacy: *Hormones*, above n 119, para 215; *Salmon*, above n 121, paras 163–4.

decision-makers. It is much less obviously amenable to being used as a sword, to constrain substantive discretion, in an action claiming that regulation is insufficiently precautionary. If nothing else, the precautionary principle leaves a broad margin of discretion to decision-makers, and in these circumstances judicial review is limited to a consideration of whether a decision is 'vitiated by a manifest error or a misuse of power or whether the Community institutions clearly exceeded the bounds of their discretion'.[137] The EC Courts have however shown themselves willing to assess action by reference to the precautionary principle, albeit subject to a certain deference, particularly an inclination to interpret the relevant legislation consistently with the precautionary principle.[138] There is also a hint from the CFI in its decision in *Artegodan* that the precautionary principle could be used more proactively. Confirming the discretion of an authority to choose the appropriate level of protection, the Court nevertheless states:

> That choice *must*, however, comply with the principle that the protection of public health, safety and the environment is to take precedence over economic interests (emphasis added)[139]

Shortly after that proposition, the Court states that the precautionary principle:

> *requires* the suspension or withdrawal of a marketing authorisation where new data give rise to serious doubts as to either the safety or the efficacy of the medicinal product in question (emphasis added).[140]

As discussed above, this may be easier said than done in many cases; nevertheless, and although in this case the legislative context places human health at the forefront of concerns,[141] the wording is suggestive of an expansive role for the precautionary principle.

To conclude, the potential of the precautionary principle has not yet been fully explored by the EC institutions. It brings out yet again debates between technical CBA and risk assessment and more political approaches to environmental issues; it also reminds us of the impossibility of seeking simple solutions. Although it is a tool of risk management, the use of the precautionary principle revolves around scientific risk assessment. The precautionary principle's recognition of the limitations of science could still give it a role in the mediation between scientific and lay perspectives on risk. That is, however, subject to the development of the WTO perspective on the principle.

---

[137] This is a well-used formula, but see for example *Alpharma*, above n 10, para 177.
[138] *Monsanto*, above n 97; *Greenpeace*, above n 97. See MG Doherty, 'Hard Cases and Environmental Principles: An Aid to Interpretation?' vol 3 *Yearbook of European Environmental Law* 57, for a more wide ranging discussion of the use of the environmental principles in legal interpretation.
[139] *Artegodan*, above n 94, para 186.
[140] *Ibid*, para 192.
[141] *Ibid*, paras 175–7.

THE WTO, RISK AND SCIENCE

Membership of the WTO imposes certain limits on risk regulation.[142] The most significant provisions for current purposes are contained in the 1994 Sanitary and Phytosanitary (SPS) Agreement. Whilst the SPS Agreement provides certain incentives for reliance on internationally agreed standards,[143] it confirms also the legitimacy of members setting their own standards for the protection of animal and plant life and health, or human life and health. This autonomy is, however, subject to conditions, most importantly that the measures are necessary, not arbitrarily or unjustifiably discriminatory, and do not constitute artificial restrictions on international trade. To ensure this end, the SPS Agreement institutes a wholeheartedly science-based regime: any measure must be 'based on scientific principles and [...] not maintained without sufficient scientific evidence',[144] a question assessed on a case by case basis.[145] This requirement for 'sufficient scientific evidence' is read together with the requirement in the SPS Agreement for risk assessment.[146] The absence or insufficiency of a risk assessment is a 'strong indication' that the measure is not concerned with protection of health, but with trade restrictions.[147] The Appellate Body does not draw a distinction between risk assessment and risk management, which means that no inherent limitations on political decision-making are implied by the use only of the phrase 'risk assessment'.[148] Nevertheless, the focus of the Appellate Body so far has been on the importance of the scientific risk assessment process.

Although now joined by other important decisions, the *Beef Hormones* dispute remains instructive of the WTO prioritisation of scientific justifications for regulatory measures. The EC banned the production or import of hormone fed beef, with the aim of protecting the health and safety of consumers.[149] The fact that the EC could not demonstrate that adequate risk assessment was carried out before it instituted its ban was central to the conclusion that the ban was unlawful. The scientific evidence relied on was inadequately specific, involving not studies of the

---

[142] See ch 9 below, which considers also the GATT and the Agreement on Technical Barriers to Trade.

[143] Domestic measures that 'conform with' certain international standards are presumed to be lawful, Art 3.2, whilst higher standards have to be justified under the SPS Agreement. The WTO Appellate Body has however been very cautious in enhancing incentives for compliance with international standards, see J Scott, 'International Trade and Environmental Governance: Relating Rules (and Standards) in the EU and the WTO' (2004) *European Journal of International Law* 307.

[144] Art 2.2.

[145] *Japan Apples*, above n 122, para 164.

[146] Art 5.1. See *Hormones*, above n 119, para 193; *Japan — Measures Affecting Agricultural Products* WT/DS76/AB/R, 22 February 1999, para 76.

[147] *Salmon*, above n 121, para 166.

[148] The Appellate Body in *Hormones*, above n 119, rejects this distinction, which was drawn by the Panel in that dispute 'to achieve or support what appears to be a restrictive notion of risk assessment', para 181. Note also the quotation from *Salmon* set out in the text above at n 121, in which the Appellate Body distinguishes between risk assessment and the 'determination of the appropriate level of protection'.

[149] *Hormones, ibid*. The EU also argued that consumer anxieties and preferences were legitimate factors supporting its ban.

effects of eating hormone fed beef, but studies of the effects of hormones[150]; the 'pathway' of the risk apparently needs also to be considered. The Appellate Body's willingness to examine the detail of risk assessments relied on by members is clear. In a pre-cursor to the CFI's rejection of 'hypothetical risk', the Appellate Body also found that 'theoretical uncertainty', the absence of proof that a substance will never have adverse effects, did not provide an adequate basis for a ban.[151] In response to the EC's argument in *Hormones* that it was following a policy of 'pre-caution', the Appellate Body determined that appeal to the precautionary principle cannot justify measures that are 'otherwise inconsistent' with the Agreement. The principle does not 'override' provisions requiring an 'assessment ... of risks', which rest predominantly on available scientific evidence.[152]

The apparent assumption of the WTO Appellate Body that decisions can be based on 'facts' may be troubling for the prospects of autonomous decision-making in areas of uncertainty, and particularly for the role of non-scientific criteria in decision-making.[153] This is, if anything, reinforced by more recent cases. It has become clear that the *possibility* of harm is not a sufficient basis for protective measures: likelihood or probability has to be evaluated, and '*some* evaluation of the likelihood or probability' does not suffice.[154] In addition, WTO rules require a 'rational relationship' between measures taken and the risk assessment,[155] and apparently the absence of such a relationship can in appropriate cases be demonstrated by a 'clear disproportion' between 'negligible' risk and measures taken.[156] This introduction of a proportionality type enquiry has the potential to enable quite invasive review of domestic risk regulation.

Although the prioritisation of scientific risk assessment is clear, the Appellate Body has also made it clear that the evaluation of likelihood or probability need not lead to a quantitative evaluation, nor need it establish a 'certain magnitude or threshold level or degree of risk',[157] although the development of a proportionality requirement would require some nuancing of that position. Nor does the evidence have to be 'monolithic'[158]; measures can be taken when opinions diverge or are uncertain. It is clearly possible to look to minority scientific evidence, as well

[150] See also *Japan Apples*, above n 122, on the need to focus on the risk posed specifically by apples, para 203. Note however that in *Asbestos*, above n 120, albeit in the different legal context of the GATT rather than the SPS Agreement, the fact that information on the particular form of asbestos (chrysotile) was not available did not invalidate the risk assessment. The analysis may well be more complex in less clear cut risks than asbestos.

[151] *Hormones*, above n 119, para 186.

[152] *Hormones*, *ibid*, para 124

[153] For detailed criticism, see VR Walker, 'Keeping the WTO from Becoming the "World Trans-Science Organization": Scientific Uncertainty, Science Policy, and Factfinding in the Growth Hormones Dispute' (1998) 31 *Cornell International Law Journal* 251.

[154] *Salmon*, above n 121, paras 123–4, relying on SPS Agreement, Annex A, para 4. Note also the question of 'negligible risk', *Japan Apples*, above n 122.

[155] *Hormones*, above n 119; *Japan Agricultural Products*, above n 146.

[156] See above n 122.

[157] *Hormones*, above n 119, para 186; *Salmon*, above n 121, para 124.

[158] *Hormones*, *ibid*, para 194.

as '"mainstream" scientific opinion', although the Appellate Body, like the EC judiciary, is prepared to consider whether the 'divergent opinion' is from 'qualified and respected sources'.[159] The Appellate Body also allows for the indeterminacy of effects, referring to the 'actual potential for adverse effects on human health in the real world where people live and work and die'; although sufficient evidence of that 'real world' effect may be demanded.[160]

Article 5.7 of the SPS Agreement puts in place a rather conservative version of the precautionary principle. It provides:

> In cases where relevant scientific evidence is insufficient, a Member may provisionally adopt sanitary or phytosanitary measures on the basis of available pertinent information [...] In such circumstances, Members shall seek to obtain the additional information necessary for a more objective assessment of risk and review the sanitary or phytosanitary measure accordingly within a reasonable period of time.

This provision has been considered by the Appellate Body on two occasions.[161] Four cumulative requirements apply to the use of Article 5.7: the relevant scientific evidence must be insufficient; the measure must be adopted on the basis of available pertinent information; the Member that adopted the measure has to seek the additional information necessary for a more objective assessment of risk; and has to review the measure within a reasonable period of time.[162] With respect to the insufficiency of scientific evidence, the Appellate Body has confirmed a Panel's assertion that this relates to situations in which there is 'little, or no, reliable evidence ... available on the subject matter at issue'.[163] In response to the concern that this excludes cases subject to a mass of scientific investigation, but continued uncertainty, the Appellate Body emphasises the question of 'reliability' of the available evidence.[164] Quite how that will be developed remains to be seen: a link is drawn with the requirement for risk assessment, in that the evidence is insufficient 'if it does not allow, in quantitative or qualitative terms, the performance of an adequate assessment of risks'.[165] The level of confidence with which the evidence is considered by the experts also seems to be relevant.[166] Leaving aside the appropriateness of the conclusion in the particular case, this is a very narrow approach, in particular calling into question the role of minority or unorthodox views. The limitation of Article 5.7 to provisional measures, something taken on board by the European Commission,[167] reinforces the shallow perspective on scientific uncertainty, assuming primarily a problem of 'data gaps'; indeed the Appellate

---

[159] *Ibid.*

[160] *Ibid*, para 187; the risk that farmers would fail to observe good veterinary practice was dismissed, in the absence of risk assessment on this specific issue, paras 207–8.

[161] *Japan — Agricultural Products,* above n 146; *Japan Apples,* above n 122.

[162] *Japan — Agricultural Products, ibid,* para 89; *Japan Apples, ibid,* para 176.

[163] *Japan Apples, ibid,* paras 183–5.

[164] *Ibid,* para 185.

[165] *Ibid,* para 179.

[166] *Ibid,* para 173.

[167] Commission, above n 8. See also Reg 178/2002, above n 9, Art 7. Art 5.7 was not argued in *Hormones* because of the provisionality requirement.

Body emphasises that Article 5.7 is not concerned with scientific uncertainty at all, but with 'insufficient' evidence.[168] The 'reasonable period of time' within which measures must be reviewed should be considered 'on a case-by-case basis' and can depend on 'the difficulty of obtaining the additional information necessary for the review *and* the characteristics of the provisional SPS measures'.[169] The return, under the WTO approach to the precautionary principle, to scientific authority tends to downplay any non-scientific elements of risk regulation, including any potential to take a more inclusive and expansive approach to decision-making. In general, any prospect of using Article 5.7 to look beyond science seems to be diminishing.

Article 5.7 does not however exhaust the relevance of the precautionary principle, and the Appellate Body concedes that:

> Responsible, representative governments commonly act from perspectives of prudence and precaution where risks of irreversible, eg life-terminating, damage to human health are concerned.[170]

It does not, however, expand on what might be involved in those 'perspectives' of prudence and precaution. Similarly, when stating that the precautionary principle may be relevant beyond Article 5.7, reference was made only to the 'reflection' of the precautionary principle in provisions that allow WTO members to choose their own appropriate standards of protection.[171] Whether that choice can be exercised on grounds that go beyond scientific risk assessment is a key unanswered question; the prioritisation of science by the Appellate Body in its general approach to risk assessment, and in its approach to Article 5.7, suggests that the answer could be negative.

The WTO agreements, binding on the EU and its Member States, prioritise scientific knowledge, interpreting such knowledge as objective and neutral. The demand for a scientific basis to decisions is 'essential' for the 'delicate and carefully negotiated balance' between the 'interests of promoting international trade and of protecting the life and health of human beings'.[172] Albeit that there are ambiguities in the Reports, and space for legal argument and future development, politics is on the whole treated with some suspicion.

It remains to be seen whether and how the very modest EU efforts to incorporate non-scientific factors into risk regulation decisions will be reconciled with the WTO's scientific focus, which places yet further pressure, to add to the home-grown pressure, on decisions based on 'other factors'. Reconciliation is not out of the question, given particularly how open much of the still young WTO law is. Indeed, finding a way to expand the legitimate basis for decisions, without prejudicing

---

[168] *Japan Apples*, above n 122, para 184.
[169] *Japan — Agricultural Products*, above n 146, para 93. The Commission is of the view that the period will not expire until further scientific evidence can be attained. Commission, above n 8, para 6.3.5.
[170] *Hormones*, above n 119, para 124.
[171] Sixth paragraph of the preamble and Art 3.3: *Hormones, ibid*, para 124.
[172] *Hormones, ibid*, para 177.

trade discipline, may be less problematic than finding a way to maintain the vitality and legitimacy of the WTO in the absence of an acknowledgement of national democratic politics.[173] The concern that an appeal to non-scientific factors disguises trade restrictions is, however, powerful. The major challenge for the WTO, and indeed for the EU and national administrations, is in ensuring the probity of non-scientific factors. The open expression of value based concerns is an improvement, in terms of accountability, over the obscurity of those values in an apparently technical decision. It is possible that the Community's increasing expectations of openness and public participation in decision-making, to be explored further in chapters five, six, and nine below, could be developed into tools to investigate and challenge public values and public opinion.

CONCLUSIONS

Given that there is no consensus understanding of 'risk', it is scarcely surprising that the regulation of risk is controversial. Risk regulation is even more complex at EU than at national level: general concerns about the political, distributive and value-based nature of risk are compounded by the diversity of responses to risk around the EU, and the potential for the benefits and burdens of regulation to be unevenly distributed between the Member States. In these circumstances, responding to risk crises by further centralising risk assessment, whilst it certainly simplifies free movement, seems to be something of a high risk strategy for the EU. A public that is sceptical about national risk decisions is not likely to be significantly reassured by a European decision.

The relationship between expertise and the public is an old and knotty problem, and it is entirely appropriate that it is a crucial aspect of the EU's legitimacy debates. Holding expert opinions up to scrutiny, whilst recognising the legitimate concerns provoked by a turn to manipulable, ill-defined and possibly ill-informed political opinion, is a difficult task. Moreover, as environmental law endeavours to become more proactive, more preventive and more holistic, science becomes ever more crucial, and ever less certain. The EU attempts to hold the line on risk regulation by asserting a dichotomy between the technical and the political. Whilst this allows for the political nature of risk regulation as a whole, it largely denies the political nature of the risk assessment process. However, EU risk regulation is now pervaded by an almost inescapable rhetoric of transparency and openness. If that is successfully applied to technical risk assessors in practice, some of the flaws of the dichotomy can be addressed.

---

[173] J Scott, 'European Regulation of GMOs: Thinking About Judicial Review in the WTO' forthcoming (2005) *Current Legal Problems*. See also the discussion of WTO and EC approaches to GMOs in ch 9 below.

A number of themes introduced here will be revisited in later chapters. In particular, chapter nine on GMOs provides a high profile example of a situation in which the tension between expert and political decision-making has been acute, and which is also raising WTO issues. The relative role of the experts and the public will be discussed in chapters five and six, which will also raise the possibility of investigating qualitative information on public opinion. If decision-makers understand the background to and reasons for expert and public assessments, they are in a much better position to reach good decisions.

5

European Environmental Governance and Public Participation

INTRODUCTION

RECENT YEARS HAVE seen a remarkable consensus emerge around the need for public participation in environmental decision-making. A number of justifications and explanations for public participation are available, some of which are particularly attractive in the environmental sphere, some of which are particularly attractive to European institutions. A turn to more participatory procedure, in all its complexity, is now almost an instinctive response to concerns about the legitimacy of decision-making, concerns that arise with some regularity in EC law. In the specifically environmental context, public participation has the potential to provide a response both to the disputed democratic credentials of EC environmental law, and to criticisms of the effectiveness of EC environmental law.

Notwithstanding its wide use, the meaning of 'public participation' is deeply ambiguous, and often unresolved or unexamined. The most basic form of political participation is of course voting, and the assumption of political equality on which the principle of 'one person one vote' rests should be a useful discipline through which to view other public participation initiatives[1]: in particular, who constitutes the 'public' for the purposes of participation is a crucial and often unvisited question. The intention of public participation is, however, generally to look beyond periodic elections on a bundle of issues. For current purposes, a broad understanding of public participation is appropriate, including open and transparent procedures and decisions, consultation or more intense involvement in decisions, through to possible litigation or other forms of dispute resolution or review after a decision has been taken.

Public participation need not be enormously challenging to familiar institutional arrangements. Consultation processes allow external views to be put before decision-makers, who take an autonomous decision based on their conception of the overall public interest. Cost benefit analysis (CBA) is sometimes conceptualised as a form of public participation, allowing for the aggregation of preferences and

---

[1] Although of course citizens are not equally represented in the EU: in particular, the European Parliament provides different levels of representation for citizens depending on the size of their Member State.

their intensity, through real or hypothetical markets.[2] These 'thin'[3] forms of participation, which view the 'public interest' as broadly an aggregate of individual interests, can be distinguished from the more challenging ideal of 'deliberative democracy'.

The literature on deliberation is complex, sophisticated and extensive, not to mention subject to considerable internal and external critique.[4] It is not the intention here to comment on it, or even to advocate deliberation in EC environmental law. However, the appeal of deliberative forms of democracy in EC environmental law should be noted, and certain elements of deliberation outlined before we proceed. The key to deliberation, which can be contrasted with the calculation and aggregation of interests, is rational argument, including the provision of reasons that are capable of recognition as 'reasons' by others who disagree. Unlike opinion polls, consultations, voting or CBA, deliberative processes should provide qualitative information on reasons behind opinions and values, as well as quantitative information on those opinions and interests. There is also an assumption that values can be transformed by deliberation, by contrast with the pre-formed and static private interests elicited in 'thin' forms of participation. This potential for transformation, and the search for qualitative as well as quantitative information, takes us back to Mark Sagoff's discussion of interests versus values.[5] Whilst one might disagree with Sagoff's very sharp dichotomy between the public and the private, particularly in the environmental sphere where personal behaviour has such direct impact on public goods, the notion that decisions are properly based on values, supported by reasons, rather than on competition between self-interested positions, is instinctively attractive.[6] Many environmentalists make an appeal to deliberation without significant theoretical ambition, but on the basis that reasons and argument within a broadly based process are the best way both to capture the complexity of environmental values, and to escape narrow parameters, such as efficiency or risk assessment, for decision-making.

The literature, particularly the environmental literature, often elides discussion of participation and deliberative democracy. Deliberative democracy does not

---

[2] See for example, DW Pearce, EB Barbier and A Markandya, *Blueprint for a Green Economy* (London, Earthscan, 1989).

[3] J Black, 'Proceduralizing Regulation' (2000) 20 *Oxford Journal of Legal Studies* 597, and (2001) 21 *Oxford Journal of Legal Studies* 33.

[4] On the history of deliberative democracy see 'Introduction' in J Bohman and W Rehg (eds), *Deliberative Democracy* (London, MIT Press, 1997). The seminal work on deliberation is found in Habermas (from a critical perspective) and Rawls (from a liberal perspective). See also J Dryzek, *Deliberative Democracy and Beyond: Liberals, Critics, Contestations* (Oxford, Oxford University Press, 2000); G Smith, *Deliberative Democracy and the Environment* (London, Routledge, 2003); A Dobson, *Citizenship and the Environment* (Oxford, Oxford University Press, 2003).

[5] M Sagoff, *The Economy of the Earth: Philosophy, Law and the Environment* (Cambridge, Cambridge University Press, 1988), see discussion in ch 1 above. Note also the distinction between the 'market' and the 'forum' as a locus for decision-making, which similarly brings out the effort to escape the self-interest of participants, in J Elster, 'The Market and the Forum: Three Varieties of Political Theory' in Bohman and Rehg, *ibid*.

[6] CR Sunstein, 'Preferences and Politics' (1991) 20 *Philosophy and Public Affairs* 3.

however necessarily imply direct citizen involvement; nor does direct citizen involvement necessarily imply deliberation. The commitment of the EU to participation by at least some sections of the public, at least rhetorically, is clear; the commitment to deliberation is less explicit. There seems however to be an underlying assumption that the provision of occasions (to experts, to representatives, to the public, to public interest groups) to debate, provides also a forum for deliberation.

This chapter will examine first the possible reasons for the contemporary enthusiasm for public participation in environmental decision-making, and the many attractions of public participation to the EU. Access to environmental information, participation in environmental decision-making and access to justice in environmental matters at EU level will then be discussed. These are the three 'pillars' of the high profile UN ECE Aarhus Convention, the *Convention on Access to Information, Public Participation in Decision-making and Access to Justice in Environmental Matters*,[7] the signature of which by the EC as well as all Member States is at least a significant indication of political commitment to its values; chapter six below will consider the implementation, through EC environmental law, of the Aarhus Convention at national level. Before concluding, this chapter will consider some of the main difficulties of a move to increased public participation in decision-making.

EXPLAINING PARTICIPATION

This section will look at two main categories of justification for public participation, which is generally discussed by reference to substantive or process rationales; some possibilities that fit neatly into neither category will also be discussed. Process rationales see public participation as inherently beneficial; at EC level, this tends to shade into discussion of 'democracy' and democratic deficits, but the intention need not be so ambitious. Substantive rationales make a link between public participation and improved outcomes. The intention of this section is to indicate some of the reasons for the contemporary fascination with participatory mechanisms, and particularly in the field of EC environmental law, given the effectiveness and democratic challenges faced in that discipline.

The preoccupation of the EC institutions with public participation is apparent well beyond the environmental context, forming an element of potentially momentous developments in both 'European governance' and European constitutionalism. The culmination of the 'constitutionalisation' and 'governance' debates, for now, has been the publication by the Commission of a *White Paper on European Governance*[8] and the agreement by the European Council in June 2004 of the Treaty Establishing a Constitution for Europe.[8a] Whilst there is no intention to add to or analyse the scholarly or political debates here, there has been an

---

[7] Available at http://www.unece.org/env/pp/documents/cep43e.pdf. The UN ECE is one of five United Nations regional commissions, the United Nations Economic Commission for Europe.
[8] European Commission, *White Paper on European Governance* COM (2001) 428 final.
[8a] [2004] OJ C 310/01, also available at http://europa.eu.int/constitution/index_en.htm

important mutual influence between fashionable political ideas of participation and the development of governance and constitutionalisation. A brief introduction is useful before proceeding.

'Governance' is receiving a great deal of attention at the national and international level, as well as in the EU, and is a significant element of the movement to participation in decision-making. The Commission's definition of governance as 'rules, processes and behaviour that affect the way in which powers are exercised at European level'[9] is rather vague, but usefully brings out the role of governance in decision-making. Governance emphasises the complexity of regulatory decision-making, indeed the complexity of exercising regulatory authority. As a response, governance suggests a shift away from top-down, hierarchical decision-making towards greater cooperation and shared responsibility. It is possible that 'governance' indicates a certain mistrust of 'government', implying a turn away from well-established mechanisms of governmental legitimacy; although of course one of the distinguishing features of the EU is the absence of a single 'government' to which such legitimising mechanisms can be attached.[10] The desirability of a move to governance is much debated,[11] given in particular its potential to dilute or disperse lines of accountability and responsibility.[12] Governance can also tend to downplay the importance of politics and political contest in public decision-making.[13] Although the Commission's discussion of participation in 'governance' is heavily focussed on 'democratisation', the suitability of the method for the end is contested.[14] It is also debatable whether the Commission's emphasis in the *White Paper on European Governance* on the 'Community method', and, especially, on its own place at the core of this method, fully captures the sophistication of governance more generally. For current purposes, one can simply note the centrality of a rhetoric of participation to the Commission's understanding of European governance: its five 'principles of good governance' are 'openness, participation, accountability, effectiveness and coherence'.[15] The impact of the governance project on practical arrangements for public participation will be discussed further below.

---

[9] Commission, *ibid*, p 8, fn 1.

[10] AM Sbragia, 'The Dilemma Of Governance With Government' *Jean Monnet Working Paper 3/02*.

[11] M Shapiro, 'Administrative Law Unbounded: Reflections on Government and Governance' [2001] *Indiana Journal of Global Legal Studies* 369; P Allott, 'European Governance and the Re-Branding of Democracy' (2002) 27 *European Law Review* 60; C Harlow, *Accountability in the European Union* (Oxford, Oxford University Press, 2002).

[12] Shapiro, *ibid*, argues that the use of the word governance 'announces a significant erosion of the boundaries separating what lies inside a government and its administration and what lies outside them', p 369.

[13] Consider the contrast between political accountability and governance processes in Harlow, above n 11.

[14] D Curtin, 'The Commission as Sorceror's Apprentice? Reflections on EU Public Administration and the Role of Information Technology in Holding Bureaucracy Accountable' in C Joerges, Y Meny, and JHH Weiler (eds), *Mountain or Molehill? A Critical Appraisal of the Commission's White Paper on Governance*, available at ive.it/RCAS/Research/OnlineSymposia/governance.shtml; D Wincott, 'Looking Forward or Harking Back? The Commission and the Reform of Governance in the European Union' (2001) 39 *Journal of Common Market Studies* 897; L Cram, 'Governance "to Go": Domestic Actors, Institutions and the Boundaries of the Possible' (2001) 39 *Journal of Common Market Studies* 595.

[15] Commission, above n 8, p 10.

The Convention on the Future of Europe, whose draft *Treaty Establishing a Constitution for Europe*[16] formed the basis for the Constitution agreed in June 2004, was a self-consciously deliberative and inclusive exercise, demonstrating the growing influence of this type of thinking in constitutional debate.[17] Although there have been, perhaps inevitably, serious concerns around precisely who was represented in the Convention process, including some ambivalence about the highly formalised approach to external input,[18] the Convention bears comparison to the far from perfect alternative of the closed diplomatic world of Inter-Governmental Conference (IGC). However, given the Convention's lack of formal power or indeed established social legitimacy, the final decision on Treaty reform was placed in the hands of an IGC. Although there was eventual agreement in June 2004, the reversion to self interest (to the extent that it had been escaped in the Convention) and closed fora was starkly apparent in the stalling of negotiations in December 2003, and the constant reiterations of national interest in early summer 2004. This is indicative of one of many serious challenges in the design of participatory or deliberative structures: at some point decisions have to be made, and at this stage, any real shifts of power may well be contested. The place for participation in the ultimate results of the Convention, the 2004 Constitutional Treaty, will be discussed below.

Process and Democratic Deficits

European integration was in its early years a predominantly elite project, pursued in relative isolation from the public. In the last decade or two, high profile public debate on the 'democratic deficit' has emerged, and remains fundamentally unresolved.[19] Democracy is virtually universally approved of, but its meaning is deeply contested. Without wishing to seek a definition of 'democracy', it suffices for current purposes to note that democracy has a generally accepted core that might be (vaguely) described as government by and for the people; in a practical sense, governments can be turned out of office as a result of decisions taken through the

---

[16] [2003] OJ C 169/1.

[17] Participation in the Convention itself was extensive compared to IGCs, extending to national parliamentary representatives, Member State government representatives, European Parliament and Commission representatives, plus observers from the social partners, and the European ombudsman. Accession states, including Romania, Bulgaria and Turkey were also included. There was some effort to allow participation by third parties: the Convention's website provided information and an opportunity for comment, and events were held for 'civil society'.

[18] J Shaw, 'Process, Responsibility and Inclusion in EU Constitutionalism' (2003) 9 *European Law Journal* 45; J Scott, 'The Culture of Constitution-Making? "Listening" at the Convention on the Future of Europe' (2002) 3 *German Law Journal*, available at http://www.germanlawjournal.com/.

[19] There is an enormous literature. See for example P Craig, 'The Nature of the Community: Integration, Democracy, and Legitimacy' in P Craig and G de Búrca (eds), *The Evolution of EU Law* (Oxford, Oxford University, 1999); JHH Weiler, *The Constitution of Europe* (Cambridge, Cambridge University Press, 1999); S Douglas-Scott, *Constitutional Law of the European Union* (London, Longman, 2002), pp 129–41.

ballot box. The EU's democratic deficit, which might embrace concern about the very existence of the EU as well as its decision-making mechanisms, is similarly uncertain, but with a similarly well understood core: in particular, the people on whose behalf laws are passed and implemented are unable to reject or influence legislators or government by popular vote, a deficit deepened by the obscurity of the EU's activities to many of its citizens. There is undoubtedly some nostalgia in unfavourable comparisons between EU institutions and idealised national parliamentary democracy[20]: all democratic systems compromise, for example in the interests of minority rights, or of effectiveness, as well as more pernicious compromises. The fact that national democratic systems are not ideal, however, does not diminish the defects in the EU system. Nor should it deflect attention from the contribution of EU decision-making to national democratic problems, in particular the tendency of EU decision-making to empower national courts and executives at the expense of democratic institutions.[21]

The gaps in the EU's democratic accountability resist the solutions offered by representative democracy, creating room for participatory alternatives. The democracy debate in the EU is broad, deep and sophisticated, but for current purposes it suffices to note that enhancing traditional mechanisms of representative democracy can have paradoxical effects, in particular by shifting power between institutions in complex ways. So for example, giving unitary legislative power to the European Parliament, the institution with the clearest democratic credentials, involves transferring power from national democratic bodies to a more remote, albeit elected, EU institution. Moreover, any move to purer representative democracy at EU level implies the acceptability of binding minorities to the majority will through such institutions; it is debatable whether there is a sufficiently coherent European political or community identity to take this step.[22] Similarly, establishing a government for the Parliament to hold to account implies a state-like system, with a concurrent diminution of national democratic institutions. If attempts to create parliamentary democracy at EU level would lead to a politically unlikely form of state building, the diametrically opposite possibility is to reassert the inter-governmental aspects of EU decision-making, relying on a more direct link with national democratic processes to provide legitimacy. A return to inter-governmentalism would involve increasing the legislative autonomy of Council (that is, reducing the power of the European Parliament) and reinvigorating the veto in Council. Not only would this run the risk of paralysing decision-making, however, but without corresponding reform of national parliaments, it would increase the strength of the executive over parliament at the domestic level.

[20] A Moravcsik, 'In Defence of the "Democratic Deficit": Reassessing Legitimacy in the European Union' (2002) 40 *Journal of Common Market Studies* 603, argues that the EU is legitimate compared against existing advanced industrial democracies. Others positively embrace the non-majoritarian aspects of EU decision-making, focussing on the potential for better decisions, see especially, G Majone (ed), *Regulating Europe* (London, Routledge, 1996).

[21] D Wincott, 'Does the European Union Pervert Democracy?' (1998) 4 *European Law Journal* 411.

[22] The 'no demos' problem, see especially JHH Weiler, 'Does Europe Need a Constitution? Demos, Telos and the German Maastricht Decision' (1995) *European Law Journal* 217.

Inter-governmentalism can allow governments to evade democratic (especially parliamentary) scrutiny at both national and European levels.[23] Although there are numerous more sophisticated proposals for the enhancement of democracy between these simplistic extremes, for current purposes it is important simply to observe that the consistent infeasibility of liberal democratic reforms direct attention to a range of alternative participatory mechanisms. Explicit calls are made for deliberative or republican democracy,[24] and deliberative theories are used to explain and justify the workings of different EU institutions[25]; although participatory mechanisms may turn out to face very similar challenges to those faced in representative democracy, the appeal of participation is clear.

General moves to public participation in environmental decision-making, are, then, reinforced for the EU by the intractability of the democratic deficit. This is confirmed, albeit modestly, by the new Constitution, which contains a title on 'The Democratic Life of the Union'.[26] Affirming that the 'functioning of the Union shall be founded on the principle of representative democracy', making the conventional appeal to the European Parliament and Council (accountable to national parliaments or citizens) for that claim,[27] the Constitution gives space also to the 'principle of participatory democracy'.[28] Relatively familiar commitments to openness, transparency, dialogue, consultations and exchanges of view illustrate the perceived constitutional importance of participation in the day-to-day decision-making of the EU. Provision is also made for the novel instrument of a 'citizens' initiative':

> Not less than one million citizens who are nationals of a significant number of Member States may take the initiative of inviting the Commission, within the framework of its powers, to submit any appropriate proposal on matters where citizens consider that a legal act of the Union is required for the purpose of implementing the

[23] The shift to inter-governmental decision-making under the EU's 'third pillar' is creating concern, see Harlow, above n 11.

[24] Weiler, above n 19, for example, advocates the use of more 'direct democracy' with the creation of the 'European public square' and mechanisms such as legislative ballots. See also J Cohen and C Sabel, 'Directly-Deliberative Polyarchy' (1997) 3 *European Law Journal* 313; P Craig, 'Democracy and Rule-Making within the EC: An Empirical and Normative Assessment' (1997) 3 *European Law Journal* 105; D Curtin, *Postnational Democracy* (The Hague, Kluwer, 1997); A Reale, 'Representation of Interests, Participatory Democracy and Lawmaking in the European Union: Which Role and Which Rules for the Social Partners?' *Jean Monnet Working Paper 15/03*. MA Wilkinson, 'Civil Society and the Re-Imagination of European Constitutionalism' (2003) 9 *European Law Journal* 451, discusses the claims on deliberation in EU constitutional scholarship. For a sceptical view, see D Chalmers, 'The Reconstitution of European Public Spheres' (2003) 9 *European Law Journal* 127.

[25] EO Eriksen and JE Fossum, 'Democracy through Strong Publics in the European Union?' (2002) 40 *Journal of Common Market Studies* 401, discusses the European Parliament, Comitology and the Convention; C Lord and P Magnette, 'E Pluribus Unum? Creative Disagreement about Legitimacy in the EU' (2004) 42 *Journal of Common Market Studies* 183, discusses deliberation in a number of institutions; C Joerges and J Neyer, 'From Intergovernmental Bargaining to Deliberative Process: The Constitutionalisation of Comitology' (1997) 3 *European Law Journal* 273, considers the possibility of 'deliberative supranationalism' in comitology, see also ch 4 above.

[26] Title VI.

[27] Art I–46. Note also 'the principle of democratic equality', Art I–45. See A Peters, 'European Democracy After the 2003 Convention' (2004) *Common Market Law Review* 37, for discussion.

[28] Art I–47.

Constitution. European laws shall determine the provisions for the procedures and conditions required for such a citizens' initiative, including the minimum number of Member States from which such citizens must come.[29]

The detail is to be filled in by legislation, which would dictate the practical strength of this provision. Whilst both greens and deliberative theorists mistrust these sorts of aggregative arrangements, the 'initiative' does have considerable appeal in an environmental context.[30] Popular votes are able to side-step the official agenda, often dominated by economic questions. Citizens' initiatives are also directly inclusive, escaping some of the concerns that the demands of participation actually enhance exclusion, considered below. There is however a significant danger that political and economic elites will drive, if not manipulate, the process, weakening rather than enhancing legitimacy. The normal complexities of this sort of reform are compounded at EU level. The protection of minorities is always an issue; in this case, it is unclear what would be done with vastly differing results in the different Member States. The minimum number of Member States whose citizens are involved in the initiative, and the number of citizens from each Member State, need to be filled out by highly sensitive legislation. The difficulty is that the emergence of a 'European public' for the purposes of participatory democracy is no more imminent than is a 'European public' for the purposes of representative democracy. So whilst this provision might have some appeal to those concerned by environmental protection, it can make only a limited contribution to moving beyond the democratic deficit; nor will it necessarily provide for environmentally beneficial results.

The EU does not have a monopoly on 'democratic deficits': the relationship between green political thought and democratic traditions is similarly complex, albeit at a more abstract level. Elements of ecological thought have led to the suggestion that the gravity of the environmental crisis cannot be left to democracy, and authoritarian forms of government begin to look like the only solution. Even if this authoritarian streak has been exaggerated,[31] the acceptability of only environmentally beneficial outcomes has at least an uncomfortable relationship with liberal democracy's commitment to value pluralism, notwithstanding a range of arguments supporting the necessity of environmental constraints on democracy.[32] The solution is again to turn to various forms of participatory or deliberative democracy. The faith of some that deliberation, rational argument, and public participation will necessarily lead to green outcomes is probably misplaced.

---

[29] Art I–47(4).

[30] See the discussion of referenda and initiatives in Smith, above n 4, pp 93–8.

[31] A Dobson, *Green Political Thought* (London, Routledge, 2000) warns against too hasty a link between green thought and authoritarianism, pp 114–24. B Doherty and M de Geus, 'Introduction' in B Doherty and M de Geus (eds), *Democracy and Green Political Thought — Sustainability, Rights and Citizenship* (London, Routledge, 1996) discusses the evolution of green political thought and democracy from rather inauspicious beginnings.

[32] See for example, the contributions to Doherty and de Geus, *ibid*. See also Dobson, above n 4, and the argument that liberalism should be committed to strong sustainability as a means to keep open the widest possible range of ways to pursue the good life in the future.

Nevertheless, even if green outcomes cannot be guaranteed, deliberation and participation are seen as an important way to allow the expression of green values, as well as to ensure that environmental issues receive attention alongside other priorities.[33] This approach is also able to acknowledge the plurality of values within what can only loosely be called 'the' environmental movement.[34]

Another dimension to the green democratic deficit is the very common delegation, at the national level, of environmental decision-making to independent agencies that have at best only indirect and weak links to electoral processes. This delegation is justified by the need for technical and scientific expertise in environmental decision-making. However, for reasons discussed in chapter 4 above in respect of risk, environmental decisions are not simply technical questions, but involve political value judgments and divided interests. The most common response to the distance between agencies and the electorate is to turn to participatory mechanisms such as transparency, consultation and review. The imposition of procedural obligations on national regulators through EC environmental law will be discussed in detail in chapter six below, and it should for now simply be noted that the prospect of enhancing the legitimacy of EC environmental legislation through national participation is highly appealing to the EC institutions. National participatory mechanisms can however only ever partially reverberate at EU level. First of all, national participation in respect of policies that will be developed at EU level is mediated by majority voting in Council, the involvement of other institutions, and the ability of national representatives to escape national scrutiny. Secondly, participation in national implementation measures takes place after certain crucial policy decisions have been taken, when the national or local body may be subject to binding legal obligations.

From the starting point that the EU developed as a 'regulatory order',[35] rather than as a distributive institution, analogies are drawn between the constitutional challenges posed by delegation of power to agencies within the state, and delegation of power to a regulatory power beyond the state. Proponents of this 'administrative model' of the development of the EU have at times argued that because technical decision-making is isolated from politics, particularly redistributive politics, (EU) regulation can and must be sheltered from democratic pressures; legitimacy is achieved by the quality of decisions, or by the 'credibility' of the institutions.[36] In recognition of the inevitable political and distributive impact of regulatory decisions, this approach also provides a procedural route through the legitimacy debate, albeit one that stops short of ambitious 'democratisation' rhetoric. Procedural standards of openness and review focus not on democratising major decisions, but on the legitimacy of a bureaucracy.

---

[33] Different approaches to environmental democracy can be found in J Dryzek, *The Politics of the Earth* (Oxford, Oxford University Press, 1997); Smith, above n 4; M Sagoff, above n 5; Doherty and de Geus, *ibid*.

[34] Smith, *ibid*.

[35] Majone, above n 20.

[36] G Majone, 'The Regulatory State and its Legitimacy Problems' (1999) 22 *West European Politics* 1.

In short, criticisms are made of the democratic credentials of both EU decision-making and of environmental decision-making more broadly. The problems identified do not respond well to familiar solutions from liberal representative democracy, and participatory alternatives exercise a powerful sway. The enthusiasm does however raise its own questions, some of which will be discussed below.

Substance and Problem-Solving

The main alternative approach to public participation looks at substantive results, the outcome of decision-making.[37] At its most basic, the intention is simply to increase the information available to decision-makers, providing them with otherwise dispersed expertise, including especially local knowledge,[38] and a range of perspectives on the problem. This could involve quite minimal levels of consultation, with little interaction between participants and decision-maker. An attempt jointly to resolve controversial problems in the public interest could, however, go beyond gathering information on technical matters and pre-formed interests, to a more deliberative approach.[39] The multi-faceted nature of decisions with environmental impacts, particularly if sustainable development is the objective, reinforces the need to move beyond a technical approach to decisions, suggesting a broadly based decision-making process.

A different perspective on substantive rationales for public participation, often dominant at EU level, revolves around the implementation of decisions.[40] Changes in individual behaviour may be essential for the success of certain policy measures, for example as to waste production or energy use. 'Public participation' can become a very passive exercise from this perspective, limited to the implementation of pre-determined policy, but acknowledgement of the need for public participation in implementation may also point towards prior engagement in policy-making. In addition, environmental education and awareness-raising may be positive by-products of public participation in policy making,[41] an environmental reflection of the argument that deliberative democracy more generally raises

---

[37] For example, Dryzek above n 33.

[38] F Fischer, *Citizens, Experts, and the Environment: The Politics of Local Knowledge* (London, Duke University Press, 2000). See also B Wynne, 'May the Sheep Safely Graze? A Reflexive View of the Expert-Lay Knowledge Divide' in S Lash, B Szerszynski and B Wynne (eds), *Risk, Environment and Modernity: Towards a New Ecology* (London, Sage, 1996); Dryzek, above n 33.

[39] J Steele, 'Participation and Deliberation in Environmental Law: Exploring a Problem-solving Approach' (2001) 21 *Oxford Journal of Legal Studies* 415.

[40] The Commission's proposal for the ratification of the Aarhus Convention by the EU, for example, makes much of the implementation potential of the access principles, European Commission, *Proposal for a Council Decision on the Conclusion, on behalf of the European Community, of the Convention on Access to Information, Public Participation in Decision-making and Access to Justice in Environmental Matters* COM (2003) 625 final.

[41] See for example, J Barry, 'Sustainability, Political Judgement and Citizenship: Connecting Green Politics and Democracy' in Doherty and de Geus, above n 31; Elster, above n 5, argues that these can only ever be side products, and will evaporate if they become the point of the exercise.

democratic and civic awareness. These and other educational measures may have a more profound impact than the use of superficial financial signals to influence individual behaviour.[42] Still in the realm of implementation, many regulation scholars see third party involvement and transparency as a way to keep regulators and regulated on the straight and narrow,[43] and the EC legal system is of course no stranger to reliance on individuals to ensure the application of the law. It is also suggested that a level of consensus on regulation improves implementation[44]; whilst this often stresses the acceptability of regulation to the regulated industry, easing relationships between an installation's operators and neighbours can be a very real benefit from a fully participative process.[45]

The substantive effect of public participation should be testable by reference to the actual outcomes of decisions. This is far from straightforward. It assumes first of all that there is some level of consensus as to the objectives of the decision, and so what constitutes a good outcome. And even if one assumes that a good outcome is the most environmentally protective outcome, there is legitimate disagreement about what environmental protection requires in any particular case, given the trade-offs and uncertainties involved in environmental protection. Moreover, a 'good' decision will inevitably incorporate other facets of the public interest, if only within the rubric of sustainable development. Even if the objective of a particular decision is clear, judgment is difficult: hindsight helps only to a limited degree. For example, a bad outcome does not necessarily mean that a decision was wrong[46]; the question of acceptable risk is only marginally less controversial retrospectively than prospectively. Revisiting and re-assessing decisions and the ways in which they were reached is an important part of environmental learning. Nevertheless, given the likelihood that the 'quality' of a decision is a contentious and normative question, rather than a simple empirical inquiry, the best thing that can be attempted is to fit decision-making to the nature of the decisions. There is no guarantee of environmentally positive outcomes, but the task should be to provide a process that incorporates a wide range of values.

---

[42] Dobson, above n 4. Dobson acknowledges that market instruments may also be useful.

[43] See for example, I Ayres and J Braithwaite, *Responsive Regulation* (Oxford, Oxford University Press, 1992); M Gunningham and P Grabosky, *Smart Regulation: Designing Environmental Policy* (Oxford, Oxford University Press, 1998); see ch 3 above.

[44] Note that this has been particularly influential in the US given the concern about high levels of litigation in that jurisdiction, and in that context does attempt to pre-empt dissent from environmental groups as well as industry. The purported benefits of consent are disputed, see C Coglianese, 'Is Consensus an Appropriate Basis for Regulatory Policy?' in EW Orts and K Deketelaere (eds), *Environmental Contracts: Comparative Approaches to Regulatory Innovation* (Boston, MA, Kluwer, 2000); GF Gaus, 'Reason, Justification and Consensus: Why Democracy Can't Have it All' in Bohman and Rehg, above n 4. This will be discussed further in the context of 'environmental agreements' in ch 8 below.

[45] See for example, J Petts, 'Waste Management Strategy Development: A Case Study of Community Involvement and Consensus-Building in Hampshire' (1995) 38 *Journal of Environmental Planning and Management* 519; N Stanley, 'Contentious Planning Disputes: An Insoluble Problem' [2000] *Journal of Planning and Environmental Law* 1226; Fischer, above n 38.

[46] Steele, above n 39.

In brief, the depth and variety of criticisms of the effectiveness of EC environmental law means that the 'substantive' rationale provides a powerful reinforcement of the process rationale for public participation in this context.

Conclusion: Between Substance and Process

The elusiveness of a majoritarian solution to the EU's democratic deficit increasingly turns scholarly discussion towards the 'new speak of transparency, responsibility, accountability and participation',[47] whilst the inability of regulators alone to deal convincingly with persistent environmental problems provokes a search for alternative sources of knowledge and problem-solving. The intention here is not to advocate one of the myriad approaches to participation or deliberation, but to try to identify what EC environmental law is doing with these very popular concepts.

Whether the distinctive understandings of the purpose for public participation are always consistent is of course a different issue. So for example, a search for 'good' decisions may have a narrower conception of the public than a search for more democracy; the nature of the debate within the participatory exercise is also likely to be different. Chapter six will discuss the potential for technical debate to drown out the lay public participation that one might expect from a 'democratising' perspective. Of course, the best way to achieve some reconciliation of the two perspectives is to keep in mind that environmental decisions are not technical, but normative, and so good decisions, as much as democratic decisions, require non-expert contributions.

So far, substance and process rationales have been considered separately. Some explanations of public participation might be placed between substance and process. In particular, the dominance of sustainable development in environmental policy has encouraged 'bottom up' solutions from the time of the Brundtland Report.[48] Not only does the 'justice' limb of sustainable development imply a 'democratising' ambition, the inherent value of public involvement, but sustainable development is also a multi-faceted, complex and normative objective, crying out for multiple perspectives and a range of knowledge. Principle 10 of the Rio Declaration states that '[e]nvironmental issues are best handled with the participation of all concerned citizens', and emphasises the importance of access to environmental information, 'the opportunity to participate in decision-making processes' and opportunities for legal redress and remedy[49]; more recently, the Johannesburg

---

[47] A Tomkins, 'Transparency and the Emergence of a European Administrative Law' (1999) 18 *Yearbook of European Law* 217, p 218; Harlow, above n 11. Chalmers, above n 24, even goes as far as to say that 'the strength of participation in its political processes has increasingly become the yardstick against which the legitimacy of the European Union is measured', p 127.

[48] World Commission on Environment and Development, *Our Common Future* (Oxford, Oxford University Press, 1987). See ch 2 above.

[49] *Rio Declaration on Environment and Development* (1992) available at http://www.un.org/documents/ga/conf151/aconf15126-1annex1.htm.

Declaration states that sustainable development requires 'broad-based participation in policy formulation, decision-making and implementation at all levels'.[50]

The Aarhus Convention on public participation begins to elaborate on the participatory aspect of sustainable development.[51] It does not, however, commit itself to any particular rationale for participation, and the recitals recognise diverse motivations, including the enhancement of 'the quality and the implementation of decisions' and 'public awareness of environmental issues', and the aim 'to strengthen public support for decisions on the environment'. The Convention is also intended to 'contribute to strengthening democracy'. Although the Aarhus Convention has very mixed motives, perhaps the clearest and strongest link is with improving environmental protection; not only are there no guarantees, but the success of this objective is not always clear retrospectively. The Aarhus Convention also draws links between human rights and public participation, confirming the existence of a human right, for present and future persons, to an environment 'adequate to his or her health and well-being'.[52] The now reasonably familiar conceptualisation of procedural environmental rights as human rights may enhance the gravity of procedural rights.[53] One of the reasons for linking environmental rights with procedure is the difficulty of putting in place rights to environmental quality. In particular, the definition of environmental quality involves difficult questions of prioritisation between different environmental goods, and between environmental protection and other public goods. As both an anthropocentric and an individualistic concept, however, the ability of human rights to protect either the collective good in the environment, or the environment itself, in anything other than a marginal and contingent manner is open to question.

Talk of rights in the Aarhus Convention seems to be mainly a substantive claim on participation: the rights are to enhance environmental quality. In the context of 'rights', a brief mention should be made of the possible relationship between process rights and emerging notions of citizenship, be that EU citizenship,[54] 'ecological citizenship'[55] or a combination of the two.[56] In this context, rights suggest more of an inherent value to participation. International and EU arrangements

---

[50] *Johannesburg Declaration on Sustainable Development* (2002), para 26, available at http://www.un.org/esa/sustdev/index.html.

[51] Above n 7.

[52] Art 1.

[53] The European Court of Human Rights, for example, also considers environmental rights in broadly process terms: *Guerra v Italy* (1998) 26 EHRR 357 considered the relationship between the provision of information on a facility and the right to a private and family life; *Lopez Ostra v Spain* (1995) 20 EHRR 277 required a fair balance to be struck between the area's economic interest and the applicant's effective enjoyment of her right to respect for her private and family life. Note that the Constitution provides for EU accession to the ECHR, Art I–9, and that Part II of the Constitution, incorporating the Charter on Fundamental rights includes a number of rights that may be called on in environmental law.

[54] See S Douglas-Scott, above n 19, pp 479–514; P Craig and G de Búrca, *EU Law: Text, Cases and Materials* (Oxford, Oxford University Press, 2003) pp 755–62.

[55] Dobson, above n 4.

[56] C Hilson, 'Greening Citizenship: Boundaries of Membership and the Environment' (2001) 13 *Journal of Environmental Law* 335; D McGillivray and J Holder, 'Locating EC Environmental Law' (2001) 20 *Yearbook of European Law* 139.

for public participation in environmental decision-making begin to expand notions of citizenship on environmental issues beyond the nation state. In the environmental sphere it is particularly important to match of citizenship rights with duties[57]; not only does a right to be heard imply a duty to listen, but public participation is claimed to enhance active environmental citizenship, in the form both of contribution to public debate and of taking environmentally responsible private decisions.

PUBLIC PARTICIPATION IN DECISION-MAKING AND THE EU

The Aarhus Convention applies to Community level decision-making, and although limited to environmental content, is not limited to bodies with specific roles in relation to the environment. As such it has a potentially extensive impact on EC decision-making, and provides a good framework for the examination of EC level public participation. Although the early response of the EC legislators to the Aarhus Convention was to push implementation to the national level,[58] they have now begun to take responsibility for its implementation at EC level. In particular, the Commission has put forward a proposal for the application of the Convention to EC institutions and bodies.[59]

The Aarhus Convention, notwithstanding a certain deference to national, or here regional, law and practice, rests on a basic expectation of extensive involvement in environmental decision-making at all levels. One of the most significant elements of the Aarhus Convention is its assumption that environmental interest groups are able to take advantage of the 'access principles', and their express inclusion in the definition of the 'public' or the 'public concerned'.[60] Given that involvement of the regulated industry is the starting point for much contemporary regulatory reform,[61] this distinct role for environmental interest groups provides a valuable alternative input, albeit subject to certain concerns developed below.

---

[57] Dobson, above n 4.

[58] See M Lee, 'Public Participation, Procedure and Democratic Deficit in EC Environmental Law' vol 3 *Yearbook of European Environmental Law* 193.

[59] European Commission, *Proposal For A Regulation of the European Parliament and of the Council on the Application of the Provisions of the Aarhus Convention on Access to Information, Public Participation in Decision-making and Access to Justice in Environmental Matters to EC Institutions and Bodies* COM (2003) 622 final.

[60] One the most significant elements of the Aarhus Convention is its clear valuing of environmental interest groups as bearers of the public interest. The 'public' is defined as 'natural or legal persons, and, in accordance with national legislation or practice, their associations, organisations or groups', Art 2(4). The 'public concerned', which features in most of the harder participatory rights, is 'the public affected or likely to be affected by or having an interest in, the environmental decision-making ... non-governmental organizations promoting environmental protection and meeting any requirements under national law shall be deemed to have an interest', Art 2(5).

[61] Think for example of the fashion of 'negotiated rule making' and 'co-regulation', in which regulators and regulated (with or often without external input) agree regulatory standards, see Orts and Deketelaere, above n 32; Commission, above n 8, p 21. Environmental agreements are discussed in ch 8 below.

The Aarhus Convention has three 'pillars', access to environmental information, participation in environmental decision-making and access to justice in environmental matters. This section will review EC implementation of each of these pillars in turn.

Access to Environmental Information

Access to information is a crucial element of a democratic society, a precondition of basic rights such as the right to vote, the right to free speech, the right to participate in decision-making, and certainly of any form of deliberation. The widespread perception that secrecy leads to mistrust, and that openness is the way to regain public confidence in government action is also very apparent in EC discussion of public participation.[62] Legislation on general access to documents at EC level seems to assume that openness has an inherent value, and is related to taking decisions close to the citizen.[63] Implementation of the Aarhus Convention at EC level, by contrast, seems to be justified largely on instrumental grounds, concentrating on the potential for improved implementation of environmental measures.[64] In this context, open access to information allows the public to police the environmental performance of polluters and public regulators, who in turn are aware that their decisions are subject to public scrutiny.[65] Particularly when public authorities are required actively to provide and disseminate information, environmental information tends to be seen as a tool by which to enhance environmental awareness, improving the likelihood of positive environmental decisions by individuals.

Access to information is the most detailed pillar of the Aarhus Convention. In common with most access to information regimes, subject to a number of exceptions, there is a right of access to environmental information without an interest having to be stated.[66] The detail of the Aarhus Convention's provisions on access to information will be discussed in chapter six below, in the context of rules on access to environmental information held by Member States.

[62] Much of the Commission's governance work could be cited here; see also ch 4 above.
[63] See the recitals to Reg 1049/2001 Regarding Public Access to European Parliament, Council and Commission Documents [2001] OJ L 145/43, especially Recitals 1 and 2; Declaration No 17 to the *Maastricht Treaty on European Union*. Note also Case C–58/94 *Netherlands v Council* [1996] ECR I–2169: 'openness of decision-making processes constitutes an innate feature of any democratic system and the right to information, including information in the hands of the public authorities, is a fundamental right of the individual', Opinion of AG Tesauro, para 6, and ECJ, para 35. Other decisions drawing links between democratic principles and access to information include Case T–14/98 *Hautala v Council* [1999] ECR II–2498, especially paras 80–3; Case C–353/99P *Council v Hautala* [2001] ECR I–9565; Case T–174/95 *Svenska Journalistforbundet v Council* [1998] ECR II–2289, para 66; Case T–211/00 *Kuijer v Council* [2002] ECR II–485, para 52.
[64] See the recitals to Commission, above n 40; Commission, above n 59.
[65] Note that the *Protocol to the Aarhus Convention on Pollutant Release and Transfer Registers*, Kiev 2003, available at http://www.unece.org/env/pp/prtr.htm introduces the idea that access to information can enhance 'corporate accountability'.
[66] Aarhus Convention, Art 4.

In order both to implement the Aarhus Convention, and to achieve consistency with Member State obligations in respect of access to environmental information,[67] the Commission has proposed that general Community law on access to information be adjusted in respect of 'environmental information',[68] the definition of which for these purposes closely follows the broad approach taken in the Aarhus Convention.[69] The changes felt necessary by the Commission are however rather marginal. For example 'institution' in the Regulation is to be read in respect of environmental information as 'community institution or body'; whilst this provides welcome clarity, the general rules have already had an impact on bodies other than the triumvirate of Commission, Council and Parliament.[70] The Proposal also provides access to documents regardless of nationality, as required by the Aarhus Convention; again, that seems to be the usual practice in any event.[71]

The position on general access to information in the EU has moved from a culture of secrecy, reflecting the diplomatic nature of international decision-making, through voluntary initiatives, to formal legal obligations of access to Community documents.[72] The value of 'transparency' is recognised by Treaty,[73] and would be enhanced by the Constitutional Treaty, which links transparency with 'good governance' and 'the participation of civil society' in the context of 'The Democratic Life of the Union'.[74] Transparency is also given increasing attention by the EC judiciary, which even uses the language of fundamental rights in respect of access to information.[75] The contribution of the European Ombudsman illustrates the additional potential of less legalistic approaches.[76] Whilst the principle of transparency is forcefully recognised, however, its implementation remains controversial. Rules on public access to documents have now been laid down by Regulation

---

[67] Dir 2003/04 on Public Access to Environmental Information and Repealing Council Directive 90/313/EC [2003] OJ L 41/26.

[68] Commission, above n 59.

[69] *Ibid*, Art 2(1)(e).

[70] For example, Reg 1049/2001 now applies directly to the European Environment Agency via an amendment to its constituting regulation, see Reg 1210/90 on the Establishment of the European Environment Agency and the European Environment Information and Observation Network [1990] OJ L 120/1, as amended, Art 6. Comitology committees also fall within the Regulation, because they have no independent existence beyond the Commission, Case T–188/97 *Rothmans International BV v Commission* [1999] ECR II–2463. The limit in the Commission's proposal is drawn at bodies acting in a judicial or legislative capacity, as per Art 2(2) Aarhus Convention.

[71] Aarhus Convention, Art 3(9); Commission, above n 59, Art 3; in respect of transboundary public participation at national level, see ch 6 below.

[72] See A Roberts, 'Multilateral Institutions and the Right to Information: Experience in the European Union' (2002) 8 *European Public Law* 255.

[73] Art 255 EC.

[74] Art I–50; see also Art III–399.

[75] Above n 63. Note that the cases referred to in this section generally discuss the institutional initiatives that preceded the current legislation.

[76] So for example the Ombudsman was largely responsible for the Commission's (admittedly limited) moves towards increased openness on Art 226 processes, see ch 3 above. For critical assessment of the Ombudsman's work in this field, see R Rawlings, 'Engaged Elites: Citizen Action and Institutional Attitudes in Commission Enforcement' (2000) 6 *European Law Journal* 28; PG Bonnor, 'Institutional Attitudes in Context: A Comment on Rawlings' Engaged Elites — Citizen Action and Institutional Attitudes in Commission Enforcement' (2001) 7 *European Law Journal* 114.

1049/2001,[77] which provides a right of access, within specified time limits,[78] and a requirement for reasoned decisions.[79]

Regulation 1049/2001 applies to documents, rather than information as in the Aarhus Convention, but the broad definition of 'document', extending to any medium including 'sound, visual or audiovisual recordings', means that this is less problematic than might be expected.[80] The right of access applies not only to documents produced by the institution, but also those received. This brings a crucial element of transparency to public participation in decision-making; the public has a right to know not only the position of the institutions, but also who is communicating with them and how. The obligation to list documents in a public register goes some way to reinforcing the monitoring of third party involvement in decision-making, although the content of the register is rather unspecified in the Regulation.[81]

Rights of access to information are generally subject to exceptions to allow for the protection of competing public interests. The grounds for refusing access to documents are set out in three main categories in the Regulation.[82] *First,* access shall be denied if it would undermine protection of the public interest in public security, defence and military matters, international relations or the financial, monetary or economic policy of the Community or a Member State, or if it would undermine the protection of the 'privacy and integrity of an individual'. *Secondly,* if access to documents would undermine the protection of commercial interests, court proceedings and legal advice, or the purpose of inspections, investigations and audits, access shall be refused, subject to a test of overriding public interest in disclosure. *Thirdly,* access to documents relating to a matter in which the decision has not been taken, or preparatory documents after the decision has been taken, shall be refused if disclosure would 'seriously undermine the institution's decision-making process', unless there is an overriding public interest in disclosure. In all cases, only harm to a recognised interest justifies denial of access[83]; the exceptions are not about the convenience of government, but about specific conflicting interests. The limitation of the third category of exceptions to cases in which the

---

[77] Reg 1049/2001, above n 63.

[78] Applications must be handled promptly, and within 15 working days, Reg 1049/2001, *ibid,* Art 7(1), extendable in exceptional circumstances by a further 15 working days, *ibid,* Art 7(3).

[79] *Ibid,* Art 7(1).

[80] *Ibid,* Art 3(a).

[81] *Ibid,* Art 11.

[82] *Ibid,* Art 4. Note also Art 9, limiting the personnel who can deal with a request for access to 'sensitive' documents. For statistical information on the use of the exceptions, see European Commission, *Report on the Implementation of the Principles in EC Regulation No 1049/2001 Regarding Public Access to European Parliament, Council and Commission Documents* COM (2004) 45 final. Those parts of a document not subject to an exception should be severed and disclosed, *ibid,* Art 4(8), previously *Hautala,* above n 63.

[83] See also Joined Cases C–74/98 and 189/98P *Netherlands and Van der Wal v Commission* [2002] ECR I–1 confirming that before denying access to any document, it must be established that disclosure would in fact harm the public interest, and that the institutions must assess documents *individually* not as a category; *Kuijer,* above n 63, provides that the risk of the public interest being undermined must be reasonable foreseeable and not purely hypothetical, para 56.

relevant interest is 'seriously undermined' emphasises that access is not to be lightly denied. The Commission has however observed the difficulty of distinguishing between 'undermining' an interest and 'seriously undermining' that interest,[84] particularly given that in either case, the harm to the recognised interest should nevertheless be incurred if the public interest in disclosure is overriding. Both the second and third categories of exception require documents to be disclosed if the public interest in disclosure is overriding. This is welcome; it appears, however, that an overriding public interest has never been used to justify going beyond the exception.[85]

The final exception to the duty to provide access to documents appears to contain no requirement either to establish harm to a recognised interest or to consider an overriding public interest in disclosure.[86] The Regulation allows a Member State to 'request the institution not to disclose a document originating from that Member State without its prior agreement'.[87] This exception has the potential to be highly restrictive of access rights, and its absolute character is inconsistent with the approach taken in the Aarhus Convention. The intention of this exception is to allow Member States to maintain their national rules on access to information, avoiding the granting of access by the back door.[88] Given that all Member States have commitments to the Aarhus Convention, not to mention obligations on access to environmental information under EC legislation,[89] the restriction should not cause problems in an environmental context. The nature of obligations in respect of environmental information could nevertheless be more transparent.

The Proposal for compliance with the Aarhus Convention would not affect the exceptions in the Regulation,[90] which go beyond the provisions of the Aarhus Convention in a number of ways, in addition to Member State 'requests' that information be withheld. First and most generally, the Aarhus Convention contains an obligation to interpret the exceptions in a restrictive way, which is not directly reflected in the Regulation, although the jurisprudence provides for restrictive interpretation of exceptions.[91] Secondly, the EC level access to information regime does not reflect the Aarhus Convention's expectation, discussed further in chapter six below, that requests for information relating to emissions

---

[84] Commission, above n 82, p 23.

[85] *Ibid*, p 24.

[86] Case T–76/02 *Messina v Commission*, 17 September 2003, not yet reported.

[87] Reg 1049/2001, above n 63, Art 4(5). The scope of this exception is somewhat restricted by the Council's restrictive interpretation of the concept of 'document originating from a Member State', to exclude the work of Member State representatives in the Council or its committees, on the basis that they are not outside the institution, Commission, above n 82, p 25.

[88] See also Reg 1049/2001, *ibid*, Art 5, requiring consultation in respect of access through the Member States to documents originating in the Community.

[89] Dir 2003/04 on Public Access to Environmental Information and Repealing Council Directive 90/313/EC [2003] OJ L41/26, see ch 6 below.

[90] Commission, above n 59.

[91] *Kuijer*, above n 63; *Van der* Wal, above n 83; Case T–105/95 *World Wildlife Fund UK v Commission* [1997] ECR II–313, para 56; Case T–124/96 *Interporc v Commission* [1998] ECR II–231.

into the environment will be treated more favourably than other information. And thirdly, the Aarhus Convention simply contains no exception relating to 'financial, monetary or economic policy'. Whilst case law deals with the first issue, it is perhaps anticipated that the final two issues will not arise: that information on emissions will generally be held at the national level, and that 'financial, monetary or economic policy' will not lead to environmental information disputes. Nevertheless, in this area if in no other, greater transparency would be welcome.[92]

On a slightly different note, it is surprising that the Commission did not include in its proposal an additional exception to allow, as under the Aarhus Convention, a refusal of access if the information would harm the environmental interest being protected; the example given in the Convention is information on the breeding sites of rare species. The Community institutions are not likely to generate this sort of information, and if it comes from a Member State, the Member State can prevent disclosure without having to give a reason.[93] There could however be problems if the relevant information comes from an external source other than the Member State. This is a potentially important omission, and the European Parliament has proposed an amendment to remedy it.[94]

To conclude, the EU's provisions on general access to environmental information go some way to complying with the requirements of the Aarhus Convention. The Commission has proposed some relatively low key amendments, and there are some further concerns that it is to be hoped are addressed as the legislation progresses.

As well as the right of access to existing information, the Aarhus Convention imposes duties on public authorities actively to collect and disseminate environmental information.[95] Under Regulation 1049/2001, the institutions are obliged to produce a register of documents, an important but under-specified obligation. Under the Proposal for the implementation of the Aarhus Convention, environmental information is to be organised 'with a view to its active and systematic dissemination to the public, in particular by means of computer telecommunication and/or electronic technology'.[96] The sort of information that should be available is set out a little more clearly, including an obligation on the Commission to publish reports on the state of the environment every four years. The Aarhus Convention 'where appropriate' also requires parties to establish:

> a coherent, nationwide system of pollution inventories or registers on a structured, computerized and publicly accessible database compiled through standardized reporting.[97]

---

[92] The European Parliament has proposed amendment on the emissions point, European Parliament First Reading, 31 March 2004.
[93] Reg 1049/2001, above n 63, Art 4(5).
[94] Above n 92.
[95] Aarhus Convention, Art 5.
[96] Commission, above n 59, Art 4(1).
[97] Aarhus Convention, Art 5(9).

This obligation has subsequently been developed by a *Protocol on Pollutant Release and Transfer Registers*.[98] It is implemented at EC level through the Integrated Pollution Prevention and Control (IPPC) Directive, which requires the Commission to publish an 'inventory of principle emissions and sources' every three years.[99] This inventory takes the form of the European Pollutant Emission Register (EPER).[100] The EPER is an important step towards the positive collection of useful environmental information. It is however limited to information on facilities regulated under the IPPC Directive (primarily large industrial installations), to emissions into air and water, and to substances regulated under IPPC, falling short of the Aarhus Convention and its Protocol in each of those respects. The Commission recognises the need to expand the principles behind the register.[101] The limitations of the EPER are perhaps simply an indication of the limitations of providing broad rights of access to environmental information through existing mechanisms. In the case of the IPPC Directive, the focus on particular industrial operations is the limitation; in the case of Regulation 1049/2001, it is the contentious and disputed nature of the right to access, something that should in principle have been settled in respect of environmental information at the time of signature of the Aarhus Convention.

Finally, it should be noted that rights of access to information do not automatically provide transparency. In particular, the ability of the lay public to process information depends on its presentation, which may be accessible only to experts, or only to the highly educated and highly motivated.[102] Documents under the Regulation are simply provided as they exist. Some element of 'translation'[103] is inevitable if technical information is to be used by lay participants, albeit that this enhances the political sensitivity of control of information. In respect of environmental information, the Aarhus Convention says very little, and the Commission's proposal for implementation simply makes Community bodies

---

[98] Above n 65. The Protocol is not yet in force. Like the Aarhus Convention itself, it requires 16 ratifications. See http://www.unece.org/env/pp/prtr.htm.

[99] Dir 96/61 on Integrated Pollution Prevention and Control [1996] OJ L 257/26, Art 15(3). The IPPC Directive is discussed in ch 6 below.

[100] Commission Decision 2000/479 on the Implementation of A European Pollutant Emission Register (EPER) According to Article 15 of Council Directive 96/61/EC Concerning Integrated Pollution Prevention and Control (IPPC) [2000] OJ L 192/36. The EPER is available at http://www.eper.cec.eu.int/.

[101] European Commission, *On the Road to Sustainable Production: Progress in Implementing Council Directive 96/61/EC concerning Integrated Pollution Prevention and Control* COM (2003) 354 final, p 24; European Commission, *Towards a Thematic Strategy on the Prevention and Recycling of Waste* COM (2003) 301 final, sees this as an opportunity to improve access to information, p 24. Note also Decision 280/2004 Concerning a Mechanism for Monitoring Community Greenhouse Gas Emissions and for Implementing the Kyoto Protocol [2004] OJ L 49/1, providing for Member States to report anthropogenic greenhouse gas emissions to the Commission, which draws up a Community inventory.

[102] Whilst it is not suggested that this is a question of presentation, it appears that the *general* right of access to documents at EC level is exercised primarily for academic purposes or professional purposes, for example by 'lobbies trying to influence decision-making', presumably including environmental interest groups, Commission above n 82, p 11. Whilst one might not expect individual requests, it is perhaps surprising that journalists make very little use of the right.

[103] Black, above n 3.

subject to the same obligation as national bodies to provide 'up to date, accurate and comparable' environmental information. There is more concern with 'user friendliness' in respect of positive dissemination of environmental information, as for example in the EPER.

Public Participation

The EU has certain relatively long-standing arrangements for formal consultation or involvement of particular interests,[104] as well as many less formal relationships. Further formalisation of consultation or public participation in EC decision-making has been prominent in efforts to respond to the democratic deficit, and the Commission is particularly strongly implicated. The Treaty of Amsterdam introduced a duty on the Commission to consult widely before issuing proposals[105]; this is being pursued in the context of the *European Governance* project, which quite explicitly intends to feed into efforts at democratisation of the EU.[106]

The Aarhus Convention provides for public participation in decision-making at three stages: 'decisions on specific activities'[107]; 'plans, programmes and policies relating to the environment[108]; and 'the preparation of executive regulations and/or generally applicable legally binding normative instruments'.[109] Any could implicate the EC institutions; the first is however most commonly relevant at Member State level, and will be discussed in more detail in chapter six below.[110] Participation in relation to 'plans, programmes and policies relating to the environment' is subject to Article 7 of the Aarhus Convention. On plans and programmes, Parties shall make:

> appropriate practical and/or other provisions for the public to participate during the preparation of plans and programmes relating to the environment, within a transparent and fair framework, having provided the necessary information to the public.

[104] The 'social dialogue' is the most formalised participatory process, Arts 138–9. The Economic and Social Committee (ESC) as a form of institutionalised interest representation should also be considered. Its expansion from predominantly industry and worker representation suggests a role in the current debate. See S Smismans and L Mechi, *The ESC in the Year 2000* (Brussels, Economic and Social Committee, 2000). On the ESC's own efforts regarding civil society, see S Smismans, 'European Civil Society: Shaped by Discourses and Institutional Interests' (2003) *European Law Journal* 473. The role of the ESC in consultation is confirmed in European Commission, *Towards a Reinforced Culture of Consultation and Dialogue — General Principles and Minimum Standards for Consultation of Interested parties by the Commission* COM (2002) 704 final.

[105] Protocol No 7 to the Treaty of Amsterdam on the Approach of the Parties to Subsidiarity and Proportionality, para 9.

[106] See the Commission's website on the subject, especially http://europa.eu.int/comm/governance/ governance_eu/index_en.htm; European Commission, *Preparatory Work for the White Paper*, also available on the governance website.

[107] Aarhus Convention, Art 6.

[108] *Ibid*, Art 7.

[109] *Ibid*, Art 8.

[110] Note the discussion of EC level authorisation of GMOs in ch 9 below.

Provisions on 'reasonable time frames', the requirement for 'early' and 'effective' public participation, and the obligation to take 'due account' of the outcome of the public participation are also incorporated. The Aarhus Convention's provisions on 'policies relating to the environment' involve simply the obligation to 'endeavour' to provide opportunities to participate 'to the extent appropriate'. Article 8, on 'executive regulations and other generally applicable legally binding rules' requires parties to 'strive to promote effective public participation at an appropriate stage, and while options are still open'. The provisions on policies and executive regulations are, then, negligible in terms of formal obligation, although they suggest the desirability of inclusive processes across the board.

The Commission's Proposal for the implementation of the Aarhus Convention at EC level is concerned only with 'plans and programmes', and requires all Community institutions and bodies to make arrangements for public participation during the preparation of 'plans and programmes relating to the environment'.[111] The arrangements would have to provide for reasonable time frames, early and effective consultation, and for 'due account' to be taken of the outcome of the participation. The plans or programmes affected are those that 'contribute to or are likely to have significant effects on, the achievement of the objectives of Community environmental policy' as laid down in environmental action programmes; the environmental action programmes themselves are also included. Plans and programmes are not defined.[112] The assumption throughout Aarhus and Aarhus implementation seems to be that distinguishing plans and programmes from other measures, particularly 'policies', which are not subject to legislative intervention, will be without incident; that remains to be seen. 'Financial or budget plans or programmes' are explicitly excluded from the Proposal, on the basis that they 'do not as such have a significant direct effect on the environment'.[113] Given the recurrent controversy over funding of environmentally damaging initiatives, and the general policy of integration of environmental considerations into other areas, this is a startlingly blunt conclusion.

The obligation on the institutions will be to formalise policy on public participation, a project currently most advanced in the Commission, through the European governance project. The *White Paper on European Governance* is permeated by the desirability of 'opening up the policy making process to get more people and organisations involved in shaping and delivering EU policy'.[114] 'Civil society',[115] largely composed of organised interest groups, seems to be the prime beneficiary of the Commission's focus on public participation. There are optimists

---

[111] Commission, above n 59.

[112] Commission, *ibid*, defines them as plans or programmes prepared or adopted by a community institution or body, required by 'legislative, regulatory or administrative provisions', Art 2(f).

[113] *Ibid*, p 9.

[114] Commission, above n 8, p 3.

[115] The Commission provides a lengthy list, including: 'trade unions and employer's organisations ("social partners"); non-governmental organisations; professional associations; charities; grass-roots organisations; organisations that involve citizens in local and municipal life with a particular contribution from churches and religious communities', *ibid*, p 14. G de Búrca and N Walker, 'Law and

in the search for real direct engagement of the lay public in decision-making, and a number of cheering examples of public involvement at local and national (or why not supranational) level can be identified.[116] However, it is probably realistic of the Commission not to expect widespread direct participation of individual citizens in EU policy setting. The complexity and specialist conduct of the policy debate is likely to exclude, even if the complexity and specialist nature of the EU institutions does not. That is not to say that efforts to engage individuals should not be pursued. However, in the meantime, the recognition, through the Aarhus Convention and the governance project, that environmental groups have interests in the environment, and rights capable of being infringed, goes some way to filling an important gap, in particular because industry is always likely to be closely involved in environmental decision-making.

Since the White Paper, the Commission has set out minimum standards of consultation, the 'overall rationale' of which 'is to ensure that all relevant parties are properly consulted'.[117] This is the type of approach foreseen by the Commission for all institutions and bodies in respect of the implementation of the Aarhus Convention.[118] The Commission's minimum standards of consultation apply to major policy initiatives across the board,[119] rather than specifically to environmental plans and programmes, and the Commission has undertaken to complete this framework in order to comply with the Aarhus Convention,[120] which in particular is not limited to 'major policy initiatives'.

One of the key requirements of the Commission's minimum standards on consultation is that the Commission ensure 'adequate coverage' in a consultation process of 'those affected by the policy; those who will be involved in implementation of the policy; or bodies that have stated objectives giving them a direct interest in the policy', taking also into account 'the wider impact of the policy on other policy areas, eg environmental interest', as well as 'the need to involve non-organised interests, where appropriate'.[121] Along similar lines, the Commission's Proposal for Aarhus implementation, consistently with the Aarhus Convention, would require the Community institution or body to *identify* 'the public which may participate ... including relevant non-governmental organisations, such as those promoting environmental protection and other organisations concerned.'[122]

Transnational Civil Society: Upsetting the Agenda?' (2003) 9 *European Law Journal* 387, provides a brief history of the idea; see K Armstrong, 'Rediscovering Civil Society: the European Union and the White Paper on Governance' (2002) 8 *European Law Journal* 102, on the ambiguity of the phrase.

[116] See for example, Fischer, above n 38.
[117] Commission, above n 104, p 3.
[118] Commission, above n 59.
[119] Major policy initiatives are those initiatives subject to 'extended impact assessment', which is decided on the basis of the Commission's Annual Policy Strategy or Work Programme, taking into account 'substantial economic, environmental and/or social impact on a specific sector', 'significant impact on major interested parties' and whether a proposal represents a 'major policy reform'. See European Commission, *Impact Assessment* COM (2002) 276 final.
[120] Commission, above n 59, p 15.
[121] Commission, above n 104, p 20.
[122] Commission, above n 59, Art 8(d).

The selection of participants raises obvious concerns about the extent of institutional control over 'public' participation. In particular, the likely favouring of familiar and predictable groups creates incentives for civil society not to rock the boat. Groups with challenging ecological viewpoints could easily be excluded as unhelpful or unconstructive. Similarly, notwithstanding the Commission's acknowledgement of the value of the non-Brussels standpoint,[123] it is clear that the Commission prefers to work with pan-European organisations.[124] Aside from the perhaps legalistic point that the Aarhus Convention does not permit discrimination as to 'citizenship, nationality or domicile, and, in the case of a legal person, as to where it has its registered seat or an effective centre of its activities',[125] there may be concerns if local, *ad hoc*, or poorly resourced organisations are marginalised by transnational, highly bureaucratic organisations. The latter are likely to be more distant from the broader public,[126] meaning that an overall dilution of participatory democracy is possible.[127] Notwithstanding these reservations, however, an obligation to look for participants does recognise that public participation does not simply happen, and that some thought needs to be paid to who should be involved; public participation is not, from the institution's perspective, a passive exercise.

The Commission's minimum standards on consultation also place some emphasis on the 'proper balance' between representatives of 'social and economic bodies', 'large and small organisations or companies', 'wider constituencies ... and specific target groups' and 'organisations in the European Union and those in non-member countries'.[128] Possible responsibilities in this respect are hinted at by the Court of First Instance (CFI) in *UEAPME*.[129] This case involved binding employment legislation adopted by Council, but following negotiations between the 'social partners', rather than the normal legislative process.[130] The legislation was challenged by a group excluded from the negotiations. The factual

---

[123] Commission, above n 104, pp 11–12.

[124] Note that funding is targeted at environmental groups 'active at a European level'. Decision 466/2002 Laying Down a Community Action Programme Promoting Non-Governmental Organisations Primarily Active in the Field of Environmental Protection [2002] OJ L 75/1 requires 'activities covering at least three European countries', although two is acceptable in certain circumstances, Art 2(b).

[125] Aarhus Convention, Art 3(9).

[126] See Reale, above n 24, on pan-European employment groups, which may have no direct connection at all with individuals, and only a weak link with member organisations. The European Environmental Bureau is an environmental interest group based in Brussels that brings together national environmental groups, in a 'federation'. For details, see the EEB website: http://www.eeb.org/Index.htm.

[127] See Armstrong, above n 115, suggesting that transnational organised civil society may suffer from the same sorts of legitimacy problems as transnational governance more generally. Also Cram, above n 14, on the importance of considering the relationship between European and national levels of 'governance'.

[128] Commission, above n 104, p 20.

[129] Case T–135/96 *Union Europeenne de L'Artisanat et des Petites et Moyennes Entreprises (UEAPME) v Council* [1998] ECR II–2335.

[130] Under Art 139 EC. For discussion, see Reale, above n 24; B Bercusson, 'Democratic Legitimacy and European Labour Law' (1999) 28 *Industrial Law Journal* 153.

context is very different from that considered here, and the CFI bases its decision at least in part on the absence of the European Parliament from the legislative process, which is by no means the suggestion in the context of the Aarhus Convention. Nevertheless, the decision brings to the fore the legitimacy of the participation of outsiders in lawmaking, and the CFI was willing to review in a fairly intensive manner the institutions' consideration of the cumulative representativeness of the participants. Judicial recognition of the need to give a thought to who is engaged in a process, from the perspective of democratic principles and legitimacy, is important. The application of the notion of representativity by the CFI is however decidedly brisk. The identification of the interests at stake in a decision, and the way in which they should be represented, is not only very complex, but also very far from more familiar notions of democracy and equality.

One manifestation of the 'democratisation' talk in governance is a specifically European approach to arguments that public participation (especially deliberative participation) enhances political or civil awareness, and encourages 'active citizenship'. The Commission hopes that involvement of civil society will 'Europeanise' society, channelling public views to decision-makers, getting 'citizens more actively involved in achieving the Union's objectives', and indeed raising European consciousness generally.[131] There is a considerable element of wishful thinking here. Aside from anything else, 'civil society', and specifically environmental interest groups, may be unable or unwilling to perform an awareness-raising role[132]; nor can the necessary level of connection with the grassroots be assumed. This instrumental view of civil society as an agency for democratisation is unconvincing, but there is also a more general gap between the rhetoric of the governance project and the mechanisms provided. The *White Paper on European Governance* does not go far beyond a 'business as usual' approach to consultation, aiming to elicit the pre-formed views of recognised groups.[133] Environmental interest groups in no way represent the public, and they are not necessarily well-connected with their own membership. Nor do environmental interest groups, in any straightforward way, represent the public interest, because a range of legitimate public interests compete with environmental protection. Even the environmental interest is multi-dimensional: for example, it cannot be assumed that local and international environmental groups share interests, particularly if a measure that is arguably environmentally progressive on a global scale imposes an environmental burden on a particular and identifiable community.[134]

---

[131] Commission, above n 8, especially p 15.

[132] A Warleigh, '"Europeanising" Civil Society: NGOs as Agents of Political Socialisation' (2001) 39 *Journal of Common Market Studies* 619.

[133] See de Búrca and Walker, above n 115; Curtin, above n 14, criticises the concentration on selected groups and fixed stages in decision-making, which misses more open and dynamic debate; P Steinberg, 'Agencies, Co-Regulation and Comitology: And What About Politics' in Joerges, Meny and Weiler, above n 14; P Magnette, 'European Governance and Civic Participation: Can the European Union be Politicised?' in Joerges, Meny and Weiler, *ibid*.

[134] For example, energy from waste incinerators, rail freight depots, wind farms.

The Commission attempts to provide incentives for interest groups to reflect on their role, proposing an exchange: 'partnership arrangements' would be established in particular areas, 'committing the commission to additional consultation in return for more guarantees of openness and representativity of the organisations consulted'.[135] Civil society groups would be expected to follow 'the principles of good governance', that is 'openness, participation, accountability, effectiveness and coherence', as well as proving their 'capacity to relay information' or 'lead debates in Member States'.[136] This sort of oversight has risks, particularly the co-option of a social movement.[137] It could change the nature of the movement, involving the moderation of environmental demands, and the adoption of the institutional agenda. Increased bureaucratisation and Europeanisation enhances risks of a loss of contact with membership.[138] If the role of voluntary action and free debate is reduced by organisation, an overall dilution of participatory democracy is the paradoxical possibility. The Commission's subsequent minimum standards on consultation seem to be somewhat less intrusive. It must 'be apparent' in respect of participants both 'which interests they represent' and 'how inclusive that representation is'; this is crucial minimum transparency in participation, 'who is being consulted and why'.[139] The rush to grant rights to interest groups raises the distinct possibility that groups will be formed specifically to take advantage of those rights; not all such groups will be pursuing the sorts of public interests we might expect, and the emergence of 'public interest groups' pursuing an industry agenda is perfectly feasible. In these circumstances, the Commission's concern about who a lobby represents becomes extremely important. The Commission also maintains that the intention is not 'to create new bureaucratic hurdles in order to restrict the number of those that can participate in consultation processes', but that participation remains open to all.[140] The risk of undue interference nevertheless remains, as does the risk that the Commission will only speak to a narrow section of self-consciously European society. Although the Commission's governance proposals are framed in terms of greater inclusion, they carry with them matching risks of exclusion, particularly of groups unable or unwilling to make the arrangements that the Commission seeks.

The importance of public interest groups in EC decisions is not new. The political dynamics of early European integration,[141] including the relative weakness of

---

[135] Commission, above n 8, p 4. See *UEAPME*, above n 129, which concentrates on collective representativeness of groups consulted.
[136] Commission, *ibid*, p 17.
[137] J Dryzek *et al*, *Green States and Social Movements: Environmentalism in the United States, United Kingdom, Germany and Norway* (Oxford, Oxford University Press, 2003).
[138] Armstrong, above n 115; B Hicks, 'Setting Agendas and Shaping Activism: EU Influence on Central and Eastern European Environmental Movements' in J Carmin and SD VanDeveer (eds), *EU Enlargement and the Environment: Institutional Change and Environmental Policy in Central and Eastern Europe* (New York, Frank Cass Publishers, 2004) discusses the dangers in central and eastern Europe.
[139] Commission, above n 104, p 17.
[140] *Ibid*, p 11.
[141] S Mazey and J Richardson, 'Environmental Groups and the EC: Challenges and Opportunities' (1992) 1 *Environmental Politics* 109.

the European Parliament in terms of both legitimacy and power, together with the small size of the Commission and its resulting need for external expertise, is thought to have favoured public interest groups. Fragmented decision-making also increased access points to decision-makers, and environmental interest groups did not face the same barriers to EU cooperation as firms in economic competition. Notwithstanding their historical significance, however, environmental interest groups face clear weaknesses relative to industry, in terms both of resources and of influence in sections of institutions that are not explicitly 'environmental'.[142] There is a danger that formal equality between environmental interest groups and industry, coupled with practical differences, creates simply an illusion of full involvement. Public funding achieves some parity of resources with industry groups, but enhances concerns about independence and autonomous priority setting,[143] not to mention vulnerability to changes in government priorities. The governance White Paper is marked by the desire of the Commission to consolidate its own centrality in the Community decision-making process. It is important that civil society is not used to legitimise the Commission bureaucracy, without a meaningful change in participatory practice.

To conclude, important steps are being taken that should allow environmental interests a clearer representation in decision-making. The Commission's approach, however, raises certain concerns, in particular about further exclusion and about over ambitious claims.

Access to Justice

The third pillar of the Aarhus Convention imposes obligations in respect of 'access to justice'. Rules on standing govern who is permitted to invoke the judicial process to challenge the breach of, for current purposes, environmental law. Standing in the environmental sphere has required considerable thought in all jurisdictions, mainly because traditional approaches allow recourse to the law only if individual interests or rights are harmed. This rarely captures the collective and diffuse nature of harm to environmental interests. Environmental harms can affect one or a small group disproportionately or very severely, but often, for example chronic air pollution or loss of biodiversity, affect large numbers of people in not readily perceptible ways.

The access to justice pillar of the Aarhus Convention is closely tied to the other two pillars. Article 9(1) provides for review of a refusal or failure to respond to a request for access to information, discussed above. Appeal under Regulation 1049/2001 takes the form of a 'confirmatory application' to the institution that

---

[142] See the detailed discussion in W Grant, D Matthews and P Newell, *The Effectiveness of European Union Environmental Policy* (Basingstoke, MacMillan Press, 2000), ch 2; P Newell and W Grant, 'Environmental NGOs and EU Environmental Law' (2000) *Yearbook of European Environmental Law* 225.

[143] The Commission does fund environmental interest groups. See Decision 466/2002, above n 124.

made the decision, asking it to revisit the decision, with a subsequent right to take action before the ombudsman or CFI.[144] Article 9(2) of the Aarhus Convention provides for the challenge of substantive or procedural legality in any decision subject to Article 6 (decision-making on projects), and also 'where so provided for under national law' any decision subject to 'other relevant provisions' of the Convention. Standing depends on the question of 'sufficient interest' or 'impairment of a right', depending on domestic law; environmental interest groups that comply with the Convention definition of 'the public concerned'[145] are explicitly deemed to have a 'sufficient interest' or 'rights capable of being impaired'. Finally, Article 9(3) provides for access to administrative or judicial procedures to challenge acts and omissions by private and public bodies that contravene domestic law relating to the environment; it is for national (or EC) law to lay down the criteria for standing. This hints at rights of action against private polluters; no such innovation has been put in place at EC level.

Generally, with the possible exception of review of failure to provide access to environmental information, access to justice in the Aarhus Convention is strongly boxed in by reference to national law. There is undoubtedly an assumption that broad standing is desirable, but restricted access to justice is perhaps more at odds with the spirit than the letter of the Convention.

Article 230 EC provides for claims against the Community institutions. The Member States and institutions are 'privileged' applicants, with absolute access. Ordinary private litigants can challenge only 'a decision addressed to that person' or a more general measure that is 'of direct and individual concern'.[146] The interpretation by the European Court of Justice (ECJ) of 'direct and individual concern' excludes most litigation over diffuse interests, paradigmatically environmental protection. 'Direct concern' requires that the Community measure directly affects the legal situation of the litigant, and leaves no discretion to those who have the task of implementing it. For natural and legal persons to be regarded as 'individually concerned' by a measure not addressed to them, the measure must affect their position by reason of certain attributes peculiar to them, or by reason of a factual situation which differentiates them from all other persons and distinguishes them individually.[147] The EC judiciary has said very little on public interest litigation, that is the standing of an environmental interest group in representation of the public interest. As such, environmental interest groups have to claim access on the same grounds as individuals, with very apparent limitations.[148]

This very conservative approach to locus standi has undergone some fairly dramatic reversals of fortune in recent cases. The *Greenpeace* case is the infamous

---

[144] Reg 1049/2001, above n 63, Arts 7(2) and 8.
[145] See above n 60.
[146] Art 230 EC.
[147] Case 25/62 *Plaumann v Commission* [1962] ECR 207. For detailed examination of the complex case law, see for example F Ragolle, 'Access to Justice for Private Applicants in the Community Legal Order: Recent (R)evolutions' (2003) 28 *European Law Review* 90.
[148] C Harlow, 'Towards a Theory of Access for the European Court of Justice' (1993) 12 *Yearbook of European Law* 213. Note also that 'individuals' are generally corporate litigants, *ibid*.

starting point.[149] In this case, Greenpeace, together with local individuals and local groups, attempted to challenge a Commission decision to grant funding to Spain for the construction of two power stations, arguing breach of environmental law. Standing was denied to both Greenpeace and the local residents on the basis of the conservative interpretation of 'individual concern' outlined above.[150] Greenpeace was denied standing on the basis that the members it claimed to represent lacked standing: none of the local residents was affected in a way that distinguished them from 'all the people who live or pursue an activity in the areas concerned'.[151] This approach extends even to the potential for personal injury. For example, standing was denied in respect of an attempted challenge against nuclear testing in the Pacific, because the applicants were not affected any differently from all other inhabitants of Polynesia[152]; apparently, the more extensive the environmental harm, the less accessible the legal remedy.

Two recent cases provided the opportunity for a rethink.[153] *Unión de Pequeños Agricultores (UPA)*[154] involved a challenge to a regulation on the common organisation of the market in oils and fats. In *Jégo-Quéré*,[155] a fishing company applied to the Court for the annulment of provisions requiring certain fishing vessels to use nets with a minimum mesh size. In *UPA*, the CFI held the application to be manifestly inadmissible on the ground that the members of the association were not individually concerned by the provisions of the regulation. Advocate General Jacobs, on appeal to the ECJ, took a more liberal approach to standing, and his Opinion clearly exercised a considerable influence on the CFI in its subsequent decision in *Jégo-Quéré*.

The Advocate General's Opinion and the CFI judgment bring out very clearly the difficulties of the orthodox, narrow approach to standing. *Greenpeace* assumes that litigants have alternative routes to court, specifically either proceedings before a national court plus a reference to the ECJ for a preliminary ruling under Article 234 EC, or an action based on the non-contractual liability of the Community. As only the Community Courts are able to make a ruling of invalidity of a Community measure, some route to Luxembourg is crucial. The preliminary ruling procedure may not, however, provide adequate and effective judicial protection for a number of reasons, including especially the gap in protection if there is no national implementing act that could form the basis of an action before national courts. The CFI emphasises that using illegality as a defence after violating the

---

[149] Case T–585/93 *Stichting Greenpeace Council v Commission* [1995] ECR II–2205; Case C–321/95P *Stichting Greenpeace Council v Commission* [1998] ECR I–1651.

[150] There was also a question as to the 'directness' of concern of the funding (rather than the construction) decision. For criticism, see L Kramer, *Casebook on EU Environmental Law* (Oxford, Hart Publishing, 2002), pp 403–12.

[151] Case T–585/93, above n 149, para 54.

[152] Case T–219/95 *Danielsson v Commission* [1995] ECR II–3051.

[153] For discussion, see JA Usher, 'Direct and Individual Concern — an Effective Remedy or a Conventional Solution?' (2003) 28 *European Law Review* 575; Ragolle, above n 147.

[154] Case C–50/00P *Unión de Pequeños Agricultores v Council* [2002] ECR I–6677.

[155] Case T–177/01 *Jégo-Quéré and Cie SA v Commission* [2002] ECR II–2365.

rules laid down in Community law 'does not constitute an adequate means of judicial protection. Individuals cannot be required to breach the law in order to gain access to justice.'[156] The delay implied by reliance on Article 234 could in any event make all the difference in a case such as *Greenpeace*.[157] Nor would an action for damages against the Community institutions satisfactorily protect the interests of the individual affected. It cannot 'result in the removal from the Community legal order of a measure', and would not address 'all the factors which may affect the legality of that measure, being limited instead to the censuring of sufficiently serious infringements of rules of law intended to confer rights on individuals.'[158] The CFI emphasised the importance of the right to an effective remedy in its citation of both the European Convention on Human Rights, and the Charter of Fundamental Rights.

Both Advocate General Jacobs and the CFI would reinterpret 'individual concern' in a more liberal manner. According to the Advocate General:

> a person is to be regarded as individually concerned by a Community measure where, by reason of his particular circumstances, the measure has, or is liable to have, a substantial adverse effect on his interests.[159]

The CFI would define individual concern around the individual's 'legal position' rather than interests. An applicant is individually concerned:

> if the measure in question affects his legal position, in a manner which is both definite and immediate, by restricting his rights or by imposing obligations on him. The number and the position of other persons who are likewise affected by the measure, or who may be so, are of no relevance in that regard.[160]

The difference between the two propositions is difficult to assess, in particular because the concepts of interests, rights and obligations were not explored. The intention was clearly to liberalise standing, which would no doubt have been welcomed by environmental interest groups. The extent to which an environmental interest group would benefit from the reformulations, however, is not clear, and depends on whether environmental interest groups would be deemed capable of holding the relevant rights or interests, as well as the extent to which they could piggy back on the rights or interests of their members in any particular case.[161]

The developments in these two cases could have constituted a major advance in locus standi before the EU courts. However, the ECJ's decision in *UPA* confirmed

---

[156] *Jégo-Quéré, ibid*, para 45.
[157] The availability of interim relief varies around the EU. See the discussion of Jacobs AG, *UPA*, above n 154, para 44.
[158] *Ibid*, para 46.
[159] *Ibid*, para 60.
[160] *Jégo-Quéré*, above n 155, para 51.
[161] Usher, above n 153, is of the view that these alternative approaches would not liberalise public interest litigation. Note the approach of the Aarhus Convention to the holding of rights and interests by environmental interest groups, above n 60.

its longstanding case law, notwithstanding the novel approach of its Advocate General.[162] The ECJ rejected any revised approach to 'individual concern', making the highly contentious assertion that the CFI's approach would empty the phrase of meaning. The Court takes the position that it is for the Member States to fill any lacunae in access to justice at national level, and that any change on access to justice at EC level would have to come from Treaty revision.[163]

Given that Treaty reform was very much on the agenda at the time of the decision, the suggestion that the Court's very narrow approach to the Treaty reflects the will of the drafters is more convincing than usual. Modest, but somewhat unpredictable, change can be found in the Constitutional Treaty.[164] The requirement for 'individual concern' is dropped in respect of a 'regulatory act' which 'does not entail implementing measures'. This change rests on the distinction drawn in the Constitution between 'legislative acts' and 'non-legislative acts', the operation of which is not yet entirely clear.[165] A 'regulation'[166] under the Constitution is a non-legislative measure, that is an implementing or administrative measure, of general application. Access to justice under the proposed changes would be contingent on the legal nature of the act rather than the nature of the harm caused by the measure. In particular, it seems unlikely that access is widened for environmental interest groups in a case such as *Greenpeace*, discussed above.

The provisions of the Aarhus Convention on access to justice are notably deferential to national (or here EC) law, but in line with the spirit of the Convention, the Commission is proposing moves to broaden standing in the environmental context. The Commission uses the concept of the 'qualified entity' as the reference point for standing. A qualified entity is 'an independent and non-profit-making legal person, which has the objective to protect the environment', and which has been legally constituted for more than two years, with audited accounts for that period. It has to be 'active at Community level'; this implies coverage of at least three Member States.[167] Following the ECJ's conclusion that a change of approach would require Treaty amendment, providing these environmental groups with review is a delicate task. The Proposal would allow qualified entities to request an

---

[162] Following its Advocate General, the Court rejects an argument taken from the judgment in *Greenpeace*, namely that a direct action for annulment before the Community Courts will be available where it can be shown that national procedural rules do not allow an individual to bring proceedings to contest the validity of the Community measure at issue, para 43.

[163] It is notorious that the Court has not always been so cautious in its interpretation of Treaty rules on access to justice, in particular allowing Parliament standing in Case 70/88 *Parliament v Council* [1991] ECR I–4529, before the Treaty gave Parliament privileged standing.

[164] Art III–365(4). Usher, above n 153, discusses the Convention work on access to justice.

[165] Arts I–33–35. For discussion of the difficult nature of the distinction in the environmental context, see J Jans and J Scott, 'The Convention on the Future of Europe: An Environmental Perspective' (2003) 15 *Journal of Environmental Law* 323.

[166] Assuming that 'regulatory act' in Art III–365(4) implies 'regulation'.

[167] Commission, above n 59, Art 12. Qualified entities can be recognised either in advance or on an ad hoc basis; the same criteria apply in either case. Note the similar approach in respect of access to justice in the Member States, ch 6 below.

internal review of an administrative decision or omission.[168] That would lead to a decision addressed to the 'qualified entity'. There is then explicit provision for judicial review of that decision.[169] Whether this ruse proves successful at persuading the Courts to look at the disputed environmental decision behind the response to the request for review remains to be seen. In any event, the exclusion of the individual, the local and the *ad hoc* is very notable; the dominance of a small number of exclusively environmental European organisations, equally so.[170] The requirement in the Aarhus Convention that proceedings be 'timely' and especially 'not prohibitively expensive' is not directly addressed,[171] and would be a serious challenge for the EC judicial system. However, the provision for internal review goes some way to providing informal administrative justice, as indeed does access to the European Ombudsman.

Conclusions

Considerable progress has been made in responding to expectations of openness and consultation at EC level, even if talk of democratisation is somewhat ambitious. Something should be said in conclusion on reason giving, which although not a specific principle of the Aarhus Convention, does feature in support of other rights, and is also a key element of administrative probity more generally.[172] Whilst there is obviously a danger that 'boiler plate' reasons will be attached to any decision simply with an eye to judicial review, the obligation to give reasons does have potentially salutary effects on decision-making, encouraging attention to be paid to the factors that should influence a decision, as well as enhancing accountability and providing a means for challenging a decision. The broad acceptance of widespread public participation in decision-making suggests that the reasons for a decision should also be broadly based, since open participation assumes the relevance of a range of perspectives, ethical, political, economic, scientific, to environmental decisions. The appearance of neutrality and objectivity provided by scientific or technical evidence is a great comfort to decision-makers and makes the transition to more extensive grounds for decision-making difficult. This can be reinforced by legal requirements for decision-making based on expertise, as discussed in chapter four above. Clothing value judgments in technical language, however, distorts lines of accountability and transparency. If decision-makers are to rationalise their decisions in a sophisticated and accountable way, they need comparably robust information on public opinion and the range of public values: broadly based participation, providing qualitative as well as quantitative

---

[168] Commission, *ibid*, Art 9.

[169] *Ibid*, Art 11.

[170] It should also be noted that the Commission's proposals for Aarhus implementation, *ibid*, explicitly exclude Arts 226–8, that is Commission enforcement measures.

[171] Aarhus Convention, Art 9(4).

[172] Art 253 EC; there is a long line of case law. For discussion of reason-giving, see Harlow, above n 11, pp 159–65.

information, is crucial in this respect. Whilst the EU approach discussed above certainly does not preclude such an approach to public participation, there is still quite a distance to travel before it is reached.

THE PROBLEMS OF ACCESS

There are many compelling reasons to enhance public participation, in the broadest sense, in environmental decision-making. There are also however considerable challenges to be met, and it should not be assumed that an unreflective rush to public participation will lead to a happy result. In particular, participation should always maintain a concern for the risk of exclusion. Participatory mechanisms may further exclude the poor, poorly educated and unorthodox from institutions of decision-making; in the current context, one might also be anxious about the inadequately *communautaire*. Exclusion can be direct, in the sense of restricted access to the forum. There are also more insidious forms of exclusion. First of all, structures are difficult to access, and the ultimate safeguards of representative democracy are weak; deliberative democracy is most commonly invoked to justify *majoritarian* decision-making, particularly on major constitutional issues. Actually creating institutions and situations in which meaningful public participation or genuine deliberation can take place is the most challenging and urgent task.[173] And secondly, even the call for reason can marginalise the unpopular and disguise the exercise of power.[174] It is far from unusual to see limitations placed on what counts as 'legitimate' reasoning in environmental debate: most obviously, a narrow approach to 'sound science' or allocative efficiency can lead to the dismissal of every other concern as 'irrational' or 'NIMBYism'. Opposition to GMOS, for example, was for a long time dismissed as 'irrational', because it was not based on established science.

Neither the Aarhus Convention nor the implementation proposals, however, look closely at removing barriers to participation or deliberation. EC level participatory democracy suffers from similar limitations as arise in representative democracy, with restricted European 'public space' for debate.[175] The European environmental debate is inaccessible or uninteresting to all but a small, self-selecting group of self-conscious Europeans. Pan-European organised groups can fill some gaps, but may be more remote from affected individuals than equivalent local or national groups.

If the search for 'a new form of supranational, participatory democracy' is just a 'wild goose chase',[176] perhaps more modest objectives can be pursued. The

---

[173] See Smith, above n 4.

[174] Bohman and Rehg, above n 4, outlines some of the tensions.

[175] So for example, European Parliament elections continue to be fought on largely national rather than European grounds. See Douglas-Scott, above n 19. For a more positive assessment, see Eriksen and Fossum, above n 25.

[176] Harlow, above n 11, p 179.

background to the Commission's *White Paper on European Governance* invokes the 'democratising' potential of public participation; the minimum standards on consultation are however at least equally concerned with the improvement of output, and the Proposal for Aarhus implementation is similarly instrumental, looking primarily to implementation of environmental law. In this respect, the empowerment of environmental interest groups is potentially important. However, the concern that the group with the greatest resources (financial, political, technical) will win the 'lobbying' game means that the range of voices heard remains significant from the substantive perspective on public participation. A republican conception of deliberation, in which 'the prerequisite of sound government was the willingness of citizens to subordinate their private interests to the general good' is an effort to get around the manipulation of the political process by 'factions'[177]; whether deliberation will in fact to purge the selfish motivations of those involved is more problematic.[178] Whilst allowing environmental interest groups into the decision-making process has certain beneficial characteristics, particularly from a substantive perspective, considerable caution needs to be exercised in respect of some of the grander claims being made.

The Commission resists calls to put in place a legally binding instrument on consultation, basically on grounds of effectiveness:

> such an over-legalistic approach would be incompatible with the need for timely delivery of policy, and with the expectations of the citizens that the European Institutions should deliver on substance rather than concentrating on procedures. [179]

Concerns that 'output legitimacy', that is results, will be sacrificed to 'input legitimacy', that is process, are valid, and a balance must inevitably be drawn. This takes us back to Majone's argument that effectiveness is the key to legitimacy.[180] The tension between public participation and reasonably swift and decisive regulation is acute; environmental interest groups should be particularly concerned that making regulatory activity more onerous can serve simply to strengthen the status quo. However, to argue that environmental decisions can be made well without some breadth of involvement involves a mistaken understanding of environmental issues, which, as discussed in the context of risk in chapter four above, are rarely one-dimensional technical decisions. Moreover, whilst a balance needs to be struck, and at the risk of repetition, the certain involvement of industry means that environmental interest groups can make an important contribution to decision-making.

---

[177] CR Sunstein, 'Interest Groups in American Public Law' (1985) 38 *Stanford Law Review* 29, p 31.

[178] See Elster, above n 5 and Chalmers, above n 24 for expressions of scepticism; CR Sunstein, 'Deliberative Trouble? Why Groups Go To Extremes' (2000) 110 *The Yale Law Journal* 71 discusses empirical observations that like-minded groups (and individuals within them) tend to shift to extreme positions in the direction of their initial tendency following discussion.

[179] Commission, above n 117, p 10.

[180] Majone, above nn 35 and 36.

The Commission is also concerned by the potential for formal decision-making procedures to lead to excessive litigation.[181] The liberalisation of standing is one possible contributor to excessive litigation, although the intensity of review by the judiciary is probably of greater concern. Liberalised standing does however create other dilemmas. The politicisation of the judicial process could not only compromise that process, but also shift political disputes from more appropriate (political) fora.[182] In addition, it should be recalled that both *UPA* and *Jégo-Quéré* involved industry challenges of legislation, in the latter case of broadly environmentally protective legislation. Litigation is generally utilised most readily by industry; indeed whenever protections are legally entrenched, rights are invoked only by those with the resources to do so. The ECJ has been described as a 'natural magnet for the determined, well-informed and wealthy "repeat player" willing to use legal challenges systematically to protect its own interests'.[183] Whilst the analogies are far from direct, the classic discussion by Marc Galanter of 'why the haves come out ahead' is instructive.[184] Galanter's thesis suggests certain advantages to the well-organised, the well-resourced, in short the powerful, in the use of the law. The benefits enjoyed by industry and industry associations in these respects are clear. However, in the context of EC environmental law, even if a general liberalisation of standing enhances the route of industry groups to court, it also provides a recognition of environmental interest groups that is currently entirely absent. Whilst lacking industry's financial resources, environmental interest groups enjoy the advantages of 'repeat players', including experience and knowledge, and the ability to play individual conflicts or negotiations for long-term advantage. It goes without saying, however, that perspectives that fall within neither environmental interest group nor industry's perspective of what is worth fighting for, face serious difficulties in being heard at all.

Whilst it is important to consider concerns about the practical limitations of public participation, and the likely dominance of the process by certain groups, it is equally important not to start from an unduly idealistic perspective. In particular the industry view is readily heard, as indeed it should be. Efforts to expand participation, to allow a richer range of perspectives into the process, are undoubtedly a step forward. Moreover, the weakness of representative democracy at EC level renders somewhat ambivalent any concern that the access principles interfere with the formal equality provided by representative democracy. Care, however, needs to be exercised about what is claimed for participation, and it is

---

[181] Commission, above n 104, p 10. The US experience is usually cited, see R Stewart, 'The Reformation of American Administrative Law' (1975) 88 *Harvard Law Review* 1660.

[182] See especially C Harlow, 'Public Law and Popular Justice' (2002) 65 *Modern Law Review* 1.

[183] Harlow, above n 148, p 236; also M Galanter, 'Predators and Parasites: Lawyer-Bashing and Civil Justice' (1994) 28 *Georgia Law Review* 633.

[184] M Galanter, 'Why the "Haves" Come Out Ahead: Speculations on the Limits of Legal Change' (1974) *Law and Society* 95. Galanter argues that there are limits to what can be achieved by changes to substantive legal rules. Galanter would suggest a wide range of procedural rules to even up the position between the 'haves' and the 'have nots'. There are, however, also limits to what can be achieved by procedural changes.

important also to be vigilant of how participation actually functions. A move to participation cannot be viewed as a simple option; participation is no 'reform-lite',[185] but requires much more thought to be given to institutional arrangements. Finally, whilst the risk that burdensome procedural requirements will lead to inertia in decision-making should be borne in mind, that by no means implies that only industry should be involved in decision-making, or in access to justice. Public interest representation prevents diffuse interests from being lost in the battles between individual interests.

CONCLUSIONS

The inclusion of environmental groups in the American policy-making process in the early 1970s has been explained as a response to the legitimisation crisis that arose from popular 'counter-culture' movements of the late 1960s.[186] Whilst the political situation is very different, there are parallels in the enthusiasm at EU level for increased participation at a time of disputed legitimacy.[187] Whether the particular focus on *environmental* interest groups is similarly about embracing the less threatening elements of contemporary legitimacy challenges, is perhaps more contentious.

The types of mechanisms discussed here have become almost an alternative to a discussion of democracy at the EU level. And yet the mechanisms available are both weak in themselves, and strikingly inadequate for any attempt at democratisation. 'Participation', certainly as currently conceptualised by the Commission, is far from sufficiently robust an instrument to bear the weight of democratising the Union; quite heroic institutional rearrangements would be required. Talk of participatory democracy through governance is perhaps misplaced; we have an alternative form of representation, but particular functional interests are being represented rather than the 'people'. The representation and the accountability of the 'representatives' is as a result much less clear.

On the whole the Commission is rather sanguine about the limitations of participation as a tool of democracy, perhaps because it is also quite surprisingly sanguine about the EU's legitimacy problems more generally.[188] Democratisation is not, however, the only rationale for public participation, and indeed although calls for enhanced public participation are legion, the motivation and meaning of such a move remain ambiguous. Even if public participation cannot be used to avoid the increasingly urgent democracy problems at EU level, a commitment to rigorous and transparent involvement of as wide a group of participants as possible may nevertheless be important. Open participation can at least avoid a stranglehold on

---

[185] Chalmers, above n 24, p 129.
[186] Dryzek *et al*, above n 137.
[187] Note also the turn to procedure in risk regulation following intense politicisation of risk, ch 4 above.
[188] Commission, above n 8, especially p 7.

environmental policy by industry. It can also provide alternative perspectives that recognise the normative and political character of regulation, avoiding monopolisation by technocrats. In this context, the legitimacy of a broad range of reasons for a decision is important. A requirement to base a decision on a narrow rationality, for example a scientific risk assessment, or cost benefit analysis, would mean that the 'other' factors influencing decisions, including the concerns of the lay public, are likely to be hidden from view.

Finally, EC environmental law has made some significant interventions in national processes, including provisions as to public participation in decision-making. The value of local participation is, however, restricted by the background of EC legal obligations. So to mention just two examples to which we will return below,[189] local participation over the permitting of a waste incinerator, required under various provisions of EC environmental law, must take as settled the Community legislation that requires reduced reliance on landfill; similarly, national participation on the commercialisation of genetically modified organisms can find its way into the authorisation decision only through qualified majority voting in Council, and only if (at least until recently) its conclusions fit within the narrow technical rationality of the legislation. The restrictive nature of participation at EU level is far from compensating for a diminution of participation at national or local level, from a process or a substantive perspective.

---

[189] See chs 8 and 9 below.

6

Procedure, Integration and Assessment

INTRODUCTION

IT IS NOW widely accepted, as discussed in chapter five, that public participation is a crucial element of effective and democratic environmental law.
Even if the meaning of public participation remains somewhat ambiguous, it
exercises a considerable attraction over EU policy-making. Participation can
respond to disparate sources of anxiety about environmental decision-making:
the dilemma of non-majoritarian decision-making; the limitations of periodic
elections; an apparent loss of faith in representative democracy; 'green authoritarianism' and also the failings of 'green liberalism'; the quality and the implementation of environmental measures; add to this the very pragmatic desire to see
particular developments introduced with the minimum of public complaint, and
the arrival of public participation in the orthodoxy is easily understood.

International legal debate, ranging from sustainable development in the 1980s
and beyond,[1] through to the human rights perspective taken in the Aarhus
Convention in the late 1990s,[2] has been an important element of the main-
streaming of public participation in the EU. Bolstered by this general shift, EC
environmental legislation has begun to have a potentially dramatic impact on
legal arrangements for public participation at national and sub-national level. The
preoccupation with levels of public participation in the Member States rests,
however, not only on this broader trend. First, the long-standing instrumental
benefits of individual rights in EC law can be seen in the background: conferring
legally enforceable rights on individuals within the Member States has served the
integration project of the EC well and long. The current developments are necessary in part because the public and diffuse nature of environmental goods and
environmental harms has meant that the role of individual rights has developed
slowly by comparison with many other areas of EC policy. Secondly, the move to
public participation forms part of contemporary trends in EU environmental law
to 'proceduralisation'. A descriptive if ugly label, proceduralisation is subject to

---

[1] World Commission on Environment and Development, *Our Common Future* (Oxford, Oxford
University Press, 1987); *Rio Declaration on Environment and Development* (1992), Principle 10, available at http://www.un.org/esa/sustdev/documents/docs.htm; *Johannesburg Declaration on Sustainable
Development* (2002), para 26, available at http://www.un.org/esa/sustdev/index.html.
[2] *Convention on Access to Information, Public Participation in Decision-making and Access to Justice in
Environmental Matters* (1998), available at http://www.unece.org/env/pp/documents/cep43e.pdf, see
ch 5 above.

considerable theoretical debate,[3] but for current purposes it quite simply connotes the imposition of procedural constraints by EC law on national decision-makers, a development that tends to be matched by more flexible and open-ended substantive environmental obligations.[4] Forms of participation are an important element of proceduralisation, but the imposition of highly technical procedures can be equally significant.

This chapter will begin with a discussion of the influence of EC environmental legislation on the national implementation of the three pillars of the Aarhus Convention. EC legislation is capable of providing a very hard edge to the sometimes vague international commitments contained in the Convention. In turn, the Aarhus Convention has the potential to be very significant in the continued development of EC level control of national procedure; if nothing else, concerns about the appropriate role of the Community legislator in national democratic and decision-making arrangements are to a large degree defused by the simple fact of signature of the Aarhus Convention by all Member States. This chapter will then move on to discuss proceduralisation as a legal technique, and three particular 'proceduralising' areas of EC environmental law: integrated pollution prevention and control, environmental assessment and environmental management and audit systems.

THE ACCESS PRINCIPLES

The Aarhus Convention was introduced in chapter five, along with a discussion of the strength of the commitment to its principles at EC level. Many of the reservations expressed there about the overreaching rhetoric sometimes connected with participation, apply equally here. Again, the Aarhus Convention provides a useful framework within which to examine EC law's role in influencing Member State procedures, although many of the instruments discussed here were in place before the Aarhus Convention.

Access to Information

The 'hardest' law in the Aarhus Convention applies to access to environmental information. Directive 2003/04[5] implements the Aarhus Convention in respect of the rights to information held by public authorities in the Member States, replacing an earlier directive on the subject. The legislation provides a basic right of access

---

[3] For a flavour, see J Black, 'Proceduralizing Regulation' (2000) 20 *Oxford Journal of Legal Studies* 597, and (2001) 21 *Oxford Journal of Legal Studies* 33.

[4] J Scott, 'Flexibility, "Proceduralization", and Environmental Governance in the EU' in J Scott and G de Búrca (eds), *Constitutional Change in the European Union* (Oxford, Hart Publishing, 2000); R Macrory and S Turner, 'Participatory Rights, Transboundary Environmental Governance and EC Law' (2002) 39 *Common Market Law Review* 489.

[5] Dir 2003/04 on Public Access to Environmental Information and Repealing Council Directive 90/313/EC [2003] OJ L 41/26.

to environmental information held by a public authority, without an interest having to be stated.

The Aarhus Convention's definition of 'environmental information' is broad, explicitly including, as well as information on air, water and soil, information *inter alia* on 'biological diversity and its components, including genetically modified organisms', energy, noise and radiation, and measures such as environmental agreements and policies and legislation affecting or likely to affect the elements of the environment. It also recognises the importance of administrative techniques of environmental decision-making, and includes 'cost-benefit analysis and other economic analyses and assumptions used in environmental decision-making'.[6] This allows a potentially important insight into the rationales for a decision, and the opportunity to challenge and contest economic assessments should highlight any disputed or uncertain aspects before a decision is taken. The new Directive expands the EC regime's concept of 'environmental information', which in spite of a broad interpretation by the European Court of Justice (ECJ),[7] did not go as far as the Aarhus Convention. The Directive follows the Aarhus Convention very closely, with even slightly more expansive language in places.[8]

The Directive and the Aarhus Convention are both centred around public authorities, providing no right of access in respect of information held by private parties. The Aarhus Convention does require its members to 'encourage' operators to keep the public informed, 'where appropriate within the framework of voluntary eco-labelling or eco-auditing schemes'[9]: disclosure through eco-auditing will be discussed below, and eco-labelling in chapter eight. Restricting mandatory access to publicly held information is a significant limitation on legal rights of access to information, although one might expect such a compromise in an international agreement. The limitation is however compounded by the changing nature of public responsibilities: all manner of formerly public functions have passed out of government hands in recent years.[10] (Quasi) autonomous environmental regulatory agencies are brought clearly within the framework of both the Aarhus Convention and the Directive; to do otherwise would very obviously thwart much of the potential of access to environmental information.[11] The shift of information to the private sector with privatisation of formerly governmental

[6] Aarhus Convention, Art 2(3).

[7] Case C–321/96 *Mecklenburg v Kreiss Pinneberg der Landrat* [1998] ECR I–3809.

[8] For example, natural sites explicitly includes 'wetlands, coastal and marine areas', Dir 03/04, above n 5, Art 2(1)(a); the definition was also extended to include the contamination of the food chain, Art 2(1)(f), overturning in this respect Case C–316/01 *Glawischnig v Bundeskanzler* [2003] ECR I–5995 on the 1990 Directive.

[9] Aarhus Convention, Art 5(6).

[10] See A Roberts, 'Structural Pluralism and the Right to Information' (2001) *University of Toronto Law Journal* 243.

[11] The Aarhus Convention definition includes 'natural or legal persons performing public administrative functions under national law, including specific duties, activities or services in relation to the environment', Art (2)(2)(b); Dir 03/04, above n 5, is almost identical: 'any natural or legal person performing public administrative functions under national law, including specific duties, activities or services in relation to the environment', Art 2(2)(b).

activities such as utilities provision poses a more difficult dilemma,[12] and there are genuine variations in a society's conception of what constitutes a 'public' function. One might, in an attempt to assess the whether access to environmental information obligations should apply to these sorts of entities, focus on the functions of access to environmental information,[13] for example democratisation, or implementation and effectiveness of the law. This would tend, however, to take the obligation very far into the private sector, and as long as the public/private distinction persists, some inconsistency is perhaps inevitable. The Aarhus Convention nevertheless attempts to ensure that privatisation does not 'take public services or activities out of the realm of public involvement, information and participation',[14] including within the definition of public authority 'natural or legal persons having public responsibilities or functions, or providing public services, in relation to the environment, under the control of a [governmental or administrative] body or person',[15] followed very closely by the Directive.[16] A broad interpretation of 'public responsibilities or functions' and 'public services' could extend to bodies such as privatised utilities, or even waste collectors, particularly given the high level of government authority over these sorts of operations. Although the phrase 'in relation to the environment', rather than 'affecting the environment', may tend to limit the scope of the provision, it need not exclude these bodies. The precise scope of application of access to information is still to be explored.

So, there is a right of access to environmental information, broadly defined, held by a public authority. As one would expect, the Aarhus Convention contains a number of exceptions to rights of access, which, again, the Directive follows closely. The Convention provides a potentially broad exception in respect of 'material in the course of completion', or that concerning the 'internal communications of public authorities'. This exception is, however, qualified, applying only if provided for in national law 'or customary practice', and 'taking into account the public interest served by disclosure'.[17] Whilst the former qualification should prevent the *ad hoc* application of the exemption, the latter suggests that a blanket

---

[12] This is one of the main concerns highlighted in complaints lodged with the European Commission by individuals and organisations, see European Commission, *Report on the Experience Gained in the Application of Council Directive 90/313/EEC of 7 June 1990 on Freedom of Access to Information on the Environment* COM (2000) 400 final, para 3.

[13] Roberts, above n 10.

[14] S Stec and S Casey-Lefkowitz, *The Aarhus Convention: An Implementation Guide* (New York, United Nations / Economic Commission for Europe, 2000), p 32.

[15] Aarhus Convention, Art 2(2)(c). Note that the definition excludes bodies acting in a legislative or judicial capacity. See Stec and Casey-Lefkowitz, *ibid*, pp 32–4, for a detailed analysis of the definition of 'public authority'.

[16] 'Any natural or legal person having public responsibilities or functions, or providing public services, relating to the environment under the control of a body or person falling within (a) or (b)' [para (a) includes government or other public administration, para (b) is set out above n 11], Art 2(2)(c). Note the weakening of the Commission's initial proposal, which covered 'any legal person entrusted ... with the operation of services of general economic interest which affect or are likely to affect the state of elements of the environment', European Commission, *Proposal for a Directive of the European Parliament and of the Council on Public Access to Environmental Information* COM (2000) 402.

[17] Aarhus Convention, Art 4(3)(c).

approach to exceptions would be at least beyond the 'spirit' of the Convention. Other exceptions allow the refusal of access to information if its provision would adversely affect particular interests, including international relations, intellectual property rights and the confidentiality of commercial and industrial interests.[18] An interesting exception is provided in respect of protecting 'the environment to which the information relates, such as the breeding sites of rare species'.[19] The Aarhus Convention provides that all grounds for refusal are to be interpreted restrictively, 'taking into account the public interest served by disclosure' and 'taking into account whether the information requested relates to emissions into the environment'.[20] The commercial confidentiality exception cannot be a ground for refusal of 'information on emissions which is relevant for the protection of the environment'.[21]

The Directive has similar categories of exception, all subject to a public interest proviso, and all to be interpreted restrictively.[22] In every particular case, 'the public interest served by disclosure shall be weighed against the interest served by the refusal',[23] introducing an element of proportionality into the process,[24] albeit without requiring information to be disclosed where it is in the public interest to do so. The requirement for harm to a recognised interest, together with the obligation to balance this interest against the public interest in disclosure is a reminder that the exceptions are not for the convenience of government, or commercial or any other organisations: they are specifically for the protection of recognised interests that compete with rights to information. The Directive also prohibits refusal of a request for information relating to emissions into the environment, in the case of exceptions providing for the confidentiality of the proceedings of public authorities, commercial confidentiality, personal data protection, information provided voluntarily, and protection of the environment to which the information relates.[25] This goes a little further than the Aarhus Convention, which requires in most cases just that the fact that the information requested relates to emissions into the environment be taken into account; only in respect of commercial or industrial confidentiality does the Aarhus Convention state that information on emissions 'shall be disclosed'.[26] The disapplication of certain exceptions in respect of emissions has the potential to be a very significant

---

[18] Aarhus Convention, Art 4(4).
[19] Aarhus Convention, Art 4(4)(h); Dir 03/04, above n 5, Art 4(2)(h). A request may also be refused if the public authority does not hold the information requested, or if the request is unreasonable or formulated in too general a manner, Aarhus Convention Art 4(3); Dir 03/04, *ibid*, Art 4(1)(a), (b) and (c).
[20] Aarhus Convention, Art 4(4).
[21] Aarhus Convention, Art 4(4)(d).
[22] Dir 03/05, above n 5, Art 4(2). The ECJ required a restrictive interpretation of the exemptions in the old Directive, *Mecklenburg*, above n 7, para 25.
[23] Dir 03/04, *ibid*, Art 4(2).
[24] D Wilsher, 'Freedom of Environmental Information: Recent Developments and Future Prospects' (2001) 7 *European Public Law* 671, p 683.
[25] Dir 03/04, above n 5, Art 4(2).
[26] Note that, unlike the Aarhus Convention, the Directive provides no obligation to take the fact that information relates to emissions into account in respect of other exceptions.

element of the new regime, reflecting, it has been suggested, the fact that emissions lose 'their proprietary character' once they are emitted into the environment,[27] and perhaps also greater public concern about this type of environmental impact, and greater potential for direct effects on human health. Its potential to open up access to information suggests that considerable energy could be put into debating its scope, for example in respect of borderline issues such as the release of genetically modified organisms into the environment, or the deposit of solid waste in the environment.[28]

The practicalities of access are of course important, and legal rights of access do not in themselves ensure that information is transparent. Member States are also required to 'inform the public adequately of the rights they enjoy', to oblige officials to support the public and to make practical arrangements such as providing information officers.[29] Charging for access is the most abrupt limit to apparently 'open' information. On the other hand, requests for access clearly have the potential to create considerable administrative cost. Authorities are permitted to charge a 'reasonable amount' for information.[30] The ECJ has taken a purposive approach to this question, interpreting 'reasonableness' as precluding the application of a charge that is dissuasive or restrictive of the exercise of rights; nor can the entire costs of providing information, including presumably staff charges, be recovered.[31] A more subtle limitation on access to information is in its presentation, for example if information is presented in a way that only a specialist can understand, or relevant information is buried in a mass of data. The Directive provides that information has to be 'up to date, accurate and comparable',[32] but makes little comment on the presentation of requested information.

Provision of information for the purposes of public participation on particular activities takes the legislation a little further in respect of the presentation of information. The Environmental Impact Assessment Directive[33] requires information to be brought together and presented in the manner required by the Directive. An English House of Lords decision brings out the importance of these provisions, holding that 'a disparate collection of documents produced by parties other than the developer and traceable only by a person with a good deal of energy and persistence' is inadequate.[34] The Aarhus Convention and the EIA Directive also require the developer to provide a non-technical summary of the environmental

---

[27] Stec and Casey-Lefkowitz, above n 14, p 60.

[28] Stec and Casey-Lefkowitz, *ibid*, borrow the definition of 'emissions' contained in Dir 96/61 on Integrated Pollution Prevention and Control [1996] OJ L 257/26: 'direct or indirect release of substances, vibrations, heat or noise from individual or diffuse sources in the installation into air, water or land', Art 2(5).

[29] Dir 03/04, above n 5, Art 3(5).

[30] *Ibid*, Art 5; Aarhus Convention, Art 4(8).

[31] Case C–217/97 *Commission v Germany* [1999] ECR I–5087, paras 47–8.

[32] Dir 03/04, above n 5, Art 8.

[33] Dir 85/337 on the Assessment of the Effects of Certain Private and Public Projects on the Environment [1985] OJ L 175/40, as amended by Dir 97/11/EC [1997] L 073/05. Aarhus Convention, Art 6, discussed below.

[34] *Berkeley v Secretary of State for the Environment* [2001] 2 AC 603, p 617.

information collected.[35] Whilst this is necessary to allow the lay public to use information, it also increases concern that a process of information provision largely in the hands of a developer will be subject to manipulation, becoming little more than a public relations exercise. Although any presentation of information is vulnerable to manipulation, this suggests at least that 'raw data' should also be available.

In accordance with the Aarhus Convention, the Directive provides that information shall be made available 'as soon as possible or, at the latest, within one month', subject to extension by a further month if the volume or complexity of the information requires it.[36] Any refusal of access or extension of the period for decision must be accompanied by reasons.[37] The Aarhus Convention provides for access to a review procedure to protect rights in respect of access to information. Recognising the limitations of formal (and expensive) court proceedings, the Aarhus Convention requires, in addition to the possibility of review before a court or equivalent body:

> access to an expeditious procedure established by law that is free of charge or inexpensive for reconsideration by a public authority or review by an independent and impartial body other than a court of law. [38]

The Directive similarly provides both that the act or omission can be 'reconsidered' by a public authority, or 'reviewed administratively by an independent and impartial body established by law'. This process is to be 'expeditious and either free of charge or inexpensive',[39] a phrase involving difficult judgments at the margins, although one might turn to the Court's purposive approach to reasonable charges for access. In addition to this administrative review, final decisions can be made by a court 'or another independent and impartial body established by law'.[40]

As well as providing rights of access to information, the Aarhus Convention imposes an active obligation on Parties to collect and disseminate information, including a requirement to publish a national report on the state of the environment every three or four years, and to set up pollution inventories, as discussed in chapter five above.[41] The Directive also imposes positive obligations on public authorities, requiring 'active and systematic dissemination' of environmental information and data, emphasising the importance of 'computer telecommunication and/or electronic technology'.[42] Reports on 'the state of the environment' are to be published at least every four years, including information on 'the quality of, and pressures on, the environment'.[43]

---

[35] Dir 85/337, above n 33, Art 5 and Annex IV; see also Aarhus Convention, Art 6(6).
[36] Dir 03/04, above n 5, Art 3(2); Aarhus Convention, Art 4(2).
[37] Dir 03/04, *ibid*, Art 4(5); Aarhus Convention, Art 4(7).
[38] Aarhus Convention, Art 9(1).
[39] Dir 03/04, above n 5, Art 6.
[40] *Ibid*.
[41] Aarhus Convention, Art 5.
[42] Dir 03/04, above n 5, Art 7.
[43] *Ibid*, Art 7(3).

Public Participation

The Aarhus Convention provides for public participation in three types of decision: 'decisions on specific activities'[44]; 'plans, programmes and policies relating to the environment'[45]; and 'the preparation of executive regulations and/or generally applicable legally binding normative instruments'.[46] The Aarhus Convention assumes public participation far beyond familiar techniques of consulting neighbours over siting decisions.

Decisions permitting certain activities listed in the Convention,[47] or other activities likely to have a 'significant effect' on the environment, require public participation under Article 6. The listed activities relate to specific projects, with predominantly local impact, and this is the most detailed and formalised aspect of the second pillar of the Convention. Article 6 requires 'the public concerned' to be informed, 'early in an environmental decision-making procedure, and in an adequate, timely and effective manner' of a number of matters relating to the permit application, including the envisaged procedure, opportunities for public participation, and whether the activity is subject to environmental assessment; the public concerned must also be provided with a description of the site, the activity and its significant effects on the environment, and a non-technical summary of this information. This obligation actively to provide detailed information on particular proposals, as discussed above, intensifies the access to information elements of the Aarhus Convention. The need for reasonable time frames for public participation is stressed, and there must be 'early public participation, when all options are open and effective public participation can take place.'[48] 'Due account' must be taken of the outcome of the public participation,[49] and a reasoned decision provided.[50]

The somewhat less tightly defined provisions of the Aarhus Convention in respect of plans, policies, programmes and executive regulations were discussed in chapter five above. To recap briefly, 'plans, programmes and policies relating to the environment' are covered by Article 7. Parties are required to make 'appropriate practical and/or other provisions' for the public to participate during the preparation of plans and programmes relating to the environment, 'within a transparent and fair framework, having provided the necessary information to the public'. Provisions on 'reasonable time frames', the requirement for 'early' and 'effective' public participation, and the obligation to take 'due account' of the outcome of the public participation are incorporated by reference to Article 6. The Aarhus Convention is much less demanding in respect of 'policies' under the second part of Article 7 and 'executive regulations' under Article 8. On 'policies relating to the

---

[44] Aarhus Convention, Art 6.
[45] *Ibid*, Art 7.
[46] *Ibid*, Art 8.
[47] *Ibid*, Annex I.
[48] *Ibid*, Art 6(4).
[49] *Ibid*, Art 6(8).
[50] *Ibid*, Art 6(9).

environment', a party must simply 'endeavour' to provide opportunities to participate 'to the extent appropriate'. Article 8, on 'executive regulations and other generally applicable legally binding rules' requires parties to 'strive to promote effective public participation at an appropriate stage, and while options are still open'.

The Aarhus Convention clearly aims to increase participation within processes that might otherwise be closed, and envisages 'real' participation with the potential to exert a genuine influence on decisions. It says little on institutional arrangements for public participation, and provides only limited support for anything more than the provision of information and the opportunity to provide comments, even in respect of specific activities. A 'public hearing or inquiry with the applicant' should be provided 'as appropriate'[51]; there is also a requirement 'where appropriate' to 'encourage prospective applicants to identify the public concerned, to enter into discussions' before they apply for a permit.[52] Even in the most intensive provisions on public participation, a narrow reading is possible, and only fairly low-key changes to EC law have been felt necessary. The legislation nevertheless provides space to experiment with more innovative participative processes at the local level.

EC law dictates public participation in Member State environmental decision-making on activities, and plans and programmes, that is Article 6 and part of Article 7 of the Aarhus Convention. The procedures provided for environmental assessment and integrated pollution prevention and control are particularly pertinent, and will be discussed further below. Public participation on 'policies' has been deemed too politically sensitive for EC legislation, and is considered to be a matter for representative bodies in any event. One might also note that the EIA Directive does not apply to 'projects the details of which are adopted by a specific act of national legislation'.[53] The assumption that all necessary information, and presumably all necessary process legitimacy, is inherent to legislative and policy making procedures, is a familiar enough position, although how convincing it is will of course depend on the particular case.

Access to Justice

The provisions of Article 9 of the Aarhus Convention on access to justice were introduced in chapter five above. This is perhaps the most obviously sensitive access principle for implementation by EC legislation. Article 9 makes provision for review in three circumstances. First of all, the most hard-edged element of Article 9 is in respect of refusal of access to information, or failure to respond to a request for access to information, and the approach of the access to environmental information Directive was discussed above. Secondly, Article 9(2) of the Aarhus Convention provides for the challenge of substantive or procedural legality

---

[51] *Ibid,* Art 6(7).
[52] *Ibid,* Art 6(5).
[53] Dir 85/337, above n 33, Art 1(5).

in any decision subject to Article 6 (decision-making on activities), and also 'where so provided for under national law' any decision subject to 'other relevant provisions' of the Convention. Standing depends on the question of 'sufficient interest' or 'impairment of a right', depending on domestic law; environmental interest groups that comply with the Convention definition of 'the public concerned'[54] are explicitly deemed to have a 'sufficient interest' or 'rights capable of being impaired'. Finally, Article 9(3) provides for access to administrative or judicial procedures to challenge acts and omissions by private and public bodies that contravene domestic law relating to the environment; it is for national (or EC) law to lay down the criteria for standing.

Community law has introduced access to justice in respect of substantive or procedural illegality in decisions subject to environmental impact assessment (EIA) or integrated pollution prevention and control (IPPC), that is broadly the Article 6 activities.[55] EC legislation does not provide specifically for access to justice in respect of decisions subject to Article 7 rights, for example under the Strategic Environmental Assessment Directive.[56] The justification is that this is not clearly required by the Aarhus Convention; the inconsistency of the commitment to individual rights is rather perplexing, although these questions may fall within the more general access to justice provisions discussed in this section below.

Standing under EIA and IPPC revolves around the possession of a 'sufficient interest' in the matter, or the 'impairment of a right', if 'required by national law'.[57] These provisions, as in the Aarhus Convention, will be filled out by the Member States. Public interest groups 'promoting environmental protection and meeting any requirements under national law' are deemed to have sufficient interest or rights capable of being impaired.[58] As well as addressing interest group standing, this legislation to some degree overtakes judicial activity on the invocability of certain directives. The EIA Directive famously provided the locus for very significant developments in the doctrine of direct effect before the European Court of Justice (ECJ).[59]

As well as the consideration of access to justice in specific Directives, the Commission has put forward a more general proposal on access to justice in environmental matters, extending beyond activities covered by Article 6 of the Aarhus

---

[54] The 'public concerned' is 'the public affected or likely to be affected by or having an interest in, the environmental decision-making ... non-governmental organizations promoting environmental protection and meeting any requirements under national law shall be deemed to have an interest', Aarhus Convention, Art 2(5). The 'public' is more broadly defined as 'natural or legal persons, and, in accordance with national legislation or practice, their associations, organisations or groups', Art 2(4).

[55] Dir 2003/35 Providing for Public Participation in Respect of the Drawing Up of Certain Plans and Programmes Relating to the Environment and Amending with Regard to Public Participation and Access to Justice Council Directives 85/337/EEC and 96/61/EC [2003] OJ L 156/17.

[56] Dir 2001/42 on the Assessment of the Effects of Certain Plans and Programmes on the Environment [2001] OJ L197/30.

[57] Dir 85/337, above n 33, new Art 10a; Dir 96/61, above n 28, new Art 15a.

[58] Dir 85/337, *ibid*, new Art 1(2); Dir 96/61, *ibid*, new Art 2(14).

[59] See the discussion of the line of cases arising out of Case C–72/95 *Aanemersebedrijf PK Kraaijeveld BV v Gedeputeerde Staten van Zuid-Holland* [1996] ECR I–5403 in ch 3 above.

Convention.[60] The proposal would provide for review of procedural or substantive breaches of EC 'environmental law'[61] by public authorities.[62] This is a minimum scheme and so a broader approach remains open to the Member States, but the Commission proposes to remain within the requirements of the Aarhus Convention, on subsidiarity grounds. A two-tiered approach is taken to review, involving first notice to the relevant public authority, allowing for reconsideration of the decision, followed by administrative or judicial review procedures.[63] There is no provision for action directly against a private party, nor would the proposal apply to legislative instruments. The standing of environmental interest groups is a crucial aspect of the Aarhus Convention, and as in the EU level measure, discussed in chapter five above, the Commission turns to the concept of 'qualified entities'. A qualified entity is: 'an independent and non-profit-making legal person, which has the objective to protect the environment'; possesses 'an organisational structure which enables it to ensure the adequate pursuit of its statutory objectives'; and has been constituted and actively working for environmental protection for a period to be fixed by the Member States of up to three years, with audited accounts for that period.[64] Individuals have standing if they have a sufficient interest or can maintain the impairment of a right.[65] 'Qualified entities' have standing if the matter 'is covered specifically by the statutory activities of the qualified entity and the review falls within the specific geographical area of activities of that entity'.[66]

The practical limitations on access to justice are often far more problematic than the legal limitations. The requirement in the Aarhus Convention that proceedings be 'fair' and 'equitable' should not lead to too much soul searching.[67] The requirement for 'adequate and effective remedies, including injunctive relief as appropriate' is also likely to be relatively straightforward for EC Member States, although the availability of interim relief provokes consistent concern in an environmental context. If the environmental resource at issue has been destroyed by the time litigation has been completed, litigants get something of an empty victory. And although interim relief must in principle be available for the protection of Community law rights,[68] the conditions for the grant of relief are with the Member States, subject only to the provisos that procedural rules are

---

[60] European Commission, *Proposal for a Directive on Access to Justice in Environmental Matters* COM (2003) 624 final.

[61] Defined reference to the objective of the law, together with an indicative list of subject matter, including soil protection and biotechnology, Commission, *ibid*, Art 2(g).

[62] Defined as: 'the public administration of Member States including administration at national, regional or local level, but excluding public prosecutors and bodies, administrations or institutions acting in a judicial or legislative capacity', Commission, *ibid*, Art 2(1)(a).

[63] Commission, *ibid*, Arts 6 and 7. In an application for interim relief, there is no obligation to go through both stages, Arts 4(2) and 5(3).

[64] Commission, *ibid*, Art 8.

[65] *Ibid*, Art 4

[66] *Ibid*, Art 5.

[67] Aarhus Convention, Art 9(4).

[68] Case C–213/89 *R v Secretary of State for Transport, ex p Factortame (No 2)* [1990] ECR I–2433.

non-discriminatory (by comparison with equivalent national provisions), and do not render the protection of the right excessively difficult or virtually impossible.[69] It is very common for the grant of interim relief to be subject to the provision by the applicant of financial guarantees, in order to compensate the party submitting to the interim relief in case the applicant is ultimately unsuccessful. Such requirements seem to be acceptable in EC law, but can be particularly problematic in the environmental field, given the stretched resources of environmental interest groups.[70]

The requirement in the Aarhus Convention that proceedings be 'timely' and especially 'not prohibitively expensive' is particularly challenging. The meaning of 'prohibitively expensive' is of course open to some debate, but it is simply true that in many cases, litigation is not pursued because it would financially cripple the protaganist, even with a good case, and even if successful. This is an extraordinarily sensitive topic, going deep into national welfare states and national legal systems. The rather hands off exhortation in the Commission's proposal that environmental proceedings be 'adequate and effective ... objective, equitable, expeditious and not prohibitively expensive'[71] is only to be expected, given the enormous resource implications of more radical interventions. The Community institutions have, however, been less reticent in respect of civil and commercial 'cross-border disputes', requiring legal aid to be provided in certain cases.[72] An alternative way to begin to address the expense and delay of litigation is by arrangements for less formal, inexpensive administrative review of some kind. The requirement in the Commission's Proposal that contested decisions be reconsidered goes some way to providing an informal and inexpensive mechanism for access to justice.[73] Nevertheless, the realistic opportunity for the majority of individuals and interest groups to litigate should be borne in mind.

The Commission's proposal would be a major intervention in national procedural rules, a subject on which the appropriate balance between autonomy and control often proves difficult to find. The Commission's explanation of its proposal rests heavily on the prospects for improved implementation of environmental law by access to justice; its earlier working paper refers more bluntly to the 'enforcement'

---

[69] See generally S Douglas-Scott, *Constitutional Law of the European Union* (London, Longman, 2002), pp 312–23; C Kilpatrick, T Novitz and P Skidmore (eds), *The Future of Remedies in Europe* (Oxford, Hart Publishing, 2000).

[70] For example, in Case C–44/95 *R v Secretary of State for the Environment, ex parte RSPB (Lappel Bank)* [1996] ECR I–3805, the ECJ took a strongly protective stance, but in the absence of interim relief, the site had been destroyed by the time of the decision. The environmental interest group seeking the interim injunction did not have the means to make the requisite financial guarantee. For discussion, see LM Warren, 'Nature Conservation and Development in the Rural Environment' in N Herbert-Young (ed), *Law, Policy and Development in the Rural Environment* (Cardiff, University of Wales Press, 1999), pp 114–16.

[71] Commission, above n 60, Art 10.

[72] Dir 2002/8 to Improve Access to Justice in Cross-Border Disputes by Establishing Minimum Common Rules Relating to Legal Aid for such Disputes [2003] OJ L 26/41. To simplify, if there are no other mechanisms available, the Member State where the cross border litigation takes place must provide legal aid to those without the financial resources to pay the costs themselves, Art 5. Note that this does not apply to public law litigation such as considered in this chapter.

[73] Note also the two tier approach in respect of Dir 03/04, above n 5.

of EC environmental law in the Member States.[74] The 'privatisation' of certain aspects of enforcement is nothing new in EC law, which has openly relied on individuals and national courts to ensure *effet utile* ever since *Van Gend en Loos*.[75] The co-option of individuals and the national judiciary aims both to supplement Member State enforcement mechanisms on the ground and to mitigate some of the shortcomings of Commission enforcement under Article 226, conserving public resources, and avoiding problems of effectiveness, efficiency and capture in public regulation. The Commission's focus on the well-organised and well-resourced as primary beneficiaries of rights reflects this instrumental approach to the access principles. It should nevertheless be recalled that supplementary enforcement by the private sector is not necessarily a simple regulatory tool, and the balance between adequate discretion for regulators and meaningful review by third parties is delicate.[76]

PROCEDURALISATION

It is possible to identify a change of approach in EU environmental law, away from setting detailed substantive standards, towards setting overall objectives that leave considerable flexibility for the Member States, combined with enhanced procedural obligations. Whilst proceduralisation can be a theoretically very sophisticated concept, for now, proceduralisation indicates a statutory reliance on procedural standards alongside, or instead of, substantive environmental standards. This 'proceduralisation' responds to a number of influences in EC environmental law. Perhaps most importantly, procedural obligations are perceived to provide a balance to substantive de-centralisation in environmental law.[77]

A number of pressures point to de-centralisation of environmental law. Legitimacy centred subsidiarity concerns would tend to encourage fewer centralised decisions, moving decisions 'closer to the people'. 'Effectiveness' type subsidiarity concerns, which level of government will do the best job, exercise a similar effect, on the basis of arguments that centralised standard setting responds poorly to varying environmental and economic conditions. These sorts of pressures are only likely to increase with enlargement, and increased diversity, as well as with the increased representation of euro-sceptic views in the European Parliament since the 2004 elections. However, it should become apparent that EC environmental law is not yet engaged in outright de-centralisation, but in highly

---

[74] European Commission, *Working Paper, Access to Justice in Environmental Matters*, 11 April 2002. Along similar lines, note the Commission's Explanatory Memorandum to the draft Directive on environmental liability: 'the main benefit expected from the proposal is improved enforcement of environmental protection standards in line with the "polluter pays" principle', European Commission, *Proposal for a Directive on Environmental Liability with Regard to the Prevention and Restoration of Environmental Damage* COM (2002) 17 final, p 6.

[75] Case 26/62 *Van Gend en Loos* [1963] ECR 1. See the discussion of third party contributions to the enforcement of environmental law in ch 3 above.

[76] See the discussion in ch 3 above.

[77] Macrory and Turner, above n 4; Scott, above n 5; J Scott, 'Flexibility in the Implementation of EC Environmental Law' (2000) 1 *Yearbook of European Environmental Law* 37.

conditional flexibility. It should also be noted that there is still very significant legislation setting detailed centralised substantive standards: some of the waste directives discussed in chapter eight below spring to mind.

Legislative obligations for public participation are an important aspect of proceduralisation. Some procedural mechanisms however seem to point in the opposite direction from enhanced public participation, formalising and concretising technical decision-making processes. There are, as with public participation, combined process and substantive rationales for this development.[78] Substantively, using the 'best' technical methodologies should lead to the 'best' decision; in process terms, the aim is to enhance transparency and accountability by reference to very clear scientific or bureaucratic methodologies, such as specified approaches to cost benefit analysis or risk assessment. This formalisation of decision-making is a recurring theme in EU environmental policy. It has the potential to close alternative interests out of decision-making, both by shifting the debate to a language and forum remote from the public, and by making it more difficult for values and concerns that do not fit within the technical perspective to be included in the final decision. Whilst one of the attractions of procedural law is its apparent neutrality in the face of polarised views, and highly contested and uncertain facts, that appearance of neutrality can be misleading. Defining an issue in a particular way (technical, ethical, scientific, economic) involves not only positioning participants within the decision-making process, but also defining the acceptable grounds for a decision. Given the undoubted importance of technical information in environmental law, the effort should be for technical discourse to inform the public debate on values, and vice versa, for technical and participatory procedures to be linked.[79]

One important aspect of the substantive rationale for proceduralisation in specifically EC environmental law is undoubtedly the challenge of the implementation gap.[80] First, proceduralisation may enhance implementation of substantive law. Proceduralisation provides more than policing by private parties. In addition, much procedural law involves obligations of reporting and information exchange between Member States, providing not only opportunities for mutual learning, but also an element of peer review. Secondly, it is hoped that procedural law will be more easily implemented, and more easily monitored, than traditional legal mechanisms. The indirect impacts of procedural law on social actors are supposed to be to a large degree 'self-implementing'. Procedural legislation nevertheless might ultimately pose formidable substantive environmental challenges for operators, demanding rigorous regulatory activity; for example, the implementation of IPPC in existing installations appears to be going slowly.[81] Practical implementation of procedural law by the Member State can also be extremely

---

[78] See ch 5 above.
[79] Ch 4 above.
[80] See ch 3 above and C Knill and A Lenschow (eds), *Implementing EU Environmental Policy: New Directions and Old Problems* (Manchester, Manchester University Press, 2000).
[81] European Commission, *On the Road to Sustainable Production: Progress in Implementing Council Directive 96/61/EC Concerning Integrated Pollution Prevention and Control* COM (2003) 354 final.

demanding, extending very deeply into national administrative structures.[82] Even apparently familiar obligations can be challenging in practice,[83] but when serious reforms of administrative structures and habits are necessary, meaningful change is particularly onerous. This is an issue, which whilst undeniably a challenge for the fifteen 'old' Member States, may arise acutely in coming years. Participatory mechanisms make real demands of stretched administrations, and some of the new Member States face particular difficulties in this respect.[84] Participatory mechanisms similarly rely very heavily on well-resourced and well-informed environmental interest groups. Whilst there is a strong history of environmental activism in some of the new Member States, the maintenance of that momentum is a matter of some concern.[85] These difficulties are compounded, given the role of access to justice in proceduralisation, in countries where former involvement in political repression undermines the authority of the judiciary.[86] Notwithstanding high hopes that 'a new age of environmental democracy' might be ushered in to central and eastern Europe via the Aarhus Convention, care needs to be taken that superficial legal changes are not put in place without changing old habits.[87]

Proceduralisation is moreover not just a phenomenon associated with the decentralisation of EC environmental law. It is a much more general trend, and the procedures involved are very often directed at the regulated, as well as the regulators. Proceduralisation follows the argument that conventional regulatory techniques have picked the low hanging fruit, and now respond only inadequately to persistent, complex or diffuse environmental problems. There is a danger that efforts to tackle these problems through direct regulation lead to ever more intrusive, complex and inflexible rules. In this more general sense, proceduralisation is often associated with theories of 'reflexive law'.[88] Rather than dictating the objectives to be achieved, or principles to be followed, reflexive law provides structures for self-reflection and self-criticism by those involved. Reflexive law emphasises the limits of law in addressing complex problems. It does not seek to determine the outcome of social processes, but to enhance the self-referential capacities of those subject

---

[82] See the discussion of 'goodness of fit' in C Knill and A Lenschow, 'Do New Brooms Really Sweep Cleaner? Implementation of New Instruments in EU Environmental Policy' in Knill and Lenschow, above n 80.

[83] C Knill and A Lenschow, 'Change as "Appropriate Adaptation": Administrative Adjustment to European Environmental Policy in Britain and Germany' *European Integration Online Papers* (1998) 2. The UK expected EIA to fit very easily into its existing well developed land use planning regime; in fact implementation was very slow, see M Stallworthy, 'Planning Law as a Tool of Environmental Protection: the United Kingdom's Slow Embrace of Environmental Assessment' (1998) 10 *Journal of Environmental Law* 361.

[84] See for example J Caddy, 'Implementation of EU Environmental Policy in Central European Applicant States: the Case of EIA' in Knill and Lenschow, above n 80.

[85] See the discussion in ch 1 above.

[86] A Antypas, 'A New Age for Environmental Democracy: The Aarhus Convention in Hungary' (2003) 11 *Environmental Liability* 199.

[87] Antypas, above n 86.

[88] See generally EW Orts, 'Reflexive Environmental Law' (1995) 89 *Northwestern University Law Review* 1227; G Teubner, L Farmer and D Murphy, *Environmental Law and Ecological Responsibility: The Concept and Practice of Ecological Self-Organisation* (Chichester, Wiley, 1994).

to regulation. In an environmental context, the objective is to create a firm (or an individual or regulatory institution) that continually thinks critically about its own environmental performance. It is not necessary to agree with all elements of reflexive law, or 'systems theory' on which it rests, to value its insights into mechanisms that encourage institutions to learn, to revisit decisions, and to absorb new information. This question of institutional learning and simple good practice has added resonance in the context of perceived disparities in levels of implementation between the Member States.

PROCEDURALISING DIRECTIVES

A number of directives could be identified as part of the move to 'proceduralisation', both in the sense of the access principles of the Aarhus Convention, and the more technical approaches introduced above. This section will look first at integrated pollution prevention and control, before moving on to environmental assessment. It will end with a discussion of environmental management systems, which look at the control of procedure within the regulated entity.

Integrated Pollution Prevention and Control

The Integrated Pollution Prevention and Control (IPPC) Directive[89] has become representative of the shift to procedure in EC environmental legislation, away from the emphasis of early legislation on rigid standards of environmental quality or performance. Nevertheless, in many senses, the IPPC Directive provides a very traditional legal mechanism. The basic command and control principle applies, obliging operators to apply for a permit for listed activities, which, again in a fairly conventional manner, are primarily major industrial activities, rather than diffuse sources of pollution. Within this traditional mechanism, however, IPPC does not set out methods of environmental protection to be adopted by installations, or indeed anticipate that national regulators will do so. Nor does the Directive provide emission standards to be met by installations.

The key requirement of the IPPC Directive is that regulators ensure that installations meet the emission standards achievable by 'best available techniques' (BAT).[90] BAT is:

> the most effective and advanced stage in the development of activities and their methods of operation which indicate the practical suitability of particular techniques for providing in principle the basis for emission limit values designed to prevent and,

---

[89] Dir 96/61, above n 28.

[90] *Ibid*, Art 3(a) requires that: 'all appropriate measures are taken against pollution, in particular through application of the best available techniques'. Other requirements under Art 3 relate to waste prevention, energy use, accidents and decommissioning. Art 3(b) requires that 'no significant pollution is caused'.

where that is not practicable, generally to reduce emissions and the impact on the environment as a whole.[91]

This definition is hardly elegant, but begins to demonstrate both the dynamism of BAT, that is its evolution as techniques and conditions change, and its effort at a holistic approach to the environment. The definition of BAT is supplemented by definitions of each element of BAT.

Best is 'the most effective in achieving a high general level of protection of the environment as a whole', an open-ended standard that reinforces the interconnectedness of the environmental media of air, water and soil. This 'integration' attempts to overcome the tendency for the more traditional media-specific approaches to regulation to transfer pollution from one environmental medium to another, for example because the stringency of regulation or its enforcement is uneven. The recitals to the Directive make much of links between 'integration' and 'sustainable development'. From an environmental perspective, however, IPPC is a narrow approach to the 'integration' principle found in Article 6 EC,[92] an approach that integrates environmental regulation, rather than an approach that integrates environmental considerations into other sectors. The relevance of economic analysis to environmental standards in BAT is made clear in the definition of 'available' techniques, which are 'those developed on a scale which allows implementation in the relevant industrial sector, under economically and technically viable conditions, taking into account the costs and advantages'. 'Techniques' includes technology used, and 'the way in which the installation is designed, built, maintained, operated and decommissioned', another inclusive definition that picks up on the holistic aims of the Directive, a 'cradle to grave' approach albeit that the impact of the installation's product is not addressed.

Whilst there is considerable detail in the Directive on BAT, that detail is rather open-ended. So for example, costs and advantages are clearly to be taken into account, but there is no further detail on either which costs and advantages might be relevant, or the appropriate response to those costs and advantages.[93] Nor is the assessment of 'economically and technically viable conditions' self-explanatory.[94] Annex IV to the Directive provides a wide range of further considerations to be taken into account in determining BAT, 'bearing in mind the likely costs and benefits of a measure and the principles of precaution and prevention'. These considerations include such matters as the use of low waste technology and the consumption and nature of raw materials, including water, as well as emissions and environmental risk.[95] Again, how these issues are to be weighed up and traded off is very open. The importance of local conditions in BAT creates still further space for flexibility. In all, BAT prescribes a number of relevant factors in an overall

[91] *Ibid*, Art 2(11).
[92] See ch 2 above.
[93] Scott, above n 4.
[94] The Commission, above n 81, states that this should be assessed on the basis of EU wide sectoral affordability.
[95] Dir 96/61, above n 28, Annex IV.

decision-making process that has a relatively open conclusion. This assumption of flexibility is not limited to regulators, but applies also to regulated entities. Regulators are required to set emission limit values to be applied to certain pollutants in individual permits.[96] The level of emissions achievable through BAT will be the target, 'but without prescribing the use of any technique or specific technology'.[97] Operators are not required to comply with specified procedures, as long as they meet the target. This possibility for operators facing different conditions and different costs to choose their own method of implementation is generally thought to be a more efficient way of achieving environmental objectives. These 'technology based standards' are however often simply implemented in the regulated entity by applying the technology on which they are based.

Whilst the IPPC Directive is formally highly flexible, actual flexibility in the determination of what can be achieved by BAT may be compromised. Joanne Scott, whilst focusing on the novel approach to regulation in the IPPC Directive, also notes the 'equivocal' nature of the commitment to flexibility[98]; Christian Hey argues that rather than avoiding centralised substantive standards, the IPPC Directive has in practice simply changed the forum for the centralised standard setting, from legislation to committees.[99] The extent of the flexibility turns around the role of 'BAT reference notes', or BREFs, centrally determined documents that set out BAT for particular sectors or issues. BREFs, which are not mentioned in the Directive, have emerged from the Commission's interpretation of its responsibility to report on BAT on the basis of the Directive's requirements for information exchange.[100] The BREF for each sector or issue is written by committees composed of representatives of the Member States, industry and environmental interest groups. BREFs may well turn out to be a very effective way of re-centralising standard setting. The BREFs are not formally binding on Member State permitting authorities, and should simply be a factor to take into account when determining BAT[101]; the impact of local conditions does moreover receive constant attention in the Directive. However, BREFs may well provide a very tempting reference point in a technically very demanding permitting process, particularly in Member States with fewer resources to devote to environmental regulation.[102] The BREFs carry considerable scientific, if not legal, authority, and the appeal of such scientific authority to decision-makers was discussed in chapter four above. The Commission has even indicated that it would consider challenging the application of lower standards in the absence of justification.[103] Although a

---

[96] *Ibid,* Art 9(3).

[97] *Ibid,* Art 9(4).

[98] Scott above n 4, p 266.

[99] C Hey, *Towards Balancing Participation* (Brussels, European Environmental Bureau, 2000).

[100] Dir 96/61, above n 28, Art 16. The Commission has contracted out this task to the IPPC Bureau in Seville, although it remains ultimately responsible. See the discussion of the Sevilla process in Commission, above n 81.

[101] Dir 96/61, *ibid,* Annex IV.

[102] They are likely also to have fewer resources to devote to the BREF committees.

[103] N Emmott, S Bar and RA Kraemer, 'Policy Review: IPPC and the Sevilla Process' (2000) 10 *European Environment* 204.

challenge under the terms of the legislation would require a more sophisticated analysis of the Member State's actual BAT process, BREF in these circumstances provides something of a fail safe for Member States, in what is proving to be a far from easy piece of legislation.

In itself the authority gained by the BREF process is not problematic, and it may simply indicate the quality of the BREFs. This *de facto* centralisation of standard setting does however raise very significant questions as to the reality of local participation in subsequent permitting decisions. The inclusiveness of the BREF drafting process also becomes much more important. Membership of BREF committees does include environmental interest groups, and draft BREFs are posted on the internet, allowing broader feedback. This goes beyond the requirements of the Directive, which refers just to an exchange of information between Member States and industry.[104] The balance between industry and environmental representation is nevertheless open to question. Poor representation of environmental interest groups, because of lack of resources or institutional constraints, would create a risk that IPPC will simply formalise a complex negotiation between industry and regulators.[105] There is certainly a danger that the BREF process is unduly influenced by industry interests, and the Commission seems to acknowledge that industry's access to resources of expertise and information gives it a certain influence. In particular, the 'most comprehensive information'[106] on BAT comes from industry; more worryingly, economic data is crucial for the determination of BAT, but industry often does not make this data available, or if it does, it proves very difficult to cross check.[107] The likelihood that resource intensive negotiations on BREF will be dominated by larger and wealthier Member States should also be borne in mind.

The 'soft harmonisation'[108] inherent in BREFs is not the only control kept by the centre. First, European-wide emission limit values may be set by Council where 'the need for Community action has been identified',[109] replacing local flexibility with centralised standards. What constitutes 'need' is an open question. The Commission has stated that a proposal should be put forward where 'it becomes clear that in one or more Member States the authorities systematically set emission limit values that are too lenient and not based on BAT'.[110] This could be based either on a calculation that competition is distorted, or concern about adequate environmental quality. The Commission suggests that Community wide

---

[104] Dir 96/61, above n 28, Art 16.
[105] Hey, above n 99. Bettina Lange's study of the BREF decision-making process suggests that interest representation (and hence negotiation and compromise, rather than simple fact finding) can be expected in the BREF committees, B Lange, 'From Boundary Drawing to Transitions: The Creation of Normativity under the EU Directive on Integrated Pollution Prevention and Control' (2002) 8 *European Law Journal* 246. Note the similarity with concerns about the other committees operating in the EU, see ch 4 above.
[106] Commission, above n 81, p 17.
[107] *Ibid.*
[108] *Ibid*, p 7.
[109] Dir 96/61, above n 28, Art 18(1).
[110] Commission, above n 81, p 23.

standards should be rare, as they would undermine both decentralisation and, by looking at individual substances, environmental integration.

Secondly, flexibility in the determination of BAT is conditional: if meeting an independent environmental quality standard would require an operator to go beyond BAT, that standard must nevertheless be provided in the permit.[111] The backstop of quality standards provides a reassurance to the centre in the context of flexibility. Quality standards are also the most flexible of available standards.[112] Nevertheless, a quality standard for a particular environmental medium (air, soil or water) and for a particular pollutant eats into the principle of integration, as these elements of the permit are not subject to the 'environment as a whole' analysis.[113] Nor do quality standards prevent the export of pollution. More generally speaking, proceduralising directives require a new approach to be found to address the transboundary effects of pollution, which is after all perhaps the most fundamental justification of EC environmental standard setting. The IPPC Directive explicitly requires the permit to contain conditions on the 'minimization of long-distance or transboundary pollution'.[114] The participatory elements of IPPC provide an alternative mechanism by which to consider transboundary pollution: if an installation is likely to have significant effects on the environment of another Member State, consultations are required between the two Member States, and there is an obligation to allow comments from the public of other Member States.[115] Whilst not mandating any particular result, these mechanisms are supposed to prompt reflection on transboundary issues, mitigating any problems of de-centralisation.

The IPPC Directive provides rights of public participation in the grant of permits for particular installations. Applications for permits have to be 'made available for an appropriate period of time to the public, to enable it to comment on them before the competent authority reaches its decision'[116]; a non-technical summary of information provided with an application for a permit has to be supplied by the applicant[117]; results of any post-authorisation monitoring required in the permit must also be made available.[118] The detail of public participation in the IPPC Directive has been amended in line with Article 6 of the Aarhus Convention.[119] The IPPC Directive now provides for 'early and effective opportunities to participate', the publication of a reasoned decision, as well as a requirement for the application for a permit to include an outline of the main alternatives con-

---

[111] Dir 96/61, above n 28, Art 10.

[112] At least in theory, although the ECJ's insistence on legally binding implementation can in practice restrict this flexibility, see Scott, above n 77.

[113] The same might be said of the separate assessment of carbon dioxide under Dir 2003/87 Establishing a Scheme for Greenhouse Gas Emission Allowance Trading Within the Community and Amending Council Directive 96/61/EC [2003] OJ L 275/32, discussed in ch 7 below.

[114] Dir 96/61, above n 28, Art 9(4).

[115] *Ibid*, Art 17, amended by Dir 03/35, above n 55. See more generally Macrory and Turner, above n 4.

[116] Dir 96/61, *ibid*, Art 15.

[117] *Ibid*, Art 6(2).

[118] *Ibid*, Art 15(2).

[119] Dir 03/35, above n 55.

sidered, if any. It also more clearly includes environmental interest groups in the participation process.

The introduction of public participation to pollution control regulation is an important recognition that pollution control is a political as well as a technical exercise, involving public values and the distribution of benefits and burdens. There are however undoubtedly barriers to significant public participation. Local participation is most meaningful in a context of local decision-making. If BREFs turn out to be more influential than their legal status would require, the centralisation of one of the key elements of the permitting process will restrict the scope of the public participation. National harmonised standard setting, rather than local standard setting, would have a similar effect, and the arrangement of domestic responsibilities is for the Member State. Even if considerable flexibility is left for the determination of BAT at a local level, moreover, the procedural elements of BAT are in any event specialist and technical in their orientation. There is likely to be some disjunction between the expression of public concern and the technical priorities of regulators, which the Directive itself does nothing to address.

And finally, the IPPC Directive also demonstrates an effort to encourage learning in regulation, in line with notions of reflexive law. Operators are required to include a range of information in applications, and 'reconsideration and updating' of permits is required independently of changes in the plant, operation, or legal standards, allowing improved knowledge, techniques or environmental changes to be reflected in permits.[120] Information available is subject to change; self-criticism is possible and decisions can always be improved. Learning is also an important aspect of BAT, which is inherently dynamic and changes with time, particularly as a result of technical progress. The information exchange provisions (BREF), as well as subsequent public participation techniques, involve the provision of information on experience and knowledge from a range of sources, and open up the possibility of deliberation. Even provision for the setting of European emission limits can be explained by 'learning': if progress is not made under the flexible core of IPPC, EU wide standards are available.

Environmental Assessment

From its earliest formal manifestation in the US National Environmental Policy Act of 1969, environmental assessment has become a widely used tool of environmental protection. The attraction of environmental assessment is entirely in procedure. Environmental assessment need set no substantive environmental standard at all, and does not even require decisions to point in an 'environmentally sound' direction. It rests instead on an assumption that the gathering of information will improve the environmental sensitivity of decisions. Through environmental assessment, public authorities are presented with environmental information

---

[120] Dir 96/61, above n 28, Art 13.

from a range of sources, and have an opportunity to reflect on the impact of their decision; the developer of a particular project produces and receives environmental information, and similarly has an opportunity to reflect upon it.

Environmental assessment can take place at a number of stages. The first development in the EU was environmental assessment of projects, followed more recently by strategic environmental assessment. To begin with the former, the Environmental Impact Assessment (EIA) Directive requires that 'projects likely to have significant effects on the environment by virtue, *inter alia*, of their nature, size or location' are subject to environmental assessment.[121] A project listed in Annex I of the Directive, mainly major industrial and infrastructure developments, is always subject to an assessment; a project listed in Annex II is subject to an assessment if the Member State determines that it is likely to have 'significant environmental effects'.[122] The submission of Annex II projects to environmental assessment is in this respect subject to considerable Member State discretion. The ECJ has however made it clear that the discretion is limited by the 'unequivocal obligation' that projects likely to have a significant effect on the environment are subject to an assessment.[123]

If a project does fall under the Directive, the developer is required to provide information on its environmental effects,[124] and the public is consulted. The request for development consent and the information provided by the developer, including a non-technical summary, have to be 'made available to the public within a reasonable time in order to give the public concerned the opportunity to express an opinion before the development consent is granted'. The results of consultations and the information gathered 'must be taken into consideration' in the decision-making,[125] an obligation reinforced by the requirement to publish the reasoning on the final decision and mitigation measures.[126] Although the public must be able to express an opinion 'before the development consent is granted', there is no provision for consultation before environmental information is produced by the developer, for example when the necessity and scope of the environmental assessment is determined. The EIA Directive, like the IPPC Directive, provides for transboundary as well as national participation.[127] And, again like the IPPC Directive, it has been amended to comply with the Aarhus Convention, clarifying the role of environmental interest groups, and making detailed changes in line with Article 6 of the Convention.[128]

---

[121] Dir 85/337, above n 33, Art 2.

[122] *Ibid*, Art 4. Annex III provides 'screening criteria', under which the need for environmental assessment can be determined either on a case by case basis or by reference to national criteria or thresholds. Member States are not allowed to exempt entire categories of project if it is not the case that every example of such a project will necessarily have no significant environmental effects, *Kraaijeveld*, above n 59.

[123] Case C–431/92 *Commission v Germany* [1995] ECR I–2189, para 39.

[124] Dir 85/337, above n 33, Art 5(1). The information required is set out in Art 5(3) and Annex IV. The developer can request a 'scoping' decision from the public authority.

[125] *Ibid*, Arts 6(2) and 8.

[126] *Ibid*, Art 9.

[127] Dir 85/337, *ibid*, Art 7.

[128] Dir 03/35, above n 55.

Environmental assessment has, for current purposes, at least two elements. Lawyers tend to concentrate on the enforceable procedural rights granted to the public through EIA, which have also featured rather heavily in EC and national litigation. The English House of Lords provides a nice example, holding that EIA is not simply about 'a right to a fully informed decision on the substantive issue', but far more fundamentally also:

> requires the inclusive and democratic procedure ... in which the public, however misguided or wrongheaded its views may be, is given an opportunity to express its opinion on the environmental issues.[129]

This very strong statement implies a value inherent to the procedure, regardless of results. Whilst it remains a useful statement of principle, it might be compared with some later cases in which the courts have taken a harder look at the trade offs involved in enforcing rigorous procedural requirements,[130] and at the environmental, rather than democratic, significance of errors in an environmental assessment.[131] This subtly moves away from the view in the earlier case that public participation has an inherent value, to a much more instrumental view of participation.

The Directive undoubtedly has a technical aspect, alongside its participatory aspect, and is in part at least a tool to assist in the technocratic assessment of projects.[132] The provision of environmental information by the developer is a technical contribution to decision-making, as is the consultation of interested (specialist) public bodies. The recitals to the initial Directive and the 1997 amendments make very little of public participation, apparently viewing the exercise simply as an opportunity to obtain extra information; the 2003 amendments, with their express aim of implementing the Aarhus Convention and also with the changing times, do shift the focus somewhat.[133] The potential tension between a technical approach to environmental assessment and adequate lay participation is unaddressed, even in the strong stance of the English House of Lords, cited above. In particular, the language of 'misguided' and 'wrongheaded' suggests something of a struggle for those who do not express themselves in the terms of the dominant framework. Moreover, it would appear that other jurisdictions downplay the participatory elements of environmental assessment, viewing procedural matters as secondary to getting the 'right' result.[134]

---

[129] *Berkeley*, above n 34, p 15, *per* Lord Hoffmann.

[130] See for example *Jones v Mansfield District Council* [2004] Env LR 21, especially the comments of Carnwath LJ, paras 56–61.

[131] See *Belize Alliance of Conservation Non-Governmental Organisations v Department of the Environment* (2004) not yet reported, especially paras 45–8.

[132] J Petts, 'Environmental Impact Assessment — Overview of Purpose and Process' in J Petts (ed), *Handbook of Environmental Impact Assessment* (Oxford, Blackwell Science, 1999) discusses competing understandings of EIA.

[133] Perhaps because of its later evolution, there is also more balance between the technical and participatory elements in Dir 01/42, above n 56, than was initially apparent in the EIA Directive.

[134] See K Ladeur and R Prelle, 'Environmental Assessment and Judicial Approaches to Procedural Errors — A European and Comparative Analysis' (2001) 13 *Journal of Environmental Law* 185.

There are serious limitations to assessing the environmental impact of projects only after overall needs and priorities have been determined. Strategic environmental assessment (SEA) is designed to fill this gap, by requiring assessment of public plans and programmes. The Strategic Environmental Assessment (SEA) Directive was a controversial initiative, taking many years to negotiate.[135] It requires assessment of all plans and programmes[136] in particular sectors, including agriculture, energy, industry, transport, if they 'set the framework for' projects either subject to EIA, or to assessment under the Habitats Directive.[137] Quite what it means for a plan or programme to 'set the framework for' a decision remains to be seen. Plans and programmes other than those listed are also subject to assessment where they 'are likely to have significant environmental effects', an important catch-all, taking assessment beyond the sectors listed in the SEA Directive or addressed by the EIA Directive, and arguably also beyond the Aarhus Convention, which is concerned with plans and programmes '*relating* to the environment', a possibly narrower concept.[138] Certain public authorities, designated by the Member State according to whether they have specific environmental responsibilities,[139] are consulted on the decision of whether environmental assessment is required.[140] Whether a plan or programme is likely to have 'significant effects' is assessed by reference to the 'characteristics of the plans and programmes' and the 'characteristics of the effects and of the area likely to be affected'.[141] SEA applies only to a plan or programme adopted or prepared by an 'authority' and 'required by legislation, regulation or administrative provisions'. There is likely to be some discussion, for example, of plans prepared by private utilities providers. A decision not to undertake an environmental assessment must be reasoned and made public.[142]

A plan or programme subject to SEA requires the production of an 'environmental report', in which 'the likely significant effects on the environment' of implementation of the plan or programme have to be 'identified, described and evaluated', as must 'reasonable alternatives'.[143] A non-technical summary is required. The Directive sets out the minimum contents of the report.[144] Public

---

[135] Dir 01/42, above n 56. For discussion, see W Sheate, 'The EC Directive on Strategic Environmental Assessment: A Much-Needed Boost for Environmental Integration' (2003) *European Environmental Law Review* 331.

[136] Dir 01/42, *ibid*, Art 2(a). If plans or programmes determine the use 'of small areas at local level', or in the case of 'minor modifications', environmental assessment is required only where they 'are likely to have significant environmental effects', Art 3(3). Note that plans and programmes the sole purpose of which is to serve national defence or civil emergency' and 'financial or budget plans and programmes' are excluded from the Directive, Art 3(8).

[137] Dir 92/43 on the Conservation of Natural Habitats and Wild Fauna and Flora [1992] OJ L 206/7.

[138] Note also that Dir 03/35, above n 55, Art 2, provides for public participation in respect of certain plans or programmes required under earlier legislation, for example Dir 75/442 on Waste [1975] OJ L 194/39, where they do not in any event fall under the SEA Directive. This does not provide for environmental assessment, just for mandatory public participation.

[139] Dir 01/42, above n 56, Art 6(3).

[140] *Ibid*, Art 3(6).

[141] *Ibid*, Annex II.

[142] *Ibid*, Art 3(7).

[143] *Ibid*, Art 5(1).

[144] *Ibid*, Annex I.

authorities are consulted in 'deciding on the scope and level of detail of the information which must be included in the environmental report'.[145]

As with EIA, there is no public participation on the scope or detail of the report. The SEA Directive provides for wider public consultation only after preparation of the environmental report. Both the draft plan or programme and the environmental report are made available to the public,[146] which is to be given 'an early and effective opportunity within appropriate time frames to express their opinion ... before the adoption of the plan or programme or its submission to the legislative procedure'.[147] The definition of 'public' in the SEA Directive makes clear the basic legitimacy of interest group involvement[148]; as in the Aarhus Convention, Member States are expected to identify the 'public' for participation in particular cases.[149] As discussed in chapter five, this raises inevitable concerns about the control of 'public' participation, and in particular concerns about exclusion or co-option of environmental interest groups. Nevertheless, it has to be recognised that public participation does not simply happen, especially at the level of plans and programmes, and that some thought needs to be paid to who should be involved. Public participation should not be a passive exercise for the responsible institution.

Under SEA, the environmental report and the opinions expressed 'shall be taken into account during the preparation of the plan or programme'.[150] This obligation is reinforced by the requirement for a statement of reasons, including not only a summary of how the environmental report and the results of consultations have been taken into account, but also a summary of how environmental considerations have been 'integrated' into the plan or programme.[151] This is a much stronger approach to reason giving than simply a directive to take environmental considerations into account, and potentially a very powerful tool for the integration of environmental considerations into other areas of policy. From the perspective of public participation in decision-making, however, one has to ask what becomes of public concern that does not address environmental questions; the nature of the reason-giving requirement suggests that it will be downplayed. If public participation is to be at all credible, and to contribute anything to the legitimacy of a process, the scope of the public participation process must be completely transparent in terms of what it is about and what it is for. Public participation on narrow environmental issues only, excluding for example social or economic issues, is a restricted and potentially frustrating exercise.

The SEA Directive includes an obligation to monitor the significance of the environmental effects of a plan or programme,[152] an obligation notably absent

[145] *Ibid*, Art 5(4).
[146] *Ibid*, Art 6.
[147] *Ibid*, Art 6(2).
[148] *Ibid*, Art 2(d).
[149] *Ibid*, Art 6(4).
[150] *Ibid*, Art 8.
[151] *Ibid*, Art 9.
[152] *Ibid*, Art 10.

from the EIA Directive. Not only does this allow for 'appropriate remedial action' to be taken, as suggested in the Directive, but is also crucial to any ideal that regulation should 'learn' from experience.

The introduction of SEA has been a long time coming, and remedies certain flaws of project-based EIA in isolation. Public participation on projects is often forced to be reactive to developers' proposals, with participants reduced to the role of objectors; done well, earlier public participation can be more proactive, and allow more constructive engagement. A broader range of issues arises at the earlier stage, and it is more likely to be feasible to seek to reduce or eliminate negative impacts.[153] Consideration not only of alternative sites, but also alternative solutions, should be possible, for example rail over road, or waste minimisation over waste disposal. This avoids the dislocation between the issues at stake and the issues open for consideration in project-based assessment: specific, localised forms of decision-making fall short when the issue at stake (climate change, nuclear power) is neither specific to that project, nor local. For the same reason, the participatory nature of the assessment process can be frustrated if it is introduced only at the final stage of a development, after the context has been set.

There are clear benefits to earlier participation, but it does also throw up some new challenges. The complexity of public participation increases as the scale of the decision expands. In particular, the non-specialist public will rarely be easily engaged by large-scale debates. The intensity of interests increases as specific outcomes (the waste incinerator, the airport extension) gets closer. The effect of plans and programmes on individual interests, whilst important, is not readily perceived; nor is it obvious to individuals what they can contribute. It is likely that organised interest groups, from industry and the environmental sector, will dominate in participation on plans and programmes. Their role is now secured by the relevant legislation. Whilst the domination of organised interest groups is to some extent inevitable, it also has a major impact on what can be claimed for public participation. In particular, and as discussed in chapter five above, there is nothing inherently more 'democratic' about these decisions. However, the most high flown claims for public participation tend to be reserved for the EU level, and the democratic deficit, rather than national level.

Environmental assessment is one of the most important legislative arrangements for public participation in environmental decision-making. Environmental assessment is not just about the public, however, but introduces a range of information generating procedures, ensuring that decision-makers are aware of the environmental implications of a decision. It constitutes an important effort at the 'integration' of environmental considerations into other policy areas. Environmental assessment is arguably more significant in this respect than IPPC, as it specifically highlights the environmental implications of other policy areas.

---

[153] Sheate, above n 135.

Self-Regulation: Environmental Management and Audit

The legislation discussed so far affects the decision-making of the regulated entity very intensely, imposing considerable procedural burdens on applicants seeking authorisation, as well as placing their ongoing decisions against a background of public information. Environmental assessment and IPPC are, however, largely tied to public administrative structures. Proceduralisation very often implies also the structuring of decision-making within the regulated entity, encouraging learning and problem solving in the societal decision-maker. The EC's voluntary Eco-Management and Audit Scheme (EMAS),[154] described as 'the purest and most consciously reflexive environmental law yet advanced',[155] moves away from government imposed command and control regulation, attempting to influence rather than direct. It provides a system whereby organisations voluntarily commit themselves to internal environmental management and independent verification of that management, a process intended to encourage self-critical reflection on environmental performance, and active engagement with environmental impacts.

To be registered under EMAS, an organisation must conduct an 'environmental review of its activities, products and services'.[156] This is extensive. It addresses not only the 'direct environmental aspects' of an organisation's operations, including issues such as transport as well as emissions, but also indirect environmental aspects, including product related issues and the environmental performance of contractors, sub-contractors, and suppliers. In the light of this review, the organisation puts in place an 'environmental management system',[157] which requires the creation of a public environmental policy, defined by 'top management', and documents the organisation's environmental objectives and targets, planning and implementation. The organisation must institute internal environmental auditing, 'designed to assess the environmental performance of the organisation'. The environmental review, management system and audit procedure are independently verified to ensure that they meet the requirements of the Regulation. The organisation finally has to produce an 'environmental statement', which pays particular attention to the results achieved against environmental objectives and targets, and the requirement for continual improvement of environmental performance. The environmental statement is independently validated and made publicly available. To remain registered, yearly validated updates of the environmental statement have to be prepared.[158]

The objectives of EMAS are, first, the evaluation and continual improvement in the environmental performance of organisations, and secondly, the provision

---

[154] Reg 761/2001 Allowing Voluntary Participation by Organisations in a Community Eco-Management and Audit Scheme (EMAS) OJ [2001] L 114/1.

[155] Orts, above n 88, p 1233.

[156] The requirements for registration are contained in Reg 761/2001, *ibid*, Art 3(2), applying detail in the Annexes to the Regulation.

[157] There is provision here for using other recognised certified management systems, Reg 761/2001, *ibid*, Art 3(a).

[158] *Ibid*, Art 3(3). Less frequent cycles are possible for small and medium sized enterprises, *ibid*.

of information to the public and other interested parties.[159] The notion of environmental improvement injects some substance into EMAS, as well as indications of dynamism and learning, but is extremely open-ended; it is also unavoidably controversial, requiring judgments about environmental priorities and trade offs that cannot be made on a purely technical basis.[160] In its second objective, EMAS extends information provision beyond obligations on public authorities, into the private sector. The emphasis on transparency is crucial to mitigate the potential for privatised schemes such as EMAS to close out public participation in setting and meeting environmental goals. More pragmatically, the influence of third parties is supposed to encourage environmentally beneficial behaviour.

A key feature of EMAS in its original form was its focus on individual industrial sites.[161] A concentration on sites brings EMAS to ground level, where pollution takes place, and usefully allows firms to experiment on single sites. The site focus is however rather narrow, and can ignore the broader impacts of the way a whole business is managed, tending to concentrate on direct environmental impacts. Entire 'organisations' can now be registered. Registration of single sites is however still possible. Commission Guidance attempts to overcome the risk of cherry picking particular sites, and as one might expect, transparency and 'public' and 'local' accountability are the key tools to this end.[162] Whether an element of cherry picking can be completely avoided is questionable; it is perhaps in the nature of a voluntary scheme that a balance has to be reached between encouraging take up and imposing challenging obligations. The other most significant change in the new EMAS Regulation is that it is no longer limited to industry, a limitation that had excluded environmentally significant sectors of the economy from the first scheme. EMAS now applies to 'any organisation dedicated to improving its overall environmental performance',[163] which might include, for example, financial institutions, whose operations can have a very serious impact on the environmental performance of the economy.[164] It also includes the public and the voluntary sector, which it has been suggested are more amenable to the sort of responses envisaged by 'reflexive regulation', in particular because environmental performance does not at every stage have to compete with the profit motive.[165]

Adequate levels of take up of a voluntary scheme like EMAS are the first requirement for its success. Member States are obliged to 'promote' participation,

---

[159] *Ibid*, Art 1.

[160] It is defined as 'the process of enhancing, year by year, the measurable results of the environmental management system related to an organisation's management of its significant environmental aspects, based on its environmental policy, objectives and targets; the enhancing of the results need not take place in all spheres of activity simultaneously', *ibid*, Art 2(b).

[161] Reg 1863/93 Allowing for Voluntary Participation by Companies in the Industrial Sector in a Community Eco-Management and Audit Scheme [1993] OJ L 168/1.

[162] See Commission Decision on Guidance for the Implementation of Regulation (EC) No 761/2001 of the European Parliament and of the Council allowing Voluntary Participation by Organisations in a Community Eco-Management and Audit Scheme (EMAS) OJ [2001] L 247/24.

[163] Reg 761/2001, above n 154, Art 3(1).

[164] BJ Richardson, 'Horizontal Instruments' vol 3 *Yearbook of European Environmental Law* 479.

[165] SE Gaines and C Kimber, 'Redirecting Self-Regulation' (2001) 13 *Journal of Environmental Law* 157.

particularly, given their historically low levels of participation in EMAS, by small and medium sized enterprises.[166] The limitations of command and control regulation in respect of small and medium sized enterprises, together with a frequent disparity between environmental aspirations and environmental performance, moreover, suggest that softer regulatory techniques may be useful.[167] 'Promotion' of EMAS can include technical assistance, financial support, and 'consideration' of how EMAS might affect procurement policies.[168] A number of more general incentives exist for participation in EMAS. The Regulation itself suggests that participants will find three elements of 'added value': 'regulatory control, cost savings and public image'.[169] The third, 'public image' is perhaps least controversial. Membership of EMAS can be used to signal environmental commitment to the public and customers[170]; pressure from powerful customers or financial institutions enhances the incentives to join. The promise of 'cost savings' assumes the discovery of win-win solutions to environmental problems, for example by reducing waste of expensive inputs. This is desirable, but one would hope that the impact of EMAS will extend beyond short-term economic advantage. It is also suggested that regulatory compliance becomes easier, for example because focused observation of the cost of compliance leads to ways to reduce those costs.[171] This leads to the question of 'regulatory control', which assumes 'light touch' regulation, and is the most controversial 'added value'. Whilst EMAS is without prejudice to EC or national environmental law,[172] and so cannot allow for the relaxation of regulatory standards, it is possible, for example, to apply less regular inspections or monitoring to registered organisations. The EMAS Regulation requires Member States to 'consider' how registration can be taken into account in implementation and enforcement of environmental legislation, 'in order to avoid unnecessary duplication of effort by both organisations and competent enforcement authorities'.[173] Relaxing regulatory inspection or monitoring of organisations registered under EMAS effectively passes regulatory control to the private 'verifier'. Under EMAS, a private verifier is contracted by the registered organisation to verify that organisation's environmental management and auditing system. Whilst privatised enforcement through enhanced standing, discussed above, involves supervising and supplementing public sector enforcement, this is more a matter of partial delegation. Verifiers are accredited under a national system, which must 'guarantee their independence and neutrality in the execution of their tasks'; there are also

---

[166] Reg 761/2001, above n 154, Art 11.

[167] See N Gunningham, 'Regulating Small and Medium Sized Enterprises' (2002) 14 *Journal of Environmental Law* 3, although he suggests self-auditing solutions of less ambitious scope than EMAS.

[168] Reg 761/2001, above n 154, Art 11.

[169] *Ibid*, Recital 9.

[170] The logo is not designed to be used on the labels of products.

[171] JJ Bouma, 'Environmental Management Systems and Audits as Alternative Policy Instruments?' in Knill and Lenschow, above n 80.

[172] A breach of 'relevant regulatory requirements regarding environmental protection' shall lead to a refusal / suspension of registration, Reg 761/2001, above n 154, Art 6(4).

[173] *Ibid*, Art 10(2). The Commission has to be informed on decisions taken in this respect.

provisions for peer review of accreditation systems.[174] Even with scrupulous accreditation, the financial relationship between verifier and organisation leads to concerns about the rigour of enforcement. Effective public scrutiny of enforcement may also be called into doubt. Nevertheless, there are obvious attractions for both regulator and regulated in pursuing less intense monitoring of EMAS registered organisations, and from the perspective of the broader public interest, it can allow regulatory attention to be focussed elsewhere, on the assumption that organisations without EMAS are higher risk.

As a supplement to more traditional regulation, EMAS is useful in its ability to turn the attention of an organisation to environmental issues. It is entirely voluntary, and involves largely autonomous setting of targets by organisations; as such its outcomes are inevitably uncertain, and it could not replace governmental responsibility. Indeed, the relative environmental performance of organisations with and without environmental management systems is surprisingly underexamined.[175] Nevertheless, the awareness-raising and reflection involved in full engagement with EMAS has the potential to take organisations beyond regulatory compliance in an economically efficient manner. Even if greater awareness does not on its own necessarily lead to significant behavioural change, particularly where improvement requires cost, disclosure provides additional, and perhaps more forceful, persuasion. Moreover, the obligation to improve environmental performance, whilst open-ended, means that EMAS implies at least a minimal check on environmental quality as well as process.

CONCLUSIONS

Proceduralisation is a crucial development in EC environmental law. It can be seen as a form of reassurance for the centre in the context of substantive flexibility. It is also an increasingly attractive option in the face of the difficulty surrounding the setting and enforcement of substantive standards. Different approaches to proceduralisation in EC environmental law are generally a response to common challenges. The most obvious challenge comes from democracy, and stresses questions of accountability, transparency and legitimacy, responding to disquiet about placing significant and controversial decisions in the hands of unelected bodies. Whilst participatory procedures attempt to provide 'surrogate political processes',[176] technical procedures attempt to allow more meaningful oversight of the performance of autonomous regulators. The challenge from effectiveness is met by the creation of a participatory decision-making process that acknowledges

---

[174] *Ibid*, Art 4.
[175] See C Demmke, 'Trends in European Environmental Regulation: Issues of Implementation and Enforcement' vol 3 *Yearbook of European Environmental Law* 329, p 350.
[176] R Stewart, 'The Reformation of American Administrative Law' (1975) 88 *Harvard Law Review* 1660, p 1712.

the richness of environmental problems; and by rigorous technical processes that allow rigorous solutions.

There have been very concerted efforts to ensure opportunities for public participation through EC environmental legislation. These efforts have received much less fanfare than equivalent measures at EU level, perhaps because the EU institutions are not concerned by any urgent democratic deficit at this level. And yet it might be argued that participation at the local level has the most to offer participatory democracy, being most likely directly to engage individual members of the lay public. There must still however be concerns about exclusion, concerns exacerbated by the ability of EU wide decision-making to set the conditions for public participation.

Of the pillars of the Aarhus Convention, EC law provides most detail on access to information, where a strong scheme has been put in place. The instrumental appeal of access to justice has long been plain, and the trend for participation has provided the impetus to secure, in particular, the ability of well resourced and well informed interest groups to contribute to the monitoring and implementation of EC environmental law. EC law also provides clear minimum obligations on public participation, which provide an important opportunity for both lay and specialist contribution to decision-making. The detail of the public participation has been tightened in some respects by Aarhus implementation, but the type of participation remains unspecified. Nothing is said on the risk of exclusion. Nor is there any commitment to deliberation or dialogue, but simply to a rather minimal information gathering exercise. Whilst the reasons behind public views may be explored and challenged in a way that can be used to explain and support non-technical decision-making, there is no requirement for such an approach. More extensive approaches to public participation are left to the Member States. This is perhaps appropriate; however, it should not be thought that we have a brave new world of environmental democracy.

Whether the EC institutions' role in national procedures should be uncritically accepted is a difficult question.[177] Proceduralisation is likely to have a major effect on national and sub-national administrative and democratic cultures, but has been accepted as if it were a minor technical matter. This phenomenon might be compared with the general equanimity that met expansion of EC competences in the 1980s. The political commitment indicated by the signature of the Aarhus Convention by all Member States means that the significance of the EU's role is at the moment being sidestepped. In addition, as long as procedural constraints are matched with substantive flexibility, they seem to be viewed as a fair exchange. The full implications of this shift are still to be explored.

---

[177] Scott, above n 4.

7

The Challenge from the Market

INTRODUCTION: COMMAND AND CONTROL
IN ENVIRONMENTAL POLICY

PROBLEMS NOW CATEGORISED as 'environmental' were for many centuries dealt with primarily by mechanisms of private law, particularly tort (non-contractual liability) and property law, supplemented by some public regulation. From the 19th century onwards, but particularly in the 1970s and 1980s, this approach was recognised to be inadequate, and public law measures were systematically introduced to control environmental degradation. Elaborate administrative systems have now been put in place, and public regulators are tasked with setting appropriate standards of environmental protection, and with monitoring performance and enforcing the law. Not surprisingly, given the timing of EC initiatives in the environmental sphere, EC environmental policy initially turned confidently to this form of public direction, commonly and loosely labelled 'command and control' regulation.[1] 'Command and control' embraces a wide range of regulatory techniques, sharing the basic characteristic that government regulation dictates a particular end or particular methododogy, and requires industry to comply. The central mechanism of command and control is the permit (or licence or authorisation), and examples abound in EC environmental law. Through the permit, regulators are able to exercise detailed and ongoing control over an activity.

In the early years of the 21st century, command and control remains the dominant form of environmental regulation; it is however subject to severe criticism. 'Command and control' is a phrase coined with derogatory intent, with connotations of soviet style interference in private life. The typical image of command and control involves a public authority dictating uniform environmental standards, across a large area, and applying prescribed methods of meeting those standards to every installation. Whilst this is undoubtedly a caricature of regulatory activity, it contains a core of truth, and successfully brings out the flaws of some traditional environmental regulation, to which I will return

---

[1] There is a large literature on 'command and control' and its critics. For a mainly British/EU perspective, see for example: R Baldwin and M Cave, *Understanding Regulation: Theory, Strategy and Practice* (Oxford, Oxford University Press, 1999); C Hilson, *Regulating Pollution* (Oxford, Hart Publishing, 2000), ch 6; J Scott, *EC Environmental Law* (London, Longmans, 1998) chs 2 and 3; J Golub, New Instruments for Environmental Policy in the EU: Introduction and Overview' in J Golub (ed), *New Instruments for Environmental Policy in the EU* (London, Routledge, 1998).

below. Notwithstanding this core of truth, however, command and control is a misleading label, failing to reflect the diversity of basic regulatory techniques, and more particularly their potential flexibility. Much of the criticism origi-nated in the United States, and reflects a particular approach to implementation and enforcement of regulation in that jurisdiction, rather than flaws with the regulatory technique itself, as well as a particular economic and political climate that was mistrustful of the role of the state.[2] Nevertheless, the term command and control is well understood, and it is arguable that with use the derogatory overtones have lessened; it is certainly a term that has been employed in this book for its virtue of familiarity, with no derogatory intent. It might however be argued that the continued legitimacy of this type of regulatory approach requires a revisiting of the language.[3] The term 'direct regulation' will be employed in this chapter.[4]

Whilst real areas of disagreement on appropriate regulatory methods remain, criticisms of direct regulation are such that the need for policy-makers at least to experiment with novel forms of regulation is virtually uncontested. A range of alternative tools is in principle available, and the use of information, the empowerment of third parties and mechanisms to promote self-examination and learning have already been discussed.[5] Externally imposed 'market' approaches to regulation provide a common theme in alternative environmen-tal instruments. A turn to the market is an effort to respond to the apparently contradictory pressures simultaneously to improve environmental quality and to reduce regulatory burdens. The intention of creating or intervening in mar-kets is to internalise environmental externalities, and/or to influence behaviour by price signals. Richard Stewart, an important observer of environmental reg-ulation, has described the difference between direct and market regulation as follows:

> command systems limit, directly or indirectly, the quantity of residuals that each actor may generate; [economic incentive systems] establish, directly or indirectly, a price that must be paid for each unit of residuals generated, but leave each actor free to decide on the level that it generates.[6]

---

[2] For one of the leading criticisms of command and control, see BA Ackerman and RB Stewart, Reforming Environmental Law' (1985) 37 *Stanford Law Review* 1333, and note also the discussion of high levels of litigation in the US context.

[3] R Macrory, 'Regulating in a Risky Environment' (2001) 54 *Current Legal Problems* 619.

[4] M Gunningham and P Grabosky, *Smart Regulation: Designing Environmental Policy* (Oxford, Oxford University Press, 1998) use this traditional term. Macrory, *ibid*, prefers 'determine and direct'. A simple use of the term 'regulation', J Dryzek, *The Politics of the Earth: Environmental Discourses* (Oxford, Oxford University Press, 1997), p 82, whilst accurate, may exaggerate the distinction between traditional approaches and alternative regulatory instruments.

[5] See particularly chs 5 and 6 above.

[6] RB Stewart, 'Economic Incentives for Environmental Protection: Opportunities and Obstacles' in RL Revesz, P Sands and RB Stewart (eds), *Environmental Law, The Economy and Sustainable Development* (Cambridge, Cambridge University Press, 2000), p 174.

The use of the market to achieve environmental goods has received some enthusiastic attention at European level. One of the central values of EC environmental policy, the polluter pays principle, is called on in support.[7] The precise meaning and application of the polluter pays principle is as difficult to pin down as the other environmental principles found in the Treaty. It certainly does not dictate any particular regulatory scheme, and often refers simply to the costs that all forms of regulation may impose on industry.[8] The polluter pays principle is, however, dominated by an economic approach to environmental protection that is consistent with a shift towards market or economic instruments and one of its key concepts is the internalisation of externalities.

The development of economic instruments have formed an important part of EC environmental policy for some years.[9] Progress has been extremely slow, but recent years have seen a modest breakthrough in the introduction of economic instruments to EC environmental law. This chapter will first consider some of the main criticisms of direct regulation from the perspective of advocates of market mechanisms, before turning to three particular economic instruments and their use in EC environmental law[10]: environmental taxation, perhaps the paradigm economic environmental instrument; 'emissions trading'; and environmental liability. The final subject of this chapter will be EU eco-labelling, and the rather splendid oxymoron of 'green consumerism'.

There are of course many objections to the use of economic instruments in environmental protection. Because of mutual efforts to reconcile economic development and environmental protection, links are often drawn between economic instruments and sustainable development. The multi-faceted normative framework of sustainable development should however remind us, if reminder is necessary, that environmental questions 'are not all economic'.[11] Environmental regulation, and the choice between different mechanisms of environmental regulation, are profoundly political exercises. Ideally, overall environmental objectives are set politically, and economic instruments used purely for implementation, allowing explicit value judgments to be made. Market instruments however assume even more strongly than direct regulation that environmental harm is a result of market failures, to be based on economic calculations. As such, there is a

---

[7] The polluter pays principle is contained in Art 174 EC; see also Recommendation 75/436 Regarding Cost Allocation and Action by Public Authorities on Environmental Matters [1975] OJ L 194/1.

[8] Recommendation 75/436, *ibid*; Note the second of Advocate General Léger's three suggested manifestations of the polluter pays principle, Case C–293/97 *R v Secretary of State for the Environment, Transport and the Regions ex p Standley* [1999] ECR I–2603: 'the costs of remedying pollution'; the costs 'arising from the implementation of a policy of prevention'; and costs where, 'in return for the payment of a charge, the polluter is authorised to carry out a polluting activity', paras 93 and 97.

[9] Decision 1600/2002 Laying Down the Sixth Community Environment Action Programme [2002] OJ L 242/1, especially Art 3. The Fifth Environmental Action Programme, *Towards Sustainability: A European Community Programme of Policy and Action in Relation to the Environment and Sustainable Development* [1993] OJ C 138/5, also made much of market instruments.

[10] Ch 8 below will discuss extended producer responsibility and voluntary environmental agreements.

[11] M Sagoff, *The Economy of the Earth: Philosophy, Law and the Environment* (Cambridge, Cambridge University Press, 1988), ch 2. See discussion in ch 1 above.

danger that the prioritisation of highly technical economic skills will tend to weaken the accessibility and accountability of even the public debate around overall environmental objectives. This is a familiar theme, but highly technical and specialised skills dominate the decision-making process, tending to exclude non-economic public values and public participation. Looking behind economic calculations to the value judgments implicit in them is extremely difficult. The fact that some environmental damage is valued more highly by its perpetrators (including individual consumers) than the cost of preventing it, does not in itself lead to the conclusion that all is therefore well with the world. And finally, there are also of course debates about the ability of economic instruments to deliver in practice on their theoretical promise. The impact of many such instruments on environmental quality is unpredictable, depending on uncertain economic calculations and on polluters behaving in economically rational ways. Whatever their benefits, they cannot be assumed to be the preferred solution in every case.

THE CHALLENGE FROM THE MARKET

The numerous criticisms of 'command and control' that emerged in the 1980s have undoubtedly been very influential across the political (and environmental) spectrum, but were initially particularly attractive to those who doubt the value of government intervention in industry, from a distinctly de-regulatory perspective. True advocates of de-regulation would expect governments to leave markets alone, doubting that government is necessary or competent to correct market failures, emphasising instead widespread regulatory failure. Alleged regulatory failures are legion and complex, including, broadly, complaints about efficiency and effectiveness, and arguments that, for a variety of reasons, regulation is carried out in the private rather than the public interest. The rise of a market approach to environmental policy can be linked with the ascendancy of market-oriented thinking generally, and with mistrust of government,[12] but economic instruments of environmental regulation are not generally de-regulatory. They rely heavily on state intervention to substitute for the failure or absence of markets,[13] and regulatory reform (rather than outright de-regulation) seems to be the dominant contemporary debate. Economic instruments are proposed as supplements to traditional mechanisms, or in areas where direct administrative intervention does not seem to be possible or helpful.

The use of economic instruments of environmental regulation rests broadly on questions about the ability of direct regulation to meet the objectives it set itself, and its ability to do so efficiently, or as cost effectively as alternative approaches. For the sake of simplicity, this section will discuss the criticisms of direct regulation from three different perspectives: first, the alleged lack of incentive to innovate; secondly, poor efficiency or cost-effectiveness from the perspective of both regulator

[12] Dryzek, above n 4, ch 6.
[13] See for example, Stewart, above n 6.

and regulated; and thirdly the apparent intractability of certain contemporary environmental problems. Whilst the main focus of this chapter will be on the effectiveness/efficiency elements of economic instruments, it should also be recalled that economic instruments also get some support from critics of the democratic accountability of environmental regulation. In particular, those who mistrust government would argue that the market, built on many small unconstrained decisions, is a more legitimate way of influencing social behaviour than direct regulation.

To turn back to efficiency/effectiveness arguments, first, fixed environmental standards are continually outpaced, both by more effective technology, and by increasingly complex environmental problems. Much direct regulation provides the regulated with no incentive to implement this new technology, or to respond to these new problems, as long as they are in compliance with the (outdated) legislation. Although it is possible to introduce more innovation into direct regulation, for example through the concept of 'best available techniques', which is potentially flexible and responsive to change,[14] this can be costly and slow, demanding considerable regulatory resources for monitoring, and probably also for amending permits.[15] Direct regulation generally provides little incentive for regulated industries to investigate innovative techniques or innovative problems ahead of regulators. By placing a cost on pollution, or a benefit on abatement, economic instruments can be designed to create a constant incentive to reduce pollution, by contrast with direct regulation and its generally fixed environmental standards.

The second major category of criticisms of direct regulation relates to its efficiency or cost-effectiveness, beginning with the burden it places on regulators. Direct regulation is resource intensive throughout the process: gathering information, setting standards, monitoring and then enforcing these standards. It may even be argued that direct regulation makes impossible demands of the regulator, which simply cannot possess and process this level of information. Briefly put, the regulator is not best placed to make detailed operational decisions.[16] By allowing the regulated party to make decisions based on the relative costs and benefits of pollution and pollution abatement, economic instruments harness the informational capacities of the regulated industry.

Direct regulation relies heavily on both the effectiveness and the enthusiasm of the public sector, and various possible failures, incompetence, capture, self-interest, could of course arise. In addition, particularly in times of economic downturn or neo-liberal politics, resources for the public sector are likely to be stretched. The automatic, mechanical nature of certain economic instruments, such as tax collection, ease concerns about adequate enforcement, as may the fewer points of negotiation in the use of economic instruments such as emissions trading. Market instruments do not however allow the public sector to escape difficult or costly procedures. Tax, for example, is rarely noted as a model of bureaucratic ease and

---

[14] See ch 6 above.
[15] Depending on whether the obligation to be alert to change is on the regulator or the regulated.
[16] Ackerman and Stewart, above n 2.

simplicity, and is also frequently perceived to be a particularly intrusive form of government intervention.[17] And to pre-empt slightly the discussion of greenhouse gas emissions allowance trading below, emissions trading is often also dependent on extremely complex and intrusive administrative arrangements; accurate monitoring of emissions is also essential, and is not cost free.[18] The assumption behind economic instruments, that everybody behaves as a rational economic calculator, emphasises the need to pay considerable attention to the possibility of cheating, and so the continued importance of monitoring and enforcement. Nevertheless, it remains the case that direct regulation makes onerous demands of the public sector, and that the resources needed to meet those demands are often vulnerable.

The efficiency or cost-effectiveness of direct regulation is also challenged from the industry perspective. The key issue is the matter of variable 'marginal abatement costs': some firms may be able to reduce pollution very cheaply; others may find it much more costly. The variability of costs depends on factors such as the age, location or scale of the plant. Requiring the same level of abatement across the sector may not be the most efficient way of reducing overall levels of pollution. Requiring different levels of performance from different operators would be a more cost-effective way of achieving the desired level of environmental quality. Because it would be extremely difficult for the regulator to calculate marginal abatement costs and apply them in direct regulation, for example in the permitting process, economic instruments are proposed as a way to allow variable levels of pollution. They are not designed to require a specific level of abatement from particular firms or installations; instead, they are designed to provide financial incentives to all firms to abate. Rational polluters will reduce pollution for as long as polluting (including the cost of the economic instrument) costs more than abatement. If the economic incentive successfully internalises all environmental externalities, pollution ceases to be economically worthwhile at the 'efficient' level of pollution, that is the level at which the total social cost of pollution meets the total social cost of abatement. Accurate calculations of environmental externalities are, however, elusive, and it is much more common to use economic instruments as a mechanism simply to place additional costs on pollution. These additional costs are designed to act as an incentive for environmental protection and innovation in pollution abatement.

The third category of critique of direct regulation argues that, whatever its achievements thus far, direct regulation has reached its limits, and is unable adequately to address new or persistent environmental challenges. The traditional licensing mechanism, with public sector monitoring and enforcement, is most well suited to point source pollution, and to obvious and visible harms. Tackling

---

[17] The direct action against the UK fuel tax in 1999 brings out the political sensitivity of taxation, particularly when perceived to affect small businesses. See the discussion in B Doherty, M Paterson, A Plows and D Wall, 'Explaining the Fuel Protests' (2003) 5 *British Journal of Politics and International Relations* 1.

[18] DH Cole, *Pollution and Property: Comparing Ownership Institutions for Environmental Protection* (Cambridge, Cambridge University Press, 2002) explains the unavailability of the necessary technology in the 1970s as a perfectly rational reason for very heavy reliance on direct regulation in this period.

diffuse harms through direct regulation is far more problematic, in practical terms, legitimacy terms, and efficiency terms. Climate change, for example, with its unusually complex environmental and economic implications, is an environmental issue often considered from the perspective of new regulatory instruments. Although a range of gases is thought to contribute to climate change (for example, nitrous oxide and methane), carbon dioxide is the major culprit, and the 'carbon economy', particularly our reliance on fossil fuels, needs to be addressed if there is to be any happy resolution. An extraordinary range of industrial, agricultural, transport and consumption activities thereby becomes the target of regulation. Whilst there is undoubtedly a role for direct regulation,[19] climate change is commonly thought to stretch direct regulation alone too far. In addition, the broad and deep economic impact of action to tackle climate change, together with continued uncertainty around the development and effects of climate change, emphasise the political imperative of identifying the least intrusive and most cost effective government action. No doubt the fact that climate change rose to prominence as an environmental problem at a similar time as new regulatory instruments came into the mainstream, and so very little entrenched traditional regulation applies to the problem, added to the appeal of alternative instruments.

There are many convincing critiques of direct regulation as currently operated, but blanket criticisms may be inappropriate. Even from a purely economic perspective, few argue that direct regulation is inefficient (produces fewer social benefits than costs) in every case, and nor is it necessarily less efficient than equivalent market instruments in every case. [20] In some cases, economic instruments seem to provide significant cost savings relative to direct regulation, and/or significant environmental advantages; in others, the effects are uncertain or absent.[21] Without entering the empirical debate, which is in any event riven with uncertainties, it is safe to say that the advantages of economic schemes over direct regulation cannot be assumed in all areas, but needs always to be examined.

It is also true that some criticisms of direct regulation are misdirected or exaggerated, particularly in underestimating the potential flexibility of direct regulation. Much of the criticism of direct environmental regulation assumes that direct regulation rests on *technical* standards,[22] which prescribe specific technologies across industry. On the contrary, it is actually rather unusual in the EU for the regulated industry to be told en masse how to operate.[23] *Emission* standards are more

---

[19] For example, both Dir 99/31 on the Landfill of Waste [1999] OJ L 182/01 and Dir 96/61 on Integrated Pollution Prevention and Control [1996] OJ L 257/26, provide direct regulation of elements of the problem: the Landfill Directive considers methane emissions from landfill, and the IPPC Directive considers energy efficiency and certain greenhouse gas emissions.

[20] Cole, above n 18 argues that it is impossible to propose one single regulatory/property form as always most efficient or effective.

[21] Stewart, above n 6, p 206, and the examples in Macrory, above n 3.

[22] Also known as specification standards or input standards. For detailed discussion of different standards, see Scott, above n 1, ch 2; Baldwin and Cave, above n 1, ch 9.

[23] DM Driesen, *The Economic Dynamics of Environmental Law* (London, MIT Press, 2003) argues that the same proviso applies in the US, and that many criticisms of regulation are accordingly based on a false premise, pp 50–4.

common, and more flexible, since whilst they dictate to an installation what it can emit, it can choose how to achieve that level. Even 'technology based standards', that is emission standards (like BAT discussed in chapter six above) set by reference to what can be achieved by a particular technology, which many choose to implement by means of the technology according to which they were set,[24] leave the opportunity for flexibility and innovation. *Environmental quality* standards set acceptable thresholds of pollution for the environmental media (air, water, soil),[25] providing considerable discretion to regulators to set different requirements for different installations depending on local conditions. And nor are economic instruments of environmental regulation the only possible response to legitimate criticisms of direct regulation. A number of others, particularly alternatives involving third parties in standard setting and enforcement, and the stimulation of learning and self-examination in regulators and regulated, have been discussed in earlier chapters.[26]

Justifications of economic instruments of environmental protection rest primarily on their efficiency relative to direct regulation and on their effectiveness, in particular their potential to stimulate continuing environmental improvement. There is an important role here for economics beyond cost benefit analysis.[27]

NEW REGULATORY INSTRUMENTS IN THE EU

At least at a rhetorical level, economic instruments have been enthusiastically embraced by the European institutions. Whether this enthusiasm is a reaction to political pressures towards de-regulation, or a more positive effort to apply new policies to new or stubborn problems, it has introduced new language, and a potential new direction for environmental policy.[28] The Sixth Environmental Action Programme continues the approach of earlier programmes by emphasising the importance of market instruments, whilst certainly not discounting the continued need for 'old' regulatory methods.[29]

Only limited use has so far been made of economic instruments in EC environmental law, however, and even Commission proposals in the environmental arena seem to be light on alternative instruments.[30] The Commission's policy to encourage Member States to make use of economic and other alternative instruments in national environmental policies can also be limited in practice by the

---

[24] RB Stewart, 'Regulation, Innovation and Administrative Law: A Conceptual Framework' (1981) 69 *California Law Review* 1259.
[25] Also called target standards or ambient standards.
[26] See especially chs 5 and 6 above.
[27] M Sagoff, 'Cows Are Better Than Condos, Or How Economists Help Solve Environmental Problems' (2003) 12 *Environmental Values* 449.
[28] B Rittberger and J Richardson, 'Old Wine in New Bottles? The Commission and the Use of Environmental Policy Instruments' (2003) 81 *Public Administration* 575.
[29] Sixth Environmental Action Programme, above n 9, especially Art 3.
[30] See the analysis in Rittberger and Richardson, above n 28.

potential for these mechanisms to clash with elements of internal market law. Notwithstanding a continued reliance on more traditional measures, however, recent years have certainly seen a number of, admittedly modest, moves to use market instruments at EC level, as well as certain efforts to facilitate their use at national level. The perhaps counter-intuitive position of the new Member States in central and eastern Europe should also be mentioned. Not only did market instruments seem to find a ready home in central and eastern Europe when those states broke with the socialist model of regulation,[31] but environmental taxes were also in place in some states much earlier; albeit that the effectiveness of market mechanisms in the absence of a functioning market is inherently limited.[32]

Environmental Taxation

Environmental taxes, designed to put a price on either emissions from, or inputs to, a process, are the economic instrument with which Member States of the EU have perhaps the most national experience.[33] At the EU level, however, there have been enormous problems in trying to introduce environmental forms of taxation. In particular, although environmental legislation is generally subject to qualified majority voting in Council, 'fiscal measures' require unanimity.[34] It is not surprising that some Member States continue to resist majority voting in the tax area[35]: tax policy goes to the heart of national sovereignty, and taxation and expenditure policies form central elements of national political debate. Nor is it surprising that reaching consensus on environmental taxation is difficult: the most pertinent policy area is the long and controversial history of EC energy or carbon tax, which implicates major and influential sectors of industry. With enlargement, the adoption of measures on the basis of unanimity is likely to become increasingly difficult.

The idea of an EC carbon tax was first introduced in a 1992 Commission White Paper, but following severe opposition by certain Member States, the 1992 proposal was withdrawn, and replaced by a far less ambitious proposal on energy products in

[31] P Jehlicka and A Tickle, 'Environmental Implications of Eastern Enlargement: the End of EU Progressive Environmental Policy?' in J Carmin and SD VanDeveer (eds), *EU Enlargement and the Environment: Institutional Change and Environmental Policy in Central and Eastern Europe* (New York, Frank Cass Publishers, 2004).

[32] T Sterner and G Kohlin, 'Environmental Taxes in Europe' (2003) 3 *Public Finance and Management* 117; Cole, above n 18.

[33] For some interesting comparisons, see Sterner and Kohlin, above n 32. See also European Commission, *Environmental Taxes and Charges in the Single Market* COM (97) 9 final. Note that 'environmental charges' are generally, unlike taxes, exchanged for services provided by the State, although it can sometimes be difficult to distinguish between the two. The Commission however refers to both taxes and charges as 'unrequited payments', under the broader term of 'levy', *ibid*, para 10.

[34] Arts 175(2)(a) and 93 EC.

[35] The Treaty Establishing a Constitution for Europe maintains the general requirement of unanimity on fiscal measures, Art III–234.

1997.[36] This was eventually agreed in modified form in 2003,[37] and will be discussed below, after a broader review of some of the debates around environmental taxation.

An environmental tax has a number of possible objectives, which are not always clearly distinguished. The aim could be to internalise all of the external costs of an activity, correcting market failure, providing efficient levels of production and fair competition. This is hardly a new instrument, being generally associated with the work of Pigou in the 1920s.[38] It is rarely if ever achieved: the calculation of externalities, which depends on profoundly uncertain and controversial economic valuations of particular predicted or actual environmental impacts, themselves uncertain, is impossibly difficult.[39] A rough approximation of some of the relevant externalities is the best that can be hoped for.[40] As an alternative to internalising externalities, taxes might be used to influence behaviour, in an effort to achieve a particular level of environmental protection at least cost. Indeed, if an environmental tax is to provide an economic incentive, it must be set at a level that exceeds marginal abatement costs, even if that exceeds the cost of externalities.[41] The setting of incentives is also, however, problematic. The capacity of a tax to change behaviour is determined by a number of uncertain and uncontrollable factors, such as the elasticity of demand, the availability of substitutes and the profits or economic efficiency of particular firms, as well as the level of the tax. The impact of the UK tax on the landfill of waste has, for example, been at best uncertain and in some cases clearly absent,[42] which some put down to the low level of the tax. Of course, getting the level right also assumes that the regulated all behave like rational economic calculators; when they do not, direct regulation has a greater potential than taxation. A third possible aim of environmental taxation, after internalising or incentivising, is to raise revenue. If revenue raising is the primary purpose of the tax, it would generally be excluded from the definition of environmental taxes. It is too easy to lose sight of the

---

[36] European Commission, *Proposal for a Council Directive Introducing a Tax on Carbon Dioxide Emissions and Energy* COM (1992) 226 final; European Commission, *Proposal for a Council Directive Restructuring the Community Framework for the Taxation of Energy Products* COM (1997) 30 final. The most persistent resistance came from the UK and Spain, predominantly on sovereignty and development grounds respectively. See A Jordan *et al*, 'European Governance and the Transfer of "New" Environmental Policy Instruments (NEPIs) in the European Union' (2003) 81 *Public Administration* 555, p 566; see also, the discussion of the 'carbon tax fiasco' in W Grant, D Matthews and P Newell, *The Effectiveness of European Union Environmental Policy* (Basingstoke, MacMillan Press, 2000), pp 122–6.

[37] Dir 2003/96 Restructuring the Community Framework for the Taxation of Energy Products and Electricity [2003] OJ L 283/51.

[38] A Pigou, *The Economics of Welfare* (London, Macmillan, 1920).

[39] A Ogus, 'Nudging and Rectifying: The Use of Fiscal Instruments for Regulatory Purposes' (1999) 19 *Legal Studies* 245. Sagoff, above n 27, discusses vastly different assessments of the benefits to be gained by improving visibility at the Grand Canyon, p 458; Macrory above n 3, discusses the different figures produced in respect of externalities produced by coal-fired power stations, p 622.

[40] Ogus, *ibid*, classifies such an approximation of a Pigovian tax as a 'rectifying measure', and compares it with a 'nudging measure' intended to influence behaviour.

[41] Driesen, above n 23, pp 68–9.

[42] A Martin and I Scott, 'The Effectiveness of the UK Landfill Tax' (2003) 46 *Journal of Environmental Planning and Management* 673; DN Pocklington and RE Pocklington, 'The United Kingdom Landfill Tax — Externalities and External Influences' [1998] *Journal of Planning and Environmental Law* 529.

environmental nature of a revenue raising tax,[43] and the environmental objective of changing behaviour conflicts with the objective of raising revenue; as behaviour changes in an environmental beneficial direction, revenue falls.[44] Nevertheless, the possibility of raising revenue for the environment, or the public purse more generally, is sometimes considered a major advantage of tax over more traditional regulation. Although some urge 'hypothecation', that is reserving certain tax revenues for certain (here environmental) purposes, hypothecation is not possible on a large scale if environmental taxation is designed to be 'fiscally neutral', offset by other taxes.[45] The opportunity to reduce tax on social 'goods' such as employment, is one of the major attractions of taxing social 'bads' such as pollution.

The question of the destination of tax revenues leads us to the controversial question of the distributive impact of environmental taxation. There are undoubtedly winners and losers in a move to market instruments; for example high energy, low employment industries lose out from a fiscally neutral energy tax. These industries are however being forced to bear some of the costs that they otherwise impose on the environment. The potentially regressive effect of environmental taxation is a more serious issue that should be considered before any whole-hearted embrace of eco-taxation. Progressive taxation is, simply put, taxation that redistributes wealth from the richer to the poorer. The principle of progressive taxation has been hard won, and should not be abandoned as an unintended side-effect of enthusiasm for environmental markets. It is impossible to determine in the abstract whether a tax is regressive, without concrete information on who pays and who receives precisely what. Broadly, however, tax on consumption, rather than income, tends to be regressive, and taxation of essentials, such as domestic fuel, is likely to have a greater effect on poorer households.[46] If revenue from environmental taxation is used to reduce the costs of employment, then the socially progressive nature of reducing unemployment should be included in the assessment of the tax.[47] Moreover, since the poor frequently suffer more from environmental degradation, doing nothing may turn out to be the most regressive measure.[48] Nevertheless, unless specific care is taken, environmental taxation may well be regressive; if care is taken, for example through

[43] Macrory, above n 3, observes how the UK government lost sight of the environmental purpose of the fuel tax escalator.

[44] Ogus, above n 39.

[45] See for example CE Jorgensen, *Environmental Fiscal Reform: Perspectives for Progress in the European Union* (Brussels, European Environmental Bureau, 2003). Note Dir 03/96, above n 37: 'Member States might decide not to increase the overall tax burden if they consider that the implementation of such a principle of tax neutrality could contribute to the restructuring and the modernisation of their tax systems by encouraging behaviour conducive to greater protection of the environment and increased labour use', Recital 11.

[46] S Tindale and C Hewitt, 'Must the Poor Pay More? Sustainable Development, Social Justice and Environmental Taxation' in A Dobson (ed), *Fairness and Futurity: Essays on Environmental Sustainability and Social Justice* (Oxford, Oxford University Press, 1999) is a very engaging analysis of this issue.

[47] Tindale and Hewitt, *ibid*.

[48] Tindale and Hewitt, *ibid*.

compensatory measures, it need not be.[49] It is also of course true that direct environmental regulation can be regressive. For example, it is sometimes argued that nature conservation tends to benefit the middle classes disproportionately, in which case nature conservation distributes social resources to the well off. This example implies a very narrow 'amenity' understanding of conservation, which potentially has much broader benefits, but the point remains that distribution is relevant both to direct regulation and economic instruments.

One final concern often expressed about environmental taxation, and economic incentives more generally, is the potential for the public to be squeezed out of decision-making. For example, tax affairs are generally confidential, although a move to market instruments is no reason to renege on commitments to access to particular environmental information, for example on emissions. More profoundly, market instruments shift the legitimate arena for particular decisions from the public to the private realm; decisions are taken within the firm or by the 'invisible hand' of the market place. Important opportunities for public discussion and for collective decision-making could thereby be lost.

Even if the overall objectives of environmental policy are set by public debate, once the market system is in place, democratic control of that process becomes very difficult[50]; this might be contrasted with the potential for public participation in and judicial control of direct regulation from legislation, through local permitting, to enforcement. And as mentioned in the introduction to this section, this raises yet again the potential for technical debate to narrow the basis for decisions and the scope for public involvement. Reliance on economic decision-making could impede accountability by obscuring the inevitable value judgments being made. Although some argue that market instruments improve accountability, because objectors are able to challenge the premises on which economic calculations are based more readily than political judgments,[51] this assumes both the objectivity of economics, and the ability of outsiders to identify and assess the judgments within the economic assessment. It is also argued that economic instruments, or more generally an economic approach to environmental regulation, enhances public participation, since all participate in the markets through which decisions are taken. Those markets include not just demand for the product subject to taxation or other environmental regulation, but also the real or hypothetical markets by which environmental externalities are calculated. This is, however, a strikingly shallow approach to public participation, reducing all political, aesthetic and ethical judgments to simple consumer choices. Environmental values are much more complex.[52]

---

[49] Tindale and Hewitt, *ibid.*

[50] E Rehbinder, 'Market-Based Incentives for Environmental Protection' in Revsez, Sands and Stewart, above n 6.

[51] See S-L Hsu, 'Fairness and Efficiency in Environmental Law' *The George Washington University Law School Public Law and Legal Theory Working Paper No 72.*

[52] See the discussion in ch 1 above.

None of this is to suggest that economic instruments should never be used. They should not be assumed always to be preferable however, and a clear effort needs to be made to ensure that public values, including distributional issues, are not sidelined.

The 2003 taxation Directive lays down minimum rates of tax for a range of energy products, including fossil fuels, and for electricity.[53] Given the reference in the Directive to obligations to limit emissions of greenhouse gases incurred under the Kyoto Protocol,[54] one assumes that the tax is designed to target behaviour rather than, or as well as, to achieve cost internalisation. The most striking thing about the Directive, aside perhaps from the mere fact of its eventual agreement, is the potential for varying the application of the tax within the terms of the Directive. Most obviously, the Directive provides for minimum levels of tax, rather than harmonisation. In addition, considerable allowances are made for derogations and transition periods in particular areas. So for example, if electricity accounts for more than 50 percent of the cost of a product, the Directive does not apply,[55] and indeed 'energy intensive business' more generally is allowed favourable treatment.[56] This type of arrangement for energy intensive business is not unusual, and is an attempt to ensure both that the tax is politically acceptable and that affected industries remain competitive. The effort to avoid economic dislocation in respect of important economic activities does, however, very considerably reduce the potential effect of the tax, given that these are the activities that contribute most to the harm targeted. The Directive also provides extensive derogations for specified Member States in particular areas.[57] The extensive derogations and exemptions made necessary by unanimity in Council are the price of retaining national control over such a sensitive policy area, but dramatically diminish the impact of the Community level instrument. More positively, the Directive allows for the exception or reduction of taxation on certain environmentally preferable forms of energy, including for example electricity 'of solar, wind, wave, tidal or geothermal origin'.[58] Differential taxation of this type could begin to provide for improved economic competition between different forms of energy. The Directive also attempts to support other 'alternative' regulatory instruments by allowing favourable treatment where voluntary agreements or tradable permit schemes have been put in place, 'as far as they lead to the achievement of environmental protection objectives or to improvements in energy efficiency'.[59]

---

[53] Dir 03/96, above n 37.
[54] *Ibid*, Recital 7.
[55] *Ibid*, Art 2(4)(b).
[56] *Ibid*, Art 17.
[57] *Ibid*, Art 18 provides one and a half pages of provisions. Note also European Commission, *Proposal for a Council Directive amending Directive 2003/96/EC as Regards the Possibility for Certain Member States to Apply, in Respect of Energy Products and Electricity, Temporary Exemptions or Reductions in the Levels of Taxation* COM (2004) 42 final, providing exemptions or reductions for the new Member States.
[58] Dir 03/96, *ibid*, Art 15(1)(b), first indent.
[59] *Ibid*, Art 17(1)(b).

The perceived need for differential rates of taxation is one of the reasons that national environmental taxes have sometimes run into problems with internal market law.[60] Article 90 EC provides that:

> No Member State shall impose, directly or indirectly, on the products of other Member States any internal taxation of any kind in excess of that imposed directly or indirectly on similar domestic products.

This is a basic prohibition of the application of different levels of taxation to national and imported products, which may raise concerns if products subject to a higher level of tax on environmental grounds are predominantly imported. Some flexibility is available, however. It is permissible to differentiate between products on the basis of objective criteria, whether or not those objective criteria can be identified in the final product, and so including the method of production.[61] The ECJ's decision in *Outokumpu* illustrates both the potential and the limitations of this concession.[62] Finnish legislation on the taxation of energy provided for differential taxation of energy produced in Finland on the basis of method of production, with lower amounts imposed on less damaging sources. Imported energy was taxed at a single rate, higher than the lowest rate applicable to domestic energy, but lower than the highest. The Court accepted that tax rates can vary according to the manner in which electricity is produced and the use of raw materials, in so far as such variation is based on environmental considerations. However, it took a strict approach to discrimination, holding that Article 90 is infringed if tax on imported and domestic products are calculated differently, leading (if only in some cases) to higher taxation of imported products.[63] Practical difficulties, including the difficulty of determining the method of production of imported energy, cannot justify breach, and in any event, the Finnish legislation did not give importers the opportunity to demonstrate that their electricity qualified for the lower rate.[64] Although this decision confirms in principle the legitimacy of using objective factors contributing to environmental protection as a basis for different rates of tax, it puts in place significant practical hurdles for the Member States. Environmental considerations do not justify discrimination in the *calculation* of the tax; the virtual impossibility of identifying the method of generation of imported electricity is treated as any other 'practical difficulty'.[65] *Outokumpu* might be unfavourably compared to

---

[60] Commission, above n 33.

[61] By contrast with the WTO Appellate Body, whose approach to distinction on the basis of production and process methods is contentious, see ch 9 below.

[62] Case C–213/96 *Outokumpu Oy* [1998] ECR I–1777.

[63] The fact that domestic energy production is taxed harder is not a relevant concern under Art 90, which does not apply to reverse discrimination.

[64] *Outokumpu*, above n 62, para 39.

[65] G van Calster, 'Greening the EC's State Aid and Tax Regimes' (2000) 21 *European Competition Law Review* 294; L Kramer, *Casebook on EU Environmental Law* (Oxford, Hart Publishing, 2002), pp 123–7; note also that the ECJ did not follow the opinion of its Advocate General, who preferred to concentrate on the 'compelling justification' for the Finnish scheme, para 56.

the Court's approach in *PreussenElektra,* in which the difficulty of determining the source of imported electricity did seem to be relevant to the finding that German measures favouring renewable energy were not incompatible with Article 28 of the Treaty.[66]

Applying lower levels of taxation to particular industries, either to protect the competitive position of particular parts of industry, or to incentivise environmentally beneficial industry, also raises state aid questions. EC law limits the grant of state aid to national industries, in order to protect competition in the internal market.[67] Direct subsidies are the most immediate target of state aid rules. Subsidies may mean that the public, rather than the polluter, pays for pollution, and indeed their impact on industry behaviour is not clear:

> a good strategy for power companies has been to increase their use of dirty coal stocks as they lobby for a regime of rewards to switch to clean coal and non-coal power generation.[68]

Nevertheless, state economic power can be a valuable way of incentivising environmentally beneficial behaviour, and state subsidy of, for example, renewable energy projects, may be necessary to kick-start development. If a state measure constitutes the grant of state aid, the Member State must give advance notification to the Commission, which has discretionary powers to decide whether the state aid qualifies for exemption.[69] The Commission has issued guidelines on state aid for environmental purposes, in an effort to pursue integration of environmental objectives into other Community policies.[70] Starting from a position of apparent scepticism, emphasising the importance of cost internalisation and the polluter pays principle, the Guidelines recognise the importance of reconciling internal market rules and economic instruments for environmental protection. Referring to the polluter pays principle, the Commission provides that state aid cannot generally be justified in respect of compliance with Community law, with possible exceptions for small and medium sized enterprises[71]; but may in certain limited conditions be justified in respect of activities that go beyond Community standards.

---

[66] Case C–379/98 *PreussenElektra AG v Schleswag AG* [2001] ECR I–2099, para 79. A number of controversial and difficult issues arise in this judgment. See S Poli, 'National Schemes Supporting the Use of Electricity Produced from renewable Energy Sources and the Community Legal Framework' (2002) 14 *Journal of Environmental Law* 209.

[67] Art 87 EC. See van Calster, above n 65.

[68] J Braithwaite, 'Rewards and Regulation' (2002) 29 *Journal of Law and Society* 12, p 24. Braithwaite argues that rewards are not generally appropriate in regulation.

[69] Art 87 EC.

[70] European Commission, *Community Guidelines on State Aid for Environmental Protection* [2001] OJ C 37/3, para 72. See H Vedder, 'The New Community Guidelines on State Aid for Environmental Protection — Integrating Environment and Competition' [2001] *European Competition Law Review* 365; G Facenna, 'State Aid and Environmental Protection' in A Biondi, P Eeckhout and J Flynn (eds), *The Law of State Aid in the European Union* (Oxford, Oxford University Press, 2004).

[71] This is a hardening of the position vis à vis the earlier guidelines, European Commission, *Community Guidelines on State Aid for Environmental Protection* [1994] OJ C 72/03.

More immediately pertinent, there is no doubt that tax breaks are capable of constituting state aids.[72] In respect of preferential tax treatment for competitiveness reasons, for example to energy intensive industry, the Commission states that 'the adverse effects of such aid can be offset by the positive effects of adopting taxes',[73] and if such treatment is necessary to allow the use of such taxes, it is acceptable, subject to conditions as to timing and amount. Similarly, the Commission allows for measures constituting state aid to promote renewable sources of energy.[74] Without going into any more detail on this complex area of law, an example might be useful. The UK's 'climate change levy' applied to non-domestic use of energy.[75] The use of natural gas in Northern Ireland was exempted for five years, in order to encourage the development of the natural gas industry, which is comparatively environmentally benign, in Northern Ireland. The Commission found the aid to be compatible with the Treaty because of its environmental effect.[76] The special energy situation in Northern Ireland, where the natural gas market was in its infancy and still marginal, and the limited time period and quantity of aid, were all important factors.[77]

Without wishing to go any further into the relationship between internal market rules and environmental taxation, it is important to observe the recurring tension between the internal market paradigm and certain economic instruments. The Community institutions are beginning to respond to the tension, but in many cases, the legal position remains somewhat uncertain. The new generation of 'trade and environment' disputes may well be provoked by economic instruments.

Emissions Trading

Emissions trading, or tradable allowances, involves the creation of a market, rather than the manipulation of existing markets.[78] Government determines the total quantity of emissions, at local, national or regional level, by setting overall emission limits. Individual allowances are allocated within that overall cap, and transferable property rights are created in allowances. Each operator can choose

---

[72] See for example Case C–143/99 *Adria Wien Pipeline GmbH v Finanzlandesdirektion fur Karnten* [2001] ECR I–8365.

[73] Commission, above n 70, paras 22 and 47 ff.

[74] Commission, *ibid*, paras 24 and 54 ff. Note that other Treaty provisions may also need to be satisfied, for example Arts 28 or 90.

[75] See BJ Richardson and KL Chanwai, 'The UK's Climate Change Levy: Is It Working?' (2003) 15 *Journal of Environmental Law* 39, for a detailed examination; also the discussion of the scheme in the Commission's decision letter, European Commission, *State Aid 660/A/2000 — United Kingdom, Exemption from Climate Change Levy for Natural Gas in Northern Ireland (Industry and Services).*

[76] Commission, *ibid.*

[77] *Ibid.* Note also the special provision for taxation of natural gas in Northern Ireland, Dir 03/96, above n 37, Art 15(1)(g).

[78] See generally Cole, above n 18; JH Lefevere, 'Greenhouse Gas Emission Allowance Trading in the EU: A Background' vol 3 *Yearbook of European Environmental Law* 149; Ackerman and Stewart, above n 2.

to emit to its allowance, to go 'beyond compliance' and sell the difference, or to purchase extra allowances on the market. Decisions depend on the price of allowances and the marginal cost of abatement; the latter will vary from firm to firm. The theory is that the same overall level of pollution reduction is achieved at a lower overall cost, as reductions take place where marginal costs of abatement are lowest. Although the incentive for those facing high marginal costs to increase pollution cancels out the incentive on those with low marginal costs to go beyond compliance, there may also be extra environmental benefits in turning pollution prevention from a 'burden' into a 'business', stimulating innovation and technology transfer.[79]

The EC has recently put in place a regime for the trading of greenhouse gas allowances, as a key part of internal climate change policy.[80] The EU was a late convert to the role of international trading in climate change policy.[81] It has very little experience with this new instrument of environmental protection, but the speed with which internal trading is being pursued should allow considerable learning opportunities before international trading starts in 2008.[82] The greenhouse gas allowances emission trading Directive appeals to the efficiency of market instruments: trading is to be permitted 'in order to promote reductions of greenhouse gas emissions in a cost-effective and economically efficient manner'[83]; reduction targets have been set independently of the trading scheme, through the Kyoto process.[84] The Directive applies initially only to carbon dioxide, but provision is made for expansion to other greenhouse gases.[85] It also applies only to certain specified categories of installation, and again there is provision for extension.[86] These installations are already regulated under integrated pollution prevention and control (IPPC),[87] and the Directive pre-empts the regulation of emission limits of carbon dioxide by IPPC, unless there is a specific problem with local pollution; the regulator may also choose not to impose energy efficiency obligations in the IPPC permit.[88]

---

[79] Lefevere, *ibid*, pp 166–7. Driesen, above n 23 doubts this, arguing that once 'equilibrium' is achieved, there is no further incentive, pp 56–68.

[80] Dir 2003/87 Establishing a Scheme for Greenhouse Gas Emission Allowance Trading Within the Community and Amending Council Directive 96/61/EC [2003] OJ L 275/32.

[81] See C Damro and P Luaces Méndez, 'Emissions Trading at Kyoto: From EU Resistance to Union Innovation' (2003) 2 *Environmental Politics* 71; Lefevere, above n 78.

[82] The EC scheme applies regardless of the fate of the Kyoto Protocol. Dir 03/87, above n 80, sets out periods of trading, from 2005–2008, and 2008–2012; further periods need to be set out by co-decision.

[83] Dir 03/87, *ibid*, Art 1, Recital 5. See also the original explanatory memorandum to the Directive, European Commission, *Proposal for a Directive of the European Parliament and Council Establishing A Scheme for Greenhouse Gas Emission Allowance Trading within the Community and Amending Council Directive 96/61/EC* COM (2001) 581 final.

[84] On the Kyoto obligations, see Decision 2002/358 concerning the Approval, on behalf of the European Community, of the Kyoto Protocol to the United Nations Framework Convention on Climate Change and the Joint Fulfilment of Community Thereunder [2002] OJ L 130/1.

[85] Dir 03/87, above n 80, Annex I, Art 30. Monitoring techniques need to be improved for the inclusion of other gases, see Commission, *ibid*, and above n 18.

[86] Dir 03/87, *ibid,* Annex I, Art 24.

[87] Dir 96/61, above n 19.

[88] Dir 03/87, above n 80, Art 26. The 'integration' objective of IPPC is hardly furthered in these circumstances: the environment is not being considered as a whole, but in separate components.

Under the Directive, national competent authorities issue 'greenhouse gas permits' to installations, setting out, *inter alia*, monitoring and reporting conditions.[89] A permit is granted only if the competent authority 'is satisfied that the operator is capable of monitoring and reporting emissions'.[90] The Member State also allocates 'greenhouse gas allowances' to individual operators. These grant permission to emit set quantities of specified greenhouse gases, and are transferable. In principle, when the scheme is complete, firms will also be able to convert credits from emission reduction projects outside the EU into allowances for the purpose of the EU scheme, albeit that 'a significant part' of the Kyoto targets must be achieved within the EU.[91] The permit contains a condition that the operator surrender at the end of the year greenhouse gas allowances sufficient to cover all emissions made in the year.[92] As well as requiring 'effective, proportionate and dissuasive' sanctions for breach of the rules implementing the Directive, the Directive specifies a fixed financial penalty to be applied against any operator that fails to surrender sufficient allowances; the name of the operator must also be published.[93] Such specific enforcement provisions are a remarkable innovation, and undoubtedly in part reflect general concern with inadequate and uneven enforcement of EC environmental law, which in this case could directly prevent an EU-wide market developing.[94] Tradable permit schemes are, however, inherently less discretionary in their enforcement than other permits: a simple single rule, that every emission must be met by a permit, applies with little if any room for negotiation. This may make a fixed penalty less problematic than otherwise; it is also particularly important in an economic incentive scheme that the cost of breach exceeds the cost of purchasing allowances.

The Directive requires every Member State to draw up a 'National Allocation Plan' setting out its overall level of emissions, and the initial allocations of allowances. The Directive provides that the plan be based on 'objective and transparent criteria', 'including' criteria set out in Annex III to the Directive, and taking 'due account' of comments from the public.[95] On the basis of the criteria in Annex III, the Commission may accept or reject national plans[96]; Annex III has been supplemented by rather complex guidance on allocation from the Commission.[97]

---

[89] Dir 03/87, *ibid*, Art 6(2)(c) and (d).

[90] *Ibid*, Art 6(1).

[91] European Commission, *Proposal for a Directive Amending the Directive Establishing a Scheme for Greenhouse Gas Emission Allowance Trading within the Community, in Respect of the Kyoto Protocol's Project Mechanisms* COM (2003) 403 final. This 'linking directive' creates a link with the 'flexible mechanisms' of the Kyoto Protocol, that is 'joint implementation' or 'clean development mechanisms'.

[92] Dir 03/87, above n 80, Art 6(2)(e), verified under Art 15.

[93] Dir 03/87, *ibid*, Art 16. Provision is made for the grant of additional non-tradable allowances in the case of force majeur.

[94] See ch 3 above.

[95] Dir 03/87, above n 80, Art 9(1).

[96] Dir 03/87, *ibid*, Art 9(3); on the basis also of Art 10, which provides for 95% and 90% free allocation.

[97] European Commission, *Guidance to Assist Member States in the Implementation of the Criteria Listed in Annex III to Directive 2003/87/EC Establishing a Scheme for Greenhouse Gas Emission Allowance Trading within the Community and Amending Council Directive 96/61/EC, and on the Circumstances in which Force Majeure is Demonstrated* COM (2003) 830 final. Note that the Directive does not cover all sources of greenhouse gas emissions, and the calculation of what is necessary to meet the Kyoto target should take into account all emissions.

The acceptable overall level of pollution, the 'cap' on pollution up to which permits will be allocated, is the most environmentally significant question in a tradable permit scheme.[98] The presence of a cap on pollution, and the associated level of certainty as to ultimate environmental performance and regulator control, contributes to the acceptability of emissions trading to environmentalists. The level of the cap is also crucial to the efficiency of the scheme, as the scarcity, or otherwise, of permits will dictate the success of the market; if too many allowances are issued, the price will collapse and no trading will take place. The setting of the cap is an overtly political question for the public regulator or legislator,[99] and is subject to a degree of public involvement and transparency.[100] Annex III of the Directive provides that total emissions under the National Allocation Plan cannot be higher than is necessary for a Member State to meet its obligations under the Kyoto Protocol.[101]

The allocation of allowances within the cap on pollution is also extremely controversial, although it is not in theory relevant for environmental or efficiency purposes: environmental protection is ensured by the cap, and the allowances in theory end up in the possession of those who value them most highly, whoever starts out with them.[102] Allocation, however, involves the distribution of significant economic goods, and so is very controversial in practice. Again, Member States must set out their approach to allocation in their National Allocation Plan, which also has to set out the installations to which the Directive applies, and the allocations to be made to them.[103] Some emission trading schemes provide for allowances to be auctioned to the highest bidder, which is a simple form of allocation that generates revenue and allocates resources where they are most valued in economic terms. Auctioning is generally resisted by industry, which perceives it as an obligation to pay for something that was previously received free, and is politically unpopular because of potential economic dislocation. Different approaches to allocation in the EU could raise internal market concerns, favouring industry in countries that allow free allocation over those that must purchase initial rights. The Directive provides for free allocation, initially of at least 95 percent of the allowances, and from 2008, of at least 90 percent.[104]

---

[98] It is possible to have a system with no cap, see Lefevere, above n 78.

[99] Hsu, above n 51; Ackerman and Stewart, above n 2. Hsu, for example, argues that the subsequent question of how these acceptable levels are achieved is not political, but one should note at least the distributional impacts of different implementation mechanisms.

[100] Text above n 95.

[101] Dir 03/87, above n 80, Annex III, criterion 1; see also Commission, above n 97, para 2.1.1. Nor can they exceed the total actual or projected emissions from the covered installations, Annex III, criterion 2; see also Commission, *ibid*, para 2.1.2. Actual or projected emissions are assessed under Decision 280/2004 concerning a Mechanism for Monitoring Community Greenhouse Gas Emissions and for Implementing the Kyoto Protocol [2004] OJ L 49/1. The overall allowances also have to take into account the 'potential' to reduce emissions, Annex III, criterion 3, Commission, *ibid*, para 2.1.3.1.

[102] Stewart, above n 6. This is a form of Coasean bargaining, and assumes costless transactions, which never exist in practice: RH Coase, 'The Problem of Social Cost' (1960) 3 *Journal of Law and Economics* 1.

[103] Dir 03/87, above n 80, Annex III, criterion 10.

[104] *Ibid*, Art 10.

Free allocation can be very complex because of efforts to get around the risks it creates of unfairness or inefficiency; the short period provided by the Directive for the submission of National Allocation Plans sets a daunting task.[105] Free allocation of permits can be based on various administrative criteria under the Directive. One possibility might be to award allowances on the basis of existing permits or existing emissions, but this could have the effect of rewarding heavy polluters and penalising those who have taken action to abate in advance of the trading system.[106] One of the other possibilities for Member States under the EC scheme is to 'benchmark' the average emissions per unit of production, and make allocations on the basis of historic, current or expected production[107]: by allocating on the basis of production rather than emissions, an advantage is given to operations with a low per unit level of emissions. The Member States may also choose more explicitly to take 'early action' (that is action going beyond legislation) into account in their National Allocation Plans.[108] Free allocation can make life difficult for new entrants, which brings with it concerns about competition, and is also an unfortunate replication of the 'command and control' problem of regulating old installations less stringently than new installations, with the perverse possibility that newer, cleaner installations cannot compete with older, dirtier ones. The National Allocation Plans have to contain information on participation by new entrants.[109] The Commission outlines three possibilities for Member States: they could require new entrants to purchase all allowances on the market; or set aside some of their allowances for periodic auctioning; or keep a reserve of allowances for free allocation to new entrants.[110]

The free allocation of allowances in national emission trading schemes can also raise state aid issues, and indeed one of the criteria for allocation contained in Annex III is consistency with Treaty state aid rules. There is no explicit guidance on this topic, but the Commission's approach to the UK emissions trading scheme is instructive.[111] Before the Directive was in place, the UK had introduced a voluntary emissions trading scheme in respect of certain greenhouse gases. It provided a financial incentive to entities entering the scheme and voluntarily taking on emissions targets. Both the free allocation of allowances and the payment of incentive money in principle constitute state aid. Holding both to be consistent with the Treaty, the Commission considered a range of factors, including: the fact

---

[105] The Directive was passed in 2003, requiring Member States to produce their National Allocation Plans by 31 March 2004, and the whole system is supposed to be up and running by 2005. By the end of June 2004, 15 National Allocation Plans had been submitted, see http://europa.eu.int/comm/environment/climat/emission_plans.htm.

[106] M Peeters, 'Emissions Trading as a New Dimension to European Environmental Law: The Political Agreement of the European Council on Greenhouse Gas Allowance Trading' [2003] *European Environmental Law Review* 82.

[107] Dir 03/87, above n 80, Annex III, criterion 3, together with Commission, above n 97, para 2.1.3.1.

[108] Dir 03/87, *ibid*, Annex III, criterion 7, together with Commission, *ibid*, para 2.1.7.2.

[109] Dir 03/87, *ibid*, Annex III, criterion 6, Commission, *ibid*, para 2.1.6.

[110] Commission, *ibid*, para 2.1.6.2. Note that Dir 03/87, *ibid*, Annex III, criterion 6 requires information on provision for new entrants.

[111] European Commission, *State Aid No N416/2001 — United Kingdom Emission Trading Scheme*.

that the scheme applies to companies going beyond existing standards 'and achieves a net environmental benefit'; the necessity of an incentive, given the voluntary nature of the scheme; and the time limits on the scheme.[112]

A couple of other controversial issues should be mentioned. First of all, emissions trading generally raises the danger that notwithstanding control of overall levels of pollution, unacceptable levels of pollution will be produced in one locality.[113] Of course direct regulation is in practice also far from flawless in this regard. This notorious 'hot spots' problem is largely avoided in respect of carbon dioxide emissions, given that climate change is a genuinely global problem, with no link between localised emissions and localised impacts; in any event, other forms of localised pollution caused by greenhouse gases can still be dealt with under the IPPC permit.[114] A different distributive issue also arises, particularly when emissions trading functions on a global scale, in respect of concerns that the rich continue to enjoy the economic fruits of their pollution, whilst the poor are forced to sell their allowances, burdening development. In respect of the internal, EU-wide operation of trading, enhanced disparities of wealth following enlargement make such issues increasingly pertinent. The accession of the new Member States is interesting in particular because economic recession in the 1990s took some countries below their Kyoto target, potentially providing opportunities for the sale of emission allowances.[115] Responses to the distributive issue include ensuring that a fair price is paid for allowances, which allows a transfer of resources to the poor, assisting rather than impeding development; and ensuring that the rich nevertheless take action to address their own lifestyles by requiring a minimum level of reduction.[116] The EU scheme leaves this problem, which admittedly is less intense within the EU than it might be globally, to the market.

Secondly, one might encounter questions as to who should participate in trading. Some schemes allow purchase only by operators, preventing outsiders from purchasing the permits, either for speculation (as permits are removed from the market, scarcity is likely to drive up prices), or to reduce overall emissions. The EU scheme in principle allows anyone to hold or transfer greenhouse gas allowances.[117] The ability of an environmental interest group to purchase and effectively 'retire' allowances is an important opportunity for environmental gain, and in economic terms allows public resources to go to the use valued most highly. There are difficulties. First, there may be an illusion of environmental involvement in the market, when in fact few environmental interest groups have the resources to make the necessary purchases. The fact that industry is willing and able to pay more to create pollution than environmental interest groups are

---

[112] Commission, *ibid*, para V2.2. Note that the Commission is clearly concerned about the compatibility of the UK scheme with the EC scheme, once it comes into force.

[113] Rehbinder, above n 50.

[114] Dir 03/87, above n 80, Art 26.

[115] G Klepper and S Peterson, 'The EU Emissions Trading Scheme: Allowance Prices, Trade Flows, Competitiveness Effects' (2004) *Kiel Working Paper 1195*.

[116] See discussion in Lefevere, above n 78.

[117] Dir 03/87, above n 80, Arts 12 and 19.

able to pay to prevent it, actually says very little about desirable levels of pollution. From the opposite perspective, environmental interest groups do not consider any other public interests, which the regulator should have had in mind when setting the cap on pollution. Rather than innovation, the scarcity of permits could lead plants to close down, bringing with it economic dislocation, loss of employment and associated social problems. This illustrates the more general point that the market can be a blunt instrument by which to assess social value; back to politics.

Environmental Liability

Environmental liability, the obligation to pay for harm done, has been on the EC policy agenda for many years, and forms a clear part of the Commission's commitment to diversifying regulatory instruments.[118] An Environmental Liability Directive was finally put in place in 2004.[119] The environmental liability scheme provided by the Directive is very modest compared to certain possibilities raised at various points of its negotiation. In particular, the final scheme is available purely in administrative law, as a tool for regulators, rather than as an element of private law; earlier consultations had considered the possibility of amending civil liability in the Member States in respect of harm caused in an 'environmental' manner.[120] This would have empowered third parties to bring claims, either by making claims brought under ordinary non-contractual liability in the Member States (for example for personal injury or property damage[121]) easier, or even by providing a claim for environmental interest groups in respect of environmental damage.[122] These proposals would have involved major interventions in national civil liability, for the promise of at best uncertain environmental benefits.[123] The Directive provides for a minimum administrative scheme for the remediation or prevention of environmental damage. Categories of 'occupational activity',[124] listed by reference to EC environmental legislation,[125] will be subject to strict liability for the costs of remedying or preventing 'environmental damage'. It is for

---

[118] See European Commission, *Green Paper on Remedying Environmental Damage* COM (93) 47 final.
[119] Dir 2004/35 on Environmental Liability with Regard to the Prevention and Remedying of Environmental Damage [2004] OJ L 143/56. See also ch 3 above.
[120] See particularly European Commission, *White Paper on Environmental Liability* COM (2000) 66 final. For discussion of earlier versions, see M Lee, 'From Private to Public: The Multiple Faces of Environmental Liability' [2001] *European Public Law* 375; M Lee, 'The Changing Aims of Environmental Liability' [2002] *Environmental Law and Management* 189.
[121] 'Traditional damage' claims in the language of the White Paper, *ibid*, which would have provided for strict liability, and considered ameliorating rules on causation.
[122] *Ibid.*
[123] Why harms caused 'environmentally' should be treated so differently from similar harm brought about by different means is a question that is not easily resolved: P Cane, 'Are Environmental Harms Special?' (2001) 13 *Journal of Environmental Law* 3.
[124] An occupational activity is 'any activity carried out in the course of an economic activity, a business or an undertaking, irrespectively of its private or public, profit or non-profit character', Dir 04/35, above n 119, Art 2(7)
[125] Dir 04/35, *ibid*, Art 3 and Annex III.

the regulator, not for individuals or environmental interest groups, to bring the action, although provision is made for judicial review.

The Directive sets out three categories of 'environmental damage': damage to protected species and natural habitats; water damage; and land damage.[126] Damage to protected species and natural habitats is 'any damage that has significant adverse effects on reaching or maintaining the favourable conservation status of such habitats or species'[127]; protected species and natural habitats are those listed under the Wild Birds or Habitats Directives, with the option for Member States to include nationally designated habitats or species.[128] Damage to water is damage 'that significantly adversely affects the ecological, chemical and/or quantitative status and/or ecological potential' of water, as defined in the Water Framework Directive.[129] Land damage is defined by reference to 'a significant risk of human health being adversely affected'[130]; the Directive's remediation provisions indicate that the impact on human health is assessed by reference to the actual use of land, rather than by reference to the most vulnerable possible use of land.[131] This has the side-effect of radically de-centralising the notion of 'land damage', since the development objectives for particular sites are most often dictated by the private sector and by local authorities.

Although there is currently no free standing legislation by which to define land damage, in the other two cases, the Directive borrows from other legislation. This emphasises the potential of liability to act as a deterrent to the breach of legislation, and so to improve implementation. It also simplifies the scheme: even if 'conservation status' and 'ecological status, ecological potential and/or chemical status' are not yet entirely clear, they are central elements of their respective legislation, and as such encourage the development of a consistent approach.

The Environmental Liability Directive provides for a core strict liability regime in respect of environmental damage caused by the operations listed in the Directive, with a subsidiary fault liability in respect of unlisted occupational activities that cause damage to protected species or natural habitats.[132] Although it is inevitably controversial, once the decision to create a scheme *specifically* to deal with environmental damage has been taken, strict liability addresses the nature of the harm far more effectively than would a requirement for fault or unreasonable behaviour: environmental damage is after all the natural, expected and indeed reasonable result of ordinary economic enterprise. Strict liability is nevertheless subject to very significant limitations in the Directive. A 'state of the art' defence may be provided by the Member States, in respect of harm resulting from:

---

[126] *Ibid*, Art 2(1). Damage is 'a measurable adverse change in a natural resource or measurable impairment of a natural resource service which may occur directly or indirectly', Art 2(2).

[127] *Ibid*, Art 2(1)(a).

[128] *Ibid*, Art 3. Dir 1979/409 on the Conservation of Wild Birds [1979] OJ L 103/1; Dir 1992/43 on the Conservation of Natural Habitats and Wild Fauna and Flora [1992] OJ L 206/7.

[129] Dir 04/35, *ibid*, Art 2(1)(b); Dir 2000/60 establishing a Framework for Community Action in the Field of Water Policy [2000] OJ L 327/1.

[130] Dir 04/35, *ibid*, Art 2(1)(c).

[131] *Ibid*, Annex II.

[132] *Ibid*, Art 3(1).

> An emission or activity ... which the operator demonstrates was not considered likely to cause environmental damage according to the state of scientific and technical knowledge at the time when the emission was released or the activity took place.[133]

The state of the art defence is intended to exclude certain unlikely damage from liability, and presumably to protect industry innovation. The risk of the unknown, of particular types of scientific uncertainty, remains with society. Again, a concentration on deterrence or enforcement can be detected here; liability for unforeseeable damage is not thought to encourage effective deterrence. More significantly from this perspective, Member States may also provide a defence in respect of harm resulting from authorised emissions or events,[134] a 'compliance' defence that places regulatory decisions at the heart of environmental liability. Neither defence applies in respect of a negligent defendant, which could raise some serious questions about the extent to which it is negligent to fail to move ahead of regulation. These two defences have the potential to restrict liability very significantly

The Directive also sets out the nature of the remediation to be required of the polluter.[135] The need for monetary valuation of environmental resources is minimised by concentrating on physical remediation.[136] 'Complementary' remediation, and 'compensatory' remediation may be required, in respect of damage that is not fully restored by primary remediation, and interim losses between damage and primary remediation. This type of remediation might include the provision of natural resources or services on an alternative site. In respect of habitats and species damage and water damage, the objective is to return the environment to its 'baseline condition'. The Directive rejects a 'multi-functional approach' to land damage, which would require land to be made suitable for any possible use. Instead, remediation must ensure that land 'no longer poses any significant risk of adversely affecting human health', on the basis of the use of land. Land use is assessed by reference to land use regulations in place when the damage occurred, or if there are none, the nature of the area; if land use changes, further measures may be necessary.

The development of environmental liability at EC level has rested very firmly on the polluter pays principle.[137] There is certainly an intuitive link between a successful liability claim and the principle, both of which take a neo-liberal, cost-internalisation approach to environmental protection. The polluter pays principle does not however dictate any particular form of regulation, let alone the detail of liability. The Environmental Liability Directive deals conservatively with the

---

[133] *Ibid,* Art 8(4) (b).
[134] *Ibid,* Art 8(4) (a).
[135] *Ibid,* Annex II.
[136] Monetary compensation may be necessary if the preferred 'resource to resource' or 'service to service' methods of calculating complementary or compensatory measures is not possible, or not possible within a reasonable time frame or at reasonable cost, *ibid,* Annex II, paras 1.22 to 1.23.
[137] *Ibid,* Art 1: 'The purpose of this Directive is to establish a framework of environmental liability based on the "polluter pays" principle, to prevent and remedy environmental damage'.

meaning of 'polluter' and 'pollution', both of which are open in the principle itself. It defines these key terms by reference to existing regulation: pollution ('environmental damage') is not only defined where possible by reference to existing legislation, but may also be subject to a defence if it is brought about by permitted emissions or activities; the polluter is deemed in most cases to be the party subject to regulation under EC environmental legislation.[138]

Whilst environmental liability in a general sense and the polluter pays principle provide economic instruments of environmental protection, both are subject to a certain tension between economic perspectives and ideas of justice, that it is 'right' that the polluter should pay. The foreword to the *White Paper on Environmental Liability* discusses the 'suffering and painful death of several hundred thousands of sea birds and other animals' in a particular pollution incident.[139] This is not an appeal to economic efficiency, but to the emotions. Similarly, the question 'should the bill for this be paid by society at large, in other words, the tax payer, or should it be the polluter who has to pay ...?',[140] appeals to notions of fairness rather than efficiency. This is perhaps consistent with common lay understandings of the polluter pays principle, and should remind us of the fundamental concern of civil liability with compensation and justice, objectives that are rarely mentioned in discussions of environmental liability. Complex jurisprudential debates consider the role of different conceptions of justice in civil liability, but even at their simplest, notions of justice can provide attractive alternatives to pure efficiency-based understandings of environmental liability, and indeed economic instruments more generally. So, for example, whilst many environmentalists feel uncomfortable with the possibility of 'buying' a right to cause environmental damage, the idea that wrongs should be righted has a much more powerful appeal.

Environmental liability can take many forms, and is able to respond to a number of the different challenges faced within EC environmental law: it can be a tool of liberal economics, internalising externalities; in private law, it can provide alternative points of access for third parties into the regulatory process, re-opening otherwise technocratic and closed decisions, simultaneously responding to changing perceptions of risk and harm[141]; liability provides funds for environmental restoration; it supplements centralised enforcement of environmental law, by providing an additional tool for regulators, or by providing additional private sector enforcers[142]; and it may provide redress for wrongs done. The role of liability depends however on the detailed design of the scheme. Many of the subtleties of environmental liability have been abandoned in the two decades it has taken to produce a Directive, as the 'implementation challenge' has overtaken other potential objectives. It is interesting in particular to observe the ways in which the

---

[138] *Ibid,* Art 3(1)(a) and Annex III.
[139] Commission, above n 120, p 5. Note also that oil pollution at sea would have been excluded from the possibilities being discussed at that stage, and is excluded from Dir 04/35, *ibid,* Art 4(2).
[140] Commission, *ibid.*
[141] See especially J Steele, 'Assessing the Past: Tort Law and Environmental Risk' in T Jewell and J Steele (eds), *Law in Environmental Decision Making* (Oxford, Clarendon Press, 1998).
[142] See ch 3 above.

Directive limits the possible advantages to be claimed from economic instruments. First, many environmental externalities will not be internalised by this instrument, because of the relatively narrow definition of damage and defendant, and the availability of defences to cut down the scope of strict liability. Secondly, if Member States choose to apply the compliance defence, liability provides no incentive for operators to go 'beyond compliance'; for the same reason, there is no stimulation of the regulated party's information, innovation or self-regulatory capacities. The very close links between liability and existing regulation limit the scope of liability, but emphasise its enforcement and implementation potential.[143] And whilst third parties are not able to bring actions against polluters, limiting private sector contributions to direct sanctioning, their rights of judicial review do allow them to monitor regulatory activity.

Conclusions

Given its enthusiasm, it is perhaps surprising that the EU has struggled to find its own voice in the provision of economic instruments of environmental protection. The EU continues to rely heavily on national environmental policy for the development of economic instruments, and even then certain difficulties are experienced as environmental instruments compete with harder-edged and better established internal market law. The mismatch between what is said and what is done raises accountability concerns, but there seem now to be intensified efforts to reconcile rhetoric and action. Some significant, if modest, market instruments have been introduced over the past few years, although direct regulation remains at the heart of environmental policy, and efforts are also being made to enhance the feasibility of national instruments. The primary objective seems to be the appropriate regulatory 'mix' and the right choice of instruments for specific problems.[144] Just as direct regulation cannot bear alone the weight of its promise, economic instruments also have their limitations.

GREEN CONSUMERISM

Much environmental harm is caused by the consumption of products and services, an activity that nobody can avoid entirely, even if some seek to reduce it. If all environmental costs are fully internalised, the market price of a product or service reflects its harmful potential: a fully competitive market would enhance incentives to reduce the negative environmental impact of a product, even if the consumer does not consciously purchase on environmental grounds. Economic

---

[143] Note that tying the legislation to existing legislation also helps to ease concerns about subsidiarity, which would be intense in respect of some of the more ambitious suggestions in the White Paper, above n 120.

[144] See also Stewart, above n 6; Cole, above n 18; Gunningham and Grabosky, above n 4.

instruments, such as taxes and subsidies, are then amongst the tools used to stimulate preferential consumption of environmentally more benign goods. Because markets do not work on the basis of full cost internalisation, an important strand of market thinking on environmental protection relies on the 'green consumer', who consciously purchases on environmental grounds. However, the environmental quality of a product is not evident when purchases are made. In order to capitalise on perceived consumer interest in environmental protection, producers may make 'green claims' about their product, but consumers are not able to verify this information, even after purchase. The integrity of the information provided is crucial. A number of difficulties arise, aside from problems with misleading or downright inaccurate information, which could be dealt with in the same way as other consumer protection issues. So for example, information provided may not be readily comparable, making consumer selection difficult; the real nature of the claim may not be transparent; and some relevant information, for example on production rather than use, may be missing.

The EC Eco-Label Regulation is an example of legislative control of the quality of environmental information.[145] The objective of the Regulation is to 'promote products which have the potential to reduce negative environmental impacts, as compared with the other products in the same product group', an objective to be 'pursued through the provision of guidance and accurate, non-deceptive and scientifically based information to consumers'.[146] The Regulation provides an entirely voluntary scheme, whereby producers of goods or services[147] can apply to the relevant national competent authority for a label that allows them to demonstrate to consumers the environmental qualities of their goods. The Regulation sets out the broad criteria for the award of an eco-label: the product must possess 'characteristics which enable it to contribute significantly to improvements in relation to key environmental aspects', based on efforts to ascertain the 'net environmental balance between the environmental benefits and burdens ... throughout the various life stages of the products', and including 'as far as technically feasible' consideration of 'extraction or the production and processing of raw materials and energy production'.[148] The life cycle approach means that a full range of information should be taken into account.[149] The simple yes/no approach of EC eco-labelling, that is the product either receives a label or it does not, is however rather blunt when faced with such a complex range of environmental considerations. It reduces the information made available to the consumer, and requires a difficult balance in deciding eligibility. It is, however,

---

[145] Reg 1980/2000 on a Revised Community Eco-Label Award Scheme [2000] OJ L 237/1. L Kramer, 'European Community Eco-Labelling in Transition' (2000) 1 *Yearbook of European Environmental Law* 123, discusses the development of the Regulation.

[146] Reg 1980/2000, *ibid*, Art 1(1).

[147] *Ibid*, Art 1(1); this is an extension from the earlier legislation, Reg 880/90 on a Community Eco-Label Award Scheme [1992] OJ L 99/1. The initial scheme was widely criticised, see Jordan *et al*, above n 36.

[148] Reg 1980/2000, *ibid*, Art 3.

[149] See also *ibid*, Art 1(2).

simple and accessible for consumers, and may be more useful than a mass of information; simplicity is perhaps a necessary tradeoff in consumer approaches to environmental protection.

The EC Eco-Labelling Board develops detailed requirements for the award of an eco-label to different product groups, on the basis of a mandate from the Commission, and those requirements are then submitted to scrutiny through comitology.[150] The Regulation provides for a level of transparency in setting criteria for the award of an eco-label, including involvement of consumer and environmental groups, explicitly to encourage acceptability of the scheme by the general public.[151] The Eco-Labelling Board is composed of Member State competent authorities, plus a 'consultation forum', which should comprise:

> a balanced participation of all relevant interested parties concerned with that product group, such as industry and service providers, including SMEs [small and medium sized enterprises], crafts and their business organisations, trade unions, traders, retailers, importers, environmental protection groups and consumer organisations.[152]

This is an important opportunity for broad involvement in the eco-label, although the comments made elsewhere about the reality of the resources available to the different groups, and the potential for industry domination, should also be borne in mind.[153]

Whatever the detail of the EC eco-label, which competes with a range of national labels,[154] there are limitations to 'green consumerism' as a form of environmental protection. It is sometimes argued that the market allows a much wider and more direct participation in environmental decision-making than politics. If most consumers make decisions primarily on the basis of price and performance, reducing the economic signals sent to producers, that would then suggest a lack of interest in environmental issues, and a genuine reflection of the market value of environmental protection. Alternatively however, complex value judgments may simply be difficult to capture in market transactions. The conceptualisation of 'public participation' in market approaches to environmental protection is very different from that involved in the participatory approaches to environmental protection discussed in earlier chapters; political debate allows a much more complete recognition of the nature of environmental problems than market transactions. Not only is green consumerism limited to superficial participation, but it is limited to those with the financial and social means to participate in the market.

---

[150] *Ibid*, Art 6.

[151] *Ibid*, Recital 5.

[152] *Ibid*, Art 15.

[153] See chs 5 and 6 above.

[154] Reg 1980/2000, above n 145, Art 11 seeks coordination between schemes, but confirms the possibility of a range of schemes existing side by side. Earlier Commission proposals would have provided for the gradual disappearance of national labels as product groups were established under the EC scheme, see Kramer, above n 145.

And although collective consumer responses are occasionally organised, green consumerism is largely limited to individual participation on essentially collective issues; an understanding of individual responsibility for environmental degradation is important, but there is a danger of underplaying the role of collective decision-making. These are subjects to which chapter nine will return in the specific context of genetically modified organisms; whilst green consumerism may be useful, it is rarely capable of responding to the spectrum of political concerns.

More generally, green consumerism certainly has no concept of environmental 'limits'. Modern economies rely on growth, and the environmental benefits of individual purchases are likely to be quickly outstripped by increase in consumption. Indeed, eco-labelling is a positive marketing tool, aimed at increasing consumption (albeit in theory at the expense of other more damaging products). For those concerned by the damaging effects of consumption, the idea of green consumption can seem wholly oxymoronic. Although consumer campaigns on environmental issues can be very successful, they sidestep these more fundamental questions about the relationship between environmental degradation and consumption, and as to whether particular products are necessary at all.[155] Because the EU eco-label merely ranks products within product groups, it not only discounts the 'no consumption' option, but also less damaging alternative products.[156]

There is much potential in the use of consumer power, perhaps particularly if one considers the situations in which political action falls short, for example in respect of the policies of foreign states, or the activities of corporations in foreign states, where traditional citizen political influence is very weak.[157] The thin line between information provision and marketing in the philosophy behind eco-labels, however, emphasises that eco-labelling is a far from complete response to the harm caused by products.[158]

CONCLUSIONS

The 1970s saw a major shift from private to public law as the extent of environmental problems initially caught the public attention; there is now a strange sense of 'back to the future' in efforts to return to the market to regulate environmental protection. Although taxation, tradable permits, and liability as dealt with at EC level are clearly public law instruments, their influence depends on markets rather

---

[155] For example, the campaign by environmental groups against the use of ozone depleting chemicals in consumer aerosol sprays (such as hairsprays, deodorants), was highly successful in its own terms, but paid no attention to the *need* for those products, see A Dobson, *Green Political Thought* (London, Routledge, 2000), pp 205–6.

[156] Hilson, above n 1, provides the example that the relative merits of different batteries will be considered, but not the less harmful mains operated appliance, pp 109–10.

[157] M Micheletti, A Follesdal and D Stolle, 'Introduction' in M Micheletti, A Follesdal and D Stolle (eds), *Politics, Products and Markets: Exploring Political Consumerism Past and Present* (New Brunswick, Transaction Publishers, 2004).

[158] See more generally J Holder, 'Regulating Green Advertising in the Motor Car Industry' (1991) 18 *Journal of Law and Society* 323.

than government. Other new instruments, including consumerism, contract and self-regulation,[159] are more clearly private.

Ideological conflicts about the proper role of government in commercial and private life can be identified in this area. John Dryzek makes some rather acute observations about the ambivalence towards government of those he terms 'economic rationalists'.[160] On the one hand, there is a mistrust of, and even contempt for, government, which it is assumed is populated either by individual economic calculators who manipulate the public in their own private interest, or by dupes manipulated by external economic calculators in their individual economic interest. And yet a market approach to environmental regulation requires a sophisticated government apparatus, operated by highly (economically) qualified individuals in the public interest. A similar ambivalence could begin to explain the (albeit diminishing) disparity between rhetoric and reality at EC level. The turn to market instruments was borne from a politics of de-regulation and mistrust; in practice, however, the instruments involved in market regulation require considerable regulation, and are highly sensitive in terms of national sovereignty and popular politics.

The proper role of government remains, however, a crucial question. Market instruments not only foster a perception that government is reducing its involvement in regulation; by prioritising the decision-making tools of economics, market instruments can provide, like the scientific rationality discussed in earlier chapters, an apparently inevitable response to otherwise difficult political problems. The inescapably normative nature of many environmental decisions should be kept in mind. Market instruments need not take decisions out of political hands, being merely instruments by which to achieve policy goals set by political decision-making processes, but it is important to assert the continued role of the collectivity in setting norms and monitoring their implementation. Moreover, the assumption behind market instruments, of a population of rational economic calculators, has a less than inspiring message for the future of environmental protection. In particular, price signals are likely lead to superficial changes in behaviour; when it no longer makes economic sense to protect the environment, so be it. For as long as the 'ecological citizen'[161] remains in the future, economic instruments perform a useful role. As both the benefits and limitations of market instruments become clearer, one might hope for continued scaling down of the rhetoric, along with a greater willingness to use such instruments.

---

[159] See chs 8 and 9 below and 6 above.
[160] Dryzek, above n 4, ch 6.
[161] A Dobson, *Citizenship and the Environment* (Oxford, Oxford University Press, 2003).

8

Waste: Diversity in Regulation

INTRODUCTION

W ASTE REGULATION IS a strangely engaging area of EC environmental law. Strange because eyes tend to glaze over at the mention of
waste law, which is in many respects technical and obscure. Engaging,
however, for a number of reasons. First of all, waste regulation is profoundly political. Although it does not obviously attract the level of enthusiasm that conservation issues can, or the popular antipathy of controversial new technologies like
genetic modification, waste regulation is nonetheless capable of evoking very
strong feelings, particularly when it comes to ,siting installations for the management of waste. Secondly, whilst waste regulation is based unambiguously on direct
regulation, the nature of waste invites an analysis that extends beyond licensing.
The most effective way to address waste is to reduce its rate of production, something of which 'end of pipe' control of waste management operations is manifestly
incapable. A study of waste involves a study of experiments with alternative regulatory instruments, including market instruments and self-regulation. And finally,
for better or more likely for worse, waste regulation is real lawyers' law, the very
complexity of which provides a certain intellectual challenge.

It is hardly surprising that when EC legislators began to pay serious attention to
waste in the 1970s, they largely took the production of waste as a given, turning to
typical direct regulation. The Waste Framework Directive imposes an obligation on
Member States to put in place a licensing system, under which, in principle, a
permit is required by anybody who wishes to carry out 'disposal' or 'recovery' operations on 'waste'.[1] The licensing of waste management operations, however, has
never been the limit of EC waste policy. In particular, the waste hierarchy is supposed
to underpin waste policy. Waste production is increasing and if no action is taken
seems set to continue to do so[2]; the waste hierarchy requires priority to be given to
waste reduction, then reuse, recycling and recovery, with waste disposal at the bottom of the hierarchy.[3] Breaking the link between consumption and waste production
is a crucial part of efforts to reconcile environmental protection and economic

---

[1] Dir 75/442 on Waste [1975] OJ L 194/39, amended by Dir 1991/156 [1991] OJ L 078/32, Art 9.
[2] See European Environment Agency, *Europe's Environment: The Third Assessment*, 2003, available at
http://reports.eea.eu.int/environmental_assessment_report_2003_10/en, p 151; European Commission,
Towards a Thematic Strategy on the Prevention and Recycling of Waste COM (2003) 301 final.
[3] Dir 75/442, above n 1, Art 3.

growth. The potential conflict between the objectives of economic growth and of reducing waste may be highlighted by enlargement, as historically fairly good environmental performance in certain new Member States is increasingly subjected to countervailing market forces.[4] In 2003 the Commission adopted a Communication, *Towards a Thematic Strategy on the Prevention and Recycling of Waste*,[5] which could constitute the beginnings of an effort to place waste prevention and recycling closer to the heart of waste regulation.

Whilst waste is an important topic in its own right, it also demonstrates particularly acutely many of the challenges faced in environmental law more generally, including questions as to effectiveness and efficiency and tensions between technical decision-making and public anxiety. This chapter will begin with a discussion of some of the main legal complexities in waste regulation, in particular the difficult definition of waste itself. It will then discuss efforts to move beyond the regulation of waste management and to move waste up the waste hierarchy. In particular, this section will discuss the current debate about the legal approach to recycling, and the obligation in the Landfill Directive to divert waste from landfill.[6] The widespread difficulties encountered in siting the waste installations that are needed in some Member States to cope with diversion from landfill will also be discussed here. These difficulties bring out the need for waste regulation to be alert to public opinion. The self-sufficiency principle, and the difficult relationship between waste regulation and the free movement of goods will then be considered, before turning to two particular indirect regulatory instruments: extended producer responsibility and voluntary agreements.

LAWYERS AND 'WASTE'

Stephen Tromans has described EC waste law as 'a complete mess'[7]; it is difficult to dissent. Notwithstanding fairly simple objectives, the law is extraordinarily complex, provoking litigation at the highest level, and doubtless much confusion and expense on the ground.

Tromans identifies a number of factors creating difficulties in waste law,[8] some of which apply throughout environmental law, although they may be more pronounced

---

[4] Z Gille, 'Europeanising Hungarian Waste Policies: Progress or Regression?' in J Carmin and SD VanDeveer (eds), *EU Enlargement and the Environment: Institutional Change and Environmental Policy in Central and Eastern Europe* (New York, Frank Cass Publishers, 2004).

[5] Commission, above n 2. Decision 1600/2002 Laying Down the Sixth Community Environment Action Programme [2002] OJ L 242/1, Art 4 requires the Commission to put in place seven thematic strategies by July 2005. The 'towards' documents 'set out the definition and scope of the issue and scenarios for possible solutions', letter from Margot Wallstrom to European Parliament, 29 March 2004, available at http://europa.eu.int/comm/environment/waste/wallstrom_letter.pdf .

[6] Dir 99/31 on the Landfill of Waste [1999] OJ L 182/1.

[7] S Tromans, 'EC Waste Law — A Complete Mess?' (2001) 13 *Journal of Environmental Law* 133.

[8] The five reasons for complexity identified by Tromans, *ibid*, pp 134–5, are: waste can be traded, leading to a tension with free movement of goods; waste is an emotive subject; reliable statistics on waste are not readily obtained; national policies on recycling have the potential to cause difficulties for the

in waste. First of all, waste is an emotive subject, and categorisation of a material as waste can affect public acceptability of facilities that use or treat it; the legitimacy issues that arise throughout environmental regulation are particularly acute here. Secondly, the lack of reliable information on waste makes it difficult to set targets based on 'a comprehensive environmental and economic analysis', and to monitor progress.[9] Again, this applies more generally in environmental law, reflecting a broader ignorance or uncertainty about environmental conditions. Thirdly, EC waste legislation is frequently attempting to respond to international initiatives as well as following its own agenda; again, this arises elsewhere in environmental law, but acutely in waste legislation. So for example Regulation 259/93 on shipments of waste[10] attempted to implement both the Basel Convention[11] and the OECD regime,[12] which Damien Chalmers describes as like 'trying to ride two horses galloping in opposite directions'[13]: Basel is set against the background of uncontrolled movements of waste to countries with poor regulatory standards in place, and emphasises the need to control and restrict waste transfers; the OECD regime, on the other hand, addresses states that have well developed waste management systems, for whom waste can be a valuable resource.

This leads to a further significant complicating factor, which is the status of waste. Waste is a 'good' that is traded commercially, as well as an environmental problem. However, waste receives a certain amount of 'special treatment' in internal market law, particularly by the application of the self-sufficiency and proximity principles, discussed below. The familiar tension between environmental regulation and free movement of goods arises particularly sharply in this area, however, and internal market concerns have on occasion been exacerbated by very ambitious national recycling policies, which can distort markets for recycled materials; this in turn has forced the Community to react to national initiatives, leading to difficult legislation based on political compromise. The Packaging Waste Directive,[14] for example, was famously a response to economic pressures created

---

free movement of goods, forcing the Community's hand; EC law has to take account of international waste law.

[9] Commission, above n 2, p 23. The Commission is of the view that Reg 2150/2002 on Waste Statistics [2002] OJ L 332/1, will enable a first assessment of trends in waste generation only in 2008, *ibid*. The use of poor evidence and data in EC waste policy and legislation is heavily criticised by House of Lords Select Committee on the European Union, 2002–2003 47th Report, *Waste Management Policy* HL 194.
[10] Reg 259/93 on the Supervision and Control of Shipments of Waste Within, into and out of the European Community OJ [1993] L 30/11. Note that this Regulation is subject to amendment in order, inter alia, to reflect amendments to the international regimes. See European Commission, *Proposal for a Regulation of the European Parliament and of the Council on Shipments of Waste* COM (2003) 379 final; *Amended Proposal for a Regulation of the European Parliament and of the Council on Shipments of Waste* COM (2004) 172.
[11] *Basel Convention on the Control of Transboundary Movements of Hazardous Wastes and their Disposal*, 22 March 1989, see http://www.basel.int.
[12] Especially OECD, *Decision of the Council Concerning the Control of Transfrontier Movements of Wastes Destined for Recovery Operations*, 30 March 1992.
[13] D Chalmers, 'Community Policy on Waste Management — Managing Environmental Decline Gently' (1994) 14 *Yearbook of European Law* 257, p 289.
[14] Dir 94/62 on Packaging and Packaging Waste [1994] OJ L 365/10.

by national schemes.[15] It is no coincidence that its legislative passage was extremely controversial, very heavily lobbied and subject to many compromises. The Directive that emerged was criticised by environmentalists for weakness, and over-emphasis of single market issues; but also by industry for being too vague to avoid divergent national policies.[16]

The seemingly inexhaustible line of litigation on the definition of waste is perhaps the clearest indication of the complexity of waste regulation, and, given the expense of litigation, also of the money tied up in the subject. The complexities, intricacies and inconsistencies of the definition of waste are now well-trodden ground, and need only be briefly discussed here.[17]

The polluting potential of waste has both objective and subjective dimensions, which are reflected in the definition of waste.[18] Certain waste may have *objectively* risky properties, being inherently polluting.[19] More problematically for regulation, once something is waste, its holder has no incentive to take care of it, but every incentive to get rid of it as cheaply as possible: waste is *subjectively* defined because the attitude of a holder of waste increases the likelihood of pollution. This element of waste definition becomes more important as the inherent harmfulness of the material diminishes.[20] Defining waste subjectively, that is by reference to the actions or intentions of the holder, also allows regulation to pursue resource objectives alongside pollution control. A substance that one producer would discard could be a valuable resource for another; consumer waste in the industrialised world could be needed elsewhere. Given that it is perfectly clear that the fact that a substance has a positive economic value does not preclude its classification as waste,[21] however, waste regulation cannot always be justified by the presumed carelessness of waste holders. Where a substance is valuable, and even if it does not have inherently harmful properties, its classification as waste is justified as a

---

[15] Particularly the German scheme, but also the French scheme. High levels of recycling were achieved, but in the absence of domestic markets for the recylcate, the European market was flooded with recycled packaging waste. Case 302/86 *Commission of the European Communities v Denmark* (*Danish Bottles*) [1988] ECR I–4607 was also part of the background, because whilst the Court went against the Commission, it was clear that the Danish scheme was only acceptable in the absence of EC level legislation on the issue.

[16] See M Porter, 'Waste Management' in P Lowe and S Ward (eds), *British Environmental Policy and Europe* (London, Routledge, 1998).

[17] See some interesting analysis: I Cheyne, 'The Definition of Waste in EC Law' (2002) 14 *Journal of Environmental Law* 61; D Pocklington, 'How Sustainable is the Concept of "Waste"?' (2002) 14 *Environmental Law and Management* 208; J Pike, 'Discarding Legal Certainty in the Court's Jurisprudence on 'Waste'?' in A Biondi, M Chechetti, S Grassi, M Lee (eds), *Scientific Evidence in European Environmental Rule-Making: The Case of the Landfill and End of Life Vehicles Directives* (The Hague, Kluwer, 2003).

[18] Cheyne, *ibid.*

[19] Risky waste may be a broader category than hazardous waste, which is separately regulated. The definition of hazardous waste has proved difficult, see G van Calster, 'The Legal Framework for the Regulation of Waste in the European Community' (2000) 1 *Yearbook of European Environmental Law* 161.

[20] Cheyne, above n 17.

[21] Joined Cases C–304/94, C–330/94, C–242/94, C–224/95 *Criminal Proceedings Against Tombesi* [1997] ECR I–3561 confirms that a substance is not excluded from the categorisation of waste because

means to ensure safeguards if markets for recovered substances are volatile (as they are likely to be),[22] and to ensure control over substances as they enter and leave the economic cycle, with the fluctuating intentions of holders, and changing technology. The decisions of the European Court of Justice (ECJ) in this area are characterised by a broad and purposive approach to the definition of waste. The ECJ sees waste regulation as being concerned with the protection of the environment and human health against the harmful effects of waste, and steadfastly declines to interpret the concept of waste restrictively.

Waste is defined in the Waste Framework Directive as something that 'the holder discards or intends or is required to discard'.[23] Following a temporary shift of focus (the famous '*Euro Tombesi* bypass'[24]) to the question of whether a substance is subjected to a recovery or disposal operation, the ECJ has clearly confirmed that the scope of the term 'waste' turns on the meaning of the term 'discard'.[25] The meaning of 'discard', so central to the entire operation of EC waste law, is however, undefined and far from self-explanatory.

The distinction between a substance that is being used within the normal commercial cycle (as a secondary raw material) and a substance that has been discarded and is being 'recovered' (waste) is a perennial difficulty.[26] *Palin Granit* is a useful example.[27] This case concerned mining waste, which is a particularly pertinent topic at the moment, given the significance of the extractive industry to certain

---

it has a commercial value and is collected on commercial basis; see similarly joined Cases C–206/88 and C–207/88 *Vessoso and Zanetti* [1990] ECR I–1461 on substances 'capable of economic reutilisation', para 9. Nor does the fact that a substance is an integral part of an industrial process in itself prevent its classification as 'waste', Case C–129/96 *Inter-Environnement Wallonie Asbl v Region Wallonie* [1997] ECR I–7411.

[22] Cheyne, above n 17; Tromans, above n 7.

[23] Dir 75/442, above n 1, Art 1: 'any substance or object in the categories set out in Annex I which the holder discards or intends or is required to discard'. Annex I provides a non-exhaustive list of substances and objects likely to be waste, but still subject to the 'discard, etc' requirement. Dir 75/442, *ibid*, Art 1 also requires the development of a European Waste Catalogue, which, combined with the European hazardous waste list, can now be found in Decision 2000/532 Establishing a List of Wastes Pursuant to Article 1(a) of Council Directive 75/442/EEC on Waste and Council Dir 96/689/EEC on Hazardous Waste [2000] OJ L 226/3. The European Waste Catalogue lists substances or objects that are likely to be waste, but they remain subject to the proviso that the holder 'discards or intends or is required to discard' them; things not listed may nevertheless be waste if the holder 'discards or intends or is required to discard' them. Hence the continued centrality of the Art 1 definition.

[24] See G van Calster, 'The EC Definition of Waste: The Euro-Tombesi Bypass and the Basel Relief Route' (1997) 7 *European Business Law Review* 137. The notion was developed by Advocate General Jacobs, first in *Tombesi*, above n 21.

[25] Joined Cases C–418/97 and C–419/97 *ARCO Chemie Nederland* [2000] ECR I–4475 confirmed that the fact that a substance undergoes a recovery or disposal operation does not in itself mean that a substance has been discarded. Looking at recovery or disposal operations could be somewhat circular, as indeed was accepted by Jacobs AG, *Tombesi*, above n 21, because it involves defining waste by reference to operations done to waste.

[26] The *Euro-Tombesi* bypass was not particularly helpful: distinguishing between a recovery operation (done to make productive use of waste) and a normal industrial operation (done to a secondary raw material that has not been 'discarded') is not dissimilar to distinguishing between waste and secondary raw materials, that is non-waste and desirable by-products: Jacobs AG, *Tombesi*, above n 21, para 53.

[27] Case C–9/00 *Palin Granit* [2002] ECR I–3533; Case C–114/01 *AvestaPolarit Chrome Oy* 11 September 2003, not yet reported, confirming *Palin Granit*.

new Member States.[28] Palin Granit challenged the classification as waste of the stone left over from its quarrying operations, arguing that because the leftover stone is capable of being reused (for example, in embankment work, or infilling used mines), it cannot be 'waste'. In *Palin Granit*, the Court states that waste is what falls away, rather than the end-product sought by the manufacturing process. Here, the production of leftover stone is not Palin Granit's primary objective; on the contrary, efforts are made to limit the quantity produced. Nevertheless, the Court apparently agrees that if the leftover stone is a by-product that will be exploited or marketed on advantageous terms, without any further processing prior to reuse, it is not waste. However, this applies only when the reuse is not a mere possibility but a certainty; a financial advantage to the holder provides evidence on the likelihood of reuse. The Court in this case does not conclude whether the stone at issue is or is not 'waste': it is certainly capable of being waste; on the other hand, the stone would escape classification as waste if it is certain to be advantageously reused without further processing. It is for the national court to apply this guidance. In a subsequent decision in which the ECJ (uniquely) holds quite incontrovertibly that the substance at issue is *not* waste in EC law, the intentional production of the material, and the certainty of its reuse, were decisive factors.[29] More generally, *Palin Granit* also confirms that the simple fact that something poses no risk to health or the environment and is capable of immediate use does not mean that it cannot be waste; the inherently harmful characteristics of a material are not the sole rationale for waste regulation.

The Court has consistently resisted providing an abstract definition of waste, emphasising case-by-case, purposive consideration. Given the ongoing difficulties, one might, thirty years into waste policy, ask whether this is any longer adequate. However, it seems unlikely that perfect boundaries on this question would be possible in any event. If that is the case, perhaps the Court has said enough about the application of the definition of waste on a case by case basis, and should leave the national regulatory and judicial authorities to follow what is, after all, a positive glut of decisions. The importance of good relations between the EC and national courts, particularly in the context of enlargement, and the well-known limitations of the Commission's ability to monitor compliance, again particularly in the context of enlargement, may justify the ECJ's reluctance to let go. Moreover, the Court's hesitation is based in part on deference to the legislator, and the Commission has now pronounced itself 'ready to hold a debate on the definition of waste'.[30] The

---

[28] Dir 75/442, above n 1, Art 2(1)(b) provides for the exclusion of mining waste, subject to certain conditions, including coverage by other legislation, see *AvestaPolarit, ibid.* See now European Commission, *Proposal for a Directive on the Management of Waste from the Extractive Industries*, COM (2003) 319 final.

[29] Case C–235/02 *Saetti and Frediani*, 15 January 2004, not yet reported. The case concerned petroleum coke, resulting from the refining of crude oil and used by the refinery as fuel for its combined steam and electricity power station.

[30] Commission, above n 2, p 39. See D Pocklington, 'Opening Pandora's Box — the EU Review of the Definition of "Waste"' [2003] *European Environmental Law Review* 204, for a discussion of the complexities of amending the definition of waste, which cascades through an enormous amount of legislation and policy at all levels.

Commission does however acknowledge that a free standing and watertight definition is not likely. The lack of clarity in the definition of waste at the margins, particularly troubling if one recalls that criminal penalties may be attached to non-compliance,[31] is not however the most controversial aspect of the definition of waste. Many question the broad scope of the current approach, in particular the wisdom of treating waste for recycling in the same way as waste for disposal.[32] Defining a substance as waste has major economic consequences, invoking a complex and costly regulatory regime that may make cost-efficient reuse or recycling more difficult than they need be. Whilst such arguments need to be considered against the benefits of expansive control, it is clear that using waste as a resource attracts certain regulatory costs that are not borne by the use of an equivalent raw material. The Commission, however, is clearly reluctant to accept any proposal that the label 'waste' should be restricted, arguing that the environmental benefits of extensive regulation need to be properly assessed.[33] The Commission's apparent acceptance that there will always be difficult judgments to be made, together with its unwillingness to restrict the definition, would suggest that the meaning of waste will continue to be controversial.

THE WASTE HIERARCHY

The 'waste hierarchy' is a crucial element of EC waste policy. The Waste Framework Directive requires Member States 'to encourage', as a priority 'the prevention or reduction of waste production and its harmfulness', apparently primarily by means of technological fixes, rather than radical changes in consumption.[34] Recovery of waste is next on the hierarchy 'by means of recycling, re-use or reclamation or any other process with a view to extracting secondary raw materials', or by 'the use of waste as a source of energy', that is incineration with energy recovery. The Packaging Waste Directive subsequently introduced the preference for recycling over energy recovery.[35] Disposal is at the bottom of the hierarchy.

Whilst it is broadly welcome, the waste hierarchy is not without its controversies, and its role in identifying the 'best practicable environmental option' for waste is not always clear. To take recycling as an example, a number of environmental benefits will apply in most cases. Recycling is able to contribute to the conservation of raw materials, and to lessen the negative environmental effects of landfill or incineration, including associated energy, transport and storage impacts. Recycling, however, also imposes environmental costs. It produces its own emissions and

---

[31] Waste is addressed by the initiatives on criminal law discussed in ch 3 above, see European Commission, *Proposal for a Directive on the Protection of the Environment through Criminal Law* COM (2001) 139 final, amended COM (2002) 544 final, Art 3; Council Framework Decision 2003/80/JHA on the Protection of the Environment through Criminal Law [2003] OJ L 29/55, Art 2.

[32] Tromans, above n 7; Chalmers, above n 13.

[33] Commission, above n 2, pp 38–9.

[34] Dir 75/442, above n 1, Art 3.

[35] Dir 94/62, above n 14.

residues, and also requires transport, storage, energy and clean water. The balance of benefit and burden between different waste management options will vary, from sector to sector and even from place to place; small communities in particular may accrue high environmental costs either transporting to a recycling centre, or recycling on a small scale. Citizen involvement is a further possible advantage of recycling over other forms of waste management, engaging the public and encouraging reflection on environmental questions. Equally, however, this 'feel good factor' may encourage complacency about consumption: rather than recycling my plastic water bottle, I should use fewer plastic water bottles. The risk of perverse effects elsewhere in the life-cycle of a product should also be borne in mind: for example, does the use of more easily recycled material reduce a product's energy efficiency? Similar trade-offs need to be assessed in all waste management options, including even prevention: for example, legislation requiring 'qualitative' prevention measures in respect of end of life vehicles,[36] has been controversial on the grounds that there could be environmentally perverse effects if the removal of certain hazardous substances reduces the life of a vehicle, or increases its weight, so increasing fuel consumption.[37]

Notwithstanding these difficulties, the hierarchy is extremely valuable as an overall guide, and waste prevention and recycling are generally accepted to be in almost all circumstances preferable to disposal. It would indeed be surprising if a simple 'solution' such as the waste hierarchy could be automatically applied to every manifestation of a complex environmental problem.

The Commission's consultation on its 'thematic strategy' for the prevention and recycling of waste concentrates on establishing the appropriate mix of instruments in waste policy, but could also have the effect of hardening the waste hierarchy.[38] The Commission is consulting, *inter alia*, on waste prevention targets. The setting of waste prevention targets is likely to be a controversial exercise, and has failed in the past[39]: most significantly, the level of information required for robust targets is very demanding, for example as to current patterns of waste generation and its effects, before even thinking about how best to achieve a reduction without negatively affecting the economy. Moreover, the only currently practical option is to set waste prevention targets by weight or volume, which is not necessarily linked to the environmental impact of waste.[40] Even if realistic and challenging waste prevention targets still look some way off, however, addressing

---

[36] Dir 2000/53 on End-of Life Vehicles [2000] OJ L 269/34. Waste prevention has quantitative and qualitative aspects: the former involves the reduction of the amount of waste generated; the latter, reduction of the quantity of hazardous waste generated. The relative 'hazardousness' of waste is not yet something that it is technically possible to address, see the discussion in Commission, above n 2, p 16.

[37] See D Pocklington, 'An Assessment of the Proposed Legislation for ELVs' (1998) 5 *European Environmental Law Review* 138; A Lea, 'The Scrapping of End of Life Vehicles: Is New European Legislation Necessary?' [2000] *Environmental Law Review* 65.

[38] Commission, above n 2.

[39] See the discussion in Commission, *ibid*, especially p 17.

[40] For example, lightweight packaging will not necessarily be less environmentally damaging, Commission, *ibid*, p 23.

waste production is a crucial first step in a credible waste policy, and it is encouraging to see it being taken on in a comprehensive way.[41]

The waste hierarchy has the potential to bring out the relationship between waste and resources, which is becoming increasingly important in the development of EC waste policy.[42] The extraction of primary raw materials and their conversion into products both have environmental impacts that might be avoided by the reuse or recovery of waste.[43] The creation and disposal of waste can be symptomatic of a misuse of resources. The ECJ has built on the link between waste and resource use in drawing its distinction between 'disposal' and 'recovery' operations, a distinction that has raised difficulties not dissimilar from those faced in the definition of waste.[44] The ECJ identifies the 'essential characteristic' of a waste recovery operation in its 'principal objective', which must be to ensure that the waste serve a useful purpose in replacing other materials which would have had to be used for that purpose, thereby conserving natural resources.[45] This of course inevitably raises its own problems of interpretation, particularly as to the 'principal objective' of an operation; indeed, determining whether the principal objective of an operation is to conserve natural resources or to dispose of waste can seem rather like determining whether an operation is a recovery or disposal operation. For example, the Court has held that if the incineration of household waste has the principal objective of producing energy, it is a recovery operation; if energy is created and used only as a secondary effect of incineration, incineration is waste disposal.[46] Whilst this approach is undoubtedly difficult to apply, and the denial of 'recovery' status to certain waste incineration operations came as a surprise to many,[47] for current purposes the direct link between waste policy and resource policy should be noted.

Notwithstanding the tradeoffs discussed above, recycling is high up the waste hierarchy, but has so far been dealt with by EC legislation on an *ad hoc* basis. The Commission proposes a more considered approach. Recycling targets have been set for particular waste streams, including end of life vehicles, packaging waste,

---

[41] So far, limited elements of waste prevention are addressed in respect of particular waste streams, for example Dir 00/53, above n 36, restricts the use of certain hazardous substances in vehicles. Waste and resource use are factors in assessing 'best available techniques' under Dir 96/61 on Integrated Pollution Prevention and Control [1996] OJ L 257/26.

[42] See also European Commission, *Towards a Thematic Strategy for the Sustainable Use of Natural Resources* COM (2003) 572, which strongly emphasises the links with waste prevention and recycling as considered in Commission, above n 2.

[43] Commission, above n 2, p 12, provides some examples: each tonne of recycled metal avoids the mining of several tonnes of metal ore; recycling of plastics can reduce the emissions of aerosols and particulate matter by reducing the production of virgin polymer.

[44] The Annexes to Dir 75/442, above n 1, list the most common disposal and recovery operations, but do not precisely and exhaustively specify every disposal and recovery operation covered by the Directive, Case C–600/00 *Abfall Services AG (ASA) v Bundeminister fur Umwelt, Jugend und Familie* [2002] ECR I–1961. Note that Commission, above n 2, invites comments on these definitions, p 38.

[45] *ASA, ibid.*

[46] Case C–228/00 *Commission v Germany* [2003] ECR I–1439 and Case C–458/00 *Commission v Luxembourg* [2003] ECR I–553.

[47] Waste regulation is complex and interrelated, and the new understanding has serious knock on effects, in particular in respect of recovery targets set in other legislation. See Pocklington, above n 30.

and waste electrical and electronic goods.[48] The Commission intends to develop this product focus, using 'end of life' legislation to deal with the separate collection and dismantling of complex waste, and then a material specific (for example, paper, card and plastic waste from all sources, not simply packaging) approach to setting recycling targets.[49] The setting of the targets has also to date been rather *ad hoc*. The Commission is now proposing a cost benefit approach to setting recycling targets[50]; the information demands will be daunting, and of course the advantages of cost benefit analysis are not uncontroversial.[51] It is also interesting to observe the Commission toy with the idea of an EU-wide recycling target, rather than national recycling targets.[52] This would achieve the same overall recycling rate for the EU as a whole, but would leave it to the market to determine which recycling facility can best achieve high levels of recycling. This has potentially serious implications, enhancing free movement of waste for recycling, and pointing towards EU wide operating standards for recycling facilities, to ensure high environmental standards and fair competition; the Integrated Pollution Prevention and Control Directive does not currently cover all facilities.[53] Some work may also be necessary on a common definition of recycling: if what 'counts' as a recycled product varies around the EU, there is potential for different environmental standards and unequal conditions of competition. This issue increases in significance as recycling targets are more widely used. To determine when a substance has been recycled (and so contributes to the targets), we rely on a recent ECJ judgment in which the Court followed the definition provided in the Packaging Waste Directive.[54] The Court held that a recycling process must start with a substance that is 'waste', which must undergo 'reprocessing in a production process', in order to produce new material or to make a new product.[55] That new material or product has to possess 'characteristics comparable to those of the material of which the waste was composed'.[56] If the substance has impurities, and cannot be used like the raw material, it is still waste[57]; the resource objectives of waste policy are only satisfied if a useable product results, at which stage:

> the ecological advantages which led the Community legislature to accord a degree of preference to this form of waste recovery are fully achieved, namely a reduction in the consumption of energy and of primary raw materials.[58]

[48] Dir 00/53, above n 36; Dir 94/62, above n 24; Dir 2002/96 on Waste Electrical and Electronic Equipment [2003] OJ L 37/24.
[49] Commission, above n 2.
[50] Commission, *ibid*, p 22.
[51] See particularly chs 1 and 4 above.
[52] Commission, above n 2, p 25.
[53] Dir 96/61, above n 41. See the discussion in Commission, *ibid*, p 20.
[54] Dir 94/62, above n 14, 'recycling shall mean the reprocessing in a production process of the waste materials for the original purpose or for other purposes including organic recycling but excluding energy recovery', Art 3(7).
[55] Case C–444/00 *The Queen on the application of Mayer Parry Recycling Ltd v Environment Agency, Secretary of State for the Environment, Transport and the Regions* [2003] ECR I–6163.
[56] *Ibid*, para 67; see also para 73.
[57] Applying *Arco*, above n 25.
[58] *Mayer Parry*, above n 55, para 74.

Again, waste policy and resource policy are linked. And again, we see an expansive approach to the definition of waste: a substance only ceases to be waste once quite stringent criteria are met for the completion of 'recycling'.

Ambitious and comprehensive recycling targets are to a large degree for the future; the Landfill Directive is an existing effort to move waste up the hierarchy.[59] Landfill[60] is a major destination for waste produced in the EU. The Landfill Directive is a highly technical document, containing extensive and detailed provisions on the management of landfill sites. Landfill sites are already subject to authorisation under the Waste Framework Directive, and in many cases also the IPPC Directive.[61] One might even question the need for a new directive in these circumstances,[62] and the level of detail as to the operation of landfills is certainly surprising, given the much discussed trend of increased flexibility and discretion on substantive matters in recent environmental legislation[63]; any de-centralising impetus in EC environmental law seems to have stopped at landfill. Standardised waste acceptance criteria and more detailed operational and engineering standards are designed to fill gaps in existing legislation, and to respond to concern about varying standards for landfill around the EU. Implementation may well prove challenging, however, particularly given the poor implementation of existing waste legislation.[64]

The second limb of the Landfill Directive, which moves beyond licensing of landfill sites, is more interesting for current purposes. The Landfill Directive requires reductions to be made in the amounts of certain waste being sent to landfill. It sets targets for reduction in the amount of 'municipal biodegradable waste'[65] going to landfill,[66] and places a total prohibition on landfill of particular wastes.[67] A ban on co-disposal of hazardous and non-hazardous waste, under which landfill sites will be categorised according to whether they receive inert, non-hazardous or hazardous waste[68] is a major change in countries like the UK, where 'co-disposal' has been used as a means of waste management, on

---

[59] Dir 99/31, above n 6.

[60] 'Landfill' is defined as a waste disposal site for the deposit of the waste onto or into land, Dir 99/31, *ibid*, Art 2.

[61] Dir 96/61, above n 41.

[62] S Tromans, 'EC Waste Law — A Critical Perspective' in Biondi *et al*, above n 17.

[63] See ch 6 above.

[64] European Commission, *Fourth Annual Survey on the Implementation and Enforcement of Community Environmental Law, 2002* SEC (2003) 804, pp 16–18.

[65] Municipal waste 'means waste from households, as well as other waste which, because of its nature or composition, is similar to waste from households', and biodegradable waste 'means any waste that is capable of undergoing anaerobic or aerobic decomposition, such as food or garden waste, and paper or paperboard', Dir 99/31, above n 6, Art 2. This leaves the meaning of 'municipal biodegradable waste', perhaps deliberately, rather vague.

[66] By 2006 only 75% of 1995 quantities of municipal biodegradable waste should be landfilled; by 2009, 50%; and by 2006, 35%, with provision for extension by four years for states that rely heavily on landfill, Dir 99/31, *ibid*, Art 5.

[67] Including liquid waste, imprecisely defined as 'any waste in liquid form including waste waters but excluding sludge'; waste which, in the conditions of landfill, is explosive, corrosive, oxidising, highly flammable or flammable; hospital and other clinical wastes; used tyres; and any waste which does not fulfil the acceptance criteria in the Directive, Dir 99/31, *ibid*, Art 5.

[68] Dir 99/31, *ibid*, Art 4.

the controversial basis that co-disposal assists decomposition and neutralises certain hazardous components of waste.

The obligation to divert waste from landfill is a more ambitious attempt to deal with waste than simply scrutinising operational standards. It is increasingly recognised that even well run landfill sites create a number of environmental problems. Landfill emits methane, which is thought to be a major contributor to climate change. Locally, landfill can create nuisance problems or contribute to water and soil contamination, and certain epidemiological evidence suggests that landfill may pose health risks. Reliance on landfill also raises issues of land-take, and as a relatively cheap form of disposal (when environmental externalities are not taken into account), reduces incentives to avoid waste, or to make beneficial use of waste. For these reasons, landfill is thought by many to fall at the bottom of the waste hierarchy, although there is some debate as to whether in some circumstances it constitutes the best practicable environmental option.[69]

The Landfill Directive simply fixes targets for diversion from landfill, and leaves it to the Member States to choose how to implement those targets. The preference would be to move from landfill up the waste hierarchy, ideally to waste prevention. The Directive, however, says nothing about either waste prevention or recycling. It is a little perplexing that recycling often seems to be the only form of waste management that is required to pay its own way,[70] but environmentally meaningful recycling does rely on the existence of market, or at least a use, for the recycled product. Not only is the Directive silent on the subject of markets, but even the Commission's consultation on the 'thematic strategy' for waste prevention and recycling concentrates on the supply side rather than the demand side of recycling.[71]

In any event, even if strategies for the reduction and recycling of waste are extremely successful, it seems inevitable that Member States that rely heavily on landfill will shift some waste from landfill to incineration. Incineration could be a form of recovery, if its primary objective is to produce energy[72]; it might equally be another form of waste disposal, whose hierarchical relationship with landfill is far from clear cut.[73] There seems to be a real danger that the Landfill Directive will require the devotion of significant resources to the diversion of waste from one form of disposal to another, or at best to a form of recovery only slightly higher in the waste hierarchy. Even if one accepts that waste incineration is generally preferable to landfill, this is a strange prioritisation of resources. The Commission has said that landfill bans should in the future be carefully assessed to ensure that the incentive is to recycling not to incineration.[74]

[69] House of Lords Select Committee on the European Communities, 17th Report 1997–98, *Sustainable Landfill*, HL 83.
[70] House of Commons Select Committee on Environment, Transport and Regional Affairs, Fifth Report 2000–2001, *Delivering Sustainable Waste Management*, HC 36–I, para 67.
[71] Commission, above n 2.
[72] *ASA*, above n 44.
[73] See van Calster, above n 19, pp 207–8.
[74] Commission, above n 2, pp 35–6.

The difficulties faced by the UK in the implementation of the Landfill Directive's diversion targets illustrate the politicisation of waste regulation.[75] Waste management facilities (including recycling or composting facilities) rarely make popular neighbours. The label 'waste'[76] is said to carry considerable stigma when it comes to siting a facility, although it is not evident that simply changing the language would necessarily make people happier about new industrial facilities on their doorsteps.[77] Siting of incinerators, to which much waste is to be diverted, is particularly difficult. Public concern about the impact of incinerators upon human health is intense in the UK. Emissions include pollutants with known toxic properties (such as dioxins and nitrous oxides), as may the ash left after combustion, which must be disposed of.[78] Incineration is also relatively unfamiliar in the UK, which mainly for geological and historical reasons has always relied heavily on landfill. Incineration tends to imply large scale facilities that accept waste from outside the local area for technical reasons. Each of these factors is likely to enhance the public's perception of the risk associated with waste incineration.[79]

Every new waste management facility requires planning permission, probably with environmental impact assessment, and many will also be subject to integrated pollution prevention and control.[80] Each of these processes provides an opportunity for public participation. The authenticity of the participation is problematic: in particular, consultation takes place after one significant option (the *status quo*, continuing with landfill) has been taken out of the equation. Public participation is essentially limited to the siting of facilities. There is a danger that it is reduced to an 'opportunity to object', causing the delay and bad feeling that we are indeed witnessing.

The choice between landfill and energy from waste incineration is enormously complex. Amongst other things, however, it is a choice between a form of waste management that contributes to global climate change, and a form of waste management that emits carcinogens into the local environment. This is perhaps a simplistic way of putting the question, but it illustrates the unavoidability of profoundly political questions of risk acceptability and risk distribution. The appropriate balance between landfill and incineration (and indeed recycling, re-use and

---

[75] S Tromans, 'Alternatives to Landfill — Can the Planning System Deliver?' [2001] *Journal of Planning and Environmental Law* 257.

[76] Let alone 'hazardous waste', which has not hitherto been a big issue in countries that practise co-disposal.

[77] There may be a general reluctance to see an industrial facility in a neighbourhood. House of Lords Select Committee, above n 69, suggests that siting waste facilities is no more problematic than the siting of any other industrial facility.

[78] A scandal broke out in the UK in 2001 when ash from an incinerator in the north east of England was discovered to have been deposited on paths and allotments rather than properly disposed of. See House of Commons Select Committee on Environment, Transport and Regional Affairs, above n 70, para 95.

[79] Ch 4 above.

[80] Dir 85/337 on the Assessment of the Effects of Certain Private and Public Projects on the Environment [1985] OJ L 175/40, as amended by Dir 97/11/EC [1997] L 073/05; Dir 96/61 above n 41. See ch 6 above.

reduction) is not readily addressed at the project stage. In particular, without a publicly acceptable approach to the role of waste incineration, the acceptability of individual facilities is always going to be problematic. The EU level decision to restrict landfill was never likely to involve the communities that have to host waste facilities. Even taking that decision as a given, public participation before the siting stage can at least address the relative role of incineration in coping with diversion. The UK government did undertake a long consultation exercise over its national waste strategy, and local authorities also consult over their smaller scale waste management plans, a 'plans and programmes' aspect of public participation that has recently been legally reinforced by EC environmental legislation.[81] However, the example of waste demonstrates that traditional consultation mechanisms at this level are likely to be ineffective when it comes to 'delivery' at the project level, if only because there is often a considerable change of constituency between plans and programmes participation and the siting of specific proposals. Consultation on waste management generally is likely to be limited to established public interest groups and industry; broader interest is sure to be quickened when a leaflet comes through the letterbox explaining proposals to build a waste incinerator in the area. If industry and government wish to avoid confrontation, thoughtful approaches to public participation are crucial.[82] Even if it is unlikely that a large number of members of the public will wish to devote the necessary time and energy to waste planning, a slower and deeper involvement of a cross-section of stakeholders is thought to have considerable potential.[83] And we may even end up with improved policy: much of the opposition to incineration focuses on recycling and prevention as preferable strategies.

Waste policy in the UK is still encumbered by these problems, with continued warnings of looming disaster as existing facilities find themselves unable to cope and new facilities are not provided.[84] Without wishing to return to the promises and limitations of public participation discussed in chapters five and six, it suffices to note that 'the public' is crucial to the success of waste management: not only are we all involved very directly in waste production and waste management

---

[81] Dir 2003/35 Providing for Public Participation in Respect of the Drawing Up of Certain Plans and Programmes Relating to the Environment and Amending with Regard to Public Participation and Access to Justice Council Directives 85/337/EEC and 96/61/EC [2003] OJ L 156/17; Dir 2001/42 on the Assessment of the Effects of Certain Plans and Programmes on the Environment [2001] OJ L197/30. See ch 6 above.

[82] See for example J Petts, 'Waste Management Strategy Development: A Case Study of Community Involvement and Consensus-Building in Hampshire' (1995) 38 *Journal of Environmental Planning and Management* 519; N Stanley, 'Contentious Planning Disputes: An Insoluble Problem?' [2000] *Journal of Planning and Environmental Law* 1226; C Snary, 'Risk Communication and the Waste-to-energy Incinerator Environmental Impact Assessment Process: A UK Case Study of Public Involvement' (2002) 45 *Journal of Environmental Planning and Management* 267; Royal Commission on Environmental Pollution, 21st Report, *Setting Environmental Standards* (CM 4053, 1998), ch 7.

[83] Petts, *ibid.* Experiments with compensating local residents, or allowing them ongoing involvement, such monitoring powers, could also be helpful.

[84] See for example Institution of Civil Engineers, *The State of the Nation 2004: An Assessment of the State of the UK's Infrastructure*, available at http://www.ice.org.uk, which received considerable media attention at the beginning of June 2004; M McCarthy, 'Where Will It Go?' (2004) 3 *Your Environment*, the Environment Agency's magazine, available at http://www.environment-agency.gov.UK, on anticipated problems managing hazardous waste in particular.

(separating and recycling, for example), but communities must also host facilities; the role of those facilities needs to be broadly acceptable.

SELF SUFFICIENCY, WASTE AND FREE MOVEMENT

The principle that 'environmental damage should as a priority be rectified at source' is found in Article 174 EC. Generally, this is about requiring facilities to bear all and only their own costs, internalising externalities.[85] In a waste context, the source principle takes the more concrete form of the 'proximity' and 'self-sufficiency' principles. The Waste Framework Directive requires Member States to put together a network of waste sites, to 'enable the Community as a whole to become self-sufficient in waste disposal' and allowing the Member States 'to move towards that aim individually'.[86] The proximity principle follows, providing that waste should 'be disposed of in one of the nearest appropriate installations'.[87]

The purpose of the self-sufficiency principle is not entirely clear. When defined along state or internal administrative boundaries, one assumes that it is based on cost internalisation. If we are concerned with the environmental impact of transport, administrative boundaries are not the most obvious determining factor, as greater distances may be travelled within borders than across borders[88]; hence the importance of 'proximity'. Moreover, if the inherently environmentally damaging impact of transport is the concern, or the risks of transporting dangerous waste, one might wonder whether the same does not apply to the movement of any, or any dangerous, goods. The self-sufficiency principle is at least in part concerned with 'environmental dumping', the flooding of waste to the cheapest waste disposal sites, which are likely to be the less well engineered and operated sites. Concerns about environmental dumping, however, should have relatively little purchase in the heavily regulated EU context. Indeed, notwithstanding the much-discussed decline of detailed centralised standards, the role of common operating standards for waste facilities is rather pronounced.[89] And even in respect of the persistent variation in standards, which it is possible will increase with enlargement, one might ask whether similar concerns do not apply in many other areas of the internal market.[90]

---

[85] Case C–293/97 *R v Secretary of State for the Environment, Transport and the Regions ex p Standley* [1999] ECR I–2603.

[86] Dir 75/442, above n 1, Art 5(1).

[87] Art 5(2).

[88] DaimlerChrysler, challenging a requirement under German legislation to have its waste treated in most circumstances at one of two specified German incineration centres, argued that shipping the waste to the prescribed German installations, one of which is 600 to 800 kilometres from its factories, added greatly to its costs, Case C–324/99 *DaimlerChrysler AG v Land Baden-Wurttemberg* [2001] ECR I–9897.

[89] Detailed standards have been set in respect of incineration, see Dir 2000/76 on the Incineration of Waste [2000] OJ L 332/91; and for landfill, see Dir 99/31, above n 6. Commission above n 2 considers the possibility of common standards for recycling.

[90] P von Wilmowsky, 'Waste Disposal in the Internal Market: The State of Play after the ECJ's Ruling on the Walloon Import Ban' (1993) 30 *Common Market Law Review* 541.

Self-sufficiency and proximity have the capacity not only to impose considerable costs on economic operators, who may be unable to go to least cost waste facilities, but also, in effect, to divide the internal market on national lines.[91] This is most famously demonstrated in the *Walloon Waste* case.[92] Wallonia had banned the import of waste for disposal, and because waste is a 'good', this constituted a restriction on the free movement of goods. Environmental protection is not one of the justifications for a restriction to free movement provided in Article 30 EC, but does fall within the 'mandatory requirements' doctrine, developed by the Court to enable a balance to be drawn between the internal market and competing social goods.[93] The mandatory requirements doctrine, however, was thought only to apply if the restriction on free trade is the result of a non-discriminatory measure, that is if there is no discrimination between domestic and foreign goods. In this case there did appear to be discrimination between Wallonian waste, which could be disposed of in Wallonia, and imported waste, which could not. The ECJ, however, held that the relationship between waste and its production meant that imported waste is actually of a different nature from local waste, and hence the two types of waste could be treated differently without discriminating. Interpretation of this decision is difficult and controversial, and the facts of the case were highly sensitive: Wallonia was apparently being overwhelmed by waste imports, to much popular alarm.[94] However, although much restricted, the decision has not simply been confined to its facts. Waste, apparently, constitutes an exception to the paradigm of free trade, albeit only if the waste is destined for disposal, rather than recovery.[95] The relationship between free trade and waste is further refined in the legislative regime for the transport of waste.[96] This is a complex, not to mention voluminous, topic, but very broadly, Member States are able to restrict movements of waste, provided that the national measure implements the three principles of proximity, priority for recovery and self-sufficiency at Community and national levels, in a proportionate manner.[97] The Community law preference for recovery of waste rather than disposal of waste means that shipments of waste for recovery are subject to fewer restrictions than shipments of waste for disposal.

Some academic commentary disputes the logic of self-sufficiency and proximity as applied to waste for disposal, on the basis of both internal market and efficiency arguments, and it is true that waste is something of an anomoly. There seems,

---

[91] Chalmers, above n 13.

[92] Case C–2/90 *Commission v Belgium* [1992] ECR I–4431.

[93] For discussion of trade and the environment, see J Scott, *EC Environmental Law* (London, Longman, 1998), ch 4; *European Environmental Law* (Groningen, Europa Law Institute, 2000), ch VI; L Kramer, *EC Environmental Law* (London, Sweet & Maxwell, 2003), ch 3.

[94] See von Wilmowsky, above n 90; Chalmers, above n 13.

[95] Case C–203/96 *Chemische Afvalstoffen Dusseldorp BV v Minister Van Volkshuisvesting, Ruimtelijke Ordening en Milieubeheer* [1998] ECR I–4075; Case C–209/98 *FFAD, ex parte Sydhavnens Sten & Grus ApS v Kobenhavns Kommune* [2000] ECR I–3743.

[96] Reg 259/93, above n 10. For discussion see Jans, above n 93, pp 396–400; Kramer, above n 93, pp 333–8; van Calster, above n 19.

[97] These conditions were not satisfied in *DaimlerChrysler*, above n 88, which concerned a German ban on export of waste for disposal other than to waste facilities that met German standards.

however, to be considerable public unease about waste movements, even waste for recovery, which is not in principle subject to the same restrictions as waste for disposal. So for example, the 'ghost ships' saga in the UK in 2003 involved the movement of redundant ships from the United States to England for recovery, to public objections and legal controversy.[98] Although this is not an 'EU' case, it demonstrates that the political implications of waste are always present, and emphasised when the waste at issue is perceived to be somebody else's problem.

BEYOND COMMAND AND CONTROL: ALTERNATIVE REGULATORY
MECHANISMS

The use of a range of regulatory instruments has been a significant feature of waste policy in recent years, and that seems set to continue, with the Commission emphasising the need for 'an appropriate mix of instruments including legislative, voluntary and economic instruments' in this area.[99] The Commission puts forward an ambitious range of possibilities, including economic instruments, such as landfill taxes, producer responsibility, tradable certificates for recycling, and 'pay as you throw' schemes for householders.[100] This section will look at two approaches to waste regulation that are already being used in EC environmental law: extended producer responsibility and environmental agreements.

Neither the polluting potential of waste nor its resource potential can be adequately tackled by regulating waste management facilities once the waste has been produced. Influencing waste production and what becomes of the waste involves the considerable challenge of influencing a diffuse body of heterogeneous actors, which is probably more readily accessible via the market than via direct regulation. Even if effective, direct regulation of a vast range of consumption could be perceived as heavy handed, and would be a serious burden for regulators. Price signals are thought to be a crucial alternative. The 'polluter pays principle' was included in the early Waste Framework Directive, but spelled out simply as a requirement that the costs of waste disposal should be borne by the holder (or previous holders) of waste.[101] It is developed in the Landfill Directive by the requirement that all costs, including aftercare, are covered by the price charged by the operator for disposal[102]; and by producer responsibility legislation, which requires the producer of goods to bear certain costs of waste management. These provisions amount to a prohibition of state subsidy of the immediate costs of waste management, which is a fairly minimalist approach to the polluter pays principle. In particular, the low cost of disposal (especially landfill) relative to

---

[98] See *R v Environment Agency, ex parte Friends of the Earth* [2004] Environmental Law Reports 31. For discussion of the litigation and the public controversy around this issue, see D Pocklington, 'NIMBY-ism and the Spectre of Maritime Pollution' [2004] *Environmental Law and Management* 343.
[99] Commission, above n 2, p 7.
[100] Commission, *ibid*, pp 30–5.
[101] Dir 75/442, above n 1, Art 15.
[102] Dir 99/31, above n 6, Art 10.

other forms of waste management (for example recycling) is at least in part because no account is made for environmental externalities.

Producer Responsibility

Producer responsibility legislation attempts to extend the responsibility of producers through the life-cycle of a product to the post-consumption (waste) phase.[103] Manufacturers take all of the most significant decisions about the environmental performance of a product during and after its useful life. Producer responsibility attempts to harness market forces to encourage the minimisation of a product's environmental impact by putting the cost of waste into the production process, internalising what would otherwise be an externality. The price signals are intended to affect the nature and amount of waste produced, and to encourage technological innovation. As such, much of the discussion of market instruments in chapter seven above applies to producer responsibility. Producer responsibility might also be examined from the perspective of 'reflexive' law, discussed in chapter six above: rather than attempting to determine the outcome of a process, producer responsibility creates a link between the decision-maker at the manufacturing stage and waste, attempting thereby to enhance awareness of waste in the production of goods, and to set in train a virtuous process of self-examination and anticipation of problems.

Producer responsibility is a technique that has now been applied to a number of waste streams. The first initiative, the Packaging Waste Directive, was somewhat ambiguous in its attachment to producer responsibility, but most Member States chose to meet the mandatory recycling and recovery targets by means of producer responsibility.[104] The End of Life Vehicles (ELV) Directive is more explicit about producer responsibility.[105] The Directive succeeded a number of divergent Member State initiatives in the area, with associated concerns about the distortion of competition.[106] It aims to address both the environmental impact of ELVs, and the operation of the internal market, dual objectives that are common in waste regulation, reflecting the nature of waste as a traded good.

An ELV is 'a vehicle which is waste',[107] and as such, is already subject to the Waste Framework Directive. The Member States are required to ensure that economic

---

[103] KF Kroepelien, 'Extended Producer Responsibility — New Legal Structures for Improved Ecological Self Organisation in Europe' (2000) 9 *Review of European Community and International Environmental Law* 165.

[104] Dir 94/62, above n 14; Commission, above n 2, p 15. Note that producer responsibility raises certain competition issues, see Commission, *ibid*, p 32. For discussion see H Vedder, *Competition Law and Environmental Protection in Europe: Towards Sustainability?* (Groningen, Europa Law Publishing, 2003); Jans, above n 93, ch VII; S Poli, 'Legal Issues of Waste-Related Pollution in the European Community' in Biondi et al, above n 17.

[105] Dir 00/53, above n 36.

[106] M Onida, 'Challenges and Opportunities in EC Waste Management: Perspectives on the Problem of End of Life Vehicles' (2000) 1 *Yearbook of European Environmental Law* 253.

[107] Dir 00/53, above n 36, Art 2(2).

operators set up systems for the collection, treatment and recovery of ELVs and (as far as technically feasible) of waste used parts removed in repair, and to ensure the 'adequate availability' of collection facilities.[108] End users do not bear these costs, removing incentives for the dumping of vehicles, and pushing the costs up the supply chain to those with the ability to do something about vehicle design. The ELV Directive sets mandatory targets for recycling and recovery, options higher up the waste hierarchy than disposal: Member States must 'take the necessary measures to ensure' that certain re-use, recovery and recycling targets are 'attained by economic operators'.[109] These obligations on economic operators apply to producers, distributors and waste managers.[110] '[A]ll, or a significant part of, the costs' of the collection of ELVs must be met by producers of ELVs.[111] This internalises significant hitherto external costs into the costs of production, although of course the market cost of collection by no means includes all environmental externalities. The ELV Directive provides for financial responsibility, but no obligation that producers should deal with their *own* products. This inevitably weakens to some extent signals on product design, but is perhaps a necessary trade-off to ensure an effective regime.

Voluntary Agreements

Another much vaunted 'new approach' to environmental regulation is the use of voluntary agreements. From the Fifth Environmental Action Programme, there has been a commitment to move from a prescriptive to a more cooperative approach in the environmental field,[112] and the Commission's *White Paper on European Governance* proposes greater use of 'co-regulation' more generally.[113] This enthusiasm extends to the international level. In particular, the Johannesburg Summit saw the conclusion of a large number of voluntary agreements on the implementation of sustainable development goals, between parties including governments, business, and public interest groups.[114] The definition and role of partnership agreements at Johannesburg was vague, and as one would expect, these initiatives are subject to

---

[108] *Ibid*, Art 5.

[109] *Ibid*, Art 7(2). By 2015 there should be reuse and recovery to a minimum of 95% by an average weight per vehicle and year; and reuse and recycling to a minimum of 85% by an average weight per vehicle and year. Interim targets of 85% and 80% respectively are set for 2006. Lower 2006 targets are permitted for vehicles produced before 1 January 1980.

[110] 'Economic operators' are 'producers, distributers, collectors, motor vehicle insurance companies, dismantlers, shredders, recoverers, recyclers and other treatment operators of end-of-life vehicles, including their components and materials', Dir 00/53, *ibid*, Art 2(10).

[111] Dir 00/53, *ibid*, Art 5(4).

[112] Fifth Environmental Action Programme, *Towards Sustainability: A European Community Programme of Policy and Action in Relation to the Environment and Sustainable Development* [1993] OJ C 138/5.

[113] European Commission, *White Paper on European Governance* COM (2001) 428 final.

[114] For detailed discussion, see C Streck, 'The World Summit on Sustainable Development: Partnerships as New Tools in Environmental Governance' (2002) 13 *Yearbook of International Environmental Law* 63. The agreements are called 'Part II Agreements'.

competing cries of success and 'greenwash'[115]; notwithstanding more rigorous definition and constraints, similar claims are made of voluntary measures in EC law.

Whether environmental agreements are actually as novel as some would suggest is open to question; 'agreements between industry and public authorities on the achievement of environmental objectives'[116] are as old as the hills. Moreover, such agreements are rarely if ever truly voluntary, but are more commonly set against the background or the threat of more formal binding regulation. Nevertheless, a number of purported benefits are claimed for the new generation of environmental agreements.[117] These include increased flexibility for industry in meeting targets; an improved relationship between regulator and industry, which might in turn enhance the influence of the regulator on industry; greater legitimacy of the environmental objectives; improved compliance. By encouraging self-examination, it is argued that agreement may be more effective at influencing the overall management and ethos of the regulated organisation than direct regulation,[118] as well as using and valuing industry knowledge and expertise. In addition, although reaching the necessary consensus may be time consuming, it is claimed that environmental agreements can be put in place and amended more quickly than formal regulation.[119] A further possible attraction of environmental agreements is their potential to contribute to the contemporary commitment to 'participation' in environmental regulation. Clearly, the prime participant in such a mechanism is the regulated party; voluntary agreements can, however, be multi-party, with more direct and significant environmental interest group or local resident group involvement than might be possible in respect of direct regulation. The search for consensus, or at least a decision all can agree to, may also encourage committed discussion and deliberation.

These claims for a voluntary approach are clearly attractive, particularly given their ability to respond to challenges faced by the EC institutions; the extent to which environmental agreements can deliver is of course another matter.[120] The contribution of environmental agreements to public participation and deliberation,

---

[115] For a sceptical view, see N Middleton and P O'Keefe, *Rio Plus Ten: Politics, Poverty and the Environment* (London, Pluto Press, 2003).

[116] See European Commission, *Communication on Environmental Agreements* COM (96) final, p 6.

[117] See generally Commission, *ibid.*

[118] Commission, *ibid.* See particularly F Ost, 'A Game Without Rules? Ecological Self-Organisation in Firms' in G Teubner, L Farmer and D Murphy (eds), *Environmental Law and Ecological Responsibility: The Concept and Practice of Ecological Self-Organisation* (Chichester, Wiley, 1994). See the discussion of 'reflexive regulation' in ch 6 above.

[119] PM Bailey, 'The Creation and Enforcement of Environmental Agreements' [1999] *European Environmental Law Review* 170.

[120] G van Calster and K Deketelaere, 'The Use of Voluntary Agreements in the European Community's Environmental Policy' in EW Orts and K Deketelaere (eds), *Environmental Contracts: Comparative Approaches to Regulatory Innovation* (The Hague, Kluwer, 2000); C Coglianese, 'Is Consensus an Appropriate Basis for Regulatory Policy?' in Orts and Deketelaere, *ibid*, discusses a number of pathologies he claims are inherent in the institutionalisation of consensus. See Z Makuch, 'Smart Regulation and the Revised Batteries Directive: The Future of Voluntary Agreements' [2003] *European Environmental Law Review* 233, for a positive but balanced view of the role of environmental agreements as a complement to other regulatory approaches.

for example, is at best double-edged. The full expression of genuine views may not lead to consensus: 'sincere reasoners will find themselves in principled disagreements'.[121] Participants may feel pressure to self-censor in the interests of consensus, which would not necessarily lead to good or lasting agreement.[122] A search for agreement would also tend to restrict the selection of participants in decision-making, suggesting the involvement of only 'reliable' interest groups; the 'sensible' or the 'captured', depending on one's perspective. A radical environmental group that believes that a capitalist society is inherently inimical to the environmental good is not likely to be invited to the table. Asymmetries of power between the participants should also be borne in mind, as indeed in any participatory mechanism. Moreover, space for general public involvement in negotiation and monitoring of voluntary agreements, compared to more traditional forms of public regulation, may be restricted.[123] The likely exclusion of parliaments exacerbates these concerns.

Perhaps the greatest concern about environmental agreements, not unrelated to the concern that they may be sheltered from public involvement, is that they will lead to less stringent environmental targets. If there really is no compulsion, nor is there any obvious incentive to go beyond 'business as usual'.[124] Onerous commitments would simply not be taken up by industry. If the regulator or legislator is no longer the central and accountable decision-maker, the public (or the environmental) interest is no longer the highest priority, and lines of accountability become ever less well-defined. Nor is compliance as straightforward as advocates of environmental agreements suggest. One might first of all question the potential of agreement compared with more effective monitoring and sanctions of direct regulation.[125] In addition, enforceability of environmental agreements can be problematic, particularly if the agreement is not contained in a binding contract, or if the terms are unclear.[126] Although the doctrinal situation varies, in some jurisdictions only the parties to an agreement (so here government and possibly environmental interest groups) can enforce a private law contract. If the terms of the agreement and information on its monitoring are not openly accessible, third parties may not even be in a position to know of the breach, and when enforcement action is taken, private law remedies may not always be adequate. Finally, free riding, that is parts of the industry not taking part in the agreement, but relying on others to counter the need for regulation, may be a problem. A serious risk of free riding reduces the chance of successful negotiation; compelling

[121] GF Gaus, 'Reason, Justification and Consensus: Why Democracy Can't Have it All' in J Bohman and W Rehg (eds), *Deliberative Democracy* (London, MIT Press, 1997), p 231.

[122] Coglianese, above n 120.

[123] See in particular SE Gaines and C Kimber, 'Redirecting Self-Regulation' (2001) 13 *Journal of Environmental Law* 157; also Ost, above n 118.

[124] DJE Grimeaud, 'Convergence or Divergence in the Use of "Negotiated Environmental Agreements" in European and US Environmental Policy: An Overview' in NJ Vig and MG Faure (eds), *Green Giants: Environmental Policies of the United States and the European Union* (Cambridge, Mass, MIT Press, 2004), especially p 169, suggests that on the whole European environmental agreements lack environmental ambition.

[125] Coglianese, above n 120.

[126] Bailey, above n 119 considers this extensively.

free riders may on the other hand imply that private parties effectively fix the parameters of legislation that applies to other private parties.

The Commission's *Communication on Environmental Agreements*[127] attempts to respond to the most pressing concerns. So it states that guaranteed transparency is crucial for the effectiveness of environmental agreements, and that this requires 'prior consultation with interested parties' (perhaps begging the question as to who might be 'interested'). The inclusion of environmental agreements in the definition of 'environmental information' in the Directive on access to environmental information provides prima facie legal obligations of access to the terms of the agreement.[128] Transparency and consultation should contribute to accountability and public participation, and also begins to make the 'lowest common denominator' approach less politically attractive. The Communication also states that agreements should be in a binding form such as contract, that results must be monitored, and the agreement and its results published. The Commission also recommends that agreements contain 'unequivocal' quantified objectives, with interim targets to allow progress to be monitored. This Communication addresses particularly the implementation of Directives by agreement, and referring to the jurisprudence of the ECJ, states that a directive intended to create rights and obligations for third parties will not be adequately implemented by a voluntary agreement. Directives that create an obligation to 'set up reduction programmes and achieve general targets' are, however, particularly appropriate for environmental agreements. A market in the hands of relatively few producers (reducing the problem of free riders and making negotiation more practical) is also thought to be amenable to a voluntary approach.

Before the ELV Directive,[129] the regulation of ELVs in a number of Member States (beyond the normal waste licensing system) rested primarily on voluntary agreements.[130] The ELV Directive, following many of the strictures of the Communication, includes the possibility for Member States to conclude or continue agreements to implement specified elements of the Directive.[131] Some of the provisions that may be implemented by agreement are lacking in compulsion, for example requiring the 'encouragement' of particular actions,[132] and neither the Directive's quantitative recycling and recovery targets, nor the financial obligations on producers can be implemented by agreement. Certain more conclusive obligations may however be implemented by agreement, including the obligation to ensure sufficient collection facilities.[133] The ELV Directive also sets conditions

---

[127] Commission, above n 116.

[128] Dir 2003/04 on Public Access to Environmental Information and Repealing Council Directive 90/313/EC [2003] OJ L 41/26, Art 2(c), see ch 6 above.

[129] Dir 00/53, above n 36.

[130] See Onida, above n 106; note that this was also the case with packaging waste, see for example J Verschuuren, 'EC Environmental Law and Self-Regulation in the Member States: in Search of a Legislative Framework' (2000) 1 *Yearbook of European Environmental Law* 103.

[131] Dir 00/53, above n 36, Art 10.

[132] *Ibid*, Art 4(1) re the use of hazardous substances in vehicles; Art 7(1) re re-use and recovery.

[133] *Ibid*, Art 5(1); also Art 8(1) re the identification of components and materials suitable for reuse and recovery; Art 8(3) re dismantling information on new vehicles.

on the use of agreements in implementation, consistently with the Communication.[134] The agreements must: be enforceable; specify objectives and deadlines; be published in an official document; be made subject to monitoring, reporting and publicity; be subject to examination of progress by competent authorities; and be implemented by legislative, regulatory or administrative measures in case of non-compliance. These conditions are clearly designed to overcome the major criticisms of environmental agreements. The background of formal legal obligations on the Member States, together with the provisos as to enforcement, transparency, etc, will inevitably make the negotiation of agreements resemble more traditional forms of regulation, reflecting the view of the Commission that environmental agreements are a tool of implementation, rather than a tool of de-regulation. The question is the extent to which the purported advantages of voluntary agreements are still available in these circumstances. Agreements are rarely if ever truly voluntary, any more than regulation is often imposed without some level of negotiation,[135] and there is a range of policy options between direct regulation and pure self-regulation.[136] The distinction between voluntary agreements and regulation is not clear cut in EC law.

A subsequent Communication from the Commission on environmental agreements concentrates not on national agreements, but on EC level environmental agreements.[137] The Commission anticipates the negotiation of voluntary agreements in a number of areas, including waste management. It applies similar conditions on the acceptability of EC level environmental agreements as apply at the national or regional level: in particular, environmental agreements must be subject to judicial control, be transparent, and involve civil society; they must be cost-effective for the administration; monitoring and reporting is required, to quantified and staged objectives. In addition, the three pillars of sustainable development apply, and impact assessment may be required. Finally, the parties involved 'must be considered to be representative, organised and responsible by the Commission, Council and European Parliament',[138] and 'industry and their associations taking part in an agreement should represent the vast majority of the relevant economic

---

[134] *Ibid*, Art 10. The Commission, above n 116, recommends advance consultation, which is not provided for in the Directive.

[135] GC Hazard Jr and EW Orts, 'Environmental Contracts in the United States' in Orts and Deketelaere, above n 120, discuss the negotiation of 'ordinary' legislation in the litigation heavy US context. See also the comparison of the legislative auto oil programme and negotiated agreements in van Calster and Deketelaere, above n 120.

[136] D Sinclair, 'Self-Regulation Versus Command and Control? Beyond False Dichotomies' (1997) 19 *Law and Policy* 529.

[137] European Commission, *Communication on Environmental Agreements at Community Level within the Framework of the Action Plan on the Simplification and Improvement of the Regulatory Environment* COM (2002) 412 final. See also the Interinstitutional Agreement on *Better Lawmaking* in October 2003. The best known example of voluntary agreements at EC level are the agreements with associations of car makers to reduce carbon dioxide emissions from passenger cars, Commission, *ibid*. The targets have been criticised by environmental groups as unambitious, see A Jordan et al, 'European Governance and the Transfer of 'New' Environmental Policy Instruments (NEPIs) in the European Union' (2003) 81 *Public Administration* 555.

[138] Commission, *ibid*, p 11.

sector'.[139] Whilst it is important that these aspects of agreement are given explicit attention, the potential for dispute and controversy over representation is clear,[140] especially if the agreement will ultimately be extended by legislation.

The Commission puts forward two options for EC level agreement: self-regulation and co-regulation. The former would apply to an entirely voluntary undertaking from industry, and the Commission would simply acknowledge the agreement, by exchange of letters, or by means of a recommendation to allow for monitoring.[141] Co-regulation would be based on legislation. A legal act would 'stipulate that a precise, well-defined environmental objective must be reached on a given target date', and would set monitoring, enforcement and appeal mechanisms.[142] Private parties would then agree on implementation. Co-regulation has been a very controversial element of the Commission's governance project, and many of the same concerns apply as in respect of other forms of voluntary agreement, particularly as to the breadth of involvement in decision-making. The background of legislation, which will have been subject to normal processes, including European Parliament involvement, should ease some of the concern, assuming that the legislators can agree to provide for implementation by agreement. Nevertheless, implementation is far from a value free activity, and this approach may delegate significant elements of policy to private parties.

To conclude, some of the most blatant difficulties of a voluntary approach, as well as its rather long pedigree, can be seen in the UK experience with voluntary agreements in nature conservation. Briefly, until recently, the UK had a system where land could be designated as worthy of protection, and for a development project, or an industrial activity, the planning or pollution control authorities were able to prevent harm through direct regulation. However, most ordinary farming and forestry activities were not subject to planning or pollution control, in which case the only way subsequently to protect the designated land was through agreement with landowners.[143] Regulators had to persuade landowners to conserve valuable natural features, and perhaps pay them to do so. Such a scheme is not without its value. If, for political and economic reasons, more intrusive legislation was simply not possible, the provision of information to landowners at least meant that a rare chalk grassland was never ploughed up in ignorance of it being a rare chalk grassland, arguably encouraging responsibility and self-examination. The disadvantages of such a scheme are perhaps too obvious to need comment: in the words of the House of Lords, 'it needs only a moment to see that the regime is toothless'.[144]

---

[139] *Ibid.*

[140] In Case T–135/96 *Union Europeenne de l'artisanat et des Petites et Moyennes Entreprises UEAPME v Council* [1998] ECR II–2335, a party excluded from negotiations between the 'social partners' challenged the legislation arising out of those negotiations. See ch 5 above.

[141] Commission, above n 137, p 8.

[142] *Ibid.*

[143] Wildlife and Countryside Act 1981. Compulsory purchase was a possibility in respect of certain sites. See now Countryside and Rights of Way Act 2000.

[144] *Southern Water Authority v Nature Conservancy Council* [1992] 1 WLR 775, *per* Lord Mustill, p 778.

The movement of environmental agreements, and self-regulation more generally, in and out of fashion, has within it an element of conflict over the proper role of collective government. Widespread consensus decision-making involves a serious shift in public responsibilities, and broad and familiar legitimacy issues arise as decision-making moves from established fora. Similarly, a move towards compulsion is indicative of the political feasibility, and perhaps necessity, of heavier government intervention. An effort to reach agreement is not the same as an effort to protect the public interest. Public and private interests do not always or even usually, at least in the short-term, coincide.[145] The Commission's cautious welcome of voluntary agreements in these circumstances is appropriate. Many of the advantages sought by environmental agreements could equally be sought by listening to and engaging with the regulated.[146]

CONCLUSIONS

Waste might be deemed one of the less charismatic areas of environmental regulation; it certainly does not excite the imagination in the way that 'saving' forests, whales, pandas etc might, or indeed inspire the loathing of certain new technologies like genetic modification. Although the dry technical and legal aspects of waste regulation are central, however, the softer values associated with waste regulation can generate concern, debate and indeed headlines; in this sense, waste is a very visible manifestation of environmental anxiety. Waste regulation is a notoriously complex area of law, right down to the difficulty of arriving at a workable definition of the subject matter itself. As discussed above, the complexity has a number of causes; to Tromans' list of complicating factors,[147] we could perhaps add the difficulty of addressing the diverse causes of waste by familiar or traditional regulatory mechanisms. Although the waste hierarchy has been in place for many years, the EC is only now showing signs of taking much more seriously the resource use perspective on waste. Addressing waste reduction, and the subsequent use made of waste, requires the exploration of innovative mechanisms of regulation, which enhance the topic's complexity.

The main interest of waste for environmental lawyers is its acute representation of various pressing challenges in environmental regulation more generally, challenges from the public, from the market, from free trade; implementation is also a notorious problem, although it has not been dwelt on here.[148] Waste seems to attract innovative mechanisms of regulation, which take their place alongside direct regulation that sets very detailed standards of operation for installations. The

---

[145] See R Bratspies, 'Myths of Voluntary Compliance: Lessons from the Starlink Corn Fiasco' (2003) 27 *William and Mary Environmental Law and Policy Review* 591. Bratspies discusses how 'voluntary compliance' spilled over into an area that required close regulatory control, specifically the separation of a GMO not authorised from human consumption from the human food chain.

[146] Coglianese, above n 120.

[147] Tromans, above n 7.

[148] Commission, above n 64.

appearance of very detailed centralised standards even in new legislation demonstrates the limits of the move to procedure discussed in chapter six above. Waste also demonstrates that it is a mistake to perceive market instruments as a straightforward alternative to direct regulation. Extended producer responsibility, for example, depends on the entire complex structure of waste regulation. Equally, it is no more the case that environmental agreements are truly voluntary, than it is that direct regulation is simply imposed on regulated industry without some degree of negotiation.

The use of appropriate price signals has a central position in official thinking on waste.[149] This is a very important way of attempting to influence the huge number of individual decisions that create our 'waste mountain'. One might ponder whether greater efforts might be made to stimulate individual action other than through market instruments. A turn to price signals assumes that we will all behave like rational economic calculators; that must also assume that we will cheat unless there is an incentive not to (making 'pay as you throw' particularly difficult).[150] Unless enormous resources are put into preventing cheating, motives other than the purely economic are needed to stimulate behaviour: we rely on good neighbours, or 'ecological citizens' as a counterpoint to economic incentives. Whilst we may have no reason to expect an imminent rebirth of a society full of ecological citizens, this again brings out the importance of public involvement in, and especially responsibility for, waste policy.[151]

Waste regulation brings to the fore the tension at the heart of 'managerial' approaches to the environment, which recognise the need to address environmental problems, but seek to minimise changes to institutions or life style. Consumption produces waste; consumption also makes our world go round, or at least maintains economic prosperity. So for example, EC waste legislation imposes obligations to reduce the harmfulness of electrical and electronic waste, and to increase rates of recovery and recycling of this waste stream.[152] This is of course a good and progressive project in its own terms. However, to question the assumptions that drive waste production in this area would be anathema; consumption is too important a part of our economy, and the concept of 'need' just too challenging. This tension in waste policy may be considered from the perspective of the distinction drawn by Andrew Dobson between 'environmentalism', which seeks to improve management of the status quo, and 'ecologism', which implies radical change.[153] The imperative of economic growth suggests that nothing more radical can be expected; it is not difficult to understand the cynicism or despair of radical greens when faced with this sort of legislation.

---

[149] See especially Commission, above n 2.

[150] Above n 100.

[151] Note Dobson's contrast between price signals and the role of 'ecological citizenship' in fostering more profound ecological change, A Dobson, *Citizenship and the Environment* (Oxford, Oxford University Press, 2003).

[152] Dir 2002/95 on the Restriction of the Use of Certain Hazardous Substances in Electrical and Electronic Equipment [2003] OJ L 37/19; Dir 2002/96, above n 48.

[153] A Dobson, *Green Political Thought* (London, Routledge, 2000). See also ch 2 above.

9

Law, Risk and Genetically Modified Organisms

INTRODUCTION

PUBLIC ALARM AT the prospect of widespread marketing of genetically modified organisms (GMOs) met with a drastic response in the EU. From 1998, the EU essentially abandoned its regulatory framework for GMOs, introducing what amounted to a *de facto* moratorium on the marketing of GMOs in the EU.[1] This is a very uncomfortable position for the EU. Not only is the legality of the moratorium highly debatable under international trade law (not to mention EU law); there is an acute tension between this unplanned trade restriction and the significance of market integration and trade liberalisation to the EU as a polity. The perceived rejection of GM technology is also somewhat at odds with the Community's self-image as an economy built on scientific progress, as well as more specific Community ambitions with respect to biotechnology.[2] Very intense legislative and regulatory activity has been devoted by the EC institutions to trying to restart the authorisation process. The effectiveness of the enormously elaborate legislative package that has been put in place is still to be seen. The Member States remain deeply divided on the issue post-enlargement,[3] and although 2004 saw the first authorisation of a GM product since the introduction of the moratorium, the circumstances of that authorisation were enormously controversial.[4]

---

[1] A small number of crops had been authorised for commercial growing under Dir 90/220 on the Deliberate Release into the Environment of Genetically Modified Organisms [1990] OJ L 117/15, now repealed.

[2] Biotechnology is to be 'the next wave of the knowledge-based economy, creating new opportunities for our societies and economies', European Commission, *Life Sciences and Biotechnology — A Strategy for Europe* COM (2002) 27, para 1. See also *Communication to the Commission for an Orientation Debate on Genetically Modified Organisms and Related Issues* (2004), available at http://europa.eu.int /comm/food/food/biotechnology/gmfood/gmo_comm_en.pdf, especially para 1: as well as discussing the need for regulation, the Communication emphasises the need to 'harvest the potential of this high technology area', and 'reverse the exodus of researchers and rapid decline in GMO field research in the EU and the consequent negative repercussions in innovation and competitiveness of the European biotechnology industry'.

[3] No qualified majority could be reached in Committee on 16 June 2004 in respect of Monsanto's application for authorisation of GT 73 oilseed rape. Seven of the ten new Member States rejected the proposal.

[4] Discussed further below. See European Commission, *Proposal for a Council Decision Authorising the Placing on the Market of Sweet Corn from Genetically Modified Maize Line Bt 11 as a Novel Food or Food Ingredient under Regulation 258/97* COM (2004) 10 final; European Commission Press Release, *Commission Authorises Import of Canned GM-sweet Corn under New Strict Labelling Conditions — Consumers can Choose* IP/04/663. The application was made under the earlier legislation, subject to the incorporation of certain elements of the new regime. No application was made for cultivation.

The challenges faced by the EC as an environmental regulator are unusually apparent in the regulation of GMOs. In particular, the appropriate relationship between expertise and public participation is an enormous dilemma. Decisions on biotechnology demand not only expert knowledge on likely physical and economic harms and benefits, but also the consideration of fundamental questions about the sort of world in which we wish to live. Ethical concerns about the extent to which it is acceptable to interfere with nature, socio-economic and political questions about enhanced corporate control over the food sector, and distributional issues such as possible economic dislocation for small or organic farmers,[5] all go beyond the question of risk to bring into play public values. And even in respect of health and environmental protection, the adequacy of conventional risk assessment is challenged by the high political salience of both ignorance (we don't know what we don't know) and indeterminacy (the validity of knowledge depends on unpredictable human behaviour and environmental circumstances). The relevance of 'theoretical' or 'hypothetical' risks to regulatory decisions is comprehensively denied in official quarters.[6]

The new regulatory structure attempts to respond to these heterogeneous concerns, whilst at the same time responding to the competing commercial pressures, reinforced by the influence of the World Trade Organisation (WTO), which would tend to encourage regulation on the basis only of 'sound science'. In seeking to strike the very delicate balance between expert evaluations of GMOs and 'softer' public values and concerns, the EC legislation focuses largely, although not entirely, on the procedure through which GMOs shall be regulated. This turn to procedure allows a response to deeply held and opposing concerns, whilst sidestepping or delaying as much as possible final determinations on the question of values. Ultimately, however, decisions have to be taken.

This chapter will examine the legal treatment of GM food and food crops, rather than the undoubtedly equally serious questions raised by animal biotechnology or the role of biotechnology in human medicine and reproduction. There are two main strands to the new regime: a requirement for authorisation of every GMO; and an obligation to label GMOs. Two key pieces of legislation need to be examined: Directive 2001/18 on the Deliberate Release into the Environment of Genetically Modified Organisms (the 'Deliberate Release Directive')[7]; and Regulation 1829/2003 on Genetically Modified Food and Feed (the 'Food and Feed Regulation').[8] The relationship between these two pieces

---

[5] Special considerations apply with respect to developing countries, which will not be discussed here.
[6] See ch 4 above.
[7] Dir 2001/18 on the Deliberate Release into the Environment of Genetically Modified Organisms and Repealing Council Directive 90/220/EEC [2001] OJ L 106/1. See also Reg 1830/2003 concerning the Traceability and Labelling of Genetically Modified Organisms and the Traceability of Food and Feed Products Produced from Genetically Modified Organisms and Amending Directive 2001/18/EC [2003] OJ L 268/24; Reg 1946/2003 on Transboundary Movements of Genetically Modified Organisms [2003] OJ L 287.
[8] Reg 1829/2003 on Genetically Modified Food and Feed [2003] OJ L 268/1. Prior to this regulation, GM food was covered by Reg 258/97 concerning Novel Foods and Novel Food Ingredients [1997] OJ L 43/1.

of legislation is far from transparent. The Deliberate Release Directive applies to the placing on the market of GMOs as or in products, which includes their placing on the market for the purposes of deliberate release into the environment.[9] The Food and Feed Regulation applies to 'GMOs for food use', 'food containing or consisting of GMOs' and 'food produced from or containing ingredients produced from GMOs'.[10] These two pieces of legislation apply also to GM seeds for cultivation.[11]

There is clearly considerable overlap between the two pieces of legislation: many GMOs for placing on the market (Deliberate Release Directive) are also 'GMOs for food use' or 'food containing or consisting of GMOs' (Food and Feed Regulation); 'food produced from or containing ingredients produced from GMOs', however, is processed food that no longer contains actual GMOs, and so is not covered by the Deliberate Release Directive. Rather than having to apply for separate authorisations under each piece of legislation in the many cases where both could apply, the Food and Feed Regulation allows for a single application to be made.[12] In these cases of overlap, certain elements of the Deliberate Release Directive, in particular its approach to environmental risk assessment, are applied to the application under the Food and Feed Regulation. Because most of the current commercial applications of biotechnology are for food or feed use, the main exceptions being cotton and flowers, the Deliberate Release Directive is not at the moment likely to be much used for stand-alone commercial applications; the Food and Feed Regulation stands alone only in respect of its third category, 'food produced from or containing ingredients produced from GMOs'. For the sake of simplicity, this chapter will concentrate on the provisions of the Food and Feed Regulation as supplemented by the Deliberate Release Directive.[13]

This chapter will begin with an examination of the legislative authorisation process, looking first at the controversial allocation of risk assessment responsibility between national and Community level, and then at the final decision-making process. The regulation of GMOs in the EU is pervaded by a rhetoric of consumer choice, and an examination of the question of choice, labelling and co-existence will follow, before turning to the context of trade liberalisation within which GMO legislation has evolved. Not only does the need for intra-Member State free trade contribute to the rationale for (re)harmonisation of this area, but international trade pressures are a constant companion. The need to rationalise and justify environmental measures within a free trade paradigm is one of the most obvious of the many challenges faced by contemporary environmental regulators; GMOs provide a good vantage point from which to consider that challenge.

---

[9] Dir 01/18, above n 7, Art 1. Note that the former includes experimental releases.

[10] Reg 1829/2003, above n 8, Art 3(1)(a), (b) and (c).

[11] Although the Commission intends to propose separate legislation dealing with tolerance thresholds for adventitious presence of GMOs in non-GM seeds, see Communication to the Commission, above n 2.

[12] Reg 1829/2003, above n 8.

[13] References will be made to food throughout; Reg 1829/2003, *ibid*, Chapter III applies similar provisions to feed.

MULTI-LEVEL GOVERNANCE AND RISK ASSESSMENT

The political drama surrounding GMOs has made the relationship between Community and national responsibilities in the authorisation of GMOs very sensitive.

Authorisation under the Food and Feed Regulation is concerned primarily with the two issues of risk and consumer protection: GMOs must not 'have adverse effects on human health, animal health or the environment'; 'mislead the consumer'; or 'differ from the food which it is intended to replace to such an extent that its normal consumption would be nutritionally disadvantageous for the consumer'.[14] In most circumstances, consumer protection will be dealt with by mandatory labelling, placing risk assessment at the heart of regulatory authorisation. The European Food Safety Authority (the 'EFSA') plays the central role in this risk assessment.[15] Although the application for authorisation of GMOs is made to a national competent authority,[16] it is immediately passed to the EFSA, which in turn makes the application available to all other Member States and the Commission. The EFSA then provides the initial 'opinion' on the application.

The role of the national competent authorities under the Food and Feed Regulation is much reduced compared to the Deliberate Release Directive and its predecessors, under which a national body actually performed the initial risk assessment[17]; in the absence of objections from another Member State or the Commission, a positive risk assessment would have lead directly to authorisation. Under the new regime, the EFSA *may* ask a national competent body to carry out a food safety assessment or an environmental risk assessment.[18] When environmental risk assessment is a mandatory part of the application, because of overlap with the Deliberate Release Directive, the Authority is obliged to *consult* all national competent authorities.[19] If the application is for authorisation of 'seeds or other plant propagating material', the EFSA '*shall* ask a national competent authority to *carry out*' (emphasis added) the environmental risk assessment.[20]

Relative to the earlier reliance on national assessments, the role of the EFSA amounts to a real centralisation of scientific authority on GMOs. In many environmentally significant cases, the involvement of the national competent authorities in risk assessment is reduced to consultation, with no indication in the Regulation as to the influence of that consultation. As discussed in chapter four above, however, the operation of the EFSA rests on networks, and these networks, together with

---

[14] Reg 1829/2003, *ibid*, Art 4(1).

[15] See ch 4 above for discussion of the EFSA, set up under Reg 178/2002 Laying Down the General Principles and Requirements of Food Law, Establishing the European Food Safety Authority and Laying Down Procedures in Matters of Food Safety [2002] OJ L 31/1.

[16] Reg 1829/2003, above n 8, Art 5(2). In the original proposal for the Regulation, European Commission, *Proposal for a Regulation of the European Parliament and of the Council on Genetically Modified Food and Feed* COM (2001) 425 final, the application was made directly to the EFSA, Art 6(1).

[17] Dir 01/18, above n 7, Art 15(3).

[18] Reg 1829/2003, above n 8, Art 6(3)(b) and (c).

[19] *Ibid*, Art 6(4).

[20] *Ibid*, Art 6(3)(c), emphasis added.

the mandatory consultation on environmental risk assessment, do at least provide an essential opportunity for the incorporation of national perspectives on risk assessment. Given that, notwithstanding explicit responsibilities for GMOs,[21] the EFSA has only subsidiary responsibilities for the environment,[22] mandatory consultation also provides a crucial opening for a specifically environmental perspective on decision-making. Disagreements and value assumptions should also be brought into the open. When the EFSA states the reasons for its opinion, this must include the information on the opinion is based, including the responses of consulted competent authorities.[23] This transparency obligation is reinforced by the obligation of the EFSA to address diverging scientific opinions under its constituting regulation[24]; any disagreement between centralised and national risk assessors should be very clear.

The EFSA passes its opinion on the application to all Member States and the Commission. It is also made public, providing a further opportunity for scientific knowledge to be challenged, and this time not just by the elite national regulatory community. Pursuing the dichotomy between 'technical' risk assessment and 'political' risk management decisions,[25] the Food and Feed Regulation shifts the most significant Member State involvement in authorisation of GMOs from risk assessment to political representation in risk management. A 'regulatory committee', consisting of Member State representatives and chaired by the Commission, is invoked.[26] The Commission submits a draft of measures to the Committee, 'taking into account the opinion of the Authority [EFSA], any relevant provisions of Community law and other legitimate factors relevant to the matter under consideration'.[27] The public has also had the opportunity to 'make comments' before this political risk management decision.[28] The Committee delivers its decision by qualified majority: if the Committee gives a positive view, the Commission adopts the decision; if not, the proposal is passed to the Council, where a decision is again taken on qualified majority basis. If the Council fails to reach a qualified majority decision in either direction the Commission 'shall' adopt its decision, wording that suggests an absence of discretion.[29] This is precisely what happened in respect of Bt 11 sweet corn in 2004, when the Council was unable to muster a qualified majority either to accept or reject the Commission's proposal, and the

---

[21] Reg 178/2002, above n 15, Art 22.

[22] Under its constituting regulation, *ibid*, the EFSA is required to 'contribute to a high level of protection of human life and health, and in this respect take account of animal health and welfare, plant health and the environment', Art 22(3).

[23] Reg 1829/2003, above n 8, Art 6(6).

[24] Reg 178/2002, above n 15, Art 30. See ch 4 above.

[25] See the discussion in ch 4 above.

[26] Reg 1829/2003, above n 8, Arts 7(1) and 35; Decision 99/468 Laying Down the Procedures for the Exercise of Implementing Powers Conferred on the Commission [1999] OJ L 184/23, Art 5.

[27] Reg 1829/2003, *ibid*, Art 7(1); this wording will be discussed further below.

[28] *Ibid*, Art 6(7).

[29] 'Shall' appears in Decision 1999/468 above n 26, Art 5. The centrality of discretion in GMO regulation came out clearly in litigation under the previous legislation, where France was obliged to authorise a GMO at a similar stage in the proceedings, notwithstanding the emergence of great controversy during comitology, Case C–6/99 *Greenpeace v Ministère de l'Agriculture et de la Pêche* [2000] ECR I–1651.

Commission went ahead with authorisation.[30] Whilst the Commission was arguably legally compelled to adopt its proposal for authorisation, the ending of a sensitive moratorium with a high popular profile in the face of such profound divisions is nevertheless an extraordinarily controversial act. It seems likely that concern about the legality of the moratorium in WTO law was in the background.

National involvement in authorisation is, then, undermined by Member State disagreement. In any event, national involvement, and indeed policy rather than technical involvement generally, arguably comes rather late in the day in the authorisation of GMOs. The possibility for autonomous Member State action after authorisation has also been considerably reduced in the re-regulation, with the progressive tightening of the safeguard clauses that allow national restrictions on free movement. The first legislation on GMOs, Directive 1990/220 provided that a Member State with 'justifiable reasons' to consider that a product 'constitutes a risk to human health or the environment' could 'provisionally' restrict or prohibit its national use and/or sale.[31] The new Deliberate Release Directive clarifies that safeguard action requires a scientific basis, allowing the provisional restriction of use and/or sale of a GMO by a Member State only where 'new or additional information' affecting the environmental risk assessment process, or the 'reassessment of existing information on the basis of new or additional scientific knowledge' gives the Member State 'detailed grounds for considering that a GMO ... constitutes a risk to human health or the environment'.[32] The Food and Feed Regulation replaces the safeguard clause in the Deliberate Release Directive for GMOs to which it applies, and even more dramatically restricts the possibility of autonomous safeguard action.[33] 'Emergency measures' may be triggered either by an opinion from the EFSA, or when 'it is evident' that authorised products 'are likely to constitute a serious risk to human health, animal health or the environment', and 'the need to suspend or modify urgently an authorisation arises'.[34] The burden looks considerable: measures are concerned only with 'serious risk'; the requirement that it be 'evident' seems to assume a high level of proof, although in this context, the willingness of the European Court of Justice (ECJ) to interpret safeguard clauses in accordance with the precautionary principle should be noted.[35] Once emergency measures are triggered, the centralised procedure set

---

[30] Above n 4.

[31] Dir 90/220, above n 1, Art 16, see *Greenpeace*, above n 29. Quite what would have constituted a justifiable reason was not clear, although the Commission was of the view that new scientific evidence would be required.

[32] Dir 01/18, above n 7, Art 23.

[33] There is some ambiguity as to the relationship between the safeguard clauses in the Food and Feed Regulation and the Deliberate Release Directive. The Deliberate Release Directive cedes to sectoral legislation only if it contains 'a safeguard clause at least equivalent to that laid down in this Directive', Art 12(1); but the Food and Feed Regulation provides that the Deliberate Release Directive's safeguard clause shall not apply to authorisations granted under that Regulation, Art 5(5). It is debatable whether the new safeguard clause is 'equivalent'.

[34] Reg 1829/2003, above n 8, Art 34.

[35] See *Greenpeace*, above n 29, in respect of the safeguard clause in Dir 90/220, above n 1; Case C-236/01 *Monsanto Agricoltura Italia SpA v Presidenza del Consiglio dei Ministri*, 19 September 2003, not yet reported, in respect of Reg 258/97, above n 8. The ECJ views safeguard clauses 'as giving specific expression to the

out in the Food Safety Regulation applies,[36] providing for Commission action, through comitology. The possibility of autonomous Member State action exists only where the Member State has informed the Commission of the need to take emergency measures, and the Commission has not acted in accordance with the Regulation; again, the measures goes to comitology.[37]

PROCEDURALISATION

Chapter six discussed the trend in EC environmental law to regulate procedure in preference to substance, a trend very apparent and obviously attractive in the controversial regulation of GMOs. By contrast with most cases of proceduralisation in EC environmental law, where the imposition of procedural constraints on the Member States is matched by enhanced substantive flexibility, however, Member State autonomy has virtually disappeared in respect of GMOs.

The EC legislation on GMOs is light on substantive conditions, and very heavy on procedure, although the Food and Feed Regulation does introduce a substantive obligation that was absent from earlier legislation[38]: a GMO must not have 'adverse effects on human health, animal health or the environment'.[39] Whilst this certainly puts some substance into the risk assessment, procedure remains, for reasons developed below, the mainstay of the regulation.

Risk Assessment, Risk Management and Scientific Knowledge

The importance of specifying the purpose and content of the risk assessment was a lesson learned from the earlier legislation, which fell apart so comprehensively in 1998. Whilst a risk assessment had always been required, quite what that involved, as well as what might constitute an 'adverse effect', was heavily disputed.[40] In these circumstances, Member States effectively refused to recognise the adequacy of each other's risk assessments. Passing the risk assessment to the EFSA is one

precautionary principle', *Monsanto*, para 110, citing *Greenpeace*. Similar scientific rigour is applied as to Community action: protective measures 'may not properly be based on a purely hypothetical approach to risk, founded on mere suppositions which are not yet scientifically verified', *Monsanto*, para 106; measures have to be 'based on a risk assessment which is as complete as possible', *ibid*, para 107.

[36] Reg 178/2002, above n 15, Arts 53 and 54.
[37] Note that Art 95(4) and (5) EC also applies, see discussion below.
[38] Under Dir 01/18, above n 7, 'Member States shall, in accordance with the precautionary principle, ensure that all appropriate measures are taken to avoid adverse effects on human health and the environment which might arise from the deliberate release or the placing on the market of GMOs', Art 4.
[39] Reg 1829/2003, above n 8, Art 4(1)(a). It must also not mislead the consumer or 'differ from the food which it is intended to replace to such an extent that its normal consumption would be nutritionally disadvantageous for the consumer', Art 4(1)(b) and (c).
[40] In the decision that resulted in the *Greenpeace* litigation, above n 29, France had apparently not considered any potential problems caused by the presence of the antibiotic resistant marker gene, an extremely controversial element of GM technology, within its risk assessment; other Member States considered antibiotic resistance to be so important as to require resort to the Directive's safeguard clause.

response to this problem of mutual distrust; detailed provisions on the environmental risk assessment is another.

The appropriate methodology for environmental risk assessment is spelled out in some detail in the Deliberate Release Directive,[41] and it applies also to many applications under the Food and Feed Regulation. Its scope is broad: environmental risk assessment means 'the evaluation of risks to human health and the environment, whether direct or indirect, immediate or delayed, which the deliberate release or the placing on the market of GMOs may pose',[42] extending also to 'cumulative long-term effects'.[43] A non-exhaustive list of potential adverse effects is provided in the Deliberate Release Directive, in an effort to resolve the ambiguity of earlier legislation. For example, the relevance to authorisation of possible herbicide resistance on future weed management techniques was unclear under the earlier legislation; opponents of its inclusion argued that it was an economic rather than an environmental problem.[44] The Deliberate Release Directive explicitly covers 'changes in management, including, where applicable, in agricultural practices'.[45] Much less detail is provided on risk assessment in the Food and Feed Regulation,[46] although the Commission has issued detailed guidance.[47]

Turning to risk management, the level of 'acceptable risk' seems to have been clearly determined in the Food and Feed Regulation, which provides that GMOs must not 'have adverse effects on human health, animal health or the environment'.[48] The stringency of the provision is, however, not completely straightforward. First, a requirement to establish 'no adverse effects' presumably does not require proof by an applicant of absolute safety, or proof that there is no 'hypothetical risk'.[49] The EU institutions have confirmed on many occasions that this would be an unrealistic and undesirable target, and the Commission has even made a specific statement to that effect in respect of GM

See TK Hervey, 'Regulation of Genetically Modified Products in a Multi-Level System of Governance: Science or Citizens?' (2001) 10 *Review of European Community and International Environmental Law* 321. The question of antibiotic resistance is explicitly considered in the new legislation.

[41] Dir 01/18, above n 7, Annex II.

[42] *Ibid*, Art 2(8).

[43] *Ibid*, Annex II, ' "cumulative long term effects" refers to the accumulated effects of consents on human health and the environment, including inter alia flora and fauna, soil fertility, soil degradation of organic material, the feed / food chain, biological diversity, animal health and resistance problems in relation to antibiotics'.

[44] See S Carr and L Levidow, 'Negotiated Science — The Case of Agricultural Biotechnology Regulation in Europe' in M Wissenburg, G Orhan and U Collier (eds), *European Discourses on Environmental Policy* (Ashgate, Aldershot, 1999).

[45] Dir 01/18, above n 7, Annex II, C 2, para 1.

[46] The food safety assessment can be carried out by a national competent authority, Reg 1829/2003, above n 8, Art 6(3)(b). The assessment would be carried out in accordance with Regulation 178/2002 above n 15, Art 36, which is light on detail. Reg 178/2002 defines risk assessment as 'a scientifically based process consisting of four steps: hazard identification, hazard characterisation, exposure assessment and risk characterisation', Art 3(11). Risk assessment 'shall be based on the available scientific evidence and undertaken in an independent, objective and transparent manner', Art 6(2).

[47] European Commission, *Guidance Document for the Risk Assessment of Genetically Modified Plants and Derived Food and Feed* (2003) available at: http://europa.eu.int/comm/food/fs/sc/ssc/out327_en.pdf.

[48] Reg 1829/2003, above n 8, Art 4(1)(a).

[49] The discussion of risk regulation in ch 4 above is important for the discussion in this section.

food and feed.[50] The initial proposal for the Food and Feed Regulation had provided that GMO food must not 'present a risk for human health or the environment'[51]; the changed wording in the final version more clearly focuses on harm rather than risk, reinforcing the irrelevance of 'hypothetical risk'.

Whilst regulation of 'hypothetical risks' is illegitimate, it might be argued that positive evidence of *any* adverse effect would preclude authorisation, a mandatory 'zero tolerance' of harm. Combined with the precautionary principle, particularly if the precautionary principle develops in such a way as to *require*, as well as protect, precautionary action,[52] the prohibition on adverse effects could provide a very serious legal limitation on the authorisation of GMOs.[53] The Deliberate Release Directive is explicitly based on the precautionary principle,[54] which whilst not explicitly mentioned in the Food and Feed Regulation, is one of the 'general principles of food law' in the EU,[55] and has been held by the Court of First Instance (CFI) to constitute an 'autonomous principle'.[56] The precautionary principle is discussed in chapter four above; for current purposes, it is important to note that the precautionary principle entitles the Community institutions to act when the scientific evidence on harm is uncertain, and even in reliance on unorthodox or minority scientific views; the judiciary does, however, demand, and is prepared to investigate, a level of scientific cogency to any such decision.[57]

This hard line interpretation of the prohibition of 'adverse effects' could be rather startling. Human activities, including agricultural activities, inevitably have adverse effects on the environment. More specifically, many first generation GMOs involve plants that are designed to express pesticide or to be used with a particular herbicide: pesticides and herbicides undoubtedly do, in the broadest sense, have demonstrable adverse effects on the environment. The intention is unlikely to be to design legislation in such a way that would require applications for authorisation to be rejected for most, if not all, contemporary GMOs. It could be that 'no adverse effect' will be applied as if it meant 'no unacceptable adverse effect' or 'no unacceptable risk of adverse effect'.[58] A proportionality oriented interpretation to make a provision more workable is not unheard of; for example,

---

[50] Response from the Commission to Comments submitted by WTO Members under Either or Both G/TBT/N/EEC/6 and G/SPS/n/EEC/149, 26 July 2002, p 12.

[51] See Commission above n 16, Art 4(1).

[52] Cases T–74/00, T–76/00 and T–141/00 *Artegodan* [2002] ECR II–4945; the appeal to the ECJ, Case C–39/03 P *Artegodan and Others v Commission* [2003] ECR I–7785, did not provide further guidance on the precautionary principle.

[53] Although in terms of judicial review, note how unlikely it is that an objector to authorisation would even get before a court, ch 5 above.

[54] Dir 01/18, above n 7, Recital 8: 'the precautionary principle has been taken into account in the drafting of this Directive and must be taken into account when implementing it'. The precautionary principle is also a requirement of the authorisation process under Art 4.

[55] Reg 178/2002, above n 15, Art 7.

[56] Case T–70/99 *Alpharma Inc v Council* [2002] ECR II–3495; Case T–13/99 *Pfizer Animal Health SA v Council* [2002] ECR II–3305; more explicitly, *Artegodan*, above n 52.

[57] *Alpharma* and *Pfizer*, ibid.

[58] By way of example, there is evidence that crops that express the Bt pesticide are toxic to larvae of the monarch butterfly. This risk might be reduced to acceptable levels by not planting the GMOs near plants favoured by monarch butterfly larvae; it will only be eliminated by not planting the impugned crops.

the objectives of the Waste Framework Directive are not literally achievable, but do not result in the failure of all waste installations to receive authorisations.[59]

Perhaps, however, it would be easier to justify an interpretation of 'no adverse effects' that required adverse effects to be identified by reference to conventional comparators. Certainly, under the Deliberate Release Directive, the characteristics of a GMO that have potential adverse effects 'should be compared to those presented by the non-modified organism from which it is derived and its use under corresponding situations'.[60] Any such comparison involves very significant assumptions and uncertainties, not only in respect of the GMO, but also in respect of conventional agricultural practices; comparison with organic agriculture, for example, is likely to produce a very different conceptualisation of 'adversity' from comparison with industrial farming. Debate in the UK about the adequacy of risk assessment of certain GM crops illustrates the degree of professional judgment involved in the risk assessment. A UK Parliamentary committee judged the benchmark of conventional farming against which the GM crops were measured to be 'unambitious'; in respect of comparison between one particular GM crop and a conventional crop that relied on a herbicide the use of which was soon to be unlawful, that comparison was described as 'invalid'.[61] More positively, the outcry that met the assessment also illustrates the potential for transparency of scientific assessment to bring judgments and alternatives into the open.

Beyond Scientific Knowledge

One might expect that in such a dramatically polarised debate, plagued by scientific uncertainties, a serious effort would be made to encourage public participation in decision-making.[62] Indeed, EU biotechnology policy confirms the importance of public involvement,[63] and whilst the reference of the Aarhus Convention to GMOs is somewhat lacking in legal vigour,[64] it seems to assume a particular role

[59] Dir 75/442 on Waste [1975] OJ L 194/39, Art 4 requires Member States to ensure that waste is recovered of disposed of (inter alia) 'without endangering human health and without using processes or methods which could harm the environment'. Art 4 is not literally achievable, but does not result in the prohibition of all forms of waste management.

[60] Dir 01/18, above n 7, Annex II, para B. Note also that under the Cartagena Protocol on Biosafety to the Convention on Biological Diversity, available at http://www.biodiv.org/biosafety/protocol.asp, risks are 'considered in the context of risks posed by the non-modified recipients or parental organisms in the likely potential receiving environment'. Food is compared with its 'conventional counterpart' under Reg 1829/2003, above n 8, Art 5(3)(f), which is however concerned particularly with the 'consumer interests' conditions of authorisation, rather than safety.

[61] Environmental Audit Committee, 2003–2004 Second Report, *GM Foods — Evaluating the Farm Scale Trials* HC 90–I, Conclusion, paras 1 and 14.

[62] J Black, 'Regulation as Facilitation: Negotiating the Genetic Revolution' (1998) 61 *Modern Law Review* 621, discusses the need for a facilitative, integrative approach by biotechnology regulators; see also J Steele, 'Participation and Deliberation in Environmental Law: Exploring a Problem-solving Approach' (2001) 21 *Oxford Journal of Legal Studies* 415.

[63] Commission (2002), above n 2; decision-making on biotechnology is even explicitly mentioned in European Commission, *White Paper on European Governance* COM (2001) 428 final, p 19.

[64] *Convention on Access to Information, Public Participation in Decision-making and Access to Justice in Environmental Matters* (1998), available at http://www.unece.org/env/pp/documents/cep43e.pdf. Art 6

for public participation. Legislative provision for public participation in decision-making on GMOs is, however, surprisingly weak.

The new regulatory framework takes a distinctly unambitious approach to public participation. It concentrates on the most basic of the 'access principles', that is access to information. A range of documents must be made public, subject to confidentiality, including: the application for authorisation; the EFSA[65] and competent authority opinions; monitoring reports and information from the authorisation holder.[66] General access to documents and access to environmental information regimes also apply.[67] The format of the information and the means of publicity are left largely open, the requirement for a summary of the application and a public register for the logging of authorisations, being the main concessions to accessibility of information.[68]

The Food and Feed Regulation provides one explicit opportunity to make comments to the Commission, between publication of the Authority's opinion and of the Commission's draft Decision.[69] Although there is no limitation on the nature of the comments that can be made, this consultation is built around technical information, and seems to be intended to elicit information on pre-formed preferences; there is no effort to go further in seeking out public values or deliberation, and there is no indication as to the purpose or possible impact of the consultation. Any more ambitious approach to public involvement is left to the Member State; a number of Member States have indeed attempted deeper forms of public participation on this issue. The UK, for example, held an innovative effort at public deliberation in 2003, designed to elicit qualitative information on public views and values in respect of GM crops.[70] The problem is that the results of even the very best public engagement can only be imperfectly reflected in the Community decision-making process. Most obviously, each Member State is only one of 25 states involved in a joint decision;

---

does not apply automatically to GMOs under Annex I, but the public participation in decision making is explicitly stated to apply 'to the extent feasible and appropriate ... to decisions on whether to permit the deliberate release of genetically modified organisms into the environment', Art 6(11). Note that a Working Group has been convened on GMOs. The Commission proposes awaiting the outcome of these negotiations before amending participation provisions on GMOs, European Commission, *Proposal for a Council Decision on the Conclusion, on behalf of the European Commission, of the Convention on Access to Information, Public Participation in Decision-making and Access to Justice in Environmental Matters* COM (2003) 625 final, p 14.

[65] Reg 1829/2003, above n 8, Art 6(7).
[66] *Ibid,* Art 29(1).
[67] *Ibid,* Art 29.
[68] Reg 1829/2003, above n 8, Art 28. Note also Commission Decision 2004/204 Laying Down Detailed Arrangements for the Operation of the Registers for Recording Information on Genetic Modifications in GMOs, Provided for in Directive 2001/18/EC [2004] OJ L 65/20.
[69] Reg 1829/2003, *ibid,* Art 6(7).
[70] *GM Nation?* was the title of the project, and details can be found at: http://www.gmnation.org/. Whilst the project was an innovative attempt at deliberation, it has been widely acknowledged that the process was carried out more quickly than would have been ideal, that it probably needed more funding, and that it was not entirely successful in getting the involvement of people not already engaged with the issues. See in particular the evidence of the Chair of the GM Public Debate Steering Board, House of Commons Select Committee on Environment, Food and Rural Affairs, 2002–2003 18th Report, *Conduct of the GM Public Debate,* HC 1220.

whilst national governments can promise to reflect public opinion in Community decision-making fora, they cannot promise any more concrete response to national public opinion. Perhaps more central for current purposes is the ability of the deci-sion-making process to embrace the complexity of public concern. In particular, regulation preoccupied by risk to health or the environment will not take on board socio-economic, political or ethical concerns.

Both the Deliberate Release Directive and the Food and Feed Regulation seem to acknowledge the relevance of non-safety concerns. In the case of the Deliberate Release Directive, however, the final decision is made on the basis of risk assess-ment, and it is difficult to see how broader issues are taken into account.[71] There is ample opportunity for debate on safety; whether safety should really be the only point of engagement is more problematic. And it should be recalled that whilst the Deliberate Release Directive rarely applies alone to the current generation of GM crops, the technology is developing beyond food and feed. If authorisation is at some point sought for crops that have been genetically modified to produce phar-maceutical or industrial substances, we may see even more intense non-technical concern; it is not clear how this will feed into the authorisation process.

The Food and Feed Regulation, however, embraces broader objectives than the Deliberate Release Directive. In particular, it is designed to protect 'consumer interests'.[72] The precise extent of consumer interests is unclear; it might be argued that they embrace long term and inchoate issues such as the gradual impact on consumers of the extension of monocultures, or of increased reliance on a small number of patent holders for food production. When one turns to the conditions of authorisation in the Food and Feed Regulation, however, one only explicitly finds reference to possible nutritional disadvantages of GM food, and the mis-leading of consumers. In either case, labelling may be the appropriate response: on an application for authorisation, for example, the Regulation specifies that the applicant must establish either that the GM food is nutritionally no different from its conventional counterpart, or suggest appropriate labelling.[73] Both the Food and Feed Regulation and the general EU food law,[74] which spells out the question of consumer protection in a little more detail, are focussed primarily on 'informed choices'.[75] Any 'ethical or religious concerns', presumably including the presence of animal (especially bovine or porcine) genes in unexpected places, is also explic-itly linked with labelling.[76] It seems unlikely that the consumer interests rationale will feed into the authorisation process very often if at all,[77] and correspondingly

---

[71] M Lee and C Abbot, 'The Usual Suspects? Public Participation Under the Aarhus Convention' (2003) 66 *Modern Law Review* 80.

[72] Reg 1829/2003, above n 8, Art 1.

[73] *Ibid*, Art 5(3)(f).

[74] Reg 178/2002, above n 15.

[75] *Ibid*, Art 8; Reg 1829/2003, above n 8, Recital 21.

[76] Reg 1829/2003, *ibid*, Art 5(3)(g).

[77] See also J Scott, 'European Regulation of GMOs and the WTO' (2003) 9 *Columbia Journal of European Law* 213. The Commission has suggested that future developments, for example a genetic modification that makes food look fresh when it is not, or makes a food look like a different product, could feed into the authorisation process, in which case labelling may not suffice, Commission response, above n 50.

unlikely that the complex range of public concerns about GMOs will be fed into the authorisation decisions by this route.

The EU approach to risk management, discussed in chapter four, could be a more fruitful possibility than risk assessment for looking at broader concerns about GMOs. Now that the political nature of risk management has been acknowledged, there is increasing potential to expand the breadth of reasons for regulatory decisions. The distinction between risk assessment and risk management is blurred in the Deliberate Release Directive, which although providing a deliberately political rather than scientific locus for the final decision (comitology), provides no obvious space for decisions not based on risk assessment. By contrast, under the Food and Feed Regulation, the Commission's draft decision on authorisation is explicitly permitted to take account of not only the EFSA opinion and relevant provisions of Community law, but also 'other legitimate factors relevant to the matter under consideration'.[78] This wording is familiar from general food law, discussed in chapter four, according to which 'other factors legitimate to the matter under consideration' include 'societal, economic, traditional, ethical and environmental factors and the feasibility of controls'.[79] The recitals to the Food and Feed Regulation explicitly recognise that 'in some cases, scientific risk assessment alone cannot provide all the information on which a risk management decision should be based'.[80] Ostensibly, the Food and Feed Regulation allows considerable room for the incorporation into decisions of values and concern that go well beyond technical and scientific issues. More specifically, given that the Food and Feed Regulation invites public comments, it would be strange if the results of those consultations were not 'relevant'; even disregarding public opinion in itself, if the set of concerns behind public opinion could be reliably elicited, they could be taken into account. The legislation also provides for the consultation of a Committee on Ethics, and it would be similarly odd if ethical concerns were not relevant.[81] The broad ethical acceptability of the current and anticipated technology, however, seems to be largely assumed by the very framework for authorisation; questions such as eco-centric concerns around exploitation of nature seem unlikely to be considered. It is however possible that ethical issues will be revisited in respect of the use of animals, particularly once GM animals become commercially viable in agriculture; although the authorisation conditions refer only to 'animal health', the objectives of the Food and Feed Regulation embrace also 'animal welfare'.[82] By way of analogy, it might be observed that ethics seems to be a much more acceptable framework for debate in respect of human genetic technology.[83]

Notwithstanding the potential breadth of the legislative wording, a number of factors constrain political inputs into decisions on the authorisation of GMOs. Most basically, administrative powers must be exercised exclusively or primarily

[78] Reg 1829/2003, above n 8, Art 6.
[79] Reg 178/2002, above n 15, Recital 19.
[80] Reg 1829/2003, above n 8, Recital 32.
[81] *Ibid*, Art 33.
[82] *Ibid*, Art 1.
[83] See the discussion in Black, above n 62.

for purposes for which they were granted.[84] The Food and Feed Regulation in this respect takes us back to questions of adverse effects, nutritional issues and misled consumers; although the objectives of the Regulation are marginally more broadly expressed than the grounds for authorisation,[85] aside from the reference to 'animal welfare' that largely involves a revisiting of consumer interests. Relying on scientific advice also continues to hold its old appeal of apparent neutrality, and openness to external testing. These qualities are particularly attractive if decision-makers anticipate the possibility of being required to justify their position before their WTO partners. More specifically, as discussed in chapter four, EC jurisprudence tends to reinforce the role of scientific evidence in political decision-making: albeit in the context of legislation that does not contain the 'other legitimate factors' formula, the CFI has held that when a Community institution departs from the opinion of a scientific committee, it must provide 'specific reasons for its findings', and moreover that the reasons 'must be of a scientific level at least commensurate with that of the opinion in question'.[86] The precise nature of the scientific evidence required to defend disagreement with scientific advice is not clear; that it is made up of more science is. The precautionary principle, if anything, tends to confirm the likely privileging of scientific and technical information. No obvious space is provided by the precautionary principle, as interpreted in EC law, for the incorporation of ignorance or indeterminacy into the risk management process, let alone ethical or socio-economic concerns. The narrow basis for Member State safeguard action, discussed above, reinforces the conclusion that science provides the primary source of legitimacy on GMOs; Article 95 EC is also suggestive.[87] Article 95(5) provides a route for the introduction of national measures to an area subject to harmonised Community law, if those measures are necessary to protect the environment. The measures must be notified to the Commission, which can accept or reject them. The introduction of new national provisions is only acceptable if it is 'based on new scientific evidence', and the lack of such new scientific evidence was one of the factors that allowed the Commission to reject Austrian attempts to establish 'GM free zones', primarily for the protection of organic agriculture.[88]

---

[84] See for example Case C–84/94 *United Kingdom v Council* [1996] ECR I–5755, para 69; Case 331/88 *R v MAFF ex parte Fedesa* [1990] ECR I–4023.

[85] Scott, above n 77.

[86] *Pfizer*, above n 56, para 199.

[87] Art 95(5) deals with the introduction of *new* national provisions, which must be 'based on new scientific evidence relating to the protection of the environment or the working environment on grounds of a problem specific to that Member State, arising after the adoption of the harmonisation measure'. Intended measures must not constitute 'a means of arbitrary discrimination', 'a disguised restriction on trade between Member States' or 'an obstacle to the functioning of the internal market', Art 95(6). Art 95(5) is discussed by the ECJ in case C–512/99 *Germany v Commission* [2003] ECR I–845. Note that Art 95(4) provides for slightly less severe restrictions on the maintenance of existing national measures, see Case C–3/00 *Denmark v Commission* [2003] ECR I–2643. See generally H Sevenster, 'The Environmental Guarantee After Amsterdam: Does the Emperor Have New Clothes?' (2000) 1 *Yearbook of European Environmental Law* 281.

[88] Commission Decision 2003/653 Relating to National Provisions on Banning The Use of Genetically Modified Organisms in the Region of Upper Austria notified by the Republic of Austria pursuant to

In short, the entire legal context of the 'other legitimate factors' formula provides considerable incentives for the explanation of decisions by reference to (perhaps minority) scientific evidence, rather than explicitly by reference to the broader spectrum of concerns, or simple public opinion; the well known prioritisation of scientific and technical information within the WTO regime can only emphasise this ambivalence towards 'other legitimate factors'. Nevertheless, it has to be acknowledged that the Food and Feed Regulation attempts to move beyond a purely scientific or technical approach, in response to many years of complaint at the narrow basis for decisions. The precise role of 'other legitimate factors' is somewhat perplexing, and given the deeply held views on the role of politics in risk regulation, perhaps deliberately under-specified. The Commission is certainly terse in its response to its WTO partners on quite what is intended by the reference to 'other legitimate factors'.[89] If, however, this chink in technocentric decision-making is allowed to prosper, a politically reasoned decision, expressed in terms that go beyond science, would provide a far more acceptable and sophisticated response to the reality of GM technology; science-based knowledge is clearly not the sole legitimate basis for decisions in such a multi-faceted and complex area. This applies whether the decision grants or withholds authorisation; and it would be naïve not to expect such a well-resourced and well-advised industry to attempt to make use of this legal provision.

Attempts to de-politicise normative debate can erode trust and understanding, as well as blurring the accountability of decisions rationalised on grounds other than those on which they really rest. Explicit breadth to the grounds on which decisions are based should clarify responsibility for decisions; it might also rest on a recognition that the EC courts and the WTO dispute resolution bodies are increasingly willing to look at the evidence behind the stated reasons for a decision,[90] undermining the tactic of applying the language of risk to 'other' concerns. The space for politics and public opinion in WTO law will be further considered below. It is possible that a refusal to authorise a GMO on grounds of 'other factors' will need to be defended before WTO partners; the question of the evidence for and rationality of the decision will come to the fore.

Proceduralisation and GMOs

The EU appeals to at least two, not necessarily consistent, approaches to environmental proceduralisation. One manifestation of proceduralisation is a 'participatory' approach, emphasising transparency, responsiveness and even 'democratisation';

Article 95(5) of the EC Treaty [2003] OJ L 230/34. The Commission also found that the 'small structured farming systems' protected by Austria are not specific to that Member State.

[89] Response from the Commission, above n 50, pp 15–16. The Commission refers to consistency with international standards, and states that the EC has sought clarification of the role of 'other legitimate factors' at international level, without results.

[90] Scott, above n 77.

within this approach, there could be very shallow participation, concentrating on transparency and consultation over pre-formed interests, or deeper structures that approach a deliberative ideal. The participatory approach confronts what we might call a 'drowning by numbers'[91] approach to proceduralisation, which rests on the imposition of particular scientific or bureaucratic methodologies on regulators or industry, for example requirements to carry out a risk assessment in a particular way, to weigh the results of a risk assessment in a particular way, to satisfy particular burdens of proof, or to carry out a formal cost benefit analysis. Both trends are strong and worthwhile, but they can work at cross-purposes; in particular, highly technical decision-making can reduce the opportunity for meaningful lay engagement in the process.

Opportunities for public participation are limited in respect of GMOs, and the continued dominance of technical and scientific debate seems likely. Transparency, consultation and the invocation of the precautionary principle ensure, rightly, an opportunity for rigorous questioning of the technical and scientific basis of decisions. The mechanisms for the incorporation of softer values, however, are much more fragile, and in most cases these issues are simply left to the market; the assumption is that consumer choice will fill the gaps left after safety and probity have been assured.

Removed from the conflict between participation and drowning by numbers, there is a distinct 'reflexive' element to the regulation of GMOs.[92] Many elements of the legislation are designed to allow for learning from experience and regulatory evolution. Scientific information is exposed to testing from different perspectives, and multiple sources of information are encouraged. For example, a wealth of information is required in the application[93]; the risk assessor assesses that information; national officials and the public are consulted; information is exchanged and reported. The ability to revisit regulation is also significant, and closely related to the precautionary stance of the legislation: the imposition of a maximum (renewable) ten year authorisation period means that individual authorisations will always be revisited; the authorisation holder is obliged to inform the Commission of new information that might influence the safety evaluation[94]; and monitoring obligations allow assumptions to be checked following experience.[95] Along similar lines, an obligation of traceability, 'the ability to trace GMOs and

---

[91] To borrow from E Fisher, 'Drowning by Numbers: The Pursuit of Accountable Public Administration' (2000) 20 *Oxford Journal of Legal Studies* 109.

[92] See ch 6 above.

[93] See also Commission Regulation 641/2004 on Detailed Rules For The Implementation Of Regulation 1829/2003 as Regards the Application for the Authorisation of New Genetically Modified Food and Feed, the Notification of Existing Products and Adventitious or Technically Unavoidable Presence of Genetically Modified Material which has Benefited from a Favourable Risk Evaluation [2004] OJ L 102/14.

[94] Reg 1829/2003, above n 8, Art 9(3). Under Dir 01/18, above n 7, the consent holder is obliged to inform the relevant competent authority of any new information on risks to human health or the environment, and a procedure is provided for the reconsideration of consent in those circumstances, Art 20.

[95] Monitoring is an automatic condition of authorisations covered by Dir 01/18, above n 7, Art 20; under Reg 1829/2003, above n 8, monitoring may be one of the conditions of authorisation.

products produced from GMOs at all stages of their placing on the market through the production and distribution chains',[96] is an important part of responsive or precautionary legislation.

GREEN CONSUMERISM, LABELLING AND GMOs

GM food has been something of a cause célèbre for consumer power, with many major food retailers and processors rejecting GMOs in the 1990s, apparently in response to consumer demand.[97] One of the objectives of the Food and Feed Regulation is to provide a 'high level of protection of ... consumer interests'.[98] The primary tool for the protection of consumer interests is labelling, which 'enables the consumer to make an informed choice and facilitates fairness of transactions between seller and purchaser'.[99] Labelling is mandatory for all products covered by the Food and Feed Regulation, and for all other 'products consisting of or containing GMOs'.[100] The labelling obligation in the Food and Feed Regulation extends even to heavily processed foods, and so is not dependent on the presence of GM DNA or protein in the final product; EU labelling obligations are very clearly concerned with the characteristics of production, not just the characteristics of the product itself. The Food and Feed Regulation does not, however, apply to food and feed produced 'with' a GMO,[101] for example, the meat or milk of a cow fed on GM feed. Given the potential size of the market for feed, this restricts consumer influence over the cultivation of GM crops rather significantly.

The legislation provides a very important exception to mandatory labelling. Labelling is not required if a food, or an individual ingredient in a food, contains up to 0.9 per cent GM material, provided that the presence of GM material is 'adventitious' or 'technically unavoidable'.[102] The precise interpretation of this provision could have serious implications: if 0.9 per cent constitutes a baseline of 'normal' contamination, always acceptable as long as unplanned, it is likely to become widespread very quickly. However, producers wishing to take advantage

---

[96] Reg 1830/2003, above n 8, Arts 3(3) and 1. The objectives are 'facilitating accurate labelling, monitoring the effects on the environment, and, where appropriate, on health, and the implementation of the appropriate risk management measures including, if necessary, withdrawal of products'.

[97] There have been reports that Syngenta will not commercialise the sweet corn for which it received authorisation in 2004, because of consumer pressure. M Friedman, 'Using Consumer Boycotts to Stimulate Corporate Policy Changes: Marketplace, Media, and Moral Considerations' in M Micheletti, A Follesdal and D Stolle (eds), *Politics, Products and Markets: Exploring Political Consumerism Past and Present* (New Brunswick, Transaction Publishers, 2004) discusses the effectiveness and morality of consumer boycotts far more generally.

[98] Reg 1830/2003, above n 8, Art 1. This is subtly narrowed in the conditions for authorisation, Art 4. See above text at n 85.

[99] *Ibid*, Recital 17.

[100] Reg 1830/2003, above n 8.

[101] Reg 1829/2003, above n 8, Recital 16.

[102] *Ibid*, Art 12(4). The proportion is subject to being lowered by committee to reflect scientific and technical advances. Note also the 0.5% threshold re unauthorised GMOs that have been subject to a positive safety assessment, Art 47.

of the 'adventitious' or 'technically unavoidable' exception are required to provide evidence to demonstrate that 'they have taken appropriate steps to avoid the presence of such material'.[103] This suggests that to avoid labelling obligations, the efforts of the producer must aim to avoid GMOs entirely[104]; and possibly even that 0.9 per cent will be deemed to be acceptable only on an extraordinary and exceptional basis, in respect of particular 'contaminated' batches of a product. The Commission's approach to the 'co-existence' of different methods of food production, however, suggests otherwise. The Commission seems to assume that 0.9 per cent will be a norm, and it is even of the view that it would be illegitimate for a Member State to apply mandatory regulatory measures aiming below that threshold.[105] The Commission of course is not the final interpreter of the legislative language, and its understanding of the role of thresholds is open to debate.[106] However, there are presumably circumstances in which 0.9 per cent (or indeed higher proportions, but then there is no concession in respect of labelling) is technically unavoidable on a regular basis. Aside from the obligation to take 'appropriate steps', the language of the Regulation does not inherently suggest that the exception from the obligation to label should be extraordinary.

Even without this ambiguity, the consistency of thresholds with the consumer choice rhetoric, let alone with ethical concerns about genetic engineering, is somewhat tenuous. The introduction of thresholds constitutes a pragmatic recognition that once GMOs are on the market, they will be virtually impossible to avoid entirely. GM and non-GM material is mixed in fields, in storage, production, transport, and the low thresholds do require considerable efforts at segregation, the feasibility of which was initially denied by producers of grain. Pursuit of the GM free option (or the GM free 'consumer choice'), however, is in a practical sense abandoned. Thresholds are particularly controversial in the case of organic agriculture, which might be expected to attain greater levels of purity than conventional agriculture. EC legislation sets minimum standards for the accreditation of organic produce by authorised certification bodies.[107] Whilst GMOs cannot be *used* in organic agriculture, the *presence* of GMOs is unregulated. Although maximum thresholds for inadvertent contamination of organic produce are foreseen by the legislation,[108] no such thresholds have ever been

---

[103] Art 12(3).

[104] Or aim as close to zero as possible.

[105] Commission Recommendation 2003/556 Guidelines for the Development of National Strategies and Best Practices to Ensure the Co-Existence of Genetically Modified (GM) Crops with Conventional and Organic Farming C [2003] OJL 189/36: 'Measures for co-existence should be efficient and cost-effective, and proportionate. They shall not go beyond what is necessary in order to ensure that adventitious traces of GMOs stay below the tolerance thresholds set out in Community legislation', para 2.1.4.

[106] Note that under the restrictive approach to standing before the EC courts, discussed in ch 5 above, a legal challenge would probably require Member State or European Parliament action. This is not inconceivable, given the Parliament's largely cautious approach to GMOs, and the attempts of many Member States to retain a degree of autonomy on co-existence.

[107] Reg 2092/1991 on Organic Production of Agricultural Products and Indications Referring Thereto on Agricultural Products and Foodstuffs: 'GMOs and products derived therefrom are not compatible with the organic production method', Recital 10.

[108] *Ibid*, Art 23.

agreed, and it seems likely that the normal threshold (0.9 per cent) will continue to apply with respect to labelling.[109] Organic certification bodies can require their members to go beyond the minimum regulatory standards; whether that will be practical, if GM farming becomes widespread, without regulatory assistance, remains to be seen.[110]

The 'co-existence' of different types of agriculture is crucial to consumer choice. GM farming could however have a very serious impact on existing forms of agriculture, particularly if the presence of GM material affects the status or performance of non-GM food or crops.[111] According to the Commission, all forms of agriculture should be able to co-exist: 'No form of agriculture, be it conventional, organic, or agriculture using GMOs, should be excluded in the European Union'.[112] The Commission has recommended possible co-existence measures, such as separation distances or buffer zones, which whilst not guaranteeing the absence of gene flow, can be designed to minimise its extent; combined with labelling thresholds, many problems can be avoided. Co-existence measures are the responsibility of the Member States, in theory leaving the way open for distinctive national approaches.[113] However, the flexibility is placed in a framework of minimalist expectations from at least the Commission, which has issued a non-binding Recommendation and Guidelines on co-existence.[114]

The Commission presents co-existence as a purely economic issue, on the basis that any environmental or health issues related to co-existence should have been dealt with in the authorisation process.[115] Although this is consistent with the (contested) regulatory framework, understanding co-existence as a wholly economic issue has some important implications. It is perhaps likely to restrict the openness of decision-making: the lay public and NGOs have a much more obvious 'stake' in environmental decision-making than economic decision-making, and the Commission encourages 'stakeholder' rather than public involvement in decisions on co-existence.[116] Most significantly, it becomes increasingly unlikely that 'GM free' zones, other than to the extent that they emerge spontaneously

[109] The Commission intends to insert provisions into Reg 2092/91, *ibid*, clarifying that products labelled as containing GMOs cannot also be labelled as organic, and that the general thresholds apply for adventitious presence, European Commission, *European Action Plan for Organic Food and Farming* COM (2004) 415 final, Action 12.

[110] The Soil Association, the largest organic certification authority in the UK has so far pursued 'surrogate zero'. 0.1% is as low as can be detected by testing, and above that level any GMO in a product prevents its accreditation as 'organic'.

[111] The most obvious difficulty is a loss of market advantage. There may even be patent law implications: Monsanto have successfully sued a farmer in Canada for breach of their patent rights in respect of gene-flow from their patented crop to his non-GM crop, *Monsanto Canada v Schmeiser*, Supreme Court of Canada, 21 May 2004, not yet reported. See generally M Lee and R Burrell, 'Liability For The Escape Of GM Seeds: Pursuing The "Victim"?' (2002) 65 *Modern Law Review* 517.

[112] Commission Recommendation, above n 105, Recital 1.

[113] See Dir 01/18, above n 7, Art 26(a), introduced by Reg 1829/2003, above n 8, Art 43(2).

[114] Commission Recommendation, above n 105.

[115] *Communication from Mr Fischler to the Commission: Co-existence of Genetically Modified, Conventional and Organic Crops* SEC (2003) 258/4; Commission Recommendation, above n 105, Recitals 4 and 5.

[116] Commission Recommendation, *ibid*, para 2.1.2.

through farmers' agreements not to grow GMOs,[117] would be justifiable under the Treaty. Accordingly, the Commission's Guidelines provide that co-existence should be carried out on the 'appropriate scale': 'priority should be given to farm-specific management measures and to measures aimed at coordination between neighbouring farms', and co-existence measures should be specific to particular species, rather than all GMOs.[118] The regional three year ban on the use of GMOs notified to the Commission by Austria under Article 95 EC, discussed above, was primarily designed to protect organic agriculture, although also to protect conventional agriculture and biodiversity. Because the Commission interpreted the measure as relating to a socio-economic problem, the measure could not be approved under Article 95(5), which addresses only the protection of the environment and the working environment.[119]

Furthermore, if co-existence is an economic issue, purity is irrelevant as long as the market accepts impurity. The Commission's co-existence strategy is defined by reference to 'legal obligations for labelling and/or purity standards',[120] and assumes that thresholds are entirely unproblematic. The Guidelines provide that measures should be 'efficient and cost-effective, and proportionate', and in this respect should not go further than is necessary to comply with the 'tolerance thresholds' set in the legislation. At this point it is important to recall that if it is to take advantage of the 0.9 per cent adventitious or technically unavoidable exception to labelling obligations, a producer must provide evidence to establish that 'appropriate steps' have been taken 'to avoid the presence of such material'.[121] One might assume that meeting a regulatory authority's instructions on co-existence would constitute 'appropriate steps'. This bootstrapping of appropriate steps on co-existence requirements themselves *defined* by reference to the thresholds, would deprive the requirement to take appropriate steps of much of its restrictive value. A search for purity is simply not envisaged by the Commission, and any zero-tolerance 'GM free' certifiers are left out in the cold.

The intimately connected labelling, co-existence and consumer choice elements of the GMO regime supplement efforts to respond to the range of public concerns about GMOs through authorisation.[122] Whilst labelling and consumer choice are essential if GM commercialisation goes ahead, there is a danger that the rhetoric being applied is unduly optimistic. Although consumers can have a collective impact, collective action through consumption is problematic; indeed the 'market citizen' that has exercised such an enormous influence on the evolution of the EU is fundamentally individualised, with individual rights and largely economic functions.[123] One is faced with the familiar effort to force essentially public

---

[117] *Communication to the Commission*, above n 2.
[118] Commission Recommendation, above n 105, paras 2.1.5 and 2.1.6.
[119] Commission Decision 2003/653 above n 88.
[120] Commission Recommendation, above n 105, Recital 3.
[121] Reg 1829/2003, above n 8, Art 12(3).
[122] See also the language of the Commission's press release on authorisation of Bt 11 corn, above n 4.
[123] M Everson, 'The Legacy of the Market Citizen' in J Shaw and G More (eds), *New Legal Dynamics of the European Union* (Oxford, Oxford University Press, 1996).

and collective goods into an individualised framework, fudging government responsibilities. The market power of the multi-national biotechnology industry is, moreover, rather impressive, and it is not difficult to envisage a policy of aggressive pricing and marketing overcoming consumer rejection of GMOs, or at least creating consumer resignation in the face of the apparently inevitable; we are not all equal before the market.

Consumer choice is fine as far as it goes. It is true that, assuming the paradigm of the informed, active, empowered consumer, if an individual is unhappy about GMOs, or fears their health impact, that individual should be able to avoid consuming GMOs. Nor would I want to deny that consumption, and other private actions, can sometimes also be political actions. A market approach makes, however, a number of important assumptions. First of all, it assumes the adequacy of the authorisation process. The application of conventional risk analysis, which explicitly does not consider ignorance, and is likely also to over-simplify indeterminacy of effects, to GMOs is however, one of the primary concerns of opponents. The individualisation is also problematic. Consumer choice addresses an individual's concern for his/her own health or own moral probity. However, some of the mooted health impacts of GMOs are of concern species-wide, not just for the individuals who consume them. Similarly, if an individual is not simply ethically concerned about his/her own impact on the environment, but with the *overall* environmental impact or risk of GMOs, the limited effect of individual action may mean that the cost of rejecting GM is not thought to be worthwhile. This leads to the rather familiar prospect of an individual's short term consumption decisions being used to justify positions that the same individual would not support politically.[124]

Finally, and most fundamentally, the consumer choice mantra assumes that the choices available are meaningful. It is not clear why a redefinition of what we mean by 'organic' and 'GM free' is a positive conclusion to the debate on co-existence. It is contended that it is the only practical response to difficult problems; that, however, is true only once the possibility of GM free zones has been rejected. Even if global use of GMOs makes the need for some level of tolerance increasingly likely, the scale of the question rests on domestic policy. The regulatory framework assumes that widespread GM agriculture is an objective and unavoidable fact, rather than a choice.

GMOs AND TRADE

WTO rules have exercised a considerable influence over the development of the EC regime for GMOs.[125] The EC's moratorium on GMOs is currently subject to

---

[124] Note M Sagoff, *The Economy of the Earth: Philosophy, Law and the Environment* (Cambridge, Cambridge University Press, 1988), and the distinction between values and interests discussed in chs 1 and 5 above.
[125] On the influence of WTO law on the design of regulation of GMOs, see Scott, above n 77; more generally, see G de Búrca and J Scott, 'The Impact of the WTO on EU Decision-making' in J Scott and G de Búrca (eds), *The EU and the WTO: Legal and Constitutional Issues* (Oxford, Hart Publishing, 2001).

dispute settlement procedures at the WTO,[126] and the EC would face very significant problems arguing that the abandonment of its own regulatory regime in recent years is legitimate. Predicting the application of the WTO rules to the new GMO regime, assuming that it does eventually function effectively, is far more difficult.[127] The new regime implicates WTO rules in respect both of any future refusals of authorisation on grounds disputed by trading partners, and in respect of onerous regulatory requirements, including not only the obligation to apply for authorisation, but also obligations such as record keeping and labelling. The manner in which certain key elements of WTO rules would be applied to these questions remains open; even which rules would be applied is not yet clear. This section will attempt simply to outline some of the main considerations.

The WTO context parallels, and intensifies, the challenges faced at EC level in mediating between scientific and political decision-making on risk. Most obviously, it is well-recognised, subject to certain ambiguities, that the WTO prioritises scientific risk assessment as a mechanism of regulatory decision-making. The application of the Sanitary and Phyto-Sanitary (SPS) Agreement is likely to be a central element of any GMO dispute, and the discussion of that agreement in chapter four above is highly relevant here. In particular, the prioritisation of scientific and technical 'fact' makes more politically based decision-making problematic, a consideration enhanced by a shallow approach to the precautionary principle. This aspect of WTO law applies particularly to conditions or restrictions imposed on import of GMOs by reference to 'other legitimate factors' not based on scientific risk assessment.

The relationship between the preference for scientific decision-making and EC regulation of GMOs is complicated not only by certain possible openings for more evaluative decision-making in Appellate Body Reports, but also by the Cartagena Protocol on Biosafety, agreed under the auspices of the UN Convention on Biological Diversity.[128] The relationship between the Cartagena Protocol and the SPS Agreement has provoked considerable academic debate. The preamble to the Cartagena Protocol, rather unhelpfully, states both that the Protocol does not imply 'a change in the rights and obligations of a Party under any existing international agreements', and that this comment 'is not intended to subordinate this Protocol to other international agreements'. This, presumably deliberate, ambiguity essentially leaves the relationship between the two agreements to the WTO

---

[126] *European Communities — Measures Affecting the Approval and Marketing of Biotech Products,* DS291, 292, 293.

[127] There is a considerable literature on the subject. For more detail, see Scott above n 77; J Scott, 'European Regulation of GMOs: Thinking About Judicial Review in the WTO' forthcoming (2005) *Current Legal Problems*; S Zarilli, 'International Trade in Genetically Modified Organisms and Multilateral Negotiations: A New Dilemma for Developing Countries' in F Francioni (ed) *Environment, Human Rights and International Trade* (Oxford, Hart Publishing, 2001). GEC York, 'Global Foods, Local Tastes and Biotechnology: The New Legal Architecture Of International Agriculture Trade' (2001) 7 *Columbia Journal of European Law* 423; HD Heavin, 'The Biosafety Protocol and the SPS Agreement: Conflicts and Dispute Resolution' (2003) 12 *Journal of Environmental Law and Practice* 373.

[128] Cartagena Protocol, above n 60.

Appellate Body. Although it is likely that every effort will be made to interpret the Cartagena Protocol consistently with the GATT and associated agreements,[129] if it is applied, the Cartagena Protocol could make a real difference to the legality of elements of the GMO regime. The US, however, currently the primary complainant in respect of GMO regulation, is not a signatory to the Cartagena Protocol. If the relevance of multi-lateral environmental agreements between signatories is controversial, the central role of consent in international law would be directly called into question by their application to non-signatories.[130]

The Cartagena Protocol puts in place a system of 'advance informed agreement'[131] for transnational transfers of 'Living Modified Organisms' (LMOs); whilst LMOs is an unfamiliar term, the definitions of LMO in the Cartagena Protocol and GMO in the Deliberate Release Directive are not dissimilar.[132] In respect of granting or withholding agreement, the Cartagena Protocol has a similar scientific starting point to the SPS Agreement. The decision on import of GMOs must be based on a risk assessment carried out in a 'scientifically sound manner', taking into account 'recognised risk assessment techniques'.[133] This is not however the limit of the process. The Protocol explicitly also provides that certain 'socio-economic considerations', 'arising from the impact of living modified organisms on the conservation and sustainable use of biological diversity' may form part of the decision-making process.[134] Although this is not really designed for the benefit of the EU, applying 'especially with regard to the value of biological diversity to indigenous and local communities', it might provide some shelter for the Food and Feed Regulation's 'other legitimate factors'. This slight expansion of concerns is backed up by the limited support in the Cartagena Protocol for the involvement of the public in decision-making[135]; again something entirely absent from the SPS Agreement.

The approach of the Cartagena Protocol to the precautionary principle is also potentially more expansive than is found in the SPS Agreement. The Protocol

---

[129] Heavin, above n 127.

[130] The relationship between the GATT and multi-lateral environmental agreements is complex, see J Scott, 'International Trade and Environmental Governance: Relating Rules (and Standards) in the EU and the WTO' (2004) *European Journal of International Law* 307.

[131] The comparable notion of 'prior informed consent' is familiar from arrangements for trade in hazardous waste and restricted or banned chemicals; the Cartagena Protocol is exceptional and controversial in that the harmfulness of GMOs remains highly contentious.

[132] ' "Living modified organism" means any living organism that possesses a novel combination of genetic material obtained through the use of modern biotechnology'; ' "Living organism" means any biological entity capable of transferring or replicating genetic material ...'; the definition of 'modern biotechnology' specifies methods 'that overcome natural physiological reproductive or recombination barriers and that are not techniques used in traditional breeding and selection', Cartagena Protocol, Art 3(g), (h) and (i). ' "genetically modified organism" means an organism, with the exception of human beings, in which the genetic material has been altered in a way that does not occur naturally by mating and/or natural recombination'; ' "organism" means any biological entity capable of replication or of transferring genetic material', Dir 01/18, above n 7, Art 2(1) and (2).

[133] Cartagena Protocol, Art 15.

[134] *Ibid*, Art 26(1).

[135] *Ibid*, 'The Parties shall, in accordance with their respective laws and regulations, consult the public in the decision-making process regarding living modified organisms and shall make the results of such decisions available to the public', Art 23(2).

provides that '[l]ack of scientific certainty due to insufficient relevant scientific information and knowledge regarding the extent of the potential adverse effects' does not prevent a decision to refuse consent.[136] By contrast with Article 5.7 of the SPS Agreement, there is no suggestion of provisionality, and nor is there any obligation to supplement scientific knowledge. It may simply be that the Cartagena Protocol is somewhat skeletal, and can be easily supplemented by the SPS Agreement; one could argue, however, that this indicates a fundamentally different understanding of the ability of science to resolve uncertainty. Given the supreme adaptability of the precautionary principle, it might be surprising if much were made of these differences, particularly because there is some ambiguity within the Cartagena Protocol itself: the Protocol claims to be 'in accordance with the precautionary approach contained in Principle 15 of the Rio Declaration'. The Rio Declaration's limitations of 'serious and irreversible damage' and assessment of costs and benefits are however notably absent.[137]

The 'advance informed agreement' provisions would not cover every element of the EU's authorisation regime. Advance informed agreement applies only to transboundary movements of LMOs destined for deliberate release into the environment[138]; LMOs intended for direct use as food or feed or for processing are subject to domestic provisions on import, which are to be 'consistent with the objectives' of the Protocol.[139] More drastically, the Protocol does not apply at all to food and feed produced 'from' GMOs/LMOs, but just to the LMO itself; nor does the Cartagena Protocol address 'consumer interests', unless they could be squeezed within the socio-economic elements.

The scope of the objectives pursued by the EC GMO regulation, which go beyond animal, plant and human health and safety, means that any dispute could not be resolved by the SPS Agreement alone, with or without the assistance of the Cartagena Protocol. The Agreement on Technical Barriers to Trade (TBT Agreement) and the GATT itself will also be implicated in any dispute. One of the most difficult legal questions under both agreements will be the subject of 'like' products.[140] Less favourable treatment of 'like' products is *prima facie* not permissible, whilst if products are not alike, one would not necessarily expect them to be treated in similar ways. Establishing the boundaries of this concept is far

---

[136] *Ibid*, Art 10(6); Art 11(8) re foods for direct use as food or feed or for processing. The 'general principles' of risk assessment explicitly provide that 'lack of scientific knowledge of scientific consensus should not necessarily be interpreted as indicating a particular level of risk, an absence of risk, or an acceptable risk', Annex III, para 4.

[137] Ch 4 above.

[138] Cartagena Protocol, Art 10.

[139] *Ibid*, Art 11(4).

[140] 'The products of the territory of any contracting party imported into the territory of any other contracting party shall be accorded treatment no less favourable than that accorded to like products of national origin in respect of all laws, regulations and requirements affecting their internal sale, offering for sale, purchase, transportation, distribution or use', Art III(4) GATT; 'Members shall ensure that in respect of technical regulations, products imported from the territory of any Member shall be accorded treatment no less favourable than that accorded to like products of national origin and to like products originating in any other country', Art 2.1 TBT Agreement.

from a simple mechanical exercise,[141] and the WTO approach is not only controversial in its effect, but also legally uncertain. As a whole range of rules apply to GMOs, but not to conventional counterparts, it is a matter of enormous importance. Even whether GM maize differs physically from conventional maize will be controversial; foods 'containing or consisting of' GMOs, similarly. The application of the EC legislation to products produced *from* GMOs will be most controversial. In these cases, there need be no GM material in the actual product to which the legislation is applied. The highly disputed relevance of production and process methods, rather than, or as reflected in, the physical characteristics of the product itself, accordingly takes centre stage. The orthodox approach to 'like products' would be to deny the relevance of production and processing methods entirely.[142] If followed rigidly, this would be a heavy burden on the EC. It is an approach that has been subject to considerable criticism,[143] and is now subject to renewed legal debate following an Appellate Body Report suggesting a certain relaxation of the stance on like products. This Report allowed the relevance of non-trade (health) concerns to the question of 'like' products. The basis for this concession is unclear, and the question of process and production methods is not explicitly raised, but nevertheless, this may suggest some potential for a broader approach in the future.[144]

If EC provisions were found to infringe the obligation to give 'national treatment' to 'like products' under the GATT, attention would turn to the possibility of exception under Article XX. Article XX is a creature of its time: it does not address consumer interests, and has a very narrow conception of environmental protection.[145] Its

---

[141] As well as the lively debate over the approach taken by the WTO dispute resolution bodies, this might be illustrated by the famously contentious approach of the ECJ to the question of discrimination in *Wallonian Waste*, Case C–2/90 *Commission v Belgium* [1992] ECR I–4431, where waste produced in one region was distinguished from waste produced in another.

[142] The key dispute is *United States Restrictions on Imports of Tuna* (1992) 30 ILM 1598 (*Tuna/Dolphin* I); *United States Restrictions on Imports of Tuna* (1994) 33 ILM 839 (*Tuna/Dolphin* II).

[143] R Howse and D Regan, 'The Product/Process Distinction — An Illusory Basis for Disciplining "Unilateralism" in Trade Policy' (2000) 11 *European Journal of International Law* 249, p 260. Others disagree: see for example, SE Gaines, 'Processes and Production Methods: How to Produce Sound Policy for Environmental PPM-Based Measures?' (2002) 27 *Columbia Journal of Environmental Law* 383; JH Jackson, 'Comments on the Shrimp/Turtle and the Product/Process Distinction' (2000) 11 *European Journal of International Law* 303. For a recent analysis of 'likeness' more generally, se H Horn and C Mavroidis, 'Still Hazy After All These Years: The Interpretation of National Treatment in the GATT/WTO Case-Law on Tax Discrimination' (2004) 15 *European Journal of International Law* 39.

[144] *EC — Measures Affecting Asbestos and Asbestos-Containing Products* WT/DS135/AB/R, 12 March 2001. The AB found that the different health impacts of products can be taken into account to determine whether they are alike. A key question for any GMO dispute is the significance of consumer perceptions in that finding, as well as the relationship between consumer expectation and evidence of risk. See Scott, above n 77; Howse and Tuerk, above n 152; for a more conservative approach, I Musselli and S Zarrilli, 'Non-Trade Concerns and the WTO Jurisprudence in the *Asbestos* Case: Possible Relevance for International Trade in Genetically Modified Organisms' (2002) 5 *The Journal of World Intellectual Property* 373.

[145] Art XX(b) applies to measures 'necessary to protect human, animal or plant life or health'; and Art XX(g) to measures 'relating to the conservation of exhaustible natural resources if such measures are made effective in conjunction with restrictions on domestic production or consumption.' Environmental objectives can generally be squeezed into the latter category, see Gaines, above n 142, albeit rather uncomfortably.

successful application to the EC regime might seem unlikely. However, it might be more broadly significant, in suggesting a certain procedural emphasis of the WTO Appellate Body. To qualify for exemption under Article XX, domestic measures must not 'constitute a means of arbitrary or unjustifiable discrimination between countries where the same conditions prevail' or 'a disguised restriction on international trade'. In its Report on the *Shrimp/Turtle* dispute,[146] the Appellate Body emphasised in this respect the importance of negotiations with trading partners. Although the Appellate Body's prioritisation of some form of multi-lateralism[147] is not likely in itself to save the EC's GMO regime, or indeed to lead to the primacy of the Cartagena Protocol, it is likely to be revisited in any GMO dispute, given the EC's undoubted pursuit of multi-lateralism.[148] In the same case, the Appellate Body criticised in some detail the 'singularly informal and casual'[149] manner in which the disputed trade measures were applied. If this Report does indeed constitute the beginning of a 'due process' element to trade measures, it gives us some little guidance with respect to GMOs. To describe the application of the moratorium on GMOs, with no pretence even at the application of domestic law, as 'informal and casual' would be something of an understatement. By contrast, the new regime provides a certain level of protection for applicants, including case by case consideration, time limits, rights to review and reasoned opinions. Whilst the procedural aspects of *Shrimp/Tuna* can be in no way decisive of any future GMO dispute, they might begin to suggest a strategy for allowing members of the WTO a certain substantive autonomy, if that autonomy is bound within procedural obligations to consider external traders.[150]

The application of the TBT Agreement to the GMO regime is also very open, particularly as crucial provisions of the Agreement have not yet enjoyed the attention of the Appellate Body. The TBT Agreement applies to 'technical regulations', which includes 'product characteristics' and labelling obligations.[151] Technical regulations must neither create 'unnecessary obstacles to international trade' nor be 'more trade restrictive than necessary to fulfil a legitimate objective'.[152] This requirement has the potential to allow intensive scrutiny of national measures. However, from the perspective of GMO regulation, it is important to note that the TBT Agreement allows that technical regulations may legitimately pursue a

---

[146] *United States — Import Prohibition of Certain Shrimp and Shrimp Products* WT/DS58/AB/R, 12 October 1998.

[147] Scott, above n 130.

[148] Although the US is not a signatory to the Cartagena Protocol, it was influential in the negotiation.

[149] Para 181. The lack of procedural transparency and fairness was demonstrated by factors including the absence of any opportunity to make representations, the absence of reasoned decisions and the absence of any mechanism for review or appeal, para 180. See also *EC — Trade Preferences* WT/DS246/AB/R, 7 April 2004, discussed by Scott, above n 127.

[150] Scott, above n 127; Scott, above n 130.

[151] A technical regulation is a 'Document which lays down product characteristics or their related processes and production methods, including the applicable administrative provisions, with which compliance is mandatory. It may also include or deal exclusively with terminology, symbols, packaging, marking or labelling requirements as they apply to a product, process or production method', TBT Agreement, Annex I.

[152] TBT Agreement, Art 2.2. R Howse and E Tuerk, 'The WTO Impact on Internal Regulations: A Case Study of the Canada-EC Asbestos Dispute' in Scott and de Búrca, above n 125, argue for a procedural rather than a substantive review.

relatively broad range of objectives, certainly not limited to questions of risk and safety. The non-exhaustive list in the Agreement includes the prevention of deceptive practices and the protection of the environment,[153] and the Appellate Body has also allowed the legitimacy of 'market transparency, consumer protection and fair competition'.[154] This could be very important in a dispute over GMOs.

However any disputes over the new legislation are ultimately resolved, the influence of the WTO on the development of the regime on GMOs has been significant. The centrality of robust science, of transparent reason giving and of good evidence is no bad thing. There is however a broader concern that the background of the WTO rules can have a 'chilling effect' on the development of domestic social regulation.[155] Whilst debates are more subtle and sophisticated than this crude dichotomy might suggest, there are two primary responses to concern that WTO disciplines lead to the undervaluing environmental protection. One is to create a much stronger role for international standard-setting bodies, essentially the development of international rules for environmental protection. Both the SPS and the TBT Agreements encourage the use of harmonised standards to protect the interests addressed by the agreements, although the Appellate Body has so far taken a cautious approach to firming up this encouragement.[156] Whether international bodies, including the WTO Appellate Body, are ready for such a highly and visibly contentious role is far from clear, particularly in terms of their connection with and legitimacy before the people on whose behalf they would be regulating. The alternative would be for WTO bodies to defer far more readily to domestic decisions. This approach would also face legitimacy problems, albeit from the very different perspective of concern that widespread protectionist measures could result, bringing the international trade regime into disrepute.

At the heart of the response of the WTO to EC regulation of GMOs is the appropriate role of political, non-technical criteria in good decision-making. This is a topic that has plagued domestic processes for decades. The EU's GMO regime has the potential to open up some regulatory space beyond expertise, both in its concern with consumer interests, and in the introduction of 'other legitimate factors' to decisions. The dominance of scientific risk assessment in the WTO system was discussed in chapter four. The Appellate Body has avoided commenting on the appropriate response of democratic institutions to the realities of domestic politics, a question that will be clearly implicated in any legal disputes over GMOs.

---

[153] *Ibid*, Art 2.2.

[154] *European Communities — Trade Description of Sardines* WT/DS231/AB/R, 26 September 2002, para 263.

[155] De Búrca and Scott, above n 125.

[156] Domestic measures that 'conform with' (SPS Agreement, Art 3.2), or are 'in accordance with' (TBT Agreement, Art 2.5) certain international standards are presumed to be lawful, whilst higher standards have to be justified. In the absence of conformity, both Agreements also provide that national measures shall be 'based on' international standards, which implies 'a very strong and very close relationship', *Sardines*, above n 154, para 245, referring to TBT Agreement. Both Agreements anticipate legitimate reasons for not basing domestic measures on international standards. In the case of the SPS Agreement, that amounts to compliance with the science-based discipline of the Agreement. In the case of the TBT Agreement, international standards must form the basis of national measures unless they are 'ineffective' or 'inappropriate', as to which see *Sardines, ibid*, para 285. See Scott, above n 130.

There are good reasons for alarm at the prospect that political determinations, including responses to public opinion, could legitimise trade measures; the potential for manipulation and abuse is clear. However, equally, in contexts riven by uncertainty, science is not a flawless method of distinguishing legitimate from illegitimate trade measures either. To assert the absolute irrelevance of politics in a situation characterised by intense public feeling, deeply held values, and, significant scientific uncertainty, is unrealistic, distorting accountability far more than explicit reference to politics. An explicit discussion of the politics of a decision, backed up by rigorous processes that build qualitative and quantitative information on public values and opinions, could begin to provide a more solid foundation for decisions that are not purely technical. It is actually more robust, and more open to disagreement and contestation, than a decision in which public values are obscured by ostensibly technical criteria.

CONCLUSIONS

Proponents of biotechnology argue that it constitutes simply the natural next step in agricultural development; its opponents argue that it represents an extraordinary step in human intervention in nature. Those different perspectives on the world would suggest very different regulatory responses. The EU attempts to avoid staking a position in this 'big picture' debate. Faced with challenges of endemic scientific uncertainty, mistrustful publics, problematic legitimacy, and an awkward trade context, the EU has turned primarily to a procedural response to GMOs, allowing the EC legislators to steer a course between deeply divided views. Proceduralisation of GMOs provides a rigorous mechanism by which to assess, contest and debate the safety of GMOs; in the most recent regulatory developments, there are also attempts to soften the purely technical approach to risk assessment by a clearly political phase of decision-making. The depth of that political enquiry, and whether it will really ask the questions that opponents of GM want asking, is still to be seen. The barriers to political decision-making are reflected in a distinctly ambivalent approach to public participation, with the only clear commitment to lay involvement being relegated to the market.

Moreover, the proceduralisation of GMO regulation hides disturbing substantive assumptions on the future of GM technology. Deep and broad antipathy to the technology suggests any move to commercialisation will at least be slow; the requirement for 'no adverse effects' backs that up. On the other hand, WTO and commercial pressures point towards swift resolution. The Commission's *Biotechnology Strategy* bears witness to concern that the EU is somehow missing out on a wonderful opportunity[157]: whilst the Strategy makes much of the relevance of ethical perspectives and public involvement, one cannot help but get the impression that it is looking for only one 'right answer' from these alternative

[157] Commission, above n 2.

perspectives. Public involvement looks more like a tool of education (if only they understood, all would be well) or a tool to enhance trust (ditto), than an opportunity to contribute to decisions. The assumption in much of the official policy seems to be that commercialisation of GMOs is simply an objective fact to which society must adapt.[158]

Whatever the commercial ambitions with respect to biotechnology, the situation is far from resolved. The EC institutions and the Member States, rather than inexorably moving towards GM, could continue to operate outside their own regulatory structure, and take the consequences at the WTO. A *de facto* moratorium is not, however, going to get any more comfortable. Notwithstanding the highly symbolic authorisation of Bt 11 sweet corn in 2004,[159] the authorisation process continues to proceed tortuously under the new legislation, and at the time of writing still no GMOs have been authorised for cultivation since the moratorium. Member States remain reluctant to cede national control over GMOs. Although the Commission is obviously dismayed by national intervention, it is only too aware of potential problems:

> from a political point of view it could be difficult to reject these attempts at establishing GM-free zones, which are driven by strong public local concern and economic considerations (such as protection of local traditional agriculture), without offering some alternative solutions together with the necessary legal clarity and guidance to address their concerns and considerations.[160]

Given that the only 'alternative solutions', 'legal clarity' and 'guidance' proposed seem to be the application of existing legislation and further details from the Commission on co-existence, one can only agree; it is indeed difficult.

---

[158] See L Levidow and C Marris, 'Science and Governance in Europe: Lessons from the Case of Agricultural Biotechnology' (2001) *Science and Public Policy* 345.
[159] Above n 4.
[160] Communication to the Commission, above n 2, p 5.

Conclusions

By way of conclusion, some simple observations should be reiterated. First of all, EC environmental law does face some serious challenges. Those challenges are not unique to EC environmental law, but more general regulatory debates often resonate particularly strongly in this context. The complex, evolving, highly political nature of environmental problems, together with the very significant legitimacy questions being asked of the EU, invite debate about the future of EC environmental law.

Secondly, the *legal* responses to those challenges, which are not always conscious, predominantly look towards mechanisms of decision-making. EC law is busy extending the range of contributors to decision-making (contributions from the 'market', the 'people', the experts, industry itself, environmental interest groups), and attempts to influence the ways in which decisions are made throughout society. The limited accountability of alternative participants means that a responsible and accountable public decision-maker is crucial if final decisions are to look to the public interest. This perhaps rather old-fashioned point is intermittently expressed in EC environmental law, for example in the clear political responsibility for 'risk management', and is perhaps more often simply taken for granted. The tangled political accountability of the EU institutions makes neglect of this point both problematic and understandable; it also explains the tendency to push accountability mechanisms to the national and sub-national level. When attention shifts from process to substantive results, it becomes even more clear that it is simply not possible to avoid some sort of collective, public decision on controversial and difficult issues. An acceptance of the profoundly political nature of environmental decisions implies that reasonable people will disagree most intently about the best results, which involves resisting the outbreak of consensus that seems to be assumed by some new approaches to governance. And perhaps the most important observation to be made here is that the political nature of environmental decision-making is indeed broadly accepted. We see this throughout EC environmental law and policy, perhaps most explicitly in the 'other legitimate factors' formula introduced into the regulation of certain GMOs via EU food law. This has the potential to allow a transparent and sophisticated rationalisation of decisions, and an open assessment of public values and public views.

This leads however to a perhaps inevitable tension. Notwithstanding acknowledgement of public values, the temptation for final decision-makers to seek refuge (rather than enlightenment) in scientific or technical discourse such as risk assessment or cost benefit analysis is great. The legal barriers to basing decisions on factors that do not fit within a technical analysis also remain powerful. These circumstances simply enhance the urgent need to ensure that rhetoric of public participation in EC environmental policy is not used to sidestep genuine public engagement. However, just as a purely technical approach to decision-making would be radically incomplete, so abandoning the tools provided by risk assessment and economics, let alone the natural sciences, would be absurd. The challenge is to ensure that technical information is used in a way that informs, rather than usurps, political decision-making. The discomfort provoked by expressly political decision-making is legitimate, not least precisely *because* of the value-laden and interest-ridden nature of the decisions. Allowing the apparent objectivity, neutrality and external testability of decisions rationalised on a technical or scientific basis to be overtaken by 'values' leaves decisions open to protectionism, self-interest, inefficiency and simple error. It should be recalled at this point that technical and scientific opinion rarely if ever actually imbue decisions with the inevitability that is craved, but may on the contrary simply obscure the real nature of the decision. The point is not that public opinion should be followed (even if public opinion were ever so monolithic that it realistically could be), but that it should be heard and addressed. This involves both seeking general information on the opinions of the public, and attempting to examine the values and reasons behind these opinions. Again, the principle seems to be accepted in EC environmental law, but the practicle commitment is sometimes weak.

Finally, some more extreme possible responses to the sustained critique of EC environmental law should be noted. Radical de-regulation or radical de-centralisation in the environmental arena is always possible. The political attractions of outright de-regulation have largely dissipated in recent years, to be replaced by complex and often competing debates about reform. Although these replacement debates target over-regulation and demonstrate varying levels of mistrust of government activity, environmental regulation seems to be here to stay. A similar observation could be made of the possibility of radical de-centralisation, which seems largely to have been replaced by more moderate discussion of reform. The emphasis in the mainstream is very much on greater flexibility, and as with more general regulatory reform, on 'better' regulation. At the time of writing, however, there is change in the air. Ten new Member States joined the EU in May 2004; Euro-sceptic political parties promptly achieved strong results right around the newly enlarged EU in European Parliament elections characterised by a disturbingly low turn out; and after that demonstration of public anxiety, a demanding process of negotiation was completed by the signature of a popularly controversial Constitution. The impact of these developments on EC environmental law will only be seen over a period of years, but one can say that there is likely to be continuing pressure around the nature of EU activity in the environmental sphere, as elsewhere. These ongoing challenges will, one hopes, provoke continued careful thinking on the future path of EC environmental law.

Index